36
/ \
2 18
   / \
  3   6
     / \
    3   2

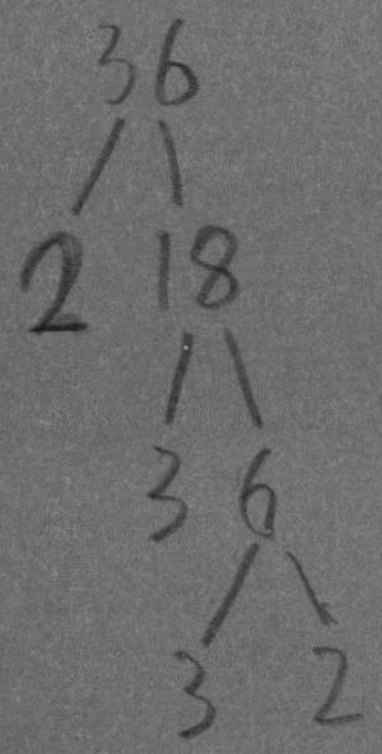

WHAT TREE IS THAT ?

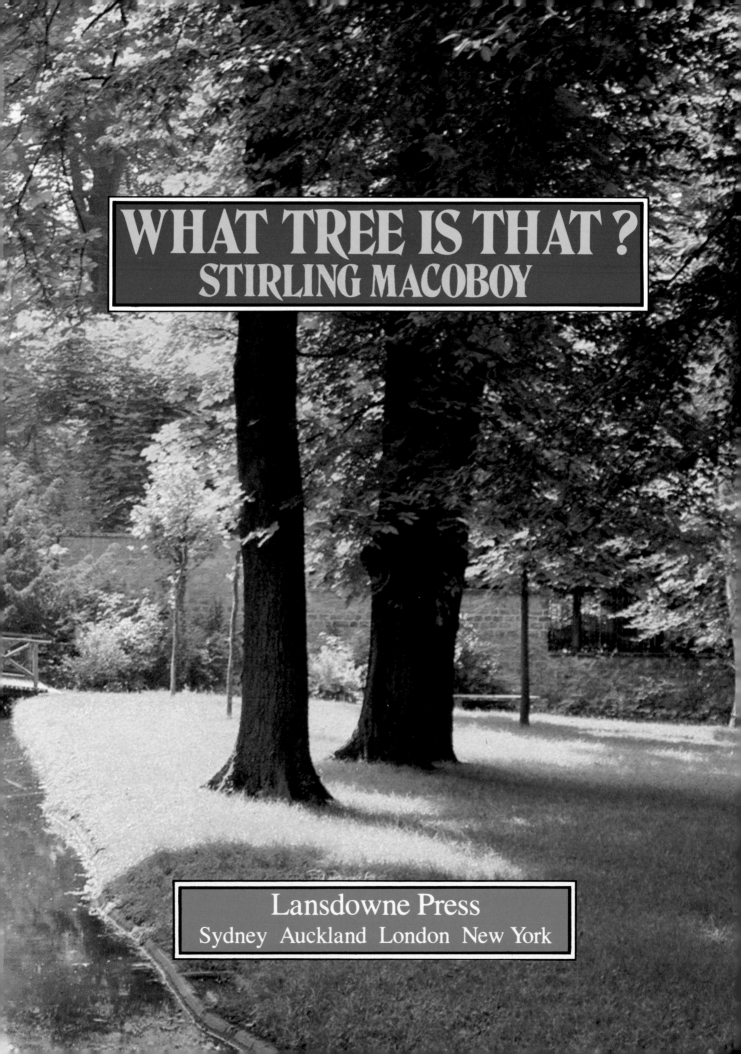

WHAT TREE IS THAT ?
STIRLING MACOBOY

Lansdowne Press
Sydney Auckland London New York

To the memory of
a grandfather I never knew:
James Harold Macoboy,
who loved trees and gardens

PHOTOGRAPHS

Half-Title page: *Erythrina variegata*, Coral tree

Title page: Trees in Empress Josephine's garden at Malmaison, France

Pages 4–5: Australia's national tree emblem, *Acacia pycnantha*, the Golden Wattle

Pages 6–7: An autumn woodland near Mohonk in New York State

Page 8: *Picea rubens Virgata* at the arboretum of Pruhonice, Czechoslovakia

Designed by Judy Hungerford
Edited by Sue Wagner

Distributed by Gary Allen Pty Ltd
15 Nowill Street, Condell Park, NSW 2200, Australia
Published by Lansdowne-Rigby Publishers,
a division of Kevin Weldon & Associates Pty Limited
372 Eastern Valley Way, Willoughby, NSW 2068, Australia

First published 1979
Reprinted 1982, 1983 (twice), 1984, 1985, 1987, 1988
© Copyright Stirling Macoboy 1979
Produced in Australia by the Publisher
Typeset in Australia
Printed in Hong Kong by South China Printing Co.

National Library of Australia Cataloguing-in-Publication Data

Macoboy, Stirling
    What tree is that?
    First published: Sydney: Ure Smith, 1979.
    Includes indexes
    ISBN 0 7018 1659 7.
    1. Trees — Identification. I. Title.

582.16

Publisher's note: A substantial amount of the material in this book is also included in *Trees for Warm and Temperate Climates,* by the same author.

CONTENTS

PREFACE

The acceptance of my earlier books on garden flowers and indoor plants has led me, in this volume, right outside the home environment and into the landscape that surrounds us in nature. There, with the help of my camera, I hope to increase your awareness of those titans of creation, the trees. To identify those that you know already; to introduce to you others that were up to this time just a blur from a car window, a name in a book.

How many of these trees there were I scarcely realized myself until I set out to capture them on film. Often I had to travel far afield to seek them out in their natural areas of vigour and display—away from the urban distractions of fences and street furniture that blight so many landscapes.

And for every tree I had on my list I discovered at least one new one that had to be included—often a tree that meant as much to the people of the country I was visiting as, say, the Eucalypt means to an Australian.

When I settled down to do the actual writing, it was with the realization that trees are great travellers too, and that we who love them, and who live around those two great basins of the Indian and Pacific Oceans, have the best of all arboreal worlds.

Whether we now call Australia, South Africa, California or New Zealand our home, the trees of a European heritage are never far away. We see them planted as garden specimens or naturalized in cooler, mountain vacation areas.

And all about us, in perfect botanical harmony, are the splendid new trees of the lands where we were born. Some of these are native only to our own countries, or to the southern hemisphere—others have migrated with man all around the world, and now grow interchangeably on five continents and many islands.

My home city of Sydney glows through a violet haze in November, when the Jacarandas flower—they are migrants from Brazil. Our nearby bushlands light up in golden wonder when the native Wattles are in bloom—but I saw the same phenomenon transported to California and the south of France. Our autumn landscapes blaze not with dying foliage, but with the scarlet blossom of the Coral Trees, signalling the end of the hot season. The *Erythrinas* come from Africa, but they now grow everywhere in Australia and have even been elected the official city tree of Los Angeles!

Exploring the world of trees has been rewarding for me, and I sincerely hope my pleasure will be shared by tree lovers everywhere.

INTRODUCTION

Trees are the most prominent, the most beautiful feature in any natural setting away from the actual polar regions of the earth. They are also the backbone, the focal point of any planned landscape design or garden.

Trees include among their many species the largest and oldest living things, and surviving members of the longest-established of all life forms, some of them relatively unchanged for millions of years.

Trees lend us shade, shelter and privacy; their wood builds our houses, our bridges, our boats. Their dead tissue has been transformed over the ages into the fossil fuels of coal and oil and gas that keep the wheels of industry turning and well lubricated, grant us the blessings of fire and warmth, and make it possible for us to be transported in comfort from one part of the world to another, by land, by sea, by air.

Almost every aspect of our lives is in some way influenced or enhanced by trees. They are the most important living things around us, and by far the slowest to reach maturity. The ancients worshipped them as symbols of life, strength and fertility. Yet daily *we* destroy them, cutting them down without replacement, without a thought for the future that seems so far off, and yet is so dangerously close.

What chance does a single tree (or even a whole race of trees) stand, when measured against the apathy of politicians, the greed of land developers, the short-sightedness of the world's farmers?

But if we are tree lovers as we claim, we *must* replant them with our children's future in mind. As they are slow to mature, we must plant them *now*, to help redress the damage that has already been done to our soil, our climate, our wildlife, our entire ecology.

Each and every one of us must speak out for the protection and replacement of the trees that were once around us, and without which our civilization could never have risen to its present heights.

We must plant trees wherever and whenever possible. Around our homes, to be sure, we can't use too many because they may become so large, but with a little shopping around we can choose from a wealth of tree species that will live and flourish in symbiosis with our families and their needs, bringing shade and beauty in only a few years.

It is my hope that this book will help us in making the choice.

Stirling Macoboy
Neutral Bay, New South Wales
June 1979

THE TREES

ABIES
(ae' bees)

The Firs

FAMILY: PINACEAE

One of the great tree genera of the world (great in stature, great in their importance to man) are the Firs or Balsams, the original Christmas trees of the northern hemisphere.

They are survivors from the last ice age, gradually retreating to the mountains of Northern Europe, Siberia, Japan and the Rocky Mountains of North America. With the spread of civilization the three dozen species scattered around the cold winter areas of the North are a dying race. Valued for their timber and their rich harvest of perfumed balsam, most Firs literally ooze with this gum which is used in pharmacy and optics, and for the fresh 'woodsy' smell of many toiletries.

In the wild, Firs grow at an astonishing rate — 1 m (3 ft) in a year is common — and reach a vast size. Firs of almost 100 m (300 ft) have been recorded. Their aptly chosen Latin name is from *abeo* — I rise!

Size would rule them out from the average garden, even if they could be persuaded to grow, but in the hill country or by the mountain weekender, they make a marvellous specimen tree — tall, straight and with a delightful fragrance.

Firs do in fact come in many shapes and sizes, and at a quick glance greatly resemble many of the other conifers, notably the Spruces (see *Picea*), but there are several details which set them apart. The leaves almost invariably bear two parallel silver lines on the underside; the cones (often colourful when young) point *upwards* like the candles on a Christmas tree, whereas on the other conifers that are similar in appearance, they hang down.

Abies grow readily from seed contained in the ripened cones.

Abies nobilis
Noble Fir

Abies homolepis
Nikko Fir

Abies alba
European Silver Fir

9

ACACIA
(ə kae' shə)

The Wattles

FAMILY: LEGUMINOSAE

Acacias seem so typically Australian that one of them (*A. pycnantha*, the Golden Wattle) has been adopted as the nation's floral symbol and wreaths the coat of arms. And yet they are by no means exclusive to the southern continent. Africa has nearly as many species, Asia and America quite a few, and Hawaii's native *A. koa* yields one of the finest of the world's timbers. There are about one thousand species throughout the world.

But Australia's *Acacias* are notably the most decorative, bursting into glowing masses of golden blossom at different times of the year according to species, but most notably in winter and spring. Viewing the dense puffball blossom for the first time, it comes as something of a surprise to learn that *Acacia* are very *un*typical members of the pea family, Leguminosae. But they do bear the same long pods as other peas, with the seeds attached alternately to either shell.

The leaves are quite a mixture. In fact most species do not bear leaves at all, merely *phyllodes* or stalks, which are generally flattened into a leaf-like shape, though in some species they may be adapted to a needle-shape or even a spine. A few species, such as the lovely Cootamundra Wattle, *A. baileyana*, do bear true leaves in their adult state, and they are very delicate fern-like affairs. Each puffball 'flower' is actually a compact globular mass of many small flowers.

Acacia blossom is generally sold as 'Mimosa' in Europe and America (where the cultivated plants were imported from Australia) but the true Mimosa is an entirely different, though related, plant. In Australia *Acacia* has always been known as Wattle, because the thin branches and trunks were often woven and then sealed with clay or mud to form walls of the earliest colonial houses. This form of construction was known in Europe as 'wattle and daub', but in Australia the name became attached to the plant.

Few Wattle species grow into large trees, or live very long. They do grow quickly, however, and are often used to provide quick colour in the new garden, or for protection from sun along fields and roads.

Acacia may be readily grown from seed, which should be heat-treated, either in boiling water or close to a fire, to split the tough casing. Some leaf-colour varieties are propagated from cuttings.

Many of the smaller *Acacia* species make useful stock fodder, particularly in times of drought, to which they are well adapted.

Acacia pendula
Weeping Myall, Boree

Acacia pycnantha
Golden Wattle

10

Acacia baileyana
Cootamundra Wattle

Acacia glaucescens
Coast Myall

Acacia terminalis
Cedar Wattle

11

Acacia giraffea
Camel Thorn

Acacia confusa
Philippine Acacia

Acacia decurrens
Black Wattle

Acacia longifolia
Sydney Golden Wattle

Acacia karroo
African Camel Thorn

Acacia koa
Koa

ACER
(ae' sə)

The Maples

FAMILY: ACERACEAE

By no means the most prolific of tree genera in terms of the number of species (*Acacia* or *Eucalyptus* would each outnumber them by at least six to one), the Maples display the most astonishing range of leaf shapes and coloration. Japanese gardeners alone catalogue hundreds of named varieties.

Native to cool temperate zones of all three continents in the northern hemisphere, they have adapted marvellously to cultivation in every part of the world away from the actual tropics, and collectively are probably the most widely planted of specimen trees.

Acer pseudoplatanus CV *'Brilliantissimum'*
Sycamore Maple

Acer saccharinum
Silver Maple

Acer griseum
Paperbark Maple

Acer negundo CV *'Elegans'*
Variegated Box Elder

13

Always with a certain delicacy, Maples come in all shapes and sizes from the low natural bonsai-habit of some dwarf Japanese varieties to the tall, fast-growing Silver and Sugar Maples of North America. Almost all of them are deciduous, producing a miraculous spectrum of colour as their leaf-chlorophyll changes in autumn. This effect is one of the world's great natural wonders in America's New England states, where an October visit is an experience never to be forgotten. But make your schedule flexible — the opening of the big colour show depends on an exact combination of sunny days and frosty nights.

While photographing for this book in Europe, I received a panic call from Boston, Massachusetts, where I had planned to arrive on 21 October. A cold snap had revised all predictions and the colour peak was expected weeks earlier. I arrived on 6 October, and the next day's country drive was a trip in every sense of the word. I was left with senses reeling from an over-indulgence in orange and scarlet, almost drunk with the vintage smell of decaying chlorophyll.

In spite of their wide variety, all Maples have several features in common. First, the leaves are sharply toothed (the name *acer* is Latin for sharp) and generally in some form digitate (resembling a spread hand), though with anything from three to thirteen lobes of varying lengths and complexity. Secondly, after a rather inconspicuous flowering, they bear masses of distinctive boomerang-shaped seeds known as *keys*. These consist of two seeds or *samaras*, each with a single wing. The precise angle of the wings to each other is one of the principal means of species identification.

The winged keys can fly quite a distance, as any Maple grower knows.

Acer saccharum
Sugar Maple

Acer japonicum CV *'Aconitifolium'*
Fern-leaf Maple

Acer platanoides CV *'Schwedleri Nigra'*
Crimson King Maple

Acer opalus
Italian Maple

Acer palmatum
Japanese Maple

Acer rubrum var. *Tridens*
Three-lobed Red Maple

Acer campestre
Field Maple

15

ACMENA
(ak mee' nə)

The Lillypilly
FAMILY: MYRTACEAE

Once upon a time, there was a beautiful race of glossy-leafed trees called *Eugenia*, after the European military leader, Prince Eugene of Savoy. Considered the largest genus of trees in nature, they were related to the Eucalypts and produced clouds of fluffy, white, many-stamened flowers in spring. But their special attraction was the profusion of showy berries, which weighed the branches down in late summer. In Australia, they were popularly known as Lillypilly.

In fact, they still are called that, although taxonomists have given many of them different botanical names which (though valid) tend to confuse the home gardener. Most are now called *Syzygium* (which see), but the old favourite Lillypilly is listed as *Acmena smithii*.

It is a tall, graceful tree, often with branches of a distinctly weeping habit. It originates from eastern Australia, but now grows in California, South Africa, Hawaii and many other places. The leaves are small and shiny, the fruit quite variable from white to mauve and only 1 cm (½ in) in diameter.

Acmena enjoys deep, rich soil with the companionship of other plants and plenty of moisture. It has, however, been successfully used as a street tree, where it adopts a rather more formal shape. The white blossoms have no petals, but do have a mass of white stamens, and look quite charming in early summer.

Propagation is from either seed or cuttings.

Acmena smithii
Lillypilly

ADANSONIA
(ad an son' ee ə)

The Baobabs
FAMILY: BOMBACACEAE

Imagine, if you can, a tree that may develop a trunk up to 10 m (30 ft) in diameter, and yet reach its branches no more than 13 m (40 ft) in the air! That's the *Adansonia* or Baobab — a native of dry, outback areas of Australia, Africa and Madagascar.

Adansonia digitata
Baobab, Dead Rat Tree

Named for a French botanist called Adanson, these trees live for an amazing length of time (some African specimens have been estimated to be over five thousand years old) and are often the only surviving vegetation for miles in times of drought. This is because the light, fleshy wood consists mostly of hollow chambers which store water from favourable seasons — up to tens of thousands of gallons of it.

No wonder they were actually worshipped in their harsh, natural African environment. A trunk full of water and handsome digitate leaves that make useful cattle fodder in hard times are only its most obvious features. The fibrous bark may be converted into paper, rope or even a rough cloth, and in processing yields a useful gum. The fruit pulp makes a refreshing acid beverage, and the seeds are almost overflowing with medicinal oil.

Adansonias are often called Bottle Trees, and some ancient specimens, hollowed out by termites, have been used as jails, storage houses or even burial chambers!

Obviously not a likely choice for the home garden, the grotesque, almost ugly *Adansonias* are such curiosities that they are often planted in botanic gardens as a tourist attraction.

AESCULUS
(aes' kyoo ləs)

The Horse Chestnuts and Buckeyes

FAMILY: HIPPOCASTANACEAE

Grown purely for aesthetic appeal, the spectacular *Aesculus* or Horse Chestnuts have no useful commercial qualities at all. Their timber is of no use, their fruit inedible, they make a terrible mess all around with a litter of spent flowers and seed capsules and yet they have become possibly the most beloved of trees in cooler parts of the northern hemisphere for parks, street planting and large gardens.

Easily grown from seed or grafted cuttings of named colour varieties, the small number of *Aesculus* species are native to various parts of Europe, North America and Asia — *Aesculus* is the original Roman name.

The most handsome of them all and the most commonly seen is *A. hippocastanum*, a tall, long-lived tree found originally in a small area of the Balkans, and imported to England in the seventeenth century. Deciduous, it grows fast and may ultimately reach 30 m (100 ft) in height, its striking, hand-shaped leaves being among the first to open in spring. These are followed by tall candles of white flowers later in the season; the flowers in turn are succeeded by round spiny fruits about the size of a golf ball. These have a passing resemblance to chestnuts, though they are inedible except to stock. In a dry year, the leaves become badly scorched about the edges, but normally they turn a clear yellow in autumn. *A. hippocastanum* has become naturalized all over Europe and much of North America, and is also grown in cool climates of the southern hemisphere.

It is often planted in conjunction with *A. X carnea*, its deep pink flowered hybrid with the smaller *A. pavia* or Red Buckeye.

Aesculus hippocastanum
spring flowers and foliage

Aesculus hippocastanum
Horse Chestnut

Aesculus californica
Californian Buckeye

Aesculus hippocastanum
late summer fruits

AGATHIS
(a gath' əs)

The Kauris

FAMILY: ARAUCARIACEAE

Scattered here and there about the Pacific, the lofty *Agathis* or Kauris are southern hemisphere conifers, but not the ordinary needle-covered, Christmas-tree type of conifer. The very name *Agathis* marks their first unusual point. It is Greek for a ball of string and that's exactly what the large fruit or cones look like — a grey ball of string or, according to the Hawaiians, a tennis ball, for they call them Tennis-ball Trees. This fruit develops on a distinct stem at the junction of branch and branchlets. The leaves are dark, sickle-shaped, and covered with wax.

Agathis species are slow-growing, and have not been much developed for timber use by modern foresters, although in earlier days they were valued by the native populations. They still give one of our finest timbers, relatively knot-free due to the trees' habit of shedding lower branches as they grow.

All parts of the Kauri are rich in a particularly long-lasting resin used in the production of linoleum-type floor coverings and varnish. This resin often outlasts the trees themselves and becomes fossilized. It is known as *copal,* and there is a small industry in New Zealand, re-claiming it from fossil beds for commercial use.

Some fifteen Kauri species are listed, originating from Australia, New Zealand, Malaysia, the Philippines, Fiji, Tonga and New Caledonia, but nowadays many botanists seem to think that they may only be adaptations (though distinctly varied) of a single, original species.

Kauris are propagated from seed.

Agathis robusta
Queensland Kauri

Agathis vitiensis
Tennis-ball Tree

Agathis moorei
New Caledonian Kauri

Agathis australis
Kauri Pine

Agonis flexuosa
Peppermint Tree

Related *A. juniperina*, the Small-leaf Willow Myrtle, is generally a taller, more slender tree, occasionally reaching 13 m (40 ft). Its foliage is finer and smaller. The white flowers are similar to those of the Willow Myrtle, but borne in clusters at the end of branchlets in mid-winter.

AGONIS
(ə goh′ nis)

The Willow Myrtles and Peppermints

FAMILY: MYRTACEAE

Light and delicate members of the Myrtle family (Eucalypts and Paperbarks are others), Western Australia's small group of *Agonis* species have found world favour as an evergreen and dry climate replacement for more delicate and deciduous willows, and other weeping trees. Outside their native continent they are now seen as both garden specimens and street trees in southern Europe, South Africa, California and many other areas.

The name *Agonis* is from the Greek *agon* meaning a collection, which is a reference to the vast number of seeds set by each tree. New plants may be propagated from these seeds in spring, or from tip-cuttings taken in summer.

A. flexuosa, the Willow Myrtle or Peppermint tree, is most commonly seen. It may reach 12 m (35 ft) in height, but is more usually a wide-spreading dwarf tree not much above the size of a large shrub. The foliage of the weeping branches is grey-green, willow-like in size and shape, and exudes a spicy peppermint odour when bruised.

Agonis juniperina
Small-leaf Willow Myrtle

AILANTHUS

(ae lan' thəs)

The Tree of Heaven

FAMILY: SIMAROUBACEAE

With *Ailanthus* there are no half measures! Either you think of it as tall and graceful, the ideal tree for smoky city air and shaded places, or as a gaunt litterer of footpaths, with the reproductive instincts of a rabbit.

In China where it originated they call it *ai-lanto,* the Tree of Heaven. In the Australian state of Victoria, it has been proclaimed a noxious weed and its cultivation forbidden.

I would take sides with the Chinese since I lived for some years in Manhattan, not exactly a 'garden city'. The view from my apartment included a grove of spindly *Ailanthus,* pushing their way out of a small yard that was otherwise all brick and concrete. Graceful in the winter with snow on their bare branches, in summer they brought blissful shade with their large pinnate leaves.

I never actually noticed my New York *Ailanthus* flowering, but their flower display is not much anyway, just small panicles of tiny, greenish blossom you can hardly see. But these flowers are followed in late summer by an absolute mass of winged seeds, orange to glowing red in colour.

Ailanthus seems happy in the sub-tropics, but grows beautifully in Paris, London, New York, Tokyo, Hong Kong, Sydney and most of the world's great cities. It may reach 20 m (60 ft) and is propagated from suckers.

There are eight other *Ailanthus* species found in various parts of Asia.

Ailanthus altissima
Tree of Heaven, Ai-lan-to

Ailanthus altissima
foliage and flowers

Ailanthus fordii
Ford's Ailanthus

ALBIZZIA
(al bit' zee ə)

The Silk Trees and Cape Wattle

FAMILY: LEGUMINOSAE

Sometimes mistaken for very large Wattles (see *Acacia)*, the related Silk Trees or *Albizzia* are a small genus found in Asia, Africa and Australia, with one unimportant species in Mexico.

Most commonly planted is the large *A. lebbek* or Siris Tree, a 25 m (75 ft) favourite for shade and shelter throughout the sub-tropical regions of the world. It bears deciduous bipinnate leaves like a Jacaranda, uninteresting panicles of greenish wattle-flowers for a few days in late spring, and then an absolute mass of brown pods. These are the tree's main display as they move and chatter ceaselessly in the wind. In the Philippines, they call it the Woman's Tongue tree!

The Australian species *A. lophantha* or Cape Wattle grows only half the size, often with a shrubby habit. Again, its leaves are bipinnate, though rather larger, and its petal-less flowers are greenish, forming bottlebrush style spikes in the leaf axils.

Prettiest of the genus is the Persian Silk Tree, *A. julibrissin*, a favourite in the Middle East, Australia, France, California and many other temperate climates. It is a short, spreading tree decked lavishly in summer with large clusters of pink puffball flowers at branch ends. It has several cultivars with deeper coloured flowers and is quite hardy down to −12°C (10°F). The timber of *A. lebbek* is much sought after for cabinet work, being heavy and beautifully figured. The bark of all species is powdered and used as soap in many primitive societies, and the leaves and seed pods are used as cattle fodder.

Albizzias were named for an Italian naturalist, Albizzi, and are readily propagated from seed.

Albizzia julibrissin
Persian Silk Tree

Albizzia lophantha
Cape Wattle

Albizzia julibrissin
close-up of blossom

Albizzia lebbek
Woman's Tongue Tree

ALECTRYON
(a lek' tree on)

The Native Quince and Titoki

FAMILY: SAPINDACEAE

A small but useful genus of trees scattered throughout the Pacific from Australia to Hawaii, *Alectryon* has only two species in general cultivation, *A. excelsa,* the Titoki from New Zealand, and *A. subcinereus*, the Native Quince from eastern Australia, both somewhat resembling the European Ash Trees (see *Fraxinus*).

The *Alectryons* are slender trees rarely exceeding 10 m (30 ft) in height and with pinnate leaves. The Titoki can be recognized from its black bark, 45 cm (18 in) leaves which are unequally pinnate (one leaflet more on one side of the leafstem) and panicles of creamy flowers. Its tough timber is valued for cabinet making and wooden toolhandles.

The Australian Native Quince (*A. subcinereus*) has grey bark and smaller pinnate leaves without a terminal leaflet. The flower panicles are short and followed by smooth berries borne in pairs, each with one shiny black seed in a red, fleshy surround.

Two native Hawaiian species have almost disappeared in recent times.

The name *alectryon* is Greek for a rooster, presumably suggesting that the arching leaf clusters resemble tail feathers.

Alectryon subcinereus
Native Quince

ALEURITES
(al yoo rai' tees)

The Candlenuts

FAMILY: EUPHORBIACEAE

Named from the Greek *aleuron* meaning floury, the striking Candlenut tree *A. moluccana* is found in hillside forests of the Pacific Islands and South-East Asia, where its pale, mealy foliage stands out from darker tropical vegetation. It is one of the great domesticated trees of the world, with a thousand uses, and has been adopted as the official tree emblem of Hawaii, where it was probably imported by the Polynesian ancestors.

The *kukui* (as Hawaiians called it) used to be as important as the Coconut Palm. The timber had many uses, particularly for canoe building. A gum extracted from it strengthened the tapa cloth they made, which was also dyed with a pigment from the roots and seed shells.

The seed shells themselves were used as beads, and their kernels, rich in oil, were threaded on coconut leaf-ribs and burnt as candles — hence the common name Candlenut Tree.

The Candlenut may reach 20 m (60 ft) in height and is densely clothed with hand-sized three- or five-lobed leaves, pale green, with a rusty fuzz on the undersides. The tiny white flowers, borne in panicles several times a year, are followed by clusters of 5 cm (2 in) nuts, which resemble a European walnut. A decorative variety, *A. moluccana var. Remui*, is valued for its deep-lobed leaves.

Several closely related but smaller species are grown in South-East Asia, principally for their commercial value. They include the Japan Wood-oil Tree, *A. cordata*, the Tung-oil Tree, *A. fordii* and the Mu-oil Tree, *A. montana*.

All may be grown from seed or cuttings under heat, and are found in gardens throughout the world.

Aleurites moluccana
Candlenut, Kukui

Aleurites moluccana
flowers and foliage

ALNUS
(al' nəs)

The Alders

FAMILY: BETULACEAE

Closely related to the slim and graceful Birches (see *Betula*), the northern hemisphere's ubiquitous Alders are, like the Birches, water babies. You see them in places where the soil is deep and wet — by riversides, along the line of underground watercourses, around the rim of marshes or in low-lying hollows. Their massive roots help protect river banks from erosion. Their timber is so water-resistant that piles cut from it have supported the city of Venice for centuries. *Alnus* was the original Roman name for the tree.

Alders are in fact so common in Europe, Asia and the Americas that their value as a garden tree has been greatly underestimated. Quite apart from their wet-soil uses mentioned above, they are remarkably attractive trees, with a light, lacy appearance in winter when they are bare, and a pleasant covering of glossy long-stemmed leaves that flutter in summer breezes.

Alders have a slim, upright shape with generally horizontal or slightly weeping branches that are festooned for much of the year with their curious flowers. The flowers are of two sorts: the female, borne in long dangling catkins; and the male, which are formed as small woody cones, rather like a conifer's.

Alders will resist a reasonable degree of frost and are quite happy in climates with up to sub-tropical temperatures, particularly the American west coast species.

Aleurites moluccana
an old tree, Queensland

Alnus oregana
Red Alder, male and female flowers

Alnus rhombifolia
White Alder, trunk detail

Alnus glutinosa
Common or Black Alder

Alnus jorullensis
Mexican Evergreen Alder

ALOË

(a loh' ae)

The Aloës

FAMILY: LILIACEAE

Aloës are generally thought of as virtually inde-structible, small to medium-size stemless plants. They have greyish succulent leaves like the *Agaves*. But *Aloë* leaves are sometimes speckled or spotted as well, and often have vici-ously spined edges. They are of the Lily family, Liliaceae, and produce tall stems of rather garish tubular flowers, usually in a combination of scarlet, orange and yellow.

In modern times, when the labour cost of maintaining a garden is such an important fac-tor, their drought-resistant qualities have made them very popular in the rock garden, in pots and in low-maintenance modern landscapes of frost-free areas.

They are taken so much for granted that it is something of a surprise to find that there are several tree members among their two hundred-odd species, and they are wonderful subjects for the desert garden or dry, sunbaked area. All of them demand good drainage and freedom from frost, and are propagated from offsets.

All Aloës are native to an area encompassing eastern Africa, Arabia and across to dry parts of southern India. The name is Arabic (*alloeh*), and for centuries the Arab peoples have cultivated them as the source of the drug, bitter aloes.

The largest tree species is *A. bainesii*, the Aloë Tree, which may reach 20 m (60 ft) in suitable surroundings. It is popular in California as well as in its native Africa, both for its dramatic land-scaping effect and its mass of rose-pink flowers produced in spring.

Other tree Aloës include *A. excelsa*, *A. plicatilis* and *A. speciosus*.

Aloe bainesii
The Aloe Tree

AMHERSTIA
(am hurst' ee ə)

The Pride of Burma

FAMILY: LEGUMINOSAE

Seldom seen away from its native India and Burma, except in botanical gardens, the gorgeous *Amherstia*, only one of its genus, has been hailed as the most beautiful flowering tree in the world. Simple, light, lacy, it grows to 13 m (40 ft) in the wild.

The graceful 1 m (3 ft) leaves are compound, with six or eight pairs of leaflets, and the new growth (like that of some other tropical trees very flaccid and colourful) is lightly speckled and often shaded with bronze, red and purple. The flowers, which are not long-lasting, hang from the branches in long racemes like inverted candelabra. Each flower develops on a red stalk, those at the top being longer than those at the bottom, so that the flower mass is shaped like a loose, inverted cone. Individual blossoms remind some people of orchids, others of hummingbirds. They are pale pink, spotted and marked in red and white, with a large splash of golden yellow on the large upper petal.

Each flower has three petals and ten arching stamens, and is followed by a crimson pea pod, though the seed is rarely viable.

Amherstias are generally propagated from cuttings and have flowered in Hawaii, the Philippines, Florida, the Caribbean, South America and even in England, under glass.

A. nobilis was named for the eighteenth century Countess Amherst, a great patron of botany.

Amherstia nobilis
Pride of Burma

ANGOPHORA
(an gof' or ə)

The Apple Gums

FAMILY: MYRTACEAE

The *Angophoras* or Apple Gums are a very small Australian genus greatly resembling the Eucalypts, with which they were once classed. Like the Eucalypts, they have achieved world popularity in other dry areas such as California and South Africa, but they are native to the rugged, fast-draining sandstone rock of the east coast of Australia.

Angophora cordifolia
Dwarf Apple Gum

They have elegant orange or pinkish bark, which peels unevenly from the trunk, and two forms of leaf — pale green, heart-shaped juvenile foliage and long drooping adult leaves up to 12.5 cm (5 in) long. The young foliage is often bright red. The flowers (invariably cream) are very largely a mass of stamens, but unlike the Eucalypts, they also have small petals. The fruits that follow are exactly like gum nuts, but ribbed. With all their decorative qualities, it is fortunate that the *Angophoras* have escaped annihilation in Australia because the timber is not of much use except for firewood.

Only two species are commonly planted, the tall and graceful *A. costata* or Smooth-barked Apple Gum, and the smaller *A. cordifolia* or Dwarf Apple Gum, which has a rugged spreading appearance and rarely exceeds 4 m (12 ft) in height.

The name *Angophora* is from the Greek words *aggos* and *phero,* and means cup-bearer, an allusion to the fruits.

ANNONA
(an noh' nə)

The Custard Apples

FAMILY: ANNONACEAE

The *Annonas* or Custard Apples include about fifty species of small trees and shrubs from the tropics of Asia, Africa and the Americas. All of them are grown world-wide in warm climates for their delicious and refreshing fruits, which are borne heavily. The name *annona* is Latin, and means 'yearly produce'.

Annonas grow readily from seed, or bud grafts, and few of the useful species will pass 8 m (25 ft) in height, and about half that in width. The alternate leaves are noticeably glossy and pleasantly scented; the flowers quite uninteresting. They would probably not be grown if it were not for the splendid fruit harvest, though many would say that these are an acquired taste.

Species commonly seen in fruitshops are the richly flavoured Custard Apple or Cherimoya, *A. cherimolia*, the refreshing and acid Soursop, *A. muricata*, the Bullock's Heart, *A. reticulata*, and the Sugar Apple, *A. squamosa*.

Curiously, in spite of their human appetite appeal, both fruits and leaves of all species have insecticidal properties.

Annona cherimolia
Custard Apple

Annona cherimolia
young trees

Annona muricata
Soursop

Annona squamosa
Sugar Apple or Sweetsop

ARAUCARIA
(a roh kah' ree ə)

The Bunya Bunya, Monkey Puzzle and Norfolk Island Pines

FAMILY: ARAUCARIACEAE

Miraculously flourishing half a world apart on both fringes of the vast South Pacific, the grand and glorious *Araucarias* are outstanding conifers, all the more remarkable for being found only in the southern hemisphere, where conifers are rare.

Named for the Araucanian natives of South America, the true Monkey Puzzle Tree was the first of these to be introduced to cultivation in 1795. A stiff and starchy construction of angular, scaled branches, it is popular in cooler climates and quite hardy in the British Isles, for which its four cousins are much too tender.

Araucaria bidwillii
Bunya Bunya

The first of these, the Bunya Bunya, *A. bidwillii,* would seem like an artist's fantasy if it did not already exist. The squat trunk, rather like a fat elephant's foot, tapers rapidly and is surrounded by stiff branches nearly as long as itself. At the top of mature trees, these open out like umbrella spokes into a great bird's nest affair. All branches develop into scaly branchlets rather like Medusa's snake-hair. The

scales themselves are razor sharp. The great fruits, which develop high up, have the size and shape of a giant pineapple, and contain scarlet seeds which were a great delicacy to the Australian Aborigines.

Araucaria bidwillii
detail of fruit

Araucaria araucana
Monkey Puzzle Tree

27

Araucaria columellaris
Cook Pine

Araucaria heterophylla
Norfolk Island Pine

The other species are: *A. columellaris*, the slender Cook Pine, found only in French New Caledonia, and nearby islets: *A. cunninghamii*, the Hoop Pine, from north-east Australia, rather like an architect's model of a tree — all green sponge rubber and fuzz; and finally the most outstanding of all, *A. heterophylla*, the Norfolk Island Pine, which grows densely on that island, but is also native to coastal areas of north-east Australia. This tree is sometimes called the Star Pine from the regular star shapes formed by its horizontal layers of branchlets. *A. heterophylla* is normally a completely salt-resistant tree, all parts being protected by a waxy coating. It was much used in earlier days for formal planting along beachfront esplanades, but in recent years, these beachfront trees have been dying in parts of eastern Australia. Dendrologists cannot be certain, but they believe this is due to the pollution of coastal waters by synthetic detergents. Sea breezes spray the trees with these detergents which eat away the protective wax, leaving the tree open to salt burn. It is the trees near big cities that are the worst affected, but they were also planted first, and it may yet prove to be just the onset of old age.

Araucarias are not cut much for timber, but are of great value in preventing seaside erosion. The leaves are modified into overlapping scales.

Araucaria cunninghamii
Hoop Pine

ARBUTUS

(ah' byoo təs)

The Strawberry Trees and Madrones

FAMILY: ERICACEAE

The name Irish Strawberry Tree must surely be a hangover from some earlier Irish joke. The fruit certainly does not look or taste like a strawberry! Birds and bugs and children playing games are likely to appreciate them, but hardly anyone else.

But the tree itself is another matter! Seek one out in autumn when the branches are almost weighed down with panicles of tiny, fragrant urn-shaped heath flowers, looking just like lily of the valley. Among the flowers, remaining from last season, are the orange and red fruits bobbing in the sunlight like colourful Chinese checkers.

Arbutus is the old Latin name for a close Mediterranean relative, and it has beautifully gnarled, reddish branches and shiny, serrated, elliptical leaves. The flowers are white or pink.

Also to be found, at the other end of Europe, is the very similar but taller *A. andrachne* of Greece and Asia Minor. Still a handsome tree, but not as spectacular in its flower display, with the flower panicles borne in an erect fashion.

Half a world away, in California, is *A. menziesii*, the Madrone or California Strawberry Tree. As befits an American version, it is the tallest of all, reaching 30 m (100 ft) in nature. Its decorative terracotta bark peels away in large flaky patches. The leaves have smoother edges, and the flower panicles appear in spring. The fruit is orange-red and smooth, without the granular texture of the European species.

Somewhere in between the European and North American species is *A. canariensis* in the Canary Islands. Its leaves are always serrated, and softer in texture; the flowers green and pink.

Arbutus unedo
Irish Strawberry Tree

Arbutus canariensis
pink flowered variety

Arbutus menziesii
Madrone, detail of trunk

ARCHONTOPHOENIX
(ah kon to fee' niks)

The Bangalow Palms

FAMILY: PALMAE

'Chief of the Date Palms' might be a rough translation of the unwieldy Greek name *archontophoenix*. They are not really Date Palms at all, but then they weren't named by the Greeks as all ten species of Bangalow Palm are native to the Australian and Malaysian areas, and have only been exported from there in the last two centuries.

Tall and slender, their trunks are completely spineless, but ridged from the scars of fallen fronds. The juvenile leaves on young plants are either single or fish-tailed in shape, but in the mature tree they are completely pinnate, like those of a Coconut Palm, and arranged in a large, weeping crown.

The inflorescence opens below this, with the flowers of both sexes appearing in the form of a drooping, many-branched spadix, surrounded by two spathes. The 1 cm (½ in) fruits that follow are bright red and do bear a slight resemblance to a bunch of dates.

Two species of *Archontophoenix* are grown in warm climate gardens of both hemispheres, both of them native to eastern Australia.

Arecastrum romanzoffianum
Queen Palm, syn. *Cocos plumosa*

ARECASTRUM
(a rə kas' trəm)

The Queen Palm

FAMILY: PALMAE

The splendid and stately Queen Palm might well be hailed as South America's answer to the Bangalow Palm (see *Archontophoenix*). There certainly is a resemblance between the two palms and Queen Palms are often erroneously sold as Bangalows and even more frequently under the outdated name of *Cocos plumosa*.

Arecastrum is native to the coastal area from South Brazil to Argentina, and is perhaps more commonly grown in the Americas than the Bangalow. It is, however, a lot smaller, rarely reaching 13 m (40 ft), and much shorter lived, hardly ever living beyond thirty-five years.

There is one species only, with a ridged brownish-grey trunk and great weeping pinnate fronds up to 5 m (15 ft) in length. Both inflorescence and fruit are yellow and larger than those of *Archontophoenix*.

The light, airy fronds are most attractive as they move in a coastal breeze, and the Queen Palm will bring your garden that splendid tropical look in winter temperatures as low as 20°C (68°F). The species usually grown is *A. romanzoffianum*.

Archontophoenix cunninghamiana
Bangalow Palm

ARTOCARPUS
(ah toh kah' pəs)

The Breadfruits

FAMILY: MORACEAE

It was the Breadfruit, as every schoolboy and MGM shareholder knows, that caused Captain Bligh's undoing in Tahiti and indirectly led to the infamous mutiny on the *Bounty*. So where do these unappetizing fruits come from? All species, of which there are nearly forty, originate in South-East Asia and only one, *A. altilis*, was carried into the Pacific during the Polynesian migrations.

They are large, tropical relatives of the humble mulberry, which they even resemble on a vast scale, and together with the Candlenut, Coconut and Paper Mulberry, they were a mainstay of Polynesian culture. The bark can be beaten into cloth, the wood made good canoes and the sap forms a gum which could be used for caulking seams, chewing and even catching birds.

The peeled fruit can be baked, boiled or pickled when unripe, and will keep for years if buried in a pit. Ripened, it becomes sweet and tangy and can be pounded into a paste for dessert. The deeply lobed leaves (possibly the most beautiful of any tree) may be 1 m (3 ft) in length, and were used for roofing, clothing and wrapping foods for the oven. The Hawaiians call it *ulu*, the Tahitians *uru*.

Artocarpus (from the Greek words *artis* meaning bread and *carpos* meaning fruit) has many leaf varieties and is propagated from cuttings or from shoots which arise spontaneously from the roots. It must have a hot, humid climate and fruits most heavily in the summer wet season.

The related *A. heterophyllus* or Jakfruit is another Malaysian tree now cultivated in many countries, and noted for bearing the largest fruit in the world. These may reach 20 kg (40 lb) in weight, and be a full metre (3 ft) in length. They appear anywhere on the trunk or older branches. The sweet, juicy pulp, which is eaten cooked or raw in the tropics, is covered with a heavy, spiky rind. The leaves are simple and dark green.

Artocarpus altilis
detail, fruit and foliage

Artocarpus altilis
Breadfruit

Artocarpus altilis
leaf variety

AVERRHOA
(av və roh' ə)

The Five-corner Fruit or Carambole

FAMILY: OXALIDACEAE

Yet another warm-climate tree genus with edible fruit, the *Averrhoas* (two species only) originate from the Indo-Malaysian area and have spread all over the world. They are well worth growing, and although members of the Oxalis family they fortunately do not have the noxious garden manners of their smaller cousins. Each of them makes a handsome specimen tree for the semi-tropical garden with deep, moist soil.

A. bilimbi, the Cucumber Tree, is the less common of the two species, and grows to about 15 m (45 ft). The leaves are pinnate with between twenty-three and forty-five leaflets, and the panicles of small red and white flowers appear from the trunk and larger branches. These are followed by 7.5 cm (3 in) waxy fruit, like small gherkins. They are juicy but very sour, and should be cooked with sugar before eating.

A. carambola, the Carambole, Five-corner Fruit or Star Fruit, is a smaller, lighter tree, reaching only 10 m (30 ft). Its leaves have five to eleven leaflets and the flowers are white and reddish-purple, appearing all over the tree from branches, trunk and twigs. The fruits, about the size of a pear, are sharply five-cornered and look as if carved from orange wax. Inside this rind is a solid mass of sweet watery pulp, tasting something like a cross between apricots and passionfruit. Delicious!

Away from the Malaysian area, they are grown commercially in California, Florida, northern Australia and parts of Africa.

Averrhoa carambola
Star Fruit, Carambole

BACKHOUSIA

(bak hou' see ə)

The Lemon-scented Myrtles

FAMILY: MYRTACEAE

Looking for a tree that's really lemon-charged? With lemon fragrance in all its parts? You don't need to go beyond *Backhousia citriodora*, a slim, neat specimen rarely reaching 8 m (25 ft).

Named for a Yorkshire nurseryman, James Backhouse, the Lemon-scented Myrtle has attracted many common names, a proof of popularity not only in its native Australia, but also in South Africa, southern USA and southern Europe: Sweet Verbena Tree, Sand Verbena Myrtle and Tree Verbena are among them.

It is easily raised from half-ripe cuttings taken in spring, and grows fast in a good, rich acid soil. *Backhousia* is deservedly popular, not only for its handsome, pointed, shiny leaves with their strong citrus fragrance, but also for the clouds of tiny four-petalled white flowers produced in early summer, both in the leaf axils and at the end of twigs. These soon fall in the warm weather, but are outlived by the tiny green calyces, which are long-lasting, and the tree's principal display.

B. citriodora is also raised commercially, the foliage being crushed to extract a volatile citrus-scented oil.

The Lemon-scented Myrtle is one of a very small botanical genus (six species only), and between them they provide quite a choice of flavours. The larger *B. anisata* or Aniseed Tree, for instance, is for aniseed fans, but is less commonly grown. All six species enjoy moisture and warmth, with a winter minimum of 2°C (36°F).

Backhousia citriodora
Lemon-scented Myrtle

BANKSIA

(banks' ee ə)

The Honeysuckles

FAMILY: PROTEACEAE

There is no written proof that Sir Joseph Banks chose this genus to be his namesake. But he was not without vanity or influence in colonial circles, and known to be immensely proud of his discovery of these curious trees, that first day ashore at Botany Bay, in April 1770.

At any rate they were named *Banksia serrata*, the Saw Banksia or Red Honeysuckle, only the first of many related species found in the southern continent in succeeding years. The Red Honeysuckle is still a feature of the Australian east coast vegetation from Tasmania to Queensland, its gnarled trunk twisting into picturesque shapes among the outcrops of sandstone.

Banksia serrata
Red Honeysuckle

Banksia serrata
seed capsules, 'Banksia Men'

33

The bark is brown and deeply furrowed, covering a striking blood-red timber. The shining leathery leaflets are sharply toothed on each margin. But *Banksia* flowerheads are the most interesting feature of the genus, stunning 15 cm (6 in) golden spikes of tubular flowers arranged in neat parallel rows. As these gradually open from the base upwards, the entire inflorescence takes on a fuzzy appearance as the wiry stamens emerge one by one. *Banksia* flowers are notably rich in nectar, and the popular name of Honeysuckle is in reference to their attraction to birds and insects. As the flowers fall, the woody cone takes on a bizarre appearance as the individual seed cells open like a series of gaping mouths. Children call these 'Banksia Men', and Australian author May Gibbs based a series of nightmarish figures on them in her children's stories.

Banksia ericifolia
Heath-leafed Banksia

Banksia integrifolia
detail of flower head

Banksias are a most useful tree in poor sandy coastal soil, and completely salt-resistant. The closely related Coastal Banksia (*B. integrifolia*) bears inflorescences of a greenish yellow tone; its leaves are smooth-edged with silver reverses, and the trunk is smooth and deep grey.

The majority of the *Banksia* species, which number about fifty, are classed as shrubs, but there are several of tree size with more spectacularly coloured flowers. They include the orange *B. ericifolia* or Heath-leafed Banksia, the silver and orange *B. menziesii* and the yellow *B. grandis*.

Banksia grandis
Bull Banksia

BARKLYA
(bah klee' ə)

The Gold Blossom Tree
FAMILY: LEGUMINOSAE

There is very little about the *Barklya* to suggest at a distance that it is a member of the pea family Leguminosae, not even the tell-tale long pods. But that's what it is — a handsome but uncommon member of the rainforest flora in New South Wales and Queensland, named for a forgotten British Colonial Governor. It is a magnificent tree, the only one of its genus, and easily propagated from seed or cuttings.

B. syringifolia may reach 20 m (60 ft) in a warm sunny position. As its specific name suggests, its leaves are heart-shaped, exactly like those of lilacs (*Syringa*). The vivid orange-yellow flowers appear in long, stiff spikes in early summer, in superb contrast to the dark trunk and foliage. They are followed by small 5 cm (2 in) pods with one or two seeds each.

Barklya seems to be able to withstand temperatures down to –2°C (28°F) and has been raised in France, South Africa and Hawaii, though not apparently on the mainland of the United States.

BARRINGTONIA
(ba ring ton' ee ə)

The Fish Poison Tree
FAMILY: BARRINGTONIACEAE

Scattered about seaside areas of the Indian and Pacific Oceans there is a tall, handsome tree that has every appearance of the American Magnolia (*M. grandiflora*). It has the same buttressed trunk and the same leathery, glossy leaves. But there the resemblance stops, for the plump flower buds at branches' end open into brilliant pink and white puffballs of fragrant stamens up to 15 cm (6 in) in diameter. How often have I tried to photograph one on the tree itself, but alas, they never appear till late evening, and drop before dawn, scattering the lawns or beach around with their fading beauty.

The tree (named for an eighteenth century naturalist called Daines Barrington) is *Barringtonia asiatica*, and the most remarkable thing about it is the heart-shaped, four-sided fruits that develop after the flowers. These consist of a corky, fibrous husk containing one seed. They are completely buoyant, and will float for long distances, thus accounting for the tree's widespread location in beachside areas.

Barklya syringifolia
Gold Blossom Tree

Barringtonia asiatica
Hotu, Fish Poison Tree

35

Native fishermen all over the Pacific use them as floats for their nets, and even more importantly, they have discovered that the grated seed, sprinkled into a lagoon, will stun fish and bring them quickly to the surface where they can be picked up by hand. Because of the seed pod's shape, the Tahitians call the tree *hotu*, meaning the human heart, from which legend tells them it sprang.

One of the *hotu*'s most attractive features is the irregular colouring and fall of the leaves, which assume brilliant autumn tones at any time of the year.

Although generally found by the shore, *Barringtonia* grows equally well inland, and makes a fine garden specimen in warm climates, as do the closely related *B. acutangula* and *B. racemosa*.

Barringtonias are propagated from seed, and need a sub-tropical climate.

Barringtonia asiatica
foliage

Barringtonia asiatica
detail of flowers and foliage

BAUHINIA
(boh hin' ee ə)

The Orchid Trees

FAMILY: LEGUMINOSAE

Bauhinia blakeana
Hong Kong Orchid Tree

In the eighteenth century, when a new genus of tree was discovered that bore uniquely twin-lobed leaves, a suitably paired name was soon forthcoming. *Bauhinia!* What inspiration in the halls of horticulture! A diligent search had revealed the names of two sixteenth century botanists, twins perhaps, brothers certainly. And so the brothers Bauhin became immortalized in the curious foliage of these lovely trees from tropical Asia, Africa, the Americas and Australia.

Most *Bauhinias* grow readily from cuttings or seed, and will thrive in any climate down to a winter minimum of 7°C (45°F). The species most commonly grown is *B. variegata*, the Orchid Tree or Mountain Ebony from India, which is a slight, graceful plant, rarely surpassing a height

Bauhinia blakeana
detail of flower

Bauhinia monandra
St Thomas Tree

of 7 m (20 ft). It is not particularly useful, although the bark is sometimes used in dyeing, and the flower buds are considered edible in India. It is cultivated worldwide for the sheer beauty of its floral display — wonderful mauve-pink blossoms with five overlapped petals, often variegated in pink or purple.

Its smaller variety *B. variegata Alba* (The White Orchid Tree) bears flowers of purest white and lime green. Both varieties flower in early spring and better after a cold winter, when the deciduous leaves drop early.

The Chinese *B. purpurea* is similar in habit, but flowers more in the purple range, while its petals are larger and quite separate. *B. monandra* is a more tropical species from Burma, and is sometimes called the Butterfly flower. Each bloom opens white, marked in red and yellow, the whole rapidly changing to pink.

Most splendid of all, the Hong Kong Orchid Tree, *B. blakeana*, is the floral symbol of that small colony. It is an evergreen sterile hybrid and bears splashy reddish purple flowers in autumn and winter, each blossom being up to 15 cm (6 in) across. The South American *B. corniculata* bears showy night-flowering white blossoms. Australian *B. hookeri* is a 12 m (36 ft) tree from tropical Queensland, its small white flowers edged with crimson.

As tree members of the pea family Leguminosae, all *Bauhinias* (with the exception of the sterile *B. blakeana*) bear long pea-like pods which turn brown and frequently hang on the branches in an unsightly fashion until the new foliage appears.

Apart from the Australian species, most Orchid Trees need encouragement and vigorous pruning to develop a tree-like shape.

Bauhinia variegata
terminal flower cluster

Bauhinia variegata
Orchid Tree

Bauhinia variegata 'Candida'
Mountain Ebony

BEAUCARNEA
(boh kah' nee ə)

The Ponytail Tree

FAMILY: AGAVACEAE

Familiar to indoor gardeners as the decorative Ponytail Plant of so many window collections, the remarkable *Beaucarnea recurvata* is in the wild a tree.

In its desert home of the southern United States and Mexico, the eyecatching bulbous trunk may reach 2 m (6 ft) in diameter at ground level and tower up to 10 m (30 ft) in the air, branching heavily. Each branch is tipped with a dense bunch of smooth grassy leaves that trail down the full height of a man, making it look rather like a stage designer's fantasy. Small white flowers appear among these terminal clusters in spring, but the tree is fancied largely for its massive trunk structure. Seen in the open it is easy to remember its other popular name, the Elephant's Foot Tree.

Beaucarnea is normally grown from seed, and is suited particularly to dry gardens of warm climate areas.

Beaucarnea recurvata
Ponytail Tree

BETULA
(bet' yoo lə)

The Birches

FAMILY: BETULACEAE

Hardiest of the deciduous broad-leafed trees, the slim and beautiful birches, 'Ladies of the Woods' as the poet Coleridge christened them, include over thirty-five species from all three continents of the northern hemisphere. Vast forests of them spread in a band across Scandinavia, the USSR and North America, thinning out and gradually shrinking into shrubby growth as their range blurs into the Arctic tundra.

In their southern limits, they tend to huddle decoratively in small groups on poor sandy soil or gravel beds along rivers, but in horticultural use they grow well in any soil as long as the drainage is good.

As a rule, birches are among the lightest of trees, tall and slender, with vividly coloured bark that tends to peel away in horizontal strips. In the species most commonly grown in cooler-climate gardens (they are no use at all in sub-tropical climates), the bark is silver-grey or white; but there are others with reddish-brown, black and yellow bark. The leaves usually are slightly more angular than oval, deeply toothed and in most species lightly borne and fluttering in the least sign of a breeze. Insignificant flowers are followed by catkins made up of a series of winged seeds. These catkins generally hang and disintegrate when ripe.

Betula pendula 'Dalecarlica'
Swedish Birch

Birches (*Betula* to give them their original Roman name) grow readily from seed except for a few fancy-leafed varieties which must be grafted. The incredibly fine branches of most species weep gracefully, and at one time were tied together as brooms, and to tan schoolboys' backsides. The deciduous leaves turn to purest gold before they fall in late autumn.

The Swedish Birch (*B. pendula* CV 'Dalecarlica') is particularly worth seeking out for its deeply cut leaves, while *B. pendula* CV 'Youngii' or Young's Weeping Birch is the perfect specimen tree for a poolside position. Its branches which weep in an exaggerated fashion will need support, however, for the tree is relatively shallow-rooted and may topple.

Birch timber is used for modern Scandinavian furniture and kitchen utensils, and is also laminated into some of the world's finest plywood. The bark of all species is remarkably tough and water-resistant and was long used by North American Indians for their canoes.

Betula pendula
detail of leaves and fruit

Betula pendula
European White Birch

Betula lenta
Cherry Birch

Betula pendula 'Youngii'
Young's Weeping Birch

Betula papyrifera
Paper or Canoe Birch

BISCHOFIA
(bis schof' ee ə)

The Toog Tree
FAMILY: EUPHORBIACEAE

One of the most important timber trees of Indonesia and South-East Asia, the Toog or Koka Tree *(Bischofia javanica)* is found in a wide tropical band well out into Polynesia. It is a popular and decorative specimen tree in warm climate gardens, growing straight and smooth to 23 m (70 ft).

The Toog tree is semi-deciduous, with bronze-green compound leaves that are divided into three pointed, long-oval leaflets which turn bright red and fall from time to time. The bark is smooth and grey, and the tiny flowers are yellowish-green and quite without petals. They appear in great, cloudy panicles, male on one tree, female on another. The female flowers later develop into clusters of tiny pea-sized fruits which may be reddish-brown, yellow or almost black.

The Samoans process the bark to extract a brown dye used in colouring their patterned tapa cloths and mats. Several parts of the tree have use in medicine and the timber, while not of the finest quality, has many uses in less sophisticated communities.

Bischofia was named for a European botanist.

Bischofia javanica
Toog Tree, Koka

BIXA
(bik' sə)

The Lipstick Tree
FAMILY: BIXACEAE

Bixa orellana
Lipstick Tree, Annatto

Grown as an ornamental in warm climate gardens everywhere, the colourful Lipstick Tree, *Bixa orellana*, is native to the Amazon region of South America. Grown easily and quickly from seed or cuttings (cuttings flower earlier), it is inclined to be bushy in shape and needs a certain amount of pruning and training to adopt tree shape in the open garden.

Bixa may reach 10 m (30 ft) in warm climates, and the evergreen heart-shaped leaves may be 17.5 cm (7 in) in length. All summer long, charming pink and white flowers, like single wild roses, appear at the tips of branches, and these are succeeded by clusters of almond-shaped red-brown fruit covered in soft spines.

For centuries, an orange dye extracted from the seed coverings has been used as body paint by South American Indians, and in the days before synthetics revolutionized industry, the tree was planted commercially for this same dye which was used to colour cheese, margarine, chocolate, fabric and paints — and of course, lipstick, hence the popular name.

Bixa is also known by the native names of Achiote and Annatto, and is valued additionally for its stem fibre (used in rope mats) and an adhesive gum which is extracted from all parts.

BLIGHIA
(blai' ee ə)

The Akee Apple
FAMILY: SAPINDACEAE

Captain Bligh may have lost his reputation over the breadfruit trees, but his name is remembered throughout the warm-climate zones of the world by another attractive fruiting tree, *Blighia sapida*, commonly known as the Akee Apple.

Originally from West Africa, but now naturalized throughout the West Indies, it is seen in tropical gardens everywhere, the only one of its genus. Growing to 13 m (40 ft) in height, it is a handsome ornamental tree with shining compound leaves consisting of up to ten oblong leaflets of graduated sizes, the largest towards the tip.

The five-petalled flowers are fragrant and greenish; the fruit, a rather pear-shaped, ribbed capsule varies from a pale apricot to ruby pink in colour. The flesh is said to be poisonous when green, but is delicious and nutritious when ripe. It is eaten raw, boiled or fried.

Blighia is related to the Australian *Harpullia* and *Cupaniopsis* (which see) and will grow in any moist, rich soil. It is propagated from seed and will stand several degrees of frost.

BOMBAX
(bom' baks)

The Silk Cotton Trees
FAMILY: BOMBACACEAE

From tropical forests of Asia, South America and Africa comes a genus of splendid specimen trees called *Bombax*. Their rather jingoistic name is in fact an ancient Greek word for cotton, although the filaments obtained from their bulky seedpods are far too fine to spin, and are used instead as a substitute for kapok.

B. malabaricum, the Red Cotton Tree from South-East Asia, is the most commonly seen species, in gardens of northern Australia, Hong Kong, Africa, Hawaii and many other places. It is a tall tree, reaching 35 m (105 ft) and more, with a widely buttressed trunk at maturity. Easily raised from seed, this *Bombax* needs deep soil and lots of moisture all year round to grow really well and produce its stunning crop of 17.5 cm (7 in) flowers in early spring. These appear at the ends of branches shortly after the tree loses its foliage for a brief period in winter.

Bombax leaves are strikingly digitate and up to 50 cm (20 in) across, consisting of three to seven widely spread leaflets. The trunk is sometimes spiny, and the tree may need a little pruning and staking when young.

Blighia sapida
Akee Apple

Bombax malabaricum
Red Silk Cotton

Bombax ellipticum
Shaving Brush Tree

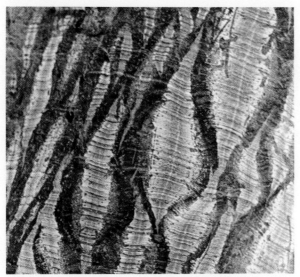

Bombax ellipticum
detail of bark, Honolulu

Bombax malabaricum
detail of flowers

BRACHYCHITON
(brak ee kai' tən)

The Lacebarks and Kurrajongs

FAMILY: STERCULIACEAE

Considered by many to be Australia's most spectacular genus of flowering trees, the Kurrajongs (*Brachychiton* spp.) are maddeningly irregular in their flowering habits. But in a good early summer, a garden specimen of the Illawarra Flame *(B. acerifolium)* is a sight never to be forgotten — a vivid scarlet blur. The effect is heightened further if it is contrasted with the mauve flowers of a nearby Jacaranda, which blooms at the same time (see *Jacaranda*).

The *Brachychitons* are most variable trees, variable in size, shape of trunk and leaves, and size and colouring of flowers, which are generally bell-shaped. Those which are native to the semi-tropical forests of Australia's moist east coast tend to grow tall and flower profusely on the bare tree after leaf fall, in summer. Others, native to the dry Australian outback, are generally smaller in size with bloated water-storing trunks. Their flowers are less showy and tend to appear under the new summer foliage which is often used for fodder in drought-stricken areas.

Brachychiton populneum
Kurrajong

43

A peculiarity of the Kurrajongs is the extreme leaf variation. On one tree of *B. populneum*, for instance, you may find simple pointed leaves, rather like a poplar's leaves and others that are long and angular, divided into anything from three to nine pointed lobes. Because of this, the tree is sometimes listed as *B. diversifolia,* though there is no true species of this name.

Brachychiton discolor
detail of summer blossom

All the Kurrajongs thrive in warm, dryish climates such as California, South Africa and the Mediterranean, but the desert species do not do well in the moister sub-tropics like Hawaii and Hong Kong.

Wood of many Kurrajong species has been used in the Australian outback for shingles and fencing, but generally they are cultivated only for their decorative and shade-giving qualities.

The name *Brachychiton* is of Greek origin. There are many intermediate hybrids, and all can be grown from seed or cuttings.

Brachychiton populneum
detail of spring flowers

Brachychiton rupestre
Queensland Bottle Tree

Brachychiton populneo-acerifolius
Pink Kurrajong

Brachychiton discolor
Queensland Lacebark

Brachychiton bidwillii
Pink Lacebark

Brachychiton acerifolium
Illawarra Flame

BRASSAIA
(bra sae' ə)

The Octopus Tree
FAMILY: ARALIACEAE

Propagated everywhere by the thousand, as befits one of the world's top ten indoor plants, Queensland's *Brassaia* or Octopus Tree gives no hint of its full potential until you've seen it growing unrestrained in a sub-tropical garden.

The handsome, umbrella-shaped compound leaves are still there but are 1 m (3 ft) in diameter and borne in long-stemmed clusters all over a many-branched tree that can reach up to 13 m (40 ft) in height. And throughout spring and summer a most extraordinary floral phenomenon appears from the heart of each leaf cluster — a series of curved and twisting flower stems looking exactly like the tentacles of a red octopus. Just like the octopus, these appear to be covered on one side with round sucker shapes, which close inspection reveals to be the heads of small red flowers.

These flowers are followed by plump, purplish-red fruit containing a number of seeds from which new plants can easily be raised. Alternatively, if you are in more of a hurry, *Brassaia* can be raised from quite large cuttings or air-layers.

The Octopus Tree enjoys warmth and plenty of water, and its normal habit is to form a single trunk with almost vertical branches appearing from quite low down. If you prefer a denser, more bushy plant, just keep cutting it back.

Brassaia is still often listed incorrectly as *Schefflera*, which is a related genus.

Brassaia actinophylla
Octopus Tree, Umbrella Tree

45

BROUSSONETIA
(broo son nae' tee ə)

The Paper Mulberry

FAMILY: MORACEAE

Not a terribly spectacular tree for decorative planting, the Chinese Paper Mulberry, *Broussonetia papyrifera* has long been one of the most valued of trees in less sophisticated societies. For its tough fibrous bark can be soaked and beaten into a useful fabric which in various cultures has functioned as paper, cloth or even shoe leather, depending on the treatment it receives.

It can be oiled to waterproof it, pulped to soften it, dyed to colour it. At the time of the European discovery of Polynesia, the wealthy wore it draped into snowy white togas, the warriors used it for remarkably strong helmets and sandals, and even the poor relied on it for their simple loincloths. It was *tapa*, the universal fabric, and even today its manufacture is quite an industry in Tonga and Samoa. Alas, it is no longer worn.

Broussonetia papyrifera
Paper Mulberry, Tapa

Broussonetia papyrifera
detail of foliage

The Paper Mulberry, also known as *tapa* tree or (in Hawaii) as *po'a'aha*, is easily propagated from seed, suckers or cuttings.

It grows quickly to 10 m (30 ft) in a frost-free climate and produces handsome, dull green leaves up to 20 cm (8 in) across. These are tremendously variable, ranging from a simple heart shape to elaborately lobed and toothed outlines as shown in our illustration.

The male flowers appear in loose, hanging, greenish catkins. The female flowers (always on a separate plant) form a fuzzy round head, almost 2.5 cm (1 in) in diameter. The red fruits look just like those of the edible Mulberry (see *Morus*).

Pierre Marie Broussonet, after whom the tree was named, was an eighteenth century professor of botany.

BROWNEA
(broun' ee a)

The Rose of Venezuela

FAMILY: LEGUMINOSAE

The huge, cabbage-sized, orange-red flower clusters of this wonderful South American tree, *Brownea grandiceps*, the Rose of Venezuela, almost play hide-and-seek among its dense foliage. Look more closely and you will notice that each head is composed of dozens of tubular, reddish blossoms with yellow stamens, fitted together very much like a hatmaker's tulle confection.

Brownea grandiceps
Rose of Venezuela

Brownea grandiceps
detail of new foliage

B. grandiceps like others of its genus was named for Patrick Brown, an Irish-born author and physician of Jamaica. It is a tall tree, growing up to 20 m (60 ft) in its jungle home, but of course not so high in cultivation. The trunk is stout, the branches greyish and woolly to the touch, and the foliage consists of great rosettes of pinnate leaves, each up to 1 m (3 ft) in length and consisting of about twelve pairs of large leaflets. When young, these great leaves are completely flaccid and often reddish-bronze in colour.

Even more spectacular in the warm-climate garden is the smaller Panama Flame, *B. mac-rophylla*. The flowers of this species are inclined to open before the foliage and are a brilliant mass of gold, pink and scarlet long-stemmed blossoms that pop directly out of the slender trunk and branches.

BUCKINGHAMIA
(buk ing ham' ee ə)

The Ivory Curl Tree

FAMILY: PROTEACEAE

A profusely flowering tree from the rainforests of southern Queensland, *Buckinghamia* has proved amenable to cultivation over quite a wide climatic range, though its size is directly related to the amount of year-round heat it gets. It has flowered successfully in areas where the temperature drops to freezing point.

Like so many of Australia's other flowering trees it is a member of the Proteaceae family, and there is only one species. This may reach 20 m (60 ft) in a suitably warm climate, but rarely passes 6 m (18 ft) in cultivation.

The glossy, leathery leaves, about 15 cm (6 in) long, have rippled edges and closely resemble those of the related *Macadamia* (which see). They are evergreen and greyish beneath. The flowers, borne in late summer, are up to 22 cm (9 in) long, and consist of long spikes of curled creamy florets, the whole reminiscent of ostrich plumes. As the florets open, the flower spikes weep under their own weight until the entire tree is a mass of fragrant blossom, almost hiding the foliage. Bees naturally adore it.

B. celsissima has been used successfully as a street tree in Queensland and New South Wales, and should do equally well in South Africa and the southern United States. It is best raised from seed.

Brownea macrophylla
Panama Flame

Buckinghamia celsissima
Ivory Curl Tree

BUTEA
(boot' ee ə)

The Dhak Tree
FAMILY: LEGUMINOSAE

A brilliantly flowering specimen tree for the warm-climate garden, the *Butea* or Dhak Tree will tolerate a much wider range of soil conditions than many of its semi-tropical relatives.

It is a slow-growing, rather gnarled tree of stark appearance until the flowers burst open in spring. These are arranged in 15 cm (6 in) racemes of curved, orange-red pea flowers with a marvellous silvery sheen to their exteriors. They are followed by typical long pea pods which are grey and furry. The foliage consists of a number of 20 cm (8 in) compound leaves, each made up of three leaflets. These have a rather silky texture and are blueish-green in colour.

In its native Bangladesh and Burma, the *Butea* (named for an eighteenth century Earl of Bute) is known also as the Pulas Tree and Flame of the Forest. The sap is valued locally as an astringent, and the entire tree yields a gum known as Bengal Kino. The flowers are often distilled into an orange dye.

A splendid choice for warm coastal gardens, *B. frondosa* will resist a degree of salt. It is also suited to saline desert soils and will even put up with an occasional light frost.

Butea frondosa
Flame of the Forest, Dhak Tree

BUTIA
(byoo' tee ə)

The Yatay Palms
FAMILY: PALMAE

A small genus of palms related to the Coconut and Date Palms, *Butias* are generally much smaller in stature and suitable for quite small gardens in a warm climate.

B. capitata (the Jelly Palm) will rarely reach 5 m (15 ft) in height, although its deeply ridged trunk may be 50 cm (18 in) in diameter. The spiny-stemmed fronds may be 3 m (9 ft) in length and are arranged in a spiral about the trunk. They are bluish-green in colour and old fronds tend to remain for a long time after browning off.

The Yatay Palm bears small greenish flowers in drooping spadices. These are followed by yellow fruits, the pulp of which is edible and said to resemble a scented jelly.

Butia capitata var. *Odorata*
Yatay or Jelly Palm

A second species, *B. yatay*, the Wine Palm, from Argentina, may also reach the same height. Its fronds are a more brilliant blue-grey and the flower spikes are almost twice as long. Its fruits are oval, orange-red and up to 3.5 cm (1¼ in) long. In spite of its popular name, I can find no reference to the fruit being used as a beverage, although it is certainly edible.

Butia grow relatively slowly from seed, but do not have the voracious root-spread that makes the Date Palms such difficult customers in the home garden.

CAESALPINIA
(says al pin' ee ə)

The Dwarf Poinciana or Barbadoes Pride

FAMILY: LEGUMINOSAE

Long spikes of flaming scarlet and yellow blossom hovering like butterflies above a mass of pale, fern-like foliage, and anywhere in a warm climate you've spotted the brilliant *Caesalpinia pulcherrima*. So universally is this small tree cultivated, its original home is unknown.

It grows readily from seed, rarely reaching more than 4 m (12 ft), and the foliage is so dense it is sometimes trimmed to hedge height and known as Barbadoes Flower Fence. What a sight it makes with gorgeous flower spikes appearing all along its length — scarlet and yellow, plain orange or pink, according to variety.

Long stamens and the flat green pods of the pea family are other points of identification on this spiky-branched sapling, the commonest, but by no means the only one of a dazzling tropical genus.

Named for sixteenth-century botanist Andrea Caesalpini, there are about thirty-five species altogether.

Next in popularity would probably be the Leopard Tree, *C. ferrea*. This grows fast to full tree size and flowers in late summer, the brilliant yellow blossoms appearing like a golden haze above a notably feathery crown that lets through plenty of light. Its special beauty is in the bark, a smooth, shadowy surface spotted in beige, grey and white, constantly changing pattern as the flakes peel away.

Caesalpinia pulcherrima
Barbadoes Pride

A rather similar tree is the Brazilwood, *C. echinata*, which has a spiny trunk and is the national tree of Brazil.

Most *Caesalpinias* are native to Central and South America, although there are representatives in India, Japan, Africa, China and northern Australia. The pods and bark of many are sought commercially for tannin and dye, while the Malaysian Sappanwood, *C. sappan*, is the source of a valuable commercial timber.

Caesalpinia ferrea
Leopard Tree

Caesalpinia spinosa
Tara

CALLICOMA
(kal lə koh' mə)

The Blackwattle

FAMILY: SAXIFRAGACEAE

From the appearance of its fluffy cream flower-clusters, it is easy to see why this tree also was given the name 'wattle' in Australia's early colonial times. They certainly do resemble the flowers of *Acacia* but in fact belong to quite a different family, the Saxifragaceae.

At one time, *Callicomas* grew densely around Sydney Harbour, but they virtually disappeared with the spread of suburbia, because they enjoy shady places and the shelter of other trees.

The 15 cm (6 in) serrated leaves, long-oval in shape, are a pleasant, light green when young. The Blackwattle ranges from shrub size to 10 m (30 ft) in height. It is shallow rooted, enjoys the same acid soils and humid conditions as Azaleas, Rhododendrons and Camellias, but grows over a much wider climatic range. It is now a popular garden specimen in many countries away from its native continent.

The name *Callicoma* is compounded from two Greek words *kallos* and *kome*, roughly translated as 'beautiful hair', a reference to the profuse golden stamens.

C. serratifolia, the name of the grown species, merely means that it has serrated leaves.

Callicoma serratifolia
Blackwattle

Callicoma serratifolia
Blackwattle

Callicoma serratifolia
detail of flowers and foliage

50

CALLISTEMON
(kal li stem' ən)

The Bottlebrushes

FAMILY: MYRTACEAE

Like so much of the natural Australian vegetation, the colourful genus *Callistemon* is part of the Myrtle family, Myrtaceae, as are *Angophora, Backhousia, Eucalyptus, Leptospermum, Melaleuca* and *Syzygium*, to list only a few of the trees represented in this book.

But the special glory of the *Callistemons* is their long spikes of flowers without petals, just a mass of clustered stamens arranged in formal rows, like a bottlebrush. The name *Callistemon* is in fact Greek for 'beautiful stamens'. These bottlebrushes appear profusely in many shades of crimson and scarlet, in cream and white, and even in pink, green or violet in less common species.

The Weeping Bottlebrush, *C. viminalis*, in particular, has become a much sought-after garden specimen in Florida, California and Hawaii, in southern England, South Africa, Hong Kong and the Mediterranean area. Like most other *Callistemons* it is found naturally in low-lying ground or even creek beds, which makes it particularly useful for badly drained sites or for planting on the low side of built-up roads and driveways.

Callistemon viminalis
Weeping Bottlebrush

Callistemon shiressi
Cream Bottlebrush

Callistemon viminalis
Weeping Bottlebrush

51

Callistemon citrinus
Crimson Bottlebrush

A fast grower with a graceful willow-like habit, it may reach 5 m (25 ft) in five or six years, and the maximum flower display is in late spring.

Another species of similar habit is the White or Willow Bottlebrush, *C. salignus*. This is perhaps a little sturdier, resisting a degree or two of frost, and quite amenable to the salt spray of coastal gardens. The bottlebrushes, borne at the end of weeping branchlets, are pale cream and contrast beautifully with the rosy pink of new foliage.

A third common species is *C. citrinus*, which bears the same scarlet flowers as *C. viminalis*, but without the weeping habit. Its foliage is distinctively lemon-scented, and the new leaves a soft pink.

Bottlebrushes are generally propagated from cuttings.

CALLITRIS
(kal li' trəs)

The Cypress Pines
FAMILY: CUPRESSACEAE

The most commonly seen conifers in the Australian landscape, the native *Callitris* or Cypress Pines are found in all states of Australia, and have been widely grown in other countries because of their resistance to dry, sandy conditions. They will survive where no self-respecting pine or spruce would think of taking a foothold, and are typically found dotting the western plains beyond Australia's coastal Great Dividing Range.

The trees are generally of tall cypress shape with extremely fine cypress-like foliage, the leaves adapted into the tiniest of scales. The bark is usually dark, the cones small and divided into six segments of variable length.

Apart from their drought-resistant qualities, the Cypress Pines are greatly valued for their pale, colourfully knot-marked timber, which is completely resistant to termites. This wood is hard and dense and takes a beautiful polish. It is often used for flooring or feature panelling.

Callitris may be propagated from seed or cuttings struck with bottom heat.

Callistemon salignus
Willow Bottlebrush

Callitris rhomboidea
Port Jackson Pine

Callitris columellaris
White Cypress Pine

CALOCEDRUS
(kal oh see' drəs)

The Incense Cedars

FAMILY: CUPRESSACEAE

Rather large and slow-growing for private gardens, there are three species of *Calocedrus* or Incense Cedars, from California and nearby states, from Taiwan, and from southern China.

They are all of similar, tall, pyramidal shape with open, upward-pointing branches and scaly leaflets arranged in flattened fern-like sprays. The cones are very small, the timber very fragrant and much used for house interiors in the Orient.

Apart from their natural range, *Calocedrus* specimens are often seen in large parks or as formal plantings by public buildings. There are some beautiful specimens thriving in Australia's capital city, Canberra.

Smaller cultivars of the American *C. decurrens* named CV *compacta* and CV *intricata* are interesting for collectors of conifers. They are, of course, propagated by cuttings.

Callitris cupressiformis
detail of fruit, foliage

Calocedrus decurrens
California Incense Cedar

53

CALODENDRON
(kal oh den' dron)

The Cape Chestnut

FAMILY: RUTACEAE

One of Africa's most delightful trees, the heavily flowering *Calodendron capense* or Cape Chestnut is now seen in gardens all over the temperate to tropical world, and will even resist winter temperatures as low as –5°C (22°F). Its botanical name is Greek for 'beautiful tree'.

Best propagated from cuttings, it will grow rapidly to 7 m (20 ft) and more slowly thereafter, particularly in cooler areas. The handsomely spotted leaves are evergreen in warm climates, but may be completely deciduous elsewhere. It will usually flower in either late summer or early spring, but more rarely at other times of the year, according to the individual tree.

The 10 cm (4 in) flowers, which appear in open panicles at branch ends, each have five curling pink petals, five crimson-spotted petaloids and five rigid pink stamens. They are highly perfumed, pick well, and are reminiscent of Rhododendron blooms.

The *Calodendron* produces a number of seeds, and seedlings are not uncommonly found nearby, but they take up to ten years to reach flowering size. Cuttings are quicker and a more reliable method of propagation.

Calodendron capense
Cape Chestnut

Calodendrons like water at all times, and are not for dry areas. They prefer the company and shelter of other trees, when they will grow to taller and more striking specimens. When exposed they tend to grow too horizontal and may fall over in a heavy wind.

It is sad to imagine such a lovely tree can be coveted for reasons other than its flower display, but in its native Africa it is felled for timber.

Calodendron capense
flowers and foliage

CANANGA
(ka nan' jə)

The Ylang Ylang

FAMILY: ANNONACEAE

Even the poor-sighted could hardly overlook a *Cananga odorata* planted nearby, or even in a garden several houses away, for its appeal is as much to the nose as to the eye. It is unfortunately purely for the warmer climate and is found naturally over a wide area from Burma down through Malaysia and Indonesia to the north of Australia.

A tall, rather narrow tree, with weeping, brittle branches, it bears the long, drooping, rippled leaves of the custard apple, to which it is related (see *Annona*). But in the leaf axils, in autumn, appear clusters of the most striking, long-lasting flowers. They are up to 7.5 cm (3 in) across, with five thin, curiously drooping petals. These are lime green at first, ripening to a warm orange after a few days, and are overpoweringly fragrant, particularly in the early morning.

In parts of its native range, *Cananga* is also known as the Perfume Tree or Ylang Ylang (which means the same thing), and individual blossoms are worn about the person or placed in cupboards to perfume linen. Earlier this century they were used to perfume coconut oil for a mens' hairdressing which was sold as Macassar oil, but it is now out of fashion. Elsewhere, the tree's trunk was used to carve drums and canoes; the bark was used for rope, and the flowers to make medicine palatable.

They are widely planted in Hawaii, but not often seen in their native Australia, which is a pity.

Cananga odorata
Ylang Ylang, Perfume Tree

CARICA
(ka' rik ə)

The Papaya or Paw Paw

FAMILY: CARICACEAE

Alas, how many warm climate gardens sport a perfectly flourishing, virgin and never fruiting Papaya! You can grow one from seed easily enough, but some Papayas bear only male flowers, some female, some hermaphroditic blossoms, and others all three kinds together.

Only the Papaya plant itself knows what sex it is until it flowers, when it is too late to make a change. Far better to buy a guaranteed bisexual plant from a reputable nursery.

The Papaya or *Carica papaya* is in fact hardly a tree at all by most criteria. It has, for instance, a rather succulent, hollow trunk which never develops into hard wood. It scarcely branches unless damaged, just grows continually taller to as high as 8 m (25 ft), dropping its old foliage as it goes, and is always topped with a palm-like crown of magnificent compound leaves.

Male Papayas (or Paw Paws as they are known in Australia) bear their creamy-green flowers in long dangling racemes. The females opt for small, neat clusters. Both appear from the leaf axils. Only female trees will fruit, of course, after the necessary preliminaries, producing masses of green or orange melon-sized fruit close to the trunk among the leaves. These have a thick, delicious pulp and are hollow.

Papayas should begin to fruit within a year of planting in a warm climate, and their fruiting life may continue for fifteen years. In spite of their tropical American origin, they are surprisingly hardy and may even be raised in cool temperate zones in a sheltered position. They will stand occasional frost, though both leaves and trunks may be badly marked.

Carica papaya
Paw Paw, Papaya

Carica papaya
ripe fruit

Carica papaya
female flowers

Carica papaya
male flowers

Carya laciniata
Shellbark Hickory

CARYA
(keə′ ry ə)

The Hickories and Pecans

FAMILY: JUGLANDACEAE

All Hickories in cultivation are North American in origin, though there are one or two Asiatic species. The shame is that so few of them *are* in cultivation outside their native area. They grow fast, straight and tall, they bear delicious nuts (Pecans ripen on one species) and they turn an unbelievable pure gold in autumn. They are however, very difficult to transplant, particularly when they reach any size.

So the only solution is to do what the squirrels do and bury the nuts. They come up in no time, but many years will pass before you can pick your own crop. Still, if you can put the idea of pecan pie and *pralinés* out of your mind and just think of the tree for its own beautiful sake, you will try to locate one among your nursery acquaintances.

Carya species like a deep, rich soil, and enjoy a surprisingly wide climatic range, from Canada's Quebec province right down into Mexico in their native North America.

The Hickories are closely related to the walnuts (see *Juglans*), and like them, bear handsome, fragrant compound leaves, each consisting of a number of spear-shaped leaflets (ranging five to seventeen according to the species). Flowers of both sexes appear on the one tree, the male in long triple catkins, the female in small spikes at ends of branches. The nuts vary in both shape and colour according to species.

C. illinoinensis, the Pecan, bears the best nuts. The Shagbark Hickory, *C. ovata*, is the most striking tree, growing twice as tall as it does wide. The trunk of a mature specimen is decorated with threads and patches of tattered bark. The Shagbarks make a fine spectacle with their brilliant autumn colour.

The scientific name *Carya*, is from *karya*, the old Greek word for their close relatives, the Walnuts.

Carya illinoinensis
Pecan

Carya glabra
Pignut

Carya illinoinensis
Pecan nuts

Carya glabra
detail of foliage and nuts

CARYOTA
(ka ree oh' tə)

The Fishtail Palms

FAMILY: PALMAE

More often seen as indoor plants, the many species of *Caryota* (from the Greek *karyotis* meaning a Date Palm), are eyecatching specimens outdoors in the tropical garden. They must have both heat and humidity, for all of them are native to an area stretching from Sri Lanka through Malaysia to Australia, and up through the Solomons to the Philippines.

They are characterized by tall straight trunks (often with a suckering habit) and great drooping bipinnate fronds, the leaflets of which are forked at the tip, just like a fish's tail.

Caryotas grow at a great rate in their native climate, but do not flower until they reach maximum height, which may take years. Then the drooping panicles of flowers are really a sight! In the case of the Wine Palm, *C. urens*, they may hang down 7 m (20 ft). Then the palm produces seed and dies, though it can be expected to produce offsets before this happens.

Caryota species vary widely in height, shape of leaflets and suckering facility. *C. rumphiana* is the giant of the family, growing to 25 m (75 ft). *C. mitis* is a lot smaller and spreads rapidly from suckers into a dense thicket.

All species may be propagated from seeds or offsets.

Caryota rumphiana
Fishtail Palm

CASSIA
(kas' see ə)

The Sennas or Shower Trees

FAMILY: LEGUMINOSAE

Possibly the most attractive of warm-climate plant genera, the Sennas or *Cassias* are certainly the most widespread. There are between four and five hundred species, native to all subtropical areas of both the northern and southern hemispheres, and blooming in a wide spectrum of colours.

Not all *Cassias* are trees of course. There are shrubs, climbers and perennials among them, but the tree species are by far the most numerous and spectacular. They all like an open sunny position and seem to do best in well-drained soil of a warm to tropical climate, though many of the North American species are reasonably frost hardy.

Cassias are a large sub-division of the pea family, Leguminosae, and in spite of their great variety have a number of points in common. They have pinnate leaves with a variable number of small leaflets appearing alternately down the leaf stalk. The flowers are five-petalled and open, with prominent stamens. They are most commonly yellow, but are also found in red, orange, white or pink.

Cassia spectabilis
Golden Wonder Tree

Cassia javanica
Apple Blossom Cassia

Cassia X *hybrida*
Rainbow Shower

Cassia X *hybrida*
Rainbow Shower

Cassia fistula
Pudding Pipe Tree

Cassia surattensis
Singapore Shower

Cassia brewsteri
Cigar Cassia

In some species the flowers appear in long, weeping sprays, and in others are rigid spikes at the end of branchlets. Some are perfumed, some not, and they cross-pollinate indiscriminately, producing many lovely hybrids.

Though different *Cassia* species flower in different seasons, almost every one is capable of gorgeous display for weeks or months on end, carpeting the ground all around with colourful blossom. The flowers are followed by long pea-like pods which are up to 60 cm (2 ft) long in some species. These are a rich source of tannin and of medicinal senna. From a gardener's point of view, the pods are the only disadvantage, hanging in unsightly masses from the branches, and finally littering the grass below.

Cassias are mostly fast growers, raised easily from seed, and their wide range means that there are suitable species for almost all gardening climates. While we are only able to illustrate a few of the best, these pictures should give some idea of the group's potential.

The name *Cassia* is from the Hebrew name for one of the species, *quetsi'oth*.

Cassia multijuga
Golden Shower

CASTANEA
(kas tan' ee ə)

The Chestnuts
FAMILY: FAGACEAE

Never a large genus at the best of times (there are fewer than a dozen species found in all three continents of the northern hemisphere), the handsome, tall-growing deciduous Chestnuts, appear to be doomed. Attacked by an Asiatic fungus that destroys the tree's circulation (very like the Dutch Elm Disease, see *Ulmus*), they have been virtually wiped out right across the North American continent, and it seems only a matter of time before the same fungus appears in Europe.

But the chestnut fungus needs other Chestnuts to live on to help it spread, so they are still a good specimen choice in parts of the world to which they are not native, particularly in the southern hemisphere.

The most loved species is the Spanish or Sweet Chestnut, *Castanea sativa*, from Europe, Asia Minor and North Africa. These are grown principally for the nutritious brown nuts which are enclosed in a prickly burr-like casing in late summer. They are often roasted as a winter delicacy, or puréed with vanilla and sugar as a delicious dessert.

The generic name *Castanea* comes from the old Greek city of *Kastanaia* in Asia, where the

Castanea sativa
Sweet or Spanish Chestnut

trees once grew densely. Ordinary Spanish Chestnuts grow easily from seed, but some better bearing, fancy varieties are grafted, as are others with fancy leaf-shapes and colours. They grow rapidly in deep, acid soil, sometimes bearing fruit in the third year from seed, and are undamaged by hot dry summers.

The profuse foliage consists of single 22.5 cm (9 in) leaves, long and pointed, sharply toothed and with downy reverses. The flowers appear in long drooping golden catkins in early summer, and the burr-encased nuts (at first green, later brown) appear late in the season and remain on the tree after leaf fall.

Mature Chestnut trees (no longer common, alas!) bear their bark in a distinctive spiral pattern and may reach 13 m (40 ft) in trunk circumference. They have been known to live several thousand years.

North American Chestnut species *C. dentata* and *C. pumila* are known as Chinquapin, from their Indian name, but are now virtually extinct in their own country as large trees.

Asiatic species *C. crenata* and *C. mollissima* are much smaller trees, raised more for timber than for nuts.

All Chestnuts sucker strongly from around the trunk, which has led to a cottage industry in Europe, where the suckers are cultivated and sold as clothes props.

Castanea sativa
detail of trunk, suckers

CASTANOSPERMUM
(kas taʰ oh spur' məm)

The Black Bean

FAMILY: LEGUMINOSAE

Named Moreton Bay Chestnuts by early British settlers, these handsome Australian trees actually have only one point of similarity to the European Chestnuts — the size and shape of their nuts, which may be roasted and eaten.

Botanists followed the settlers' lead, christening the tree *Castanospermum* meaning chestnut-seeded.

Beyond that, there is no resemblance or relationship at all. The leaves are smooth-edged and pinnate, and grow up to 45 cm (18 in) long, with five to seven pairs of leaflets. The flowers are typical pea flowers of orange and red, borne in sprays directly from the trunk or branches. These are followed by equally typical cylindrical pea pods up to 23 cm (9 in) long and about a quarter as wide. Each contains a number of the large, edible seeds.

C. australe is a handsome tree in its own right, with dense, dark foliage for most of the year and becoming partly deciduous as the flowers appear in summer. It is slow-growing, propagated from seeds or ripe cuttings, and is now raised in many warm-temperate parts of the world.

Strictly a tree for frost-free areas, it makes a striking garden specimen or street tree where there is plenty of room. It is very variable in habit, but generally wide and spreading in the open.

The timber is greatly valued in Australia's north, and has been used for fine furniture, under the name Black Bean.

CASUARINA
(kas yoo ə ree' nə)

The Sheokes

FAMILY: CASUARINACEAE

'Out of place in the wanton tropics' was how author Somerset Maugham described the *Casuarina* trees. And as usual, his description was apt; they are the sort of ghostly, leafless plants you expect to find in dry, desert areas. Yet there they are on the coasts and watercourses of many lands and islands, from East Africa, through southern India and Australia right out to far Tahiti and the South Pacific islands.

Their handsome, figured timber is as hard as the Oak which has been charmingly misspelled in their popular name; the soft needle-like foliage never ceases to move in the trade winds that murmur through the weeping branchlets making a continuous 'sshh' sound which some poetic soul has incorporated into their name. More practical botanists chose the name *Casuarina* because the foliage resembles the feathers of Australia's cassowary bird.

Castanospermum australe
Moreton Bay Chestnut

Casuarina littoralis
Black Sheoke

Casuarina spp.
flowers and foliage

Casuarina equisetifolia
Horsetail Tree, Ironwood

The *Casuarinas* are indeed strange and mysterious trees, closely related to no other, and possessed of many powers, both real and imaginary. In coastal and riverside situations their massive root systems are great sandbinders, although they take so much nourishment out of the soil that nothing can grow nearby.

The fine foliage, which consists of branchlets, not leaves, makes an excellent windbreak and gives soft, luminous shade. In older days the iron-hard timber was used for war clubs, boomerangs and other weapons, and also for carpenters' tools. It has always had magical associations, the Tahitians believing *Casuarinas* sprang from the bodies of dead warriors whose hair became foliage, and whose blood flowed again as the red sap.

Casuarinas do have leaves, but they are so small it is difficult to see them with the naked eye. They have developed into tiny scales which clothe the weeping branchlets. From the base of these scales appear the tiny flowers which cause the branchlets to turn red and fuzzy in late spring.

CATALPA
(ka tal' pə)

The Indian Bean

FAMILY: BIGNONIACEAE

The showy *Catalpas* or Indian Beans are lush trees of a most tropical appearance, and it is something of a surprise to find that they are all native to northern climes (Asia and North America) and are relatively frost-resistant.

This is the tree for your sunny lawn. And if you like heart-shaped leaves, they don't come any larger than the massive 30 cm (12 in) beauties that clothe this splendid tree most of the year. New growth is purplish; mature leaves may be green or golden according to variety. They have a slightly furry texture, and, unfortunately, in most species, a rather unpleasant smell.

The foxglove-like summer flowers appear in large fragrant clusters or spikes — white, pink or lemon according to species, generally marked in purple or yellow. These are followed by long, dangling pods which give *Catalpas* their popular names of Indian Bean and Cigar Tree.

Catalpa bignonioides
Indian Bean

Catalpa speciosa
detail of foliage, seed pods

63

CATHA

(ka' thə)

The Khat Tree

FAMILY: CELASTRACEAE

Grown in Moslem countries for centuries, this small, decorative tree is at home anywhere in warm temperate or hot, dry climates. Apart from the purely decorative effect of its slim, weeping branches, and masses of tiny white spring flowers, the leaves are much sought after in North Africa as a mild stimulant.

Dried and brewed like tea, or chewed straight from the tree, they are the Arabian equivalent of a nice cuppa, giving a pleasant start to the day, or a nice let down in the evening, both without caffein problems.

Catha edulis (from its original Arabic name, *khat*) is usually grown from seed or ripened cuttings, and does not take up too much room.

Catha edulis
Khat, Arabian Tea

Catha edulis
detail of spring flowers

CEDRELA

(see drel' ə)

The Toons

FAMILY: MELIACEAE

The delightful, small genus *Cedrela* (fewer than twenty species world-wide) from South-East Asia, the Caribbean and tropical America, is named after the giant Cedars of Lebanon, North Africa and India. *Cedrela* is the diminutive form of the Greek *kedros* meaning a Cedar, although it is not even remotely related to the Cedar. Whereas Cedars are enormous, cool-climate conifers and evergreen, the *Cedrelas* are mostly sub-tropical and deciduous.

Then how did they get their name? From the heartwood's strong resemblance to Cedar wood, in both colour and grain, and also in the aromatic fragrance which makes the timber completely insect repellent.

The *Cedrelas* more strongly resemble *Ailanthus,* to which they *are* related, but they have a slighter appearance and frequently have heavily buttressed roots. The leaves are long and pinnate with many leaflets and are generally deciduous. In the case of the Chinese Cedar or Toon (*C. sinensis*) the young foliage is a delicate pink, onion-flavoured and quite edible.

The tiny flowers are in weeping panicles and followed by small fruits from which the trees are propagated.

The South American Cigar Box Cedar (*C. odorata*) is fully tropical in its needs, while *C. sinensis* is a cooler climate tree. The Australian Red Cedar was long named *C. toona,* but is now classified under the genus *Toona* as *T. australis* (see *Toona*).

Cedrela sinensis
Chinese Toon

Cedrela odorata
Cigar Box Cedar, fruit

CEDRUS

(see'. drəs)

The Cedars

FAMILY: PINACEAE

The Cedars are one of the few genera to be known by the same name for thousands of years. To the Romans they were already *Cedrus;* to the Greeks before them *kedros;* and to the writers of the Old Testament a name very similar. They were regarded as the most precious of all timbers, a gift from God himself. 'My beloved's countenance is excellent as the cedars' the song of Solomon tells us, and again 'King Solomon built himself a chariot of the wood of Lebanon'. Noah's Ark was built of Cedar, and the fleets of Egypt's Pharaohs were laid down with its fine water-resistant timber. The great stones of the pyramids were rolled into place on mighty Cedar trunks, and later the Crusaders felled them for the construction of their palaces in the Holy Land.

As a result, the magnificent Cedars of Lebanon are today very rare in their native land, and even the survivors not as old as is often claimed. For the Cedars have the appearance if not the actuality of great age.

Cedrela sinensis
Chinese Toon

Cedrus atlantica Aurea
Golden Atlantic Cedar

Cedrus atlantica Glauca Pendula
Blue Atlas Cedar

There are four species generally recognized: the Deodar or Indian Cedar, the Atlantic Cedar, the Cedar of Lebanon and the Cyprus Cedar, all with many varieties of leaf colour and habit. Many botanists believe they are all regional remnants of a single tree species that once flourished widely from Africa across to India, and retreated into the mountains as the land dried out. But they have developed minor differences in their present native habitats. The Deodar of the Himalayas is by far the largest, reaching up to 70 m (120 ft) — a giant of a tree with a trunk girth to 12 m (35 ft) and a distinct weeping habit, particularly in young specimens. The Atlantic or Mt Atlas Cedar from the mountains of Morocco is next, with a pyramidal habit and faster growth. Its form *C.a. Glauca Pendula*, a favourite tree for parks, has blue-grey leaves and branches dragging on the ground.

Cedrus deodara
Indian Cedar, Deodar

The biblical Cedar of Lebanon is a majestic giant of a tree, flat topped and often wider than its height; while the Cyprus Cedar is a relative pygmy, dwarfed by many generations in the poor soil of its native island.

All Cedars demand a deep, rich soil for maximum growth, and particularly a porous subsoil. They are really too large for the average garden, but make splendid specimens in large mountain gardens.

Cedrus atlantica
detail of cones, foliage

Cedrus libani
Cedar of Lebanon

CEIBA
(sae' bə)

The Kapok Tree

FAMILY: BOMBACACEAE

Found in the tropic zones of both the old and the new world is a small genus of stark, gigantic deciduous trees, once of great commercial value. These are the *Ceiba* or Kapok trees, whose large hanging seed pods are filled with the fine downy fibre now largely superseded by synthetics as a stuffing for pillows and quilts. They are strange-looking trees with straight trunks that may reach 50 m (150 ft) in height and up to 3 m (9 ft) in diameter. The trunks are sometimes spiny and when leafless can be mistaken for *Chorisia* (which see). The tell-tale difference is a number of thin buttresses which surround the trunk, sometimes to a height of 10 m (30 ft) or more.

Ceiba pentandra
Kapok Tree, pods

Ceiba pentandra
Kapok Tree

Branches of *C. pentandra* (*Ceiba* is its original native name) are sparse, and generally arranged in irregular whorls around the trunk. The leaves are pinnate, with five to seven spear-shaped leaflets around 15 cm (6 in) long.

The flowers which appear in early spring when the tree is still bare are whitish and sometimes faintly pink or yellow, and notably furry on the reverses of the petals. The elliptical capsules that contain the kapok fibre may be up to 25 cm (10 in) long. Kapok trees were imported commercially to South-East Asia and old trees are often found there.

The *Ceibas* are strictly tropical, with about ten species in cultivation.

CELTIS
(kel' təs)

The Nettle Trees and Hackberries

FAMILY: ULMACEAE

Many of the Nettle Tree or *Celtis* (their ancient Greek name) species, which number over sixty, are among the world's most commonly planted street trees, with both evergreen and deciduous types to suit almost any climate. They greatly resemble the Elms (see *Ulmus*) to which they are closely related, but are generally smaller trees of quite manageable size. All are from the northern hemisphere.

Their individual leaves (which vary greatly in size according to species) may be from 3.5 to 15 cm in length (1½ to 6 in), are frequently larger on one side of their stem than the other (like Elms) and are extremely rough to the touch, exactly like the garden stinging nettles. The greenish flowers are tiny and unspectacular; the fruits (the size and colour of an edible green pea) are of little use, but are sometimes eaten in countries where food is scarce.

All *Celtis* species may be propagated from cuttings or seeds and none of them has any commercial use except as firewood. They are however, useful, fast-growing, shade trees and come into their own in autumn. In cooler climates, the serrated leaves change to a pale yellow, and the fruits may become orange, red, purple and almost black. *C. australis* with creamy-yellow leaves and indigo berries is particularly decorative at this time of year. Most *Celtis* are reasonably frost hardy.

Celtis sinensis
Chinese Hackberry, blossom

Celtis australis
Nettle Tree

Celtis occidentalis
Sugarberry, leaves and fruit

CERATONIA
(ke rə toh' nee ə)

St John's Bread, Carob Bean

FAMILY: LEGUMINOSAE

If you've ever visualized St John the Baptist munching on grasshoppers in the wilderness then think again! The locusts which sustained the good saint were the pods or fruits of the Carob or Locust tree, *Ceratonia siliqua*, a native of the Holy Land and other areas about the Mediterranean.

Hardly worth growing for purely decorative purposes, it is a useful tree for dry and perennially drought-stricken areas anywhere in a temperate climate, where its heavy foliage and spreading branches provide valuable shade, and the great crop of 20 cm (8 in) pods make a useful stock fodder. They are said to be very rich in both sugar and protein and are sometimes ground for use as a chocolate substitute.

The *Ceratonia* (from the Greek *keration* meaning a pod or horn) is evergreen, ultimately reaching a height of 15 m (45 ft), though obviously it is a slow grower in particularly arid areas. Its pinnate leaves are up to 25 cm (10 in) long; the flowers red and small, hardly noticeable under the canopy of leaves. The pods that follow develop in summer, but only on female trees. *Ceratonia* is easily grown from seed.

CERATOPETALUM
(ke ra toh pet' ə ləm)

The Coachwoods

FAMILY: CUNONIACEAE

In the coastal bushlands of New South Wales, and in many gardens of Australia, the summer Christmas season is announced by a small slender tree, *Ceratopetalum gummiferum*. As spring fades and the longest day approaches, the tree at first becomes powdered with tiny white flowers that appear in the leaf axils. The calyces (seed sheaths) behind them enlarge until they are almost 1 cm (½ in) in diameter, and then begin to change colour, flushing first a soft pink and then darkening in some local varieties to a brilliant cherry red, sometimes flushed with royal purple.

Although it has no practical use, it is beloved throughout its home state and picked lavishly for Christmas decoration. It is generally known as Redbush or Christmas Bush, and so eyecatching is the floral display, few people ever notice that behind it is a dark, slender tree with distinctive trifoliate (three-lobed) leaves of softest green. In positions with deep rich soil (so rare along this coast) it may reach 12 m (40 ft) in height.

There are four other *Ceratopetalum* species, native to the humid forests further north. One of them is of considerable importance — the Coachwood, *C. apetalum*, a splendid timber tree which may reach 30 m (90 ft) and more.

Both principal species of *Ceratopetalum* are hardy down to –2°C (28°F). They are also grown in the southern United States, usually from ripened cuttings.

Ceratonia siliqua
detail of flowers

Ceratonia siliqua
Carob Bean, St John's Bread

Ceratopetalum apetalum
Coachwood

Ceratopetalum gummiferum
New South Wales Christmas Bush

CERBERA

(sur' bur ə)

The Sea Mango

FAMILY: APOCYNACEAE

Closely related to the Frangipanis (see *Plumeria*), and resembling them in many particulars, the gawky Sea Mangoes or *Cerberas* are native to many islands of the Pacific and Indian Oceans, and southern areas of the Indo-Malaysian mainland. They are salt resistant and often used in tropical seaside gardens where the red-marked flowers make a pleasant summer display. These appear in panicles at the ends of the branches, and are followed by tennis-ball sized green or red fruits.

It would be an unfortunate man who really did mistake these for real mangoes, for like many other members of the Periwinkle family (Apocynaceae), all parts of the plant are poisonous. In fact it is believed that *Cerberas* received their botanical name in allusion to these poisonous qualities — it appears to be an adaptation of the name of Cerberus, the monstrous guardian of the gates of Hell, in Greek myths.

There are six species of *Cerbera*, of which one, *C. odollan*, may reach 15 m (50 ft). The other species rarely top 7 m (20 ft). They are propagated from cuttings or seed.

Ceratopetalum gummiferum
Redbush, flower display

Cerbera manghas
Sea Mango

CERCIS

(kur' kis)

The Judas Tree and Redbuds

FAMILY: LEGUMINOSAE

To an Australian, spring in the United States is an introduction to a new botanical world. After the generally dull tones of the Australian bush, the awakening forest of north-eastern America is a revelation with its Elms and Dogwoods and Sassafras; and everywhere, glowing in the pale sunlight, spindly many-branched trees covered in every part with brilliant rose-pink blossom. These are the Redbuds, *Cercis canadensis,* showy members of the pea family, Leguminosae.

There are seven *Cercis* species from Europe, Asia and North America, all with a strong family resemblance. They are deciduous, growing to around 15 m (40 ft) in the wild. The leaves are kidney-shaped, and their small pea-flowers, generally pink, but sometimes white or purple, appear on bare wood (often from the trunks or older branches) in stalkless clusters. They are followed by absolute masses of 10 cm (4 in) flat pods, which persist well into winter.

The name *Cercis* is from the Greek *kerkis,* the original name of the European species *C. siliquastrum.* This is sometimes known as the Judas Tree, from an old legend that it was the tree from which Judas Iscariot hanged himself after betraying Christ.

None of the genus has any commercial use. All of them are grown for the beauty of their spring blossom, particularly in cooler climates.

Cercis canadensis
Redbud, spring blossom

Cercis siliquastrum
Judas Tree, spring blossom

Cercis siliquastrum
seed pods, autumn

CHAMAECYPARIS

(cham ae kai' par əs)

The False Cypresses

FAMILY: CUPRESSACEAE

The False Cypresses, *Chamaecyparis*, form one of the smallest genera in botany — no more than about eight species. But due to their inherent instability, in both habit and coloration, the cultivated varieties developed from those eight species would fill a book. They must surely be the most popular, the most widely planted evergreens in horticultural practice.

At one time they were included by botanists among the true Cypresses (see *Cupressus*), but were placed in a separate genus of their own earlier this century; the criteria for separation included the number of seeds produced per scale, and the formation of the first juvenile leaves.

Why the name *Chamaecyparis* meaning *dwarf* Cypress was chosen is a complete mystery! None of the original species grows to less than 25 m (75 ft) in the wild, and the popular Lawson Cypress (*C. lawsoniana*) prefers to shoot up to about 70 m (200 ft) in its moist coastal forests of northern California and southern Oregon.

The Nootka Cypress (*C. nootkaensis*) comes from the same general area, the White Cypress (*C. thyoides*) from eastern North America. The others are all from Japan, China and Taiwan.

Why are these variable trees so popular in cultivation? Well, they are easy to propagate, easy to move at any size, and never need pruning. Added to which, their dainty foliage comes in almost every imaginable shade of green, gold and grey-blue, allowing for considerable colour interest in the evergreen garden.

Habits vary from dwarf and ground-hugging to tall and upright, with many nuances of spiralling, layering and weeping among them.

Chamaecyparis nootkaensis
Nootka Cypress

Chamaecyparis lawsoniana
Lawson Cypress, fruit

Chamaecyparis obtusa Crippsii
Golden Hinoki Cypress

72

CHIONANTHUS
(chai on an' thəs)

The Fringe Trees

FAMILY: OLEACEAE

An ideal choice for the cool to temperate garden, the slim and delicate Fringe Trees, *Chionanthus*, will never grow too large and outwear their welcome. An extremely small genus, with only three or four species, and only two of them are seen in cultivation, neither likely to top 5 m (15 ft).

Both species are deciduous, one from China, one from North America. The Chinese species *C. retusa* is the more dainty with slim, pointed 10 cm (4 in) leaves, dense panicles of pure white 2.5 cm (1 in) flowers in summer, and later, dark blue fruits about the size of a grape. It is frost hardy, loves a good woodsy soil in full sun, and is usually propagated from seed.

The American species *C. virginiana* is sometimes known as Old Man's Beard for its flower panicles may droop in a pointed fashion to 20 cm (8 in). Its leaves are larger, and so are the fruit.

The botanical name *Chionanthus* means snow flower, from the two Greek words *chion* and *anthos*.

Chionanthus retusa
detail of blossom

Chionanthus retusa
Chinese Fringe Tree

CHORICARPIA
(cho ri kah' pee ə)

The Brush Turpentine

FAMILY: MYRTACEAE

A fine ornamental for warm coastal areas, *Choricarpia* has been little grown outside Australia, though it would suit many climates. It will grow to 16 m (50 ft) and is quite similar to the closely related Turpentine (see *Syncarpia*) in whose genus it was once included.

The leaves are smooth, leathery and wavy-edged; rust coloured when young, but ripening to a soft green with rusty reverse. The spring blossoms, each on a long stem, appear in large arching clusters in mid-spring, great puffballs of creamy yellow stamens similar to Wattle, but much larger.

Choricarpia (the name means separate fruits) flowers when quite young, at which stage it may be mistaken for *Callicoma* (which see). But the leaves are quite different.

The beautiful Brush Turpentine has proved itself an ideal street tree in warm temperate parts of Australia.

Choricarpia leptopetala
Brush Turpentine, blossom

CHORISIA
(ko ris' ee ə)

The Floss Silk Tree

FAMILY: MALVACEAE

Unless you can get some viable seed from South America and grow *Chorisia* for yourself, you're not likely to have one. Not that the climate is unsuitable, they will grow wherever the winter temperature remains above –7°C (19°F), but they rarely seem to want to set seed away from their natural home, and won't grow from cuttings. Yet I have seen them in Sydney, in California, in Florida and in Samoa among other places and the sight of a *Chorisia* in full bloom is food for the soul — no two of them with flowers exactly the same.

That is their peculiarity. The 15 cm (6 in) flowers on one giant tree will always differ from those on another, both in colour and in structure. In the case of the best known species, the Brazilian *C. speciosa*, the flowers will be five-petalled and basically pink and resemble the related Hibiscus; but beyond that they may vary from reddish to salmon in colour, their centres white or yellow, marked in deep red or brown, the petals plain or with rippled edges.

The related *C. insignis* from Peru has basically white flowers, marked with gold, but they may also be all yellow or marked in various colours.

Both these species grow tall, 15 m (45 ft) and more, and have tapering trunks up to 2 m (6 ft) in diameter at ground level. These are liberally studded with a nightmare arrangement of barbaric thorns and spines and would be impossible to climb.

Chorisia speciosa
Floss Silk Tree

Chorisia insignis
Spiny Chorisia

Chorisia speciosa
detail of blossom

CHRYSOPHYLLUM

(kris oh fil' əm)

The Star Apple

FAMILY: SAPOTACEAE

What a wonderful group of tropical trees! Sixty or more species of them, native to warmer parts of Africa, Asia, the Americas, Hawaii and even north Australia, but alas, the only place you'll find them away from the sub-tropics is in a large greenhouse or conservatory, and you will have to actually visit the tropics to feast on their delicious many-coloured fruits.

Chrysophyllum means golden or shining leaves, and that's precisely the effect you get standing beneath them, for their evergreen foliage is backed with silky hairs which have a strangely iridescent effect; gold, copper or even silver.

The Star Apple (*C. cainito*) from Central America and the West Indies, is the most common species, now planted extensively right around the world. It is a tall tree, sometimes reaching 17 m (50 ft) in height, and at a distance has a close resemblance to the European Copper Beech (see *Fagus*). The leaves are pointed,

Chrysophyllum cainito
detail of leaf reverses

oblong and about 10 cm (4 in) in length, borne alternately on slim, often weeping branchlets. The flowers are small and white, almost undetectable beneath the leaves, but they develop into shining apple-sized fruits, bright green at first, then ripening through a rosy flush to a vivid red-violet.

They are quite delectable, full of cool, refreshing snow-white pulp with a puzzling flavour. Is it peach or persimmon? The popular name of Star Apple comes from the arrangement of the black seeds. Cut open a fruit, you'll see the seeds radiating in the form of a star.

The Star Apple's one requirement, apart from a hot climate, is year-round water. They are propagated by seeds or ripened cuttings.

Chrysophyllum cainito
Star Apple

Chrysophyllum cainito
fruit and foliage

75

CINNAMOMUM
(sin ə moh′ məm)

The Camphor Laurels

FAMILY: LAURACEAE

Marvellously fragrant in all its parts, the Asian Camphor Laurel is the most commonly grown and decorative of a large genus of aromatic trees. There are over 250 species found in the south of China, India, Malaysia and Australia, many of them highly valued in commerce as the source of a variety of gums and spices.

Cinnamomum is their botanical name (from an old Greek word), and the one all of us in frost-free parts of the world know is *C. camphora*. It is a fast-growing tree which may reach 35 m (100 ft) in a suitable position, and is rather uncomfortably large and messy for the city garden.

The trunk may reach 2 m (6 ft) in diameter, the branches are heavy and can easily span 35 m (100 ft) in a mature tree. The bark is grey and fissured, the leaves roundly pointed and a delightful apple-green in colour. The Camphor Laurel bears masses of tiny, fuzzy greenish yellow

Cinnamomum zeylanicum
Cinnamon

Cinnamomum burmanii
Padang Cinnamon

flowers in spring, followed by pea-sized black berries. But the best display is in early spring, when the entire tree performs a stunning strip tease. First there is a flush of new pink foliage from top to toe, then almost overnight, all the old leaves drop at once, making quite a litter.

Camphor Laurel leaves are not very good for compost, as they break down slowly, but they do make a delightful fragrant fire, for they are the source of medicinal camphor. The timber is also impregnated with it, so be sure to save dead branches for winter firewood. Camphorwood is light, pale and insect repellent. The Chinese have always used it for a variety of storage chests.

Other valuable species of *Cinnamomum* include *C. zeylanicum*, the Ceylon Cinnamon, principal source of the popular spice; *C. burmanii*, the Padang Cinnamon, an inferior source of the same spice; *C. cassia*, the Chinese Cassia, source of both cassia and cinnamon; and *C. loureirii*, the Saigon Cinnamon, raised for the same purpose.

Cinnamomum camphora
detail of flower buds, foliage

Cinnamomum loureirii
Saigon Cinnamon

A particularly interesting feature of all the Cinnamon Trees is that the volatile oils they contain are attractive to butterflies, which spend a great deal of time hovering about the foliage.

CITHAREXYLUM
(kith ə rək' sil əm)

The Fiddlewoods

FAMILY: VERBENACEAE

Closely related both to the shrubby Lantana and the annual Verbena, Fiddlewoods are a small genus of dainty trees from South America and the Caribbean area. They are immensely popular in warm and temperate climates worldwide and there are apparently some half a dozen species in cultivation, but they are difficult to distinguish because most of the specimens one sees are hybrids.

The most commonly seen is probably *C. quadrangulare*, the Jamaica Fiddlewood, a handsome, glossy-leafed tree valued principally for its colour in the cool winter garden, when the foliage turns a delightful golden bronze. Its branches and twigs are rectangular in section; the 10 cm (4 in) leaves are long and pointed, without teeth. The small white five-petalled flowers appear in 22 cm (9 in) racemes in spring.

Fiddlewood timber is regarded as a useful cabinet wood in its native zone. There is quite a deal of confusion about the tree's popular name. Several authorities claim it is from the French word *fidèle*, meaning merely that the timber was sound and useful. Others point to the Greek origin of its botanical name which comes from *kithara* meaning a lyre, and *xylon* meaning wood, because it was said to have been used mainly for making musical instruments.

Cinnamomum camphora
Camphor Laurel

Citharexylum quadrangulare
Jamaica Fiddlewood

CITRUS
(sit' rəs)

The Oranges and Lemons

FAMILY: RUTACEAE

In a world of orange juice, eau de Cologne and lemon-scented detergents, it's hard to imagine life without the ubiquitous Citrus fruits. But that's what Western civilization was like until the Renaissance.

All 15-odd *Citrus* species and their innumerable varieties are native to South-East Asia, and it seems likely that the first of them arrived in Europe as pot plants with the Moorish and Turkish invaders of the Middle Ages.

Since then they have been highly valued for their shiny, evergreen foliage, their fragrant and volatile oils, and most of all for the gorgeously coloured fruits, which ripen in winter from the previous spring's flowers. At least, that is what they do in the right climate, or in heated greenhouses. In cooler climates they may not ripen until the following summer.

Louis XIV of France decorated his famous *Salon des Glaces* at Versailles with lemon trees in tubs of solid silver. These were melted down in the Revolution, but some of the original trees still survive, now less extravagantly potted up in wooden containers.

Citrus grow best in a moist, humid atmosphere, and are often used in coastal areas or by large rivers. In any event they appreciate a daily spray of the foliage in dry weather, which also keeps at bay the innumerable pests attracted by their volatile leaf-oils. They like a deep rich soil, but with some sand for drainage, and plenty of manure and other fertilizer during the growing season. They are propagated from buds of the chosen variety grafted onto seedling stock, and the fruits are particularly rich in ascorbic acid (Vitamin C), which Captain James Cook discovered was the sovereign antidote to scurvy, the scourge of the eighteenth century sea traveller.

All *Citrus* species have the same dark glossy

Citrus reticulata
Mandarin Orange

Citrus aurantium
Seville Orange

Most *Citrus* trees are happy with an outdoor winter temperature as low as 7°C (45°F), though they have been known to resist short frosty spells, particularly Oranges. In colder climates they should be raised in large tubs which can be brought under shelter. That is the way it's always been done in the great houses of northern Europe where special glass-walled, heated rooms known as *orangeries* were constructed.

leaves, often with curiously bladed or winged leaf stalks. The white, or sometimes mauve-tinted flowers may appear at any time, but most heavily in spring. They are fragrant and most attractive to the bees that fertilize them. The fruits may be yellow, orange, red or green according to variety, and vary from 2.5 cm (1 in) in diameter for the Calamondin to 22.5 cm (9 in) for the Pomelo and Citron.

Citrus paradisii CV *'Marsh's Seedless'*
Marsh's Seedless Grapefruit

Citrus X tangelo 'Seminole'
Tangelo

Citrus aurantium 'Myrtifolia'
Chinotto Orange

Citrus aurantiifolia
Tahiti Lime

Citrus blossom may be
white or mauve tinted

Citrus limon CV *'Lisbon Variegata'*
Variegated Lisbon Lemon

COCCOLOBA
(kok ə loh' bə)

The Sea Grape
FAMILY: POLYGONACEAE

The Sea Grape, *Coccoloba*, was at one time used in place of writing paper by early settlers in Mexico. It was distributed in schools and in missions for childrens' throw-away writing attempts. A very handsome tree, it is used throughout the world in tropical seaside gardens for its great salt resistance and the privacy afforded by its dense foliage.

Coccoloba is grown from cuttings and seeds, and rapidly reaches 7 m (20 ft) in a warm position, the trunk thick and squat. The leaves are round and may reach 20 cm (8 in) across, giving the tree a popular name of Platterleaf. At maturity, the leaves are thick, shiny and with distinct red veins. The small greenish-white flowers appear in dense racemes up to 25 cm (10 in) long, and are followed by strings of purplish-red fruits that are quite edible.

The hard timber takes a fine polish and is used for cabinet making in the West Indies. Other parts of the plant have a variety of medicinal uses.

C. uvifera, known as the Sea Grape, is the only commonly grown species out of over 150 related plants to be found in Central and South America.

Coccoloba uvifera
Sea Grape

COCHLOSPERMUM
(kok' loh spur məm)

The Buttercup Tree or Maximiliana
FAMILY: COCHLOSPERMACEAE

Cochlospermum vitifolium
Buttercup Tree

I know of no tree that bears larger, brighter yellow flowers than Mexico's showy Buttercup Tree. At home wherever the climate is really hot, even in dry areas, the *Cochlospermum* (from the Greek words *kocklos* and *sperma* meaning shell seeds) grows easily from spring cuttings or seeds sown in the warmer weather.

It is slender and deciduous, bare for up to five months of the year, and will begin flowering when a mere metre (3 ft) in height, although it may ultimately reach 10 m (30 ft) after a number of years. A rather sparse and stiff looking tree, its leaves are handsome and larger than a dinner plate. They are five-lobed, rather like those of a grape vine or Liquidambar, and appear only in late spring after the tree's three-month blooming period.

It is in late winter that the *Cochlospermum* achieves its finest moment, as the golden-yellow, cup-sized blossoms open a few at a time, rapidly carpeting the ground all around. They are five-petalled, with a mass of golden stamens, and are followed by five-sided seed pods the size of a large egg. These have a velvety casing and contain many seeds embedded in silky fibre which is sometimes used for stuffing upholstery.

C. vitifolium is the best known species of the eighteen recorded, and is seen in hot climate gardens of India, the Philippines, Africa, California and Florida. Its cousin C. religiosum is from India and is virtually identical. The Australian species C. gillevraei has bright red flowers.

Cochlospermum vitifolium
detail of flowers

COCOS
(koh' kos)

The Coconut Palm

FAMILY: PALMAE

The very symbol of tropic enchantment and lazy island living, the ubiquitous Coconut Palm, *Cocos nucifera*, is also the very staff of life to millions of people around the global tropic zone.

It is one of the oldest trees on earth, surviving unchanged since prehistoric times, its original home unknown. Fringing all the world's great oceans, often the only tree growing on remote islands, it is rarely seen away from the sandy soil of very low altitudes, where it may ultimately reach a height of 35 m (100 ft) in favourable positions.

It has been named *Coco* (the Portuguese word for monkey) from the appearance of the end of its great hard-shelled fruit or seed. This may, in certain lights, resemble a quaint simian face.

This great seed, when ripe, is the tree's only method of propagation, remaining fertile for many months, and has been known to float thousands of kilometres. Botanists believe that this accounts for the tree's presence on so many remote islets.

Cocos nucifera
detail of fruit, flower

In many tropic lands (and at different times) the wood has been used for housebuilding, the woven fronds for walls and thatch, the fibrous husk for ropemaking. The nutshells make cups and containers, their flesh is food and drink. Young leaf-shoots are eaten as food, and from the sap is extracted toddy, an alcoholic beverage that is also a source of vinegar and sugar. The flesh of the nut is dried for copra and pressed for coconut oil, the most important ingredient of margarine, icecream, face cream, cosmetics, soap and candles. Any part of the tree left over makes splendid charcoal.

C. nucifera is the only species of its genus, and it is really happy only between the tropics of Capricorn and Cancer.

Cocos nucifera
Coconut or Coco Palm

COFFEA
(kof' fee ə)

The Coffee Tree
FAMILY: RUBIACEAE

Rarely thought of as a tree, *Coffea arabica* is usually seen pruned to shrub height to make berry-picking easier. As the source of all the coffee we drink, it is obviously of great value in commerce, but grow it as an ornamental by all means if you live anywhere in a temperate climate. It has handsome, shiny leaves, like those of the related *Gardenia,* and showy white spring blossom.

The green berries that follow turn a brilliant red. Each contains two seeds or beans that roasted, dried and ground make up your breakfast coffee. Well, with another forty-one they do!

The name *Coffea* is an approximation of the original Arabic name for this valuable plant.

Coffea arabica
detail of foliage, berries

Coffea arabica
Arabian Coffee Tree

CORDIA
(kord' ee ə)

The Bird Lime Tree
FAMILY: BORAGINACEAE

Cordia are showy tropical relatives of the temperate gardener's forget-me-nots and heliotrope, and like them easy to grow and almost trouble-free. There are at least 250 listed species, all of them found between the tropics of both the old and new worlds, in Africa, Asia, Australia and particularly in the Americas.

The commonly seen species is *C. sebestena,* the Geiger or Bird Lime Tree from the Caribbean. This is notable for its rough 20 cm (8 in) oval leaves, whose dark colouring makes a perfect foil for the vivid orange-scarlet flowers borne in terminal clusters throughout the year. The Bird Lime Tree grows easily from seed or cuttings in a sub-tropical climate, reaching 10 m (30 ft) in a few years.

Its paler-flowered cousin *C. subcordata* is the sacred *Kou* tree of Polynesia, found by seashores throughout the Indian and Pacific oceans. There is a legend that when a downpour of rain threatened to extinguish fire, the god Maui told the flames to take refuge in the *Kou* tree, hence the colour of its blossom!

C. subcordata has smooth, paler, wavy-edged leaves, and slightly less gaudy flowers which are followed by green and yellow grape-sized fruits. The decoratively figured timber was used in Polynesia for carving sacred figures and household utensils.

Cordias are named for a sixteenth century family of botanists named Cordus.

Cordia subcordata
Kou, flowers and foliage

Cordia sebestena
Bird Lime Tree

CORNUS
(kor' nəs)

The Cornels or Dogwoods

FAMILY: CORNACEAE

I shall never forget my first train ride to Virginia, speeding on the Powhatan Arrow through the Allegheny mountains in the clear light of an April morning. All along the valley route, the landscape was touched with spring — dark coal-mining towns alternating with a riot of lime green foliage, fern and fuzz. And here and there against the drab rocks the brilliance of a million flowering dogwoods, white, pink and almost red.

It was only later, in a friend's garden in Roanoke, that I discovered the inflorescence of the common Flowering Dogwood (*Cornus florida*) is not a flower at all, but a whole composite head of tiny greenish flowers with four spectacularly marked bracts enclosing the group.

When the bracts fall, the flowers develop into a cluster of bright red fruits which persist into autumn, joining the foliage in a fiery farewell to summer. *C. florida* is a slim, dark-trunked tree growing from 5 to 12 m in height (15 to 35 ft), its crepy, pointed leaves marked with conspicuous parallel veins.

There are around a hundred species of Dogwood found in cool-winter temperate parts of America and Asia, many of them shrubs with brilliantly coloured winter bark.

Other tree species of note include: *C. capitata*, a widely branched Himalayan tree of 15 m (45 ft), and partly evergreen. The bracts are creamy white, the fruit like a rather large raspberry. *C. controversa*, the Giant Dogwood from the Himalayas, grows to 20 m (60 ft). Leaves whitish beneath. Masses of pinkish flowers with cream bracts in summer. *C. kousa*, a small Japanese tree of 7 m (20 ft), deciduous, with dense masses of creamy-pink, bracted blossoms in early summer. *C. mas*, the Cornelian Cherry, another small tree from Europe and Asia. Deciduous, with yellow flowers and dark red edible fruits. It has many highly coloured leaf varieties.

Cornus florida
Flowering Dogwood, autumn

Cornus florida
Dogwood, spring blossom

Cornus florida
Dogwood, summer fruit

Cornus capitata
Himalayan Strawberry

Cornus florida Alba
White Dogwood

84

COUROUPITA
(koo roop' i tə)

The Cannonball Tree

FAMILY: LECYTHIDACEAE

Thank goodness Cannonball trees are not to be found in every garden! Dodging the head-size fruit as they come cannonading down the trunk in every rainstorm could become a real hazard, and the less said about the smell of its decaying droppings the better. They are a sight though, that every tree-lover wants to see at least once in a lifetime, and all the great warm climate arboretums make sure that we have the chance.

What a stunning botanical conversation piece! A 17 m (50 ft) tall column decked with slender flower stems all twisted and tangled like Medusa's snake hair. In season, these bear Hibiscus-sized flowers of rich apricot pink and gold. These have a curious lop-sided mass of stamens and exude a strong fruity fragrance that can be smelt from afar.

The brown, velvety fruits, when they appear in winter, cluster from top to bottom of the tree, suspended like balls on a string. They consist of a mass of seeds embedded in sickly pulp, which to Westerners smell distinctly 'off'. The South American natives, however, find it delicious, and squeeze a popular brew from it which they drink from the empty shells.

The Cannonball tree is known botanically as *Couroupita guianensis*. That is its old name in the Guianas, where this curiosity grows wild.

Cannonball Trees can be grown easily from seed in a warm climate. Just don't plant one in your garden!

Couroupita guianensis
detail of flower

Couroupita guianensis
detail of fruit

Couroupita guianensis
Cannonball Tree

CRATAEGUS
(kra tae' gəs)

The Hawthorns

FAMILY: ROSACEAE

*Gives not the hawthorn bush a sweeter shade
Than doth a rich embroidered canopy?*
Good old Shakespeare! As usual, he said it all in signalling his approval of the ubiquitous hedgerow tree of English fields, the Common Hawthorn or May, *Crataegus monogyna*.

Planted throughout the British Isles, its thorny branches make an effective barrier to man and beast, but the blow is softened in spring as it bursts into white clouds of tiny, sharp-scented, rose-like blossom. In summer the spreading branches provide welcome shade and shelter to animals and country swains alike, and the onset of frost reveals a blaze of autumn colour and a fine crop of red fruits that persist into winter.

Crataegus oxyacantha 'Coccinea Plena'
Paul's Double Scarlet Thorn

The English Hawthorn, *C. oxyacantha*, has many flower varieties both single and double, red, pink and variegated. The Mexican Thorn, *C. stipulacea*, has toothed, rose-like leaves and masses of large orange-yellow spotted fruits that hang on the tree for months. The American *C. submollis* has yellow fruits on long, hanging stems. *C. ellwangeriana* has scarlet apple-like fruits to 4 cm (1½ in) wide. *C. crus-galli*, the Cockspur Thorn, has the longest, sharpest

Crataegus monogyna
Common Hawthorn or May

Yet the Common Hawthorn is but one of perhaps a thousand species of these deciduous members of the rose family, found principally in North America, but with flourishing groups native to Europe, Asia Minor and North Africa.

They all prefer a cooler climate and are frost hardy. Most of them have decorative foliage, either lobed or rose-like, frequently associated with the most vicious thorns in the botanical kingdom. The variations between them are principally in height of growth, ranging from 5 to 15 m (15 to 45 ft), and in size and colour of fruit, varying from currant-size to that of a small apple, in every shade of red, white and pink, and a few in orange and yellow.

Crataegus X smithiana
Hybrid Thorn

spines, and the hybrid *C. X smithiana* which appeared in the Australian capital, Canberra, seems to combine the best of all possible worlds; fast growth, weeping habit, large flowers and enormous fruit clusters in a particularly glowing red.

Crataegus is from the Greek *kratos* meaning strength, referring to its hard wood. All species grow easily from seed, which takes two years to ripen. Grafting is used for fancy varieties.

Crataegus X ellwangeriana
Fruit and Foliage

Crataegus stipulacea
Mexican Thorn

CRESCENTIA
(kre·sent' ee ə)

The Calabash Tree

FAMILY: BIGNONIACEAE

The tropical American tree *Crescentia cujete* is grown today solely as an ornamental, but in earlier times it was valued highly for the storage potential of its enormous woody-shelled fruit which can easily reach 30 cm (12 in) in diameter. The Mexicans, in particular, polished and carved them beautifully, and chewed the cooked seeds inside as a delicacy.

Primitive musicians found the hollow shells made sensational rattles, and they are still used by Afro-Cuban bands and Hawaiian hula groups.

Crescentia (named for the thirteenth century Italian botanist Crescenzi) is a rather heavy tree with decorative grey bark and densely foliaged spreading branches. The shiny leaves are blunt ended and about 15 cm (6 in) long. The greenish, purple-veined flowers open at night, appearing in short clusters directly from the larger branches. There they are followed by the shining green Calabash fruit.

The wood is extremely hard and has been used in building boats and cartwheels.

C. cujete is the only one of its genus.

Crescentia cujete
Calabash Tree

CRYPTOMERIA
(krip toh meə ree ə)

The Sugi or Japanese Cedars

FAMILY: TAXODIACEAE

Cryptomeria is a Japanese coniferous genus, with only a single species but a myriad foliage varieties. Botanically it is regarded as a sort of 'missing link', a bridge between the American Sequoias and Bald Cypresses on the one hand, and the Araucarias of the South Pacific on the other.

In its normal form, it is a handsome, pyramidal tree growing as high as 50 m (150 ft) in sheltered positions with deep rich soil. Its stiff, scale-like leaves are arranged spirally in long tassels. The tiny flowers, which appear in autumn, are almost invisible. The name *Cryptomeria* is from the Greek *kryptos* meaning hidden and *meris* meaning part, in reference to these flowers. They develop into clusters of small scaly cones not much bigger than a pea.

Cryptomeria japonica
detail of cones, foliage

Cryptomerias are fairly cold hardy, but must have protection from winter winds, for they topple easily. The fancy-leafed varieties, of course, are propagated from cuttings struck in a sandy medium under heat. These varieties include: *albo-variegata,* with some white-flecked leaves; *araucarioides* with long, slender branchlets; *bandai-sugi,* a broad-growing dwarf; *elegans,* with feathery foliage that turns bronze in autumn, becomes green again in spring; *pendula,* with weeping branches; and *spiralis* with twisted branchlets.

The *Cryptomerias* are a most decorative group of conifers, suited to any cool or temperate climate. Their beautifully grained timber is one of the most highly valued in Japan.

Cryptomeria japonica
Sugi or Japanese Cedar

Cryptomeria japonica 'Pygmaea'
Dwarf Cryptomeria, foliage

CUNNINGHAMIA

(kun ning ham' ee ə)

The China Fir

FAMILY: TAXODIACEAE

China's most indispensable tree, the tall and elegant *Cunninghamia* is related both to Japan's *Cryptomeria* (see previous entry), the American Bald Cypress (see *Taxodium*) and Australia's *Araucarias*.

It is a tall, fast-growing conifer reaching up to 35 m (100 ft) and is found naturally only in China's southern provinces. Like the *Araucarias*, it is not at all cold hardy, growing only at low altitudes of a sub-tropical climate.

The fragrant timber is easily worked and much sought after for every purpose from house and boat building to the construction of coffins. The bark is scaly, red-brown and constantly peeling. The horizontally held branches are densely covered with two rows of spirally arranged, flattened needles, each about 6 cm (2 in) long. In spring the China Fir bears inconspicuous flower clusters, both male and female. These mature into scaly cones about the size of a golf ball.

Like California's related *Sequoias*, the *Cunninghamias* have the remarkable ability to renew themselves readily after felling, by sending up new shoots from the base of the trunk. *C. lanceolata* is the Chinese species, and much cultivated in warmer areas of the United States, Southern Europe and South America.

There are two other species, *C. kawakamii* and *C. konishii*, both native to Taiwan, but they are rarely seen outside that island.

The genus was named for James Cunningham, an early explorer of China.

Cunninghamia lanceolata
China Fir

Cunninghamia lanceolata
detail of bark

Cunninghamia lanceolata
foliage

CUPANIOPSIS

(koo pan' ee op sis)

The Tuckeroo

FAMILY: SAPINDACEAE

Evergreen, and native to Australia, the handsome Tuckeroo, *Cupaniopsis anacardioides* is one of about fifty species of a tree genus found only in the Western Pacific area.

Smooth and pale of bark, it may reach 13 m (40 ft) in warmer areas. Its branches are clothed all year with heavy pinnate leaves, about 25 cm (10 in) long, each consisting of about eight blunt-ended shiny green leaflets. Small white flowers are borne in panicles at branch tips, but are rarely noticeable.

The Tuckeroo's real display is in midsummer, when the hanging clusters of 2 cm (¾ in) fruits ripen. These have six cells, are orange-yellow in colour, and resemble small pumpkins. They are full of sticky red pulp and black seeds, believed to have been an Aboriginal delicacy.

The Tuckeroo has become popular in many countries with climates similar to the Australian east coast, and is much used as a street tree. It is of particular value in coastal areas, being salt-resistant. The hard pink timber is used for building in Australian country areas.

The origin of the name *Cupaniopsis* is obscure, but the specific name *anacardioides* means 'having leaves like a cashew nut', which it does.

Cupaniopsis anacardioides
autumn blossom

Cupaniopsis anacardioides syn. *anacardiopsis*
Tuckeroo, summer fruit

Cupaniopsis anacardioides
Tuckeroo

CUPRESSUS

(koo pres' səs)

The Cypresses

FAMILY: CUPRESSACEAE

As the False Cypresses are to cooler climates (see *Chamaecyparis*), so the True Cypresses, *Cupressus*, are to the mild temperate garden — the most versatile and varied group of coniferous plants. Native to southern Europe, southern USA and Central America, and parts of south-western Asia, the twenty or more species vary astonishingly from 1 to 50 m in height (3 to 150 ft), and in habit of growth.

The classic types are the tall, pencil-shaped Italian Cypress of so many Mediterranean landscapes, *C. sempervirens Stricta;* and the craggy windblown effect of California's Monterey Cypress, *C. macrocarpa.* Somewhere in between are those with a wonderful weeping habit, including *C. funebris,* the Mourning Cypress from China, and *C. lusitanica,* the Mexican Weeping Cypress.

The Asiatic Bhutan Cypress, *C. torulosa,* from the western Himalayas, has very much the habit of the Cedars, pyramidal when young, but branching into a high crown in middle age.

Foliage colours may be blue-grey as in *C. glabra,* the Arizona Cypress, or bright golden-yellow as in many of the coloured leaf varieties of *C. macrocarpa.*

As a general rule, the branchlets of True Cypresses are not held in flat planes like those of the False Cypress, and the leaves themselves are modified into scales so tiny they can hardly be distinguished from the stems. The flowers are virtually invisible and the scaly globular cones hang on the trees for several years before splitting to release the seeds.

Cupressus macrocarpa 'Brunoniana'
Golden Cypress

Very few of the Cypress genus are in the least frost hardy, and all do best in warm sheltered positions. They are generally raised from seed (except of course the fancy coloured types), but cuttings will strike if taken in late autumn. Cypresses should be planted out as small as possible, for larger specimens do not transplant at all well.

The botanical name *Cupressus* is from two Greek words meaning 'equal growth', in reference to their generally symmetrical shapes.

Cupressus sempervirens Stricta
Italian Cypress

Cupressus lusitanica 'Glauca Pendula'
Mexican Cypress, Cedar of Goa

Cupressus sempervirens 'Swane's Golden'
Golden Pencil Pine

CYDONIA
(sai doh' nee ə)

The Quince

FAMILY: ROSACEAE

More popular in the days before refrigeration, when it lasted well into winter, the deliciously perfumed fruit of the Quince is little more than a rose hip, blown up to a diameter of 12.5 cm (5 in) and more. You may even have difficulty locating a plant these days, though they're often to be found in old villages, or even out in the open fields, a sure sign of earlier habitation.

The Quince (botanically, *Cydonia*, after the old Cretan city where it grew) is native to Eastern Europe and western Asiatic countries, and has been cultivated since time immemorial.

The tree is deciduous, with woolly young shoots and leaves rather like those of an apple. It may reach 7 m (20 ft) and is usually of a rather shrubby appearance unless pruned. The flowers are perfumed and charming, single and rose-like, a delicate blush pink. The great, irregularly shaped fruits ripen in autumn, often persisting on the tree after the leaves have yellowed and fallen.

Cupressus glabra
Arizona Cypress

Cydonia oblonga
Quince

Quinces cannot be eaten raw, but can be stewed with honey or sugar, or made into delicious jams, jellies, marmalades and pies. The rather grainy-textured flesh cooks up a brilliant scarlet-pink, looking and tasting most appetizing.

C. oblonga is one of only two species in cultivation, and is by far the better of the two. A remarkably adaptable fruit-bearing tree, it is of particular use in damp, low-lying areas.

Cydonia oblonga
Quince blossom

DACRYDIUM
(dak rid' ee əm)

The Rimu and Huon Pine

FAMILY: PODOCARPACEAE

Surprisingly few of New Zealand's really remarkable trees are seen in cultivation outside that country. But one notable exception is the Rimu or Red Pine, *Dacrydium cupressinum*, a favourite specimen tree in cool, moist, frost-free areas throughout the world.

The Rimu is a slow-growing conifer which may ultimately reach a height of 25 m (80 ft) in ideal conditions, but is not really likely to exceed a third of that in an average lifetime. It is related more to the Yews and Podocarps (see *Taxus* and *Podocarpus*) than to the Pines and Firs, and like the former bears its seed in a brightly coloured acorn-type fruit. The seed is blue, the cup red. The foliage consists of tiny scale-like leaves which overlap along the length of long, weeping branchlets.

The botanical name *Dacrydium* is a diminutive form of the ancient Greek word for a tear — an allusion not to the weeping habit, but the sparkling drops of gum exuded by the tree's fruit. Like some other New Zealand flora and

Dacrydium cupressinum
Rimu, New Zealand Red Pine

fauna, the genus *Dacrydium* has related species in South America, Australia and the Malaysian area, lending belief to the theory of a one-time, ocean-spanning continent in the Pacific.

The only other cultivated species is Tasmanian *D. franklinii* or Huon Pine, now virtually extinct in mature form because of its slow growth, as little as one millimetre a year!

Both *Dacrydium* species were formerly valued for boat building (their timber is resistant to water and the boring Marine Toredo) and for cabinet making. Rimu wood is a beautifully figured rosy-yellow. Huon Pine is somewhat paler, but also attractively marked. Other members of the genus are dwarf or prostrate in habit.

Dacrydium cupressinum
detail of foliage

DAVIDIA
(dae vid' ee ə)

The Dove Tree

FAMILY: DAVIDIACEAE

Just over seventy years ago, this beautiful tree caused a botanical sensation when it flowered for the first time in the West in the garden of a French collector named de Vilmorin. This came as the climax of a race between French and English botanists to find and flower a tree reported from western China by the French missionary, Père David. It had ghostly white flowers fluttering among the foliage like handkerchiefs, or so he reported.

The race and its result are botanical history, but even before the trees were located and their seed taken back to Europe, the botanical name was never in doubt — *Davidia*, with the specific name *involucrata*, meaning that the flowers are surrounded by a bract, for the ghostly fluttering parts turned out to be not the flower itself, which is quite small.

Davidia will grow in any frost-free area short of the sub-tropics, preferring a deep, rich acid soil. It may reach 13 m (40 ft) but is usually only half that in the average garden. The flower heads are less than 2 cm (¾ in) wide, and consist of a number of greenish filaments topped with red or dark-brown stamens. These heads are each surrounded by two unequal bracts, the larger as big as a human hand.

The floral display starts just as the tree opens its spring foliage and lasts for several weeks, after which the inedible purplish green fruit appear on long stems.

DELONIX
(del' ə niks)

The Flamboyant or Poinciana

FAMILY: LEGUMINOSAE

Believed to have originated on the island of Madagascar, home of so many wonderful plants, the Royal Poinciana or Flamboyant has often been hailed as the showiest flowering tree in the world. But gardeners living further than 30° north or south of the equator will have to be content to dream about it, for it won't flower anywhere else, and requires a fully tropical climate with summer rain to put on any sort of a show.

When it does condescend to blossom, it is just like a fireworks display, as the whole tree drops its foliage and lights up literally overnight into a canopy of bright scarlet flowers, each about the size of a rose. These are quite variable in colour, shading from almost crimson to almost orange, in each case with one petal heavily spotted in either white or yellow. There is even a much rarer form, which I photographed in Tahiti, where the entire flower is yellow, one petal marked in cream.

The Poinciana (its botanical name *Delonix* is from the Greek *delos*, meaning 'obvious', and it certainly is hard to miss!) is not tall as trees go. Its limit is about 10 m (30 ft) but it may ultimately reach three times that in width, a great spreading umbrella that makes wonderful shade in tropical gardens.

The smooth grey trunk often develops large supporting buttresses; the bipinnate leaves are feathery and delicate, like those of a Jacaranda.

Davidia involucrata
Dove or Handkerchief Tree

Delonix regia
Poinciana or Flamboyant

Delonix regia
Poinciana,

Dillenia indica
Elephant Apple, Simpoh

DILLENIA
(dil len' ee ə)

The Simpoh or Elephant Apple

FAMILY: DILLENIACEAE

Visitors to warmer parts — South-East Asia, Florida, Hawaii, the Caribbean, Queensland and East Africa — often notice a heavy-looking, short-trunked tree with finely pleated leaves and fragrant white flowers the size of a Magnolia. The chances are it will prove to be the *Dillenia* or Elephant Apple, which is also known in various countries as Simpoh or Wormia.

Originally from west India, the Elephant Apple is evergreen except in dry climates where it may lose some leaves in winter. It may reach 10 m (30 ft), has few branches, and flowers principally in late spring, the great blooms appearing mostly under the foliage and visible only when you look up into the tree.

Each flower has five large petals surrounding a cushiony mass of yellow stamens with a large ovary or seed capsule in the centre. As the petals drop, the backing green sepals enlarge, covering the developing fruit. This is green, containing a number of black seeds in juicy pulp, and may reach the size of a grapefruit.

In India the sepals are used in curries, and the fruit is regarded as quite edible, that is, elephants at least enjoy them.

D. indica may be propagated from cuttings of half-ripe shoots, or from the seeds.

Dillenia indica
detail of foliage

Dillenia alata
detail of fruit and flower

95

DIOSPYROS
(dee oh spai' rəs)

The Persimmons and Ebonies

FAMILY: EBENACEAE

Tricky to eat, the luscious fruit of the Persimmon (*Diospyros kaki*) can all but paralyse the tongue unless they have reached the exact stage of squashy ripeness, when their astringent principle is converted to sugary sweetness.

The scientific name *Diospyros* is based on two Greek words meaning 'godly grain', probably an allusion to their gourmet appeal.

The Persimmon is a strikingly handsome tree, flourishing anywhere from the sub-tropics to cool temperate zones. It may reach 13 m (40 ft) in old age, but is limited to half that in the average garden. The trunk is picturesque and twisted, the branches trailing the ground in some of the named varieties. The oval 18 cm (7 in) leaves turn on a magnificent show as the cold weather approaches; orange, scarlet, even imperial purple. The small yellowish flowers are hardly noticeable, merely a necessary stage toward the gorgeous tomato-sized fruits that follow. These persist on the branches well into winter, if you can be persuaded to leave them alone. They may shade anywhere from yellow to red according to variety, and may vary from almost pear-shaped to flat and squarish.

Diospyros kaki
detail of fruit, autumn

The magnificently figured Persimmon wood is much used for precious objects in the far east, being a close relative of Ebony (*D. ebenum* from Ceylon), one of the world's great timbers.

In North American forests, the larger native *D. virginiana* or Possum Wood may tower 20 m (60 ft) or more and bears similar though smaller leaves and fruit. These are again edible, but fairly tasteless.

Persimmons and Ebonies grow from seed but the best varieties are propagated by grafting. There are about 200 species of *Diospyros* native to Asia and North America.

Diospyros virginiana
Possum Wood

Diospyros kaki
Persimmon

96

DIPLOGLOTTIS
(dip loh glot' təs)

The Native Tamarind
FAMILY: SAPINDACEAE

Diploglottis cunninghamii
Native Tamarind

Not much known outside Australia, the Native Tamarind, *Diploglottis cunninghamii* is a handsome evergreen tree from forests of the warm east coast, and could be of great value in warm temperate gardens all over the world. It grows to 12 m (36 ft), bears enormous compound leaves, each consisting of up to twelve ruffled leaflets.

The tiny yellow autumn flowers appear in decorative panicles at the end of branchlets, and are followed by yellow three-celled fruit, the size of a grape. These are full of red juicy pulp and make delicious jams and chutneys, much like the Asiatic Tamarind (see *Tamarindus*), after which it has been popularly named.

Diploglottis is grown from seed, and its botanical name means double tongue, a reference to a minor flower detail apparent only to a botanist.

DOMBEYA
(dom' bee ə)

The Natal Cherry
FAMILY: BYTTNERIACEAE

Native exclusively to eastern Africa and islands of the Indian Ocean, the *Dombeyas* are handsome but very variable trees and large shrubs, now grown in many lands and climates.

The tree species include the striking *D. tiliacea* or Natal Cherry, a slim and many-branched tree with a blackish trunk, which may reach 8 m (25 ft). It grows easily from seed or cuttings and produces a magnificent display of bloom in autumn when the entire tree becomes weighed down with clusters of white, long-stemmed, fragrant flowers — very similar to the white Japanese Cherry Blossom which suggested its popular name. The irregularly toothed 8 cm (3½ in) leaves, however, resemble those of a Poplar or Linden (see *Populus*, and *Tilia*). *D. tiliacea* is from Natal and sometimes listed as *D. natalensis*.

D. spectabilis, the Wild Pear, is deciduous, with glossy pear-like foliage, rusty on the underside. The white or pale pink blossom forms dense panicles in spring, often before the leaves.

In warmer climates you'll see the curious Mexican Rose or Pink Ball, *D. wallichii*, a shrubby small tree which may reach 10 m (30 ft). Its enormous heart-shaped leaves grow up to 30 cm (12 in) and are sometimes lobed. The crowded umbels of pink to scarlet flowers appear in ball-shaped clusters on long, hairy, hanging stems, throughout the warm weather.

Dombeya tiliacea
Natal Cherry

They are not perfumed. *D. wallichii* can be propagated from firm cuttings in spring and is often kept pruned to large shrub size.

The botanical name *Dombeya* is a tribute to an eighteenth-century French botanist, Jacob Dombey.

ELAEOCARPUS
(ə lae oh kar' pəs)

The Blueberry Ashes

FAMILY: ELAEOCARPACEAE

Was ever there a more charming small tree to complement a shady, shrubby garden? Named after the Greek words for 'olive' and 'fruit', *Elaeocarpus* are a small genus of evergreen flowering trees confined to the Indo-Malaysian area, Australia and New Zealand. Mostly slender, graceful and rather slow-growing at the outset, they bear laurel-like leaves, sometimes slightly toothed.

The fragrant flowers are borne in small sprays like lily-of-the-valley. They are usually white or pink and most delicately fringed. This spring display is followed by a heavy crop of brilliant blue fruits which persist into winter.

Species in cultivation include *E. denticulatus*, New Zealand's Hinau, with pale yellow flowers; *E. grandis*, the Silver Quandong from eastern Australia, with creamy flowers; *E. kirtonii*, the Pigeonberry Ash with white flowers; *E. reticulatus*, the Blueberry Ash, pink or white blossom; and the Malaysian *E. serratus* or Blue Olive Berry with white flowers.

All prefer moist, shaded conditions. The only recorded practical use of the trees is in India, where the dried berries are used as beads.

Dombeya spectabilis
Wild Pear

Dombeya wallichii
Mexican Rose

Elaeocarpus reticulatus
Blueberry Ash, flowers

Elaeocarpus reticulatus
Blueberry Ash, fruit

ERIOBOTRYA
(er ee oh bot' ree ə)

The Loquat
FAMILY: ROSACEAE

Eriobotrya deflexa
Nakai

Eriobotrya japonica
Loquat, Japanese Medlar

Raised in temperate to tropical climates both as an ornamental and for its succulent winter fruits, the Loquat or Japanese Medlar is out of favour in many areas because of the discovery that fruitfly larvae may survive the cold season in its fruit. But provided attention is paid to spraying, particularly in autumn when the fruit is beginning to form, there is no reason why it should not still be grown.

Only a small tree, rarely above 7 m (20 ft) in height, it is closely related to apples, pears and quinces, other fruiting trees of the rose family. The rather brittle dark foliage is evergreen, each slightly toothed leaf 25 cm (10 in) long, deeply veined and woolly beneath. The small five-petalled flowers are whitish, fragrant, and appear on rusty, woolly stems at branch tips in the autumn. The fruits ripen at various times in winter according to variety and location. They are the size of a ping-pong ball, slightly oval and a pale apricot in colour. Just rub off the slightly downy coating and eat them straight from the tree. They are very succulent, with a sweetly acid flavour, each containing several large slippery seeds.

The Loquat is known botanically as *Eriobotrya japonica* from the Greek words *erion* meaning wool and *botrys* meaning a cluster — an apt description of its flower display. It is native to China and southern Japan, and is popular in southern Europe, southern and western USA, Australia, Africa and many other places.

99

ERYTHRINA
(e rith rai' nə)

The Coral Trees

FAMILY: LEGUMINOSAE

There are some who say the showy *Erythrinas* make an appropriate floral symbol for Los Angeles, the mighty city of the Angels. All show and magnificence on top, they may scratch you badly if you try to make a grab. And the wood? Poor, weak stuff. The trees are likely to drop a branch without notice, or fall over in a high wind.

At any rate, Los Angeles *has* adopted them, and they are now planted there in great variety, though none of them is found naturally in that part of the world.

Native to many other warm temperate and tropical areas in Africa, Central America, Australia, southern Asia, the East Indies and Hawaii, they are mostly gnarled and rugged-looking trees with vicious thorns. Their wood is very light and brittle and useless for woodworking. They enjoy best a climate on the warm, dry side, but seem indifferent to winter cold short of frost.

Erythrina variegata 'Parcellii'
Variegated Tiger Claw

Erythrina vespertilio
Batswing Coral

Their flowers are mostly in brilliant scarlet, in some species shading to crimson and orange, and many of them flower in mid-winter when the trees are bare of foliage.

Australia's ubiquitous Indian Coral Bean, *E. variegata*, can be struck from large branches as an 'instant tree', but is just as likely to fall over without protection from windy weather. Its large heart-shaped leaves give wonderful summer shade.

The picturesque *E. crista-galli* or Cockscomb Coral will in time develop a wonderfully gnarled trunk, but at least in its younger days will need annual pruning back to the main branches.

E. caffra, the Kaffirboom from South Africa, makes a tall and handsome foliage tree and is deservedly popular.

Erythrina speciosa
Corallodendron

Erythrina crista-galli
Cockscomb Coral

Erythrina falcata
detail of spring flowers

Erythrina caffra
Kaffirboom

Erythrina variegata, syn. *E. indica*
Coral Bean, winter

EUCALYPTUS
(yoo ka lip' təs)

The Gum Trees or Eucalypts

FAMILY: MYRTACEAE

In Australia, the ubiquitous Gum Tree is king. To all points of the compass, and in the central desert, the great bulk of the continent's natural tree-life consists of one or another of the 600 and more recorded species of *Eucalyptus*. Often very localized by species, the Gums as a group are highly adaptable, and in fact astonishingly adapted to the rigours of life in many diverse climates.

Some species flourish in swamps, others eke out a sparse existence in barren deserts where the rainfall in one year may be nil. There are low, scrubby, many-trunked types in the sandplains, tall needle-straight giants in the forests of West-ern Australia, Victoria and Tasmania, some of them (*E. regnans*, the Mountain Ash) arguably the tallest trees on earth! The great River Red Gums send out a labyrinth of roots near water, helping combat erosion; the gnarled and hardy Snow Gums twist and sprawl on the lee side of mountains high above the snowline.

The Eucalypts have become Australia's most influential export, used for reafforestation in many of the world's most barren areas which often (but wrongly) imagine them to be their own. With very few exceptions, all the world's Eucalypts have originated from Australian seed in the last century.

You'll find them everywhere in California, in Israel, north, east and South Africa, all about the Mediterranean, and in islands as far apart as Hong Kong and Hawaii. These days Australia even imports valuable Eucalyptus oil from Africa, because of the lower labour costs there.

Eucalyptus mannifera ssp. *Maculosa*
Red-spotted Gum

Eucalyptus camaldulensis
River Red Gum

Eucalyptus citriodora
Lemon-scented Gum, bark

The exceptions which have not originated in Australia are a few tropic species from the islands north of Capricorn as far as the southern Philippines. The particularly decorative Mindanao Gum (*E. deglupta*) from the Philippines is grown in many parts of the Pacific.

Eucalypts yield several valuable oils, and because of the enormous quantities of flowers they bear, are an important source of honey. The timber of many species provides some of the best hardwoods in the world. That of the

West Australian Jarrah is used for pilings of wharves and jetties, being curiously resistant to the marine borer. The New South Wales Blackbutt has a timber so hard and strong that it was used as load-bearing columns and beams of buildings up to six storeys in height in earlier days.

Eucalypt bark may be smooth and paper thin (as in *E. citriodora*, the Lemon-scented Gum), or rough and deeply fissured as in the many Stringybarks and Ironbarks. The leaves vary widely according to species both in length and in width, ranging all the way from spear-shaped to heart-shaped, with often a recognizably different leaf-shape in juvenile foliage, which makes them very tricky to identify.

The flowers of all Eucalypt species have at least one feature found on no other tree, and that is the peculiar cup-shaped lid or operculum which covers each flower bud. This pops off and drops as the dense mass of stamens expands for the seasonal display. The pictures shown can give only a suggestion of the glorious flower colour varieties and of the vast range of this group of plants.

Eucalypts are usually grown from seed, and accordingly their flower colours and leaf-shapes are notoriously unstable. They are fast growers in garden conditions, and curiously grow quicker from small seedlings than from larger nursery-bought plants.

In common with many other Australian plants, they resent cultivation in their vicinity, and are best planted by themselves. They have one peculiarity of growth which is virtually unique in the tree world. This is the lignotuber, a vast bulb-like growth which develops at or just below ground level in many species. It serves as a storage chamber for many plant nutrients which allows the tree to survive a dry season or even regenerate completely after devastating fires have destroyed all above-ground growth.

Eucalyptus pauciflora ssp. *Niphophila*
Snow Gum

Eucalyptus racemosa
Narrow-leaf Ironbark, blossom

Eucalyptus caesia
Gungunnu, blossom

Eucalyptus leucoxylon Rosea
Pink-flowered Whitewood, blossom

Eucalyptus erythrocorys
Illyarie, blossom

Eucalyptus microcorys
Tallow-wood, blossom

Eucalyptus rhodantha
Rose Gum, blossom

Eucalyptus ficifolia
Red Flowering Gum, blossom

Eucalyptus sideroxylon Pallens
Pink-flowered Ironbark, bark

Eucalyptus deglupta
Mindanao Gum, bark

EUPHORIA
(yoo for' ee ə)

Loong Ngan or Dragon's Eye

FAMILY: SAPINDACEAE

One of Asia's most popular trees, the Loong Ngan is only known in the West as the source of a delicious canned fruit sometimes served in Chinese restaurants. The fruit greatly resembles the wonderful Lychee, though with slightly less flavour.

In fact the Loong Ngans can be grown over a far wider range, being somewhat resistant to frost and needing protection from the full tropical sun in summer. They also grow faster than the Lychee, and are altogether a more vigorous tree, reaching 13 m (40 ft) in a suitable area.

The handsome foliage consists of pinnate leaves with up to twelve pointed leaflets each, often highly coloured when young. The tiny yellow flowers appear both at the end of twigs and at the leaf bases, and are carried in brownish, furry panicles. The fruits, which ripen later than those of the Lychee, are smooth and about the size of a grape, greenish at first, but taking on a red tint as they ripen. They may be eaten fresh, preserved or dried.

Loong Ngan, the original Chinese name, means Dragon's Eye, and has been incorporated into the botanical name *E. longan*. *Euphoria* is a rough adaptation of Greek words meaning 'well-carrying'; this may be in reference to the tree's heavy crops, or to the fact that the fruit is long lasting.

The Loong Ngan can be propagated from seed, half-ripened cuttings or layers. It needs a deep, compost-rich soil and regular fertilizing, particularly when developing fruit.

FAGUS
(fae' gəs)

The Beeches

FAMILY: FAGACEAE

Not a large genus and found only in limited areas of the temperate northern hemisphere, the Beeches nevertheless include some of the biggest and most beloved of cool climate deciduous trees. In particular, the many fancy-leafed varieties of the European Beech (*Fagus sylvatica*) are among the most prized of specimens in gardens and arboretums all over the temperate world.

Beeches are deciduous and generally possessed of that most sought after of qualities, a preference for lime-rich, chalky soils. Provided there is good drainage, they romp ahead, growing to 30 m (90 ft) and reproducing rapidly from fallen seed. Left to themselves they soon form a Beech forest, for with their dense leaf canopies and surface-foraging roots, nothing else will grow in the vicinity.

Their prominence in European woodlands is reflected in many European place names, Germany's notorious Buchenwald, and England's Buckinghamshire among them. Both names come from the German *buche* meaning a Beech.

F. sylvatica is a graceful tree, tall and slim in woodland conditions, widely spreading as a specimen, often with weeping branches. The prominently veined leaves are almost translucent and covered with fine, silky hair. Their shape is a perfect pointed oval, and the colour may vary from the normal green towards either gold or purple according to variety. There are also variegated cultivars and several with finely toothed and lobed leaves.

Euphoria longan
Loong Ngan or Dragon's Eye, fruit

Fagus sylvatica
Common Beech, foliage

106

Fagus sylvatica and
Fagus sylvatica Purpurea

Fagus sylvatica Asplenifolia
Fern-leafed Beech

After a relatively insignificant flower display, the Beeches develop a crop of small triangular nuts enclosed in spiny-hairy cases which split open in autumn. These Beechnuts are relatively flavourless to humans, but a great success with pigs. The timber is popular in furniture making.

The related American Beech (*F. grandifolia*) is also an important timber tree in that country, but not grown much elsewhere. Its leaves are larger and coarsely serrated. In Japan they grow the native *F. crenata*.

Fagus sylvatica
detail of Beechnuts and foliage

Fagus sylvatica Purpurea Pendula
Weeping Purple Beech

Fagus sylvatica Purpurea
Purple Beech

FICUS
(fai' kəs)

The Figs and Banyans

FAMILY: MORACEAE

How curious that the enormous genus that includes some of the world's largest trees should be known collectively by the name of its least spectacular member. *Ficus* was the name the Romans gave to the generally small, shrubby Fig tree from Asia Minor, whose leaves the Bible tells us were worn by Adam and Eve. But both popular and botanical names stuck when its gigantic cousins were discovered later in many tropical parts of the world. Certainly the other trees, towering constructions with aerial roots and strangling branches, don't look much like the Figs of our orchards, so why are they classed in the same genus?

As is so often the case, it's a matter of the flowers. You will never see a Fig tree of any sort in flower. They produce only small hollow receptacles closed with a minuscule flapped opening or *ostiole*. The even more minute flowers are borne *inside* this receptacle. When fertilized by a small wasp (the only creature tiny enough to pierce the ostiole), the receptacle ripens into a generally pear-shaped, rather squashy fruit. The Common Fig, *F. carica*, is also the exception in being deciduous, and bears rough-textured, three-lobed leaves. Almost all the others are evergreen with handsome shiny leaves, ranging from 2.5 to 30 cm in length (1 to 12 in). Many of these are among the most reliable and popular of indoor plants, but in that form scarcely hint at their tropical grandeur.

There is *F. benjamina* for instance, the Weeping Laurel or Chinese Banyan, found all the way from India to northern Australia. Dainty little weeping plants indoors, I have seen them in Hawaii over 35 m (100 ft) in diameter and almost half that in height; or hanging their long, weeping branches 17 m (50 ft) down toward the Brisbane River. They adore humidity and should not be grown in dry areas.

F. lyrata, the Fiddle Leaf or Banjo Fig that sprouts its rough, guitar-shaped leaves dramatically in many an apartment reaches 15 m (45 ft) in the Philippines or its native Africa.

And there is the ubiquitous *F. elastica* or India Rubber Tree from northern India. One tree in Assam is said to have grown 37 m (112 ft) in just over thirty years — a good reason for *not* planting out your pet plant when it gets too big!

The Banyan, also from India, sends down aerial roots from every branch which develop into new, supporting trunks wherever they touch ground, soon forming a dense forest. One famous Banyan in India is almost half a mile in circumference (almost 1 km)!

Ficus lyrata
Fiddle Leaf Fig, Banjo Fig

Ficus elastica Variegata
Variegated Indiarubber Plant

Ficus macrophylla
Moreton Bay Fig, fruit

Ficus rubiginosa
Port Jackson Fig

Ficus carica
Common Fig

There are over 600 known *Ficus* species. Though many of them are popularly known as rubber trees, and their sticky sap can be tapped and processed into latex, they are not the trees of commercial rubber plantations. That is quite a different genus, *Hevea brasiliensis*.

Ficus religiosa
Peepul or Bo Tree

Ficus benjamina
Weeping Banyan

Ficus retusa
Chinese Banyan

109

FLINDERSIA
(flin dur' see ə)

The Australian Ashes

FAMILY: MELIACEAE

One of Australia's most valuable groups of timber trees, the handsome *Flindersias* (named for explorer Matthew Flinders), are mostly inhabitants of the moist Australian coastal forests and a few islands north to the Moluccas. The exception being the Leopardwood, *F. maculosa*, which prefers the arid outback of western New South Wales and Queensland, where it reaches a height of 15 m (45 ft).

The coastal *Flindersias* are much larger trees, and old specimens have been recorded towering to 50 m (150 ft), particularly in Queensland.

Most of them make splendid specimen or street trees in frost-free areas, and have foliage closely resembling that of the European and American Ash trees (see *Fraxinus*). That is to say, the leaves are compound, consisting of a number of coarse leaflets. Beyond that they vary greatly, bearing masses of small white flowers in late spring. These appear in branching terminal clusters, deliciously fragrant with honey. The flowers are followed by quite large seed pods, often prickly or studded with warts.

Commonly seen species include *F. australis*, the Crow's Ash, *F. pubescens*, the Silver Ash and *F. schottiana*, the Bumpy Ash. All species are propagated from seed.

Flindersia schottiana
Bumpy Ash, flowers and foliage

FRAXINUS
(frax see' nəs)

The Ashes

FAMILY: OLEACEAE

One of the most widely grown genera of largely deciduous trees from the northern hemisphere, the *Fraxinus* or Ashes have a wide climatic range spreading from quite frosty areas into hill climates of the tropics. There are over sixty species found in nature on all three continents, and many fancy cultivated varieties, particularly of the European Ash (*F. excelsior*).

Flindersia australis
Crow's Ash

Fraxinus excelsior CV *Aurea*
Golden Ash

As a genus, they are most variable in size, ranging from a small shrubby build to giants of 50 m (160 ft) and more. With very few exceptions they are resistant to all extremes of weather, provided the soil is deep and rich.

Their trademark is a foliage of decorative pinnate leaves, rarely more than 30 cm (12 in) long, and consisting of from three to thirteen leaflets, lightly toothed and with the odd one borne on the end. The small flowers appear in dense panicles, generally before the leaves, in early spring. Later, they develop into a mass of small *samaras* or seeds that hang out the end of a single, flattened wing. These are quite showy, particularly in the Mediterranean species *F. ornus* or Manna Ash.

Particularly popular in cultivation are: the Golden Ash (*F. excelsior* CV *Aurea*), which produces handsome golden-green leaves that colour brilliantly in autumn; the Weeping Ash (*F. excelsior Pendula*), a very heavy tree with branches that not only hang down, but run along the ground; *F. X 'Raywoodii'*, the Claret Ash, an Australian-raised hybrid that colours a wonderful deep red-bronze in autumn; the evergreen Mexican Ash (*F. uhdei*) and the spectacular White Ash (*F. americana*) from the eastern United States, that colours vividly in autumn with a distinct touch of mauve among the gold.

All Ashes grow readily from seed, which should be stored until spring and heat treated before sowing. They are valuable timber trees, and popular everywhere for street planting.

Fraxinus ornus
Manna Ash, fruit

Fraxinus excelsior
Common Ash, fruit

Fraxinus excelsior Pendula
Weeping Ash

Fraxinus uhdei
Mexican Evergreen Ash

111

Fraxinus spp.
Ash, bark detail

FREMONTODENDRON

(free mont' oh den dron)

The Tree Poppy

FAMILY: BOMBACACEAE

Localized in a small area of southern California, Arizona and north-west Mexico, the two showy *Fremontodendrons* make ideal specimens for dryish sheltered gardens with well-drained sandy soil. The species are *F. californicum* and *F. mexicanum;* both reach about 7 m (20 ft) and need help from the pruning shears to grow up as a tree rather than a somewhat floppy shrub.

Evergreen except in particularly dry years, they produce woolly greyish leaves, generally three-lobed on the Californian form and five-lobed on the Mexican. The Hibiscus-like flowers appear on short spurs along the branches, varying from yellow to orange in colour. Those of the Mexican species are brighter and larger.

Both *Fremontodendrons* (named for Captain Charles Fremont, explorer of the Golden West) are sometimes known as California Tree Poppy, and are propagated from seed and softwood cuttings. They cannot abide a humid climate.

Fremontodendron californicum
California Tree Poppy

Fraxinus X 'Raywoodii'
Claret Ash

Fremontodendron mexicanum
Mexican Tree Poppy

GEIJERA
(gai' jur ə)

The Wilga
FAMILY: RUTACEAE

For habitually dry areas of low rainfall, there is a tree with all the grace and charm of the water-loving willows. This is the Wilga, *Geijera parviflora*, a native of Australia's dry inland areas. Californian gardeners have discovered it, as you might expect, and it also seems to be grown in the Mediterranean lands.

Strangely enough, *Geijera* belongs to the same family as the Citrus, though you'd never guess it from the long, grey 15 cm (6 in) leaves and weeping branches. There is perhaps a hint of the relationship in the fragrant starry-white flowers, which are borne in open sprays off and on throughout the year. The timber is very hard and of a pleasant fragrance, but seems to have little use in commerce. The Wilga's principal value in cultivation is as a shapely ornamental, rarely touching 8 m (25 ft). On drought-stricken country properties, the foliage makes wonderful stock fodder.

Of the other *Geijera* species, *G. salicifolia* seems the only one in cultivation, and is more at home in moist coastal gardens. The leaves are slim and oval and densely borne, the small flowers appearing in 7 cm (2½ in) sprays. It grows to 20 m (60 ft) in nature, but only a third of that in cultivation.

The origin of the botanical name *Geijera* is uncertain. It may well be a name used by some extinct Aboriginal tribe.

GINKGO
(gin' koh)

The Maidenhair Tree
FAMILY: GINKGOACEAE

The graceful *Ginkgo* is the Rip van Winkle of botany — a tree lost in time and suddenly revived into a world changed beyond recognition.

If that hyperbole sounds melodramatic, the facts are even more so. *Ginkgo* (and other trees very similar to it in the same family) first flourished in Europe and Asia, in Australia and even in America, some 200 million years ago. The leaves have been found again and again in fossil strata from the Palaeozoic era when the earth was a jungle of steamy swamps. It was known to scientists for centuries as the ancestor of all conifers, but believed quite extinct. And so we believe it still to be, that is, in the wild. But in the gardens of certain remote and ancient Chinese temples, it lived on. The Western world first heard of it in the seventeenth century, and actually saw it in 1730 when the first living specimen was imported by Dutch traders. And so, the *Ginkgo* began life all over again, reconquering its former range, country by country.

For a tree from so ancient and tranquil a background, it does better in city conditions than almost any modern tree. Throughout polluted Tokyo you see it fresh and green, growing on some of the world's most choked and busy thoroughfares.

Geijera parviflora
Wilga

Ginkgo biloba
Maidenhair or Ducksfoot Tree

Ginkgo biloba
Ginkgo, autumn foliage

Ginkgo is cold hardy, but loves summer heat. It is quite immune to disease, fast-growing and can cope with either dry or wet conditions. It may be propagated from seed or by layering or grafting. *Ginkgo* may grow to 40 m (130 ft) in a warm climate, but around a third of that is more normal. The leaves closely resemble the Maidenhair Fern to which it owes its popular name, although the Chinese, more practically, call it the 'Duck's Foot Tree'.

On one old *Ginkgo* tree in the Tokyo Botanic Gardens, I noticed a curious feature to which I have not found reference elsewhere. These were a series of hanging protuberances like stalactites or pendulous breasts. Their purpose is a mystery.

GLEDITSIA
(gle dit' see ə)

The Honey Locusts

FAMILY: LEGUMINOSAE

I find it very difficult to remember the correct botanical name for a plant when I can't even pronounce or spell it. *Eschscholzia* for instance. Surely there was a naturalist with an easier name by which to remember the lovely California Poppy? And why name a lovely genus of trees after a man named Gleditsch, even if he was once director of the Berlin Botanical Garden?

Fortunately, reason has at last prevailed, and the name has now been mercifully simplified to *Gleditsia*, which identifies a small genus of trees in the pea family, Leguminosae, found only in Asia and North America. Small the genus may be, but *very* distinctive, widely planted as street and specimen trees all over the temperate world, both dry and wet.

Most commonly seen is the North American Honey Locust, *G. triacanthos*, which is deciduous and grows as tall as 50 m (160 ft) in its native land, though much less elsewhere. It produces bipinnate leaves with up to thirty-two leaflets, small green pea flowers in furry racemes and masses of sickle-shaped pea pods up to 45 cm (18 in) long. But its most noticeable feature is the barrier of wickedly branched spines that emerge in clusters all over the trunk. Indeed a difficult tree to climb, but how much worse to descend! Its gold-leafed cultivar 'Sunburst' is particularly decorative.

Ginkgo biloba
detail of 'aerial roots'

Gleditsia triacanthos
Honey Locust, autumn colour

Gleditsia triacanthos
detail of spines, mature tree

The Japanese species *G. japonica* is very similar though barely half the size, and with very corkscrew-twisted pods. The Persian *G. caspica* has a very warty trunk and much smaller pods, while the Chinese *G. sinensis* is similar to the Japanese type, though smaller, and with untwisted purplish pods.

All *Gleditsias* grow easily from seed, and curiously for members of the pea family, are both frost and drought hardy. Their pods, filled with sweetish pulp, are edible, hence the popular name of Honey Locust.

GLIRICIDIA
(gli ri sid' ee ə)

Madre de Cacao

FAMILY: LEGUMINOSAE

Not the source of cocoa in itself, the picturesque Madre de Cacao (Mother of Cocoa) is regarded in Central America as indispensable for the cultivation of the Cocoa plant (see *Theobroma*) which grows better in its vicinity. This interesting example of 'companioning' or symbiosis in the plant world is not an old wives' tale. The *Gliricidia*, like many of the Legume family, is particularly rich in nitrogen. Its falling leaves are turned in around the Cocoa plants as green manure, and the roots of the Madre de Cacao are covered in nitrogenous nodules which seem to enrich the soil beneath.

Madre de Cacao grows to 8 m (25 ft), with a short, gnarled trunk about 30 cm (12 in) thick. Its compact, fern-like leaves are 25 cm (10 in) long with thirteen to fifteen pairs of leaflets and an odd one on the end. The tree is very sensitive, dropping all its leaves overnight in dry weather, or at the first touch of cold. In early spring the entire tree is decked with charming, perfect pea flowers, mauve-pink with a yellow eye. These appear in small racemes directly from the branches, trunk and twigs.

The tree's botanical name *Gliricidia sepium* means 'rat poison', and the seeds are used for that purpose in Central America and the Philippines.

Gleditsia triacanthos CV 'Sunburst'
flowers and young foliage

Gliricidia sepium
Madre de Cacao

GREVILLEA
(gre vil' ee ə)

The Silky Oak
FAMILY: PROTEACEAE

If the Australian flora were known internationally for only a single tree, it would be the glorious Silky Oak, *Grevillea robusta*, which has been an outstanding success as a street tree, a garden specimen and a source of hard, beautifully-grained timber. You'll find it all over the Mediterranean area, in Africa, the southern United States and in virtually every tropical or sub-tropical corner of the world. It has been mass-planted as a timber tree in Hawaii, and is raised by millions as one of the world's most desirable indoor plants (though strangely enough never in its native Australia).

A tall grower in nature where trees of up to 50 m (150 ft) have been recorded, the Silky Oak appears spontaneously in the most unlikely places, for its winged seeds can glide for long distances. It has an upright habit with slightly upward-pointing branches decked with silver-backed fern-like leaves up to 30 cm (12 in) long.

Evergreen in moist climates, it turns deciduous in drier areas, bursting into a razzle-dazzle of vivid orange, comb-like inflorescences in summer. It is so easy to grow from seed you wouldn't think of propagating it any other way.

Several other tree species of *Grevillea*, of which there are over two hundred, are also popular in cultivation, the principal one being the Red Silky Oak, *G. banksii*, a much smaller tree of about 7 m (20 ft). This has similar fern-like leaves, but of smaller size and more heavily lobed. The floral display is in cylindrical spikes of individual red flowers, each with a curly scarlet-and-gold stamen. It is not much grown in country areas, for it seems the hairs on parts of the plants are irritating to humans and may be fatal to stock when eaten.

Grevilleas were named for Charles Greville, a friend of Sir Joseph Banks and founder of England's Royal Horticultural Society.

Grevillea banksii
Red Silky Oak, blossom

GUAIACUM
(gwae' ə kəm)

The Lignum Vitae
FAMILY: ZYGOPHYLLACEAE

So heavy it sinks in water, the hardest, finest grained timber known is cut from the *Guaiacum* or Lignum Vitae, a small tree from drier coastal areas of the Caribbean. *Guaiac* was the original Indian name of this small genus, and for centuries the cut trees were shipped from the New World for the medicinal properties of the resin in their wood. This was called 'Lignum Vitae' — 'the Wood of life'!

Nowadays they are more likely to support small cottage industries making mallets or bowling balls, but in Victorian times the wood was used for many decorative purposes (in my own

Grevillea robusta
Silky Oak

home it has been used for door handles, key plates and other miscellaneous hardware) and also in shipyards, where it was carved into splendid, long-lasting pulley blocks.

Guaiacum officinale
Lignum Vitae, foliage

Hakea laurina
Pincushion Tree or Sea Urchin

HAKEA
(hae' kee ə)

The Pincushion Tree

FAMILY: PROTEACEAE

More cold-hardy than many Australian natives, the eye-catching Pincushion Tree, *Hakea laurina* is happy down to –7°C (20°F), and even produces its flower display in the cold weather. It is not a large tree. A height of 7 m (20 ft) is about the most you can expect, and then only in dry gravelly soils, the condition it enjoys in its original West Australian setting.

Hakea is tremendously popular in the South of France and in California, and occasionally seen pruned to shrubby size as a street tree in Melbourne. But in nature, it is a loose, gangling sort of tree, the branches often weeping and densely covered with 10 cm (4 in) leathery leaves of an interesting blue-green.

The small red flowers are packed in dense 5 cm (2 in) globular heads which appear at the leaf axils. Each flower unrolls a single creamy-yellow filament, in a manner typical of the Protea family, until the whole inflorescence resembles a brightly coloured pincushion or sea urchin, both of these being among its popular names.

H. laurina is only one of a hundred or so species in the genus, although it is by far the most spectacular. The entire group were named for Baron von Hake, an eighteenth-century German professor of botany. They can be grown from either seed or ripened cuttings.

HARPEPHYLLUM
(hah' pe fil ləm)

The Kaffir Plum

FAMILY: ANACARDIACEAE

Very much a loner, South Africa's distinctive Kaffir Plum *Harpephyllum caffrum*, is rarely seen naturally in the company of other plants, for its dense canopy of foliage prevents any rain at all from reaching below its branches. Dark and glossy at a distance, it is widely cultivated in temperate climates, as both street and specimen tree.

On close inspection, the compound leaves are handsome and Ash-like, consisting of a number of shiny, pointed leaflets, each 7 cm (2½ in) in length. The fairly insignificant green flowers open in spring, and are followed by neat little clusters of fruit, nestling like a clutch of eggs in the dense foliage at branch tips. These are oval, and about the size of Cumquats. They ripen from green, through scarlet to a rich purple, and can be made into a delicious conserve.

Harpephyllum caffrum
Kaffir Plum

Harpullia arborea
Philippine Tulipwood

Most commonly seen is *Harpullia pendula*, a 15 m (45 ft) inhabitant of Australia's warm east coastal forests. It has striking Ash-like compound leaves of a vivid pale green, each consisting of four to eight pointed leaflets. The small flowers are also yellow-green, and borne in drooping panicles at branch ends. These are followed by the most curious bright orange fruits or pods. Each one consists of a pair of globular capsules joined together like a dumbbell and containing two shiny black seeds. As they mature, the paired pods split open and look for all the world like the disembodied eyes of some sinister doll. Doll's Eyes is in fact one of its popular names, Tulipwood another.

Harpephyllum caffrum
detail of fruit, foliage

HARPULLIA
(hah pool' ee ə)

The Tulipwood

FAMILY: SAPINDACEAE

Several of this small group of trees, native to South-East Asia, Australia and nearby islands, are cultivated in moist, warm-climate areas. They are valued as street or specimen trees, but also for their magnificent timber which is streaked with darkest brown and yellow, very much like the pattern of a variegated tulip.

Harpullia pendula
Doll's Eyes or Tulipwood, fruit

HETEROMELES
(het ur om' el ees)

The Toyon or California Holly

FAMILY: ROSACEAE

Without California's ubiquitous Toyon, there wouldn't be a Hollywood. For the cinema city was so named because of the widely spreading groves of this colourfully fruited tree which reminded early settlers of the cold-climate Hollies.

Alas, the groves have now disappeared beneath a landscape of neon and concrete, and the sturdy trees have emigrated to gardens in many other temperate parts of the world, where their brilliant crops of scarlet berries light up the winter landscape, and the panicles of white flowers are a delight in late summer. Its popularity can be gauged from its flock of common names including California Holly, Christmas Berry and California Maybush.

The Toyons are close relatives of both the rose and the apple; in fact the botanical name *Heteromeles arbutifolia* is a Greek-Latin mixture meaning 'different apple with leaves like the *Arbutus*'.

They grow to 10 m (30 ft), have leathery elliptical leaves and often need a bit of help from the secateurs to look more like a tree, less like a bushy shrub.

They can be propagated from seeds, cuttings or layers and are hardy in cool frost-free areas, even coastal parts of the British Isles.

Birds of all types just love the berries, and come from far around to feast in the colder months.

Heteromeles arbutifolia
Toyon or California Holly

Heteromeles arbutifolia
fruit and foliage, winter

Heteromeles arbutifolia
blossom, summer

HEVEA
(hee' vee ə)

The Para Rubber Tree

FAMILY: EUPHORBIACEAE

Rarely seen in gardens anywhere, the tall, straight-growing *Hevea* is nevertheless one of the most widely planted trees in the world — at least in humid tropical climates. For this forest denizen of the great Amazon basin is the chief source of commercial rubber, the tough elastic substance that soles your shoes, tyres your car and even keeps your clothes from falling down.

A long-living tree that grows readily from seed to a height of 20 m (60 ft) and more in eight years, it has revolutionized the economies of Malaysia, Indonesia, Ceylon and many other places where labour costs are relatively low, for the trees have to be tapped and tended by hand.

There are several species, but the Para Rubber Tree, *H. brasiliensis*, is the widest grown commercially. It bears decorative, long-stemmed,

Hevea brasiliensis
Para Rubber Tree

compound leaves consisting of three pointed leaflets, and up to 30 cm (12 in) long. These are coloured a delicate pale green. The greenish-white flowers are frizzy and without petals, followed by seed capsules with three seeds each.

From these seeds, the tree is propagated quite easily, but only, we would stress, in a fully tropical climate.

HIBISCUS
(hai bis' kəs)

The Cottonwood or Hau

FAMILY: MALVACEAE

In coastal areas of the world's tropic zone, often in swampy brackish saltwater inlets, you'll see tangled masses of the Tree Hibiscus, *H. tiliaceus*, dense as any mangrove patch. But take it into the garden, where the soil is deeper and less saline, and you have a charming warm-climate tree, often with a gnarled, picturesque trunk, and reaching a height of 7 m (20 ft).

The individual leaves are perfectly heart-shaped; smooth green above, hairy beneath and up to 30 cm (12 in) long. During the warm months, flowers appear profusely at the end of every twig and branch, each bud opening spirally to a perfect yellow Hibiscus, usually with a maroon eye. These gradually change to a burnt orange shade, and in the evening become dull red before they drop.

H. tiliaceus is known as *Hau* in Hawaii, *Purau* in Tahiti, *Mahoe* in many other places. Its bending branches were once cut in the Pacific as canoe outriggers, and even today its fibrous bark is used for ropes and baskets. Both the roots and flower buds have medicinal uses.

The Hau is winter-hardy down to –4°C (25°F), but only looks its best in a warm, humid climate.

Hibiscus tiliaceus
Hau or Tree Hibiscus

Hevea brasiliensis
rubber tapping (photo by Colin Olson)

HOWEA
(hou' ee ə)

The Sentry Palm
FAMILY: PALMAE

One of the most universally popular house plants, and certainly the easiest to propagate, the decorative *Howeas* are found naturally only on Lord Howe Island, a speck of land in the South Pacific attached politically to New South Wales. They can be raised only from seed, and the collection and export of this seed is a lucrative cottage industry in their island home.

In the nursery trade, *Howeas* are often known incorrectly as Kentias, but their accepted popular name is Sentry Palm (from their upright habit) and the botanical name *Howea* is a tribute to Lord Howe, a British Admiral in the eighteenth century.

There are actually two recognized species: *H. belmoreana* and *H. forsteriana*. The former grows to about 12 m (35 ft) in nature; the latter is altogether larger, with a heavier trunk. *H. forsteriana* is also faster-growing and the more commonly cultivated species of the two, being a popular garden subject in southern and western USA and Hawaii, as well as Australia and many other places. Both *Howeas* bear stiffly arching fronds about 2.5 m (7 ft) in length, and have bright green trunks, ringed at close intervals with the ridges from fallen fronds.

They are hardy outdoors down to a winter temperature of 10°C (50°F).

HYMENOSPORUM
(hai men oh spor' əm)

The Sweet Shade
FAMILY: PITTOSPORACEAE

Sweet shade indeed! If fragrance is your fancy, and you live in a climate as warm as coastal Australia, plant a graceful *Hymenosporum flavum* and watch it grow up and up to a height of perhaps 15 m, though it can reach 27 m (80 ft) in the wild. The foliage is neat, glossy and evergreen, massed alternately to one side or the other of the tree, and at various heights, giving it a marvellous asymmetrical appearance. And in the spring, masses of creamy Frangipani-type flowers tumble out on long stems in a profusion that almost hides the foliage. Delicately marbled with red and green, these ripen to a rich butterscotch shade and spill delicious perfume everywhere.

When mature, *Hymenosporum* is reasonably frost-resistant and is found in mountainous districts of up to 1000 m (3000 ft) and more. It apparently tastes as good as it smells, for I once made the mistake of planting one too close to a garden wall, where hungry possums regularly made short work of every flower and leaf.

The botanical name is a combination of the two Greek words *hymen* meaning a membrane and *sporum*, a seed. The seeds have a winged membrane.

Howea forsteriana
Sentry Palm

Hymenosporum flavum
Sweet Shade, Native Frangipani

IDESIA
(ai dee' see ə)

The Wonder Tree

FAMILY: FLACOURTIACEAE

One of the world's most handsome berry trees, the striking Chinese *Idesia polycarpa* can be relied on to preserve its bounty right through the cold months into spring, for birds don't seem to be interested in the fruit at all. The only catch is that you really need both a male and a female tree to get much of a display in the first place, which is undoubtedly why they are more often seen in parks than in private gardens.

Idesia is named for Eberhard Ides, an early Dutch traveller in China where the tree was discovered. It is fast-growing to above 13 m (40 ft) in height and deciduous, bearing toothed, heart-shaped leaves that may reach 25 cm (10 in) long, and hang from reddish stems. The tiny greenish flowers hang in panicles, longer on female trees, where they develop into loose clusters of grape-sized berries. These are green at first, ripening through brown to a deep red.

Idesia can be propagated from seeds, cuttings or root-cuttings, and transplants well any time. Its horizontal branches make it a popular choice as a shade tree. *Idesia* is commonly known as the Wonder Tree, but in Japan as ligiri. It is suited to both cool and warm temperate gardens.

Idesia polycarpa
Wonder Tree, ligiri

ILEX
(ai' leks)

The Hollies

FAMILY: AQUIFOLIACEAE

Of all the trees that are in the wood,
The holly bears the crown.

So runs an old Christmas carol. And it is easy to understand why Hollies exerted an almost mystical attraction to the peoples of Europe during the cold months. When forests were bare of leaves, and the ground denuded of flowers and blanketed in snow, there were the shiny pyramids of Holly catching winter sunlight with their masses of brilliantly glossy fruit.

They were sacred to many of the old pagan gods, and even after Christianity came, the Holly still played its part in cheerful Yuletide decorations in honour of our Lord's birthday. What else was there to use, in the bleak winters of the Middle Ages?

Botanically speaking, the Holly is called *Ilex* (an old Roman name) and the European species *I. aquifolium* with pointed leaves is only one of about four hundred recognized species, native to almost every part of the world except Australasia. They are found mostly in colder areas of the northern hemisphere, and by no means all of them have spiny leaves. They are not all evergreen either, but they do bear the same bright berries and tiny snow-white flowers as the European type.

That is, the female trees do. It is necessary to have trees of both sexes or a specially grafted specimen to be sure of the winter berry crop. Unfortunately, several of the most handsomely variegated species are exclusively male, can be propagated only from cuttings and will never bear fruit at all.

Hollies are best planted in very early autumn so they can make root growth before the cold weather, and so they will not suffer loss of moisture through their leaves due to a dry atmosphere. They like a sheltered but sunny position, and in warmer countries mostly prefer hill climates.

I. aquifolium grows into a magnificent pyramidal tree 25 m (80 ft) in height, but not in an average lifetime, for it is a slow grower. The fancy-leafed varieties are perhaps more commonly seen, for they make a better display when not actually in fruit. They can be trimmed or pruned in autumn to almost any shape.

In other lands, other species are more popular, and there is a great range to choose from. The Japanese like *I. pedunculata*, the Mount Fuji Holly, with long smooth-edged leaves and the berries hanging on long stems. The Chinese Holly *I. rotunda* is more popular in China and Hong Kong. It is a large, picturesquely gnarled tree of 20 m (60 ft), with dark, leathery leaves and masses of berries lasting well into spring.

The American *I. opaca* is widely seen in the United States and Canada, where it is hardy in the bleak American winter. It grows about half the height of the European species and has paler, rather twisted leaves. Its wood is used in fancy joinery and cabinet-making. South America's favourite is *I. paraguariensis*, the Paraguay Tea or Yerba Maté. It rarely exceeds 5 m (15 ft) and a popular tea-like beverage is prepared from its dried leaves.

Hollies can be propagated from seed, or in the case of fancy varieties, from grafted buds or cuttings.

Ilex aquifolium
Common Holly, spring blossom

Ilex aquifolium 'Golden King'
Variegated Holly

Ilex paraguariensis
Paraguay Tea, Yerba Maté

Ilex rotunda
China Holly

Ilex pedunculata
Mount Fuji Holly

INGA

(ing' ə)

The Pacayer
FAMILY: LEGUMINOSAE

Ingas or Yngas are a large genus of handsome tropical trees and shrubs within the pea family, Leguminosae. There are over 250 of them, native generally to the Caribbean area and northern South America, from where they have found their way to warm-climate gardens everywhere. Their name is often used (incorrectly) for similar looking shrubby plants now reclassified as *Calliandra*.

One of the most splendid tree species is *I. edulis* (known in French tropical colonies as Pacayer), a grey-barked tree of some 15 m (50 ft) or so. Its brilliantly green compound leaves each consist of six to eight leaflets about 10 cm (4 in) long. The flowers, which appear on spurs or at branch tips, are stemless with a mass of white stamens like a dandelion puffball. These are followed by thick, four-sided pods in which the seeds are embedded in a sweet white pulp.

These fruits are supremely edible and West Indian children call them 'Ice Cream Beans'.

Inga is the Caribbean native name of these great trees, which are splendidly ornamental, and generally propagated from seed.

Inga edulis
Pacayer, Ice Cream Beans

124

INOCARPUS
(in oh kah' pəs)

The Mapé or Polynesian Chestnut
FAMILY: LEGUMINOSAE

Inocarpus edulis
Mape, Polynesian Chestnut

A valuable evergreen tree from Tahiti and neighbouring islands, the *Mapé* or Polynesian Chestnut, *Inocarpus edulis* has close relatives only in Indonesia, reinforcing some theories of early Polynesian migration. It is a tall, handsome tree of humid valleys and moist swampy areas, developing a straight trunk with elaborately fluted buttresses. The leathery leaves are dark green, oblong, borne alternately, and most appetizing to stock. Since the introduction of European domestic animals, whole forests of them have been stripped of foliage to a considerable height.

The winter flowers are small, fragrant and white, appearing from the leaf axils. They are followed in spring by fibrous 5 cm (2 in) pods of a pale orange colour. These each contain one large seed or nut which, when cooked, becomes a delicacy with all the flavour and goodness of the European Chestnut, or as some would say, toasted almonds.

The clear sap turns scarlet on contact with the air, and has been used as a natural colouring for foods and artists' paints. It is also used as an astringent, and a lotion to ease the pain of jelly-fish stings.

The Latin generic name *Inocarpus* means fibrous fruit and the specific name *edulis* means edible.

The Mapé is propagated from half-ripened cuttings, but outside Tahiti and its neighbours I have seen it only in Hawaiian and Philippine gardens.

IPOMOEA
(ip oh mee' ə)

The Morning Glory Tree
FAMILY: CONVOLVULACEAE

Ipomoea arborescens
Morning Glory Tree

The world of trees is full of the most unlikely contradictions. When first I saw the handsome tree illustrated here I could hardly believe my eyes. 'In Kapiolani Park, there's a tree with weeping branches and flowers exactly like a white Morning Glory,' I tried to explain to a Hawaiian botanist friend. 'Well, naturally,' he replied, like a character from Alice in Wonderland. 'It's a Morning Glory Tree.'

And so I had to revise all my beliefs about Morning Glories being only vines or small groundcovers, for here was one right before my eyes which grows to 7 m (20 ft), has a woody trunk and branches, and yet flowers like you would never believe!

It comes from Mexico and Guatemala, where they call it Palo Blanco, and is known botanically as *Ipomoea arborescens*, a name as unlikely as the plant itself.

The Morning Glory Tree has velvety heart-shaped leaves that are deciduous, and dense clusters of open white trumpet flowers centred in red. Like others of the genus, these open at dawn and fade or drop later in the day. It seems to prefer a cool, not too humid atmosphere.

ITEA
(ai' tee ə)

The Sweetspires
FAMILY: SAXIFRAGACEAE

A small genus of slim, decorative trees for moist, temperate climates, the *Iteas* include evergreen species from Asia, and one deciduous type from North America. The species commonly cultivated is the Hollyleaf Sweetspire, *I. ilicifolia*, from western China, which is most at home in the deep, rich soil of humid coastal gardens, or a sheltered position in the hills well protected from frost.

As both its popular and botanical names suggest, the foliage resembles that of the European Holly (see *Ilex*), although individual leaves are both longer and narrower. The delicate greenish-white summer flowers are lightly fragrant, and crowded in hanging racemes up to 40 cm (15 in) in length. These racemes appear both from the leaf-axils and as terminal clusters.

I. ilicifolia rarely passes 5 m (16 ft) in height except in the most sheltered conditions, and is easily propagated from cuttings of ripe wood taken in summer.

The botanical name *Itea* is the old Greek word for the willows, with which it shares a certain delicacy of habit.

Itea ilicifolia
Sweetspire

JACARANDA
(jak ə ran' də)

The Brazilian Rosewood

FAMILY: BIGNONIACEAE

Because it is the most noticeable feature of the landscape each November, many Australians imagine the handsome *Jacaranda* to be native to their own country. But in reality it is as Brazilian as the samba, and should be pronounced more softly as *hakharanda*, as they say it in Rio.

It is found naturally in the high and dry deserts of Brazil, and many temperate gardeners have noticed that its late spring display is measurably better in a dry year, or in a neglected part of the garden. Give it too much water and the lacy, bipinnate leaves (like pale-green ostrich plumes) appear first, somewhat spoiling the startling effect of mauve trumpet flowers seen on bare grey branches.

After the flowers, conspicuous flat woody seed pods develop, and split open the following spring. *Jacarandas* seed readily, grow fast and transplant easily. One in my own garden, a scant ten years from seed, is 8 m (24 ft) high and about the same in spread.

Jacarandas are deciduous, though they do not drop their leaves until late winter, often turning a rich yellow first in cooler areas. There are white, pink and red flowered species, but by general consensus of opinion, these are not half so lovely as the beautiful mauve-blue *J. mimosaefolia*. It is a colour which really tricks the eye, and is hard to capture on the cold, analytical record of colour film.

Jacaranda is sometimes known as Fern Tree and Blue Haze Tree.

Jacaranda mimosaefolia
detail of spring flowers

JATROPHA
(jat' roh fə)

The Rose Bay

FAMILY: EUPHORBIACEAE

Mostly represented in warm temperate gardens by curiously shaped small shrubs with gouty trunks and unbelievably complex leaves, the genus *Jatropha* also includes several highly decorative small trees.

First among these, and now almost universal in its distribution, is the charming Rose Bay or Peregrina, *J. hastata*, from Cuba. Slight in habit, rarely passing 5 m (15 ft) in height, the Rose Bay

Jacaranda mimosaefolia
Brazilian Rosewood

Jatropha hastata
Rose Bay, Peregrina

has lightly weeping branches clothed in handsome velvety leaves shaped like a spear blade. The vivid cerise flowers are borne in profuse racemes at the end of branchlets.

Jatrophas are members of the botanical family Euphorbiaceae, with unpleasant milky sap. They are all mildly poisonous, but greatly valued in tropical medicine for a variety of pharmaceutical properties. In fact the very name *Jatropha* is from the Greek *iatros* meaning physician and *trophe* meaning food.

JUBAEA
(joo bae' ə)

The Wine Palm

FAMILY: PALMAE

One of the most handsome of palms, the thick-trunked, stately *Jubaea* or Wine Palm is widely planted in mild temperate gardens throughout the world, for it is far less exacting than most in its temperature requirements.

Native to coastal Chile, it is in fact closely related to the tropical Coconut Palm (see *Cocos*), which it resembles in a sort of sawn-off way. Though it bears panicles of small yellow flowers and fruit like small Coconuts, the tree's main commercial value is in its sap. This is extracted from felled trees and boiled to reduce it to a sticky substance sold as Palm Honey.

J. spectabilis, one of only two species in the genus, is named for Juba, an ancient King of Numidia.

JUGLANS
(joo' glans)

The Walnuts

FAMILY: JUGLANDACEAE

The Romans thought so highly of these splendid trees and their delicious nuts that they named them in honour of the King of all the Gods, Jupiter's Acorn, or in Latin, *jovis glans*, which has come down to us as *Juglans*, the present botanic name.

The tree they knew in Rome was *J. regia*, the Common Walnut, a native of Persia, and it is believed this had been brought to Europe with the returning armies of Alexander the Great. It is still the best species, both for nuts and for the beautifully grained and patterned timber.

The Persian Walnut grows slowly to as high as 35 m (120 ft), but not in a single lifetime. It is deciduous, bearing spicily fragrant compound leaves with up to thirteen leaflets, and flowers in small greenish catkins. The oval, pointed nut ripens in a greenish husk, which ultimately sloughs away.

The American Walnut, *J. nigra*, is native to the eastern United States, and a much larger tree, reaching 50 m (160 ft) at maturity, and very nearly as much across. Everything about it is larger: the leaves are longer and the fruit heavier and rounder (though not, gourmets insist, as tasty). It is most highly valued as a timber tree because of its fast growth.

A Californian species *J. hindsii* is much grown in the western States as a garden specimen or street tree.

Jubaea chilensis
Wine Palm, Coquito

Juglans regia
detail of nuts and foliage

Juglans hindsii
California Walnut, foliage

Other species are found in Japan, China, the Caribbean and South America.

J. regia, like others of the genus, is most readily propagated from the fresh nuts themselves, provided you get to them before the squirrels do. I had one in a Melbourne garden, many years ago, and had a fine crop of young plants every year, thanks to a forgetful squirrel which so busied itself all summer burying the nuts, that it was unable to locate them when it returned from winter quarters.

Juglans regia
Common or Persian Walnut

JUNIPERUS
(joo nip' er əs)

The Junipers
FAMILY: CUPRESSACEAE

Scattered about all continents of the northern hemisphere, particularly in areas with generally alkaline soil, are the slow-growing Junipers, one of the most widespread of coniferous genera.

There are more than fifty species, some of them with enough cultivated varieties to fill a large garden on their own. Seeing a collection of them all together, it comes as a surprise to note that they seem to have developed every possible shade of foliage short of a true, rich green.

Junipers are immensely popular for landscaping effect, and rightly so, for they thrive best in places where other lime-hating conifers cannot cope at all.

They are generally smaller trees than the related Cypresses and False Cypresses, except in their original species, which are rarely raised in gardens anyway. These include the Chinese Juniper, *Juniperus chinensis*, which may touch 20 m (60 ft); the Common Juniper, *J. communis*,

Juniperus scopulorum CV 'Cologreen'
Colorado Red Cedar

Juniperus chinensis Torulosa
Hollywood or Twisted Chinese Juniper

Juniperus communis 'Hibernica'
Irish Juniper, berries

found all over the northern hemisphere, rarely reaches 10 m (30 ft); the Colorado Red Cedar, *J. scopulorum*, again only 10 m; and the largest of all, *J. virginiana*, the Red Cedar, which has been recorded at 25 m (80 ft) and is raised commercially for pencil casings.

Adult Junipers have tiny scale-like leaves, like the True Cypress, and bear plump berry-like cones which may last on the tree for years. These are used all over the world to flavour gin.

Juniperus is the original Roman name for the genus. The species all grow readily from seed cones, which remain viable for years; the fancy-leafed varieties are propagated from cuttings.

Juniperus sabina Bermudiana
Bermuda Cedar

Juniperus chinensis 'Coasti Aurea'
Golden Chinese Juniper

KETELEERIA
(ket ə leer' ee ə)

The Keteleeria
FAMILY: PINACEAE

For mild climates where the noble Firs (or *Abies*) won't grow, there is a closely related, handsome genus of conifers from sub-tropical South-East Asia and Taiwan, the *Keteleerias*. A tall-growing genus, to 30 m (100 ft) in height, the two species are raised from seed and need protection from cold until well established.

Young trees are pyramidal in shape, though like Pines and Cedars they tend to adopt a more spreading profile as maturity sets in. The leaves are flat, rather than needle-shaped, and twice as long on the species *K. davidiana* as they are on *K. fortunei*. They are arranged spirally around the twigs in both species. The small male flowers appear in clusters at the leaf-axils, the larger female flowers on higher branches only. These develop into elegant cones about 20 cm (8 in) in length, slightly smaller on *K. fortunei*. The cones have an interesting bluish sheen when young, sometimes even with a touch of purple. They always point upwards (as in *Abies*), but do not break up when the seeds ripen.

The trees were named for a Belgian gardener of the early nineteenth century, J.B. Keteleer.

Keteleeria davidiana
Keteleeria, cones and foliage

KIGELIA
(kai jeel' ee ə)

The Sausage Tree
FAMILY: BIGNONIACEAE

Kigelia pinnata
Sausage Tree

Grown more as a novelty than anything else, and only in gardens with a sub-tropical climate, the curious *Kigelia* has no practical use in commerce that I have been able to discover, beyond the fact that its extraordinary fruits are used as some sort of poultice in its native Africa.

K. pinnata, the only one of ten species in cultivation, is a heavy-trunked tree of about 16 m (50 ft). It bears pinnate leaves in groups of three, each leaf consisting of between seven and eleven hand-sized leaflets, with the odd leaflet at the end. From the uppermost branches, long hanging stems descend to produce chains of large, night-blooming flowers of velvety red-brown. These have an unpleasant smell and are fertilized by some night-flying insect, after which they drop messily to the ground.

What follows is one of the wonders of the botanical world — long, grey, gourd-like fruits up to 1 m (3 ft) in length and as thick as your arm. These hang on their cord-like stems, up to 7 m (20 ft) long in some cases, swaying in the breeze, containing nothing but hard pulp and a few small seeds. But you can be sure somebody must love them.

Kigelia is known popularly as the Sausage Tree for fairly obvious reasons, but I have been unable to discover why it was called *Kigelia* in the first place.

They are grown from seed or from cuttings of half-ripened wood, and you'll find them in all the warm-climate botanical gardens.

Kigelia pinnata
detail of flowers and fruit

KLEINHOVIA
(klain hoh' vee ə)

The Guest Tree

FAMILY: BYTTNERIACEAE

The tall-growing *Kleinhovia* is a true butterfly of the arboreal world, for its sole function in life seems merely to be admired. Nobody has yet found any practical use for any part of it, except perhaps to keep a fire going, and it is far too beautiful to be felled for that.

Named for Dr C. Kleynhof, an eighteenth-century director of the famous Bogor Gardens in Indonesia, the Guest Tree, as it is called for

some unknown reason, is native to the whole northern area of the Indian Ocean — Africa, India and Indonesia — and is the only one of its genus, but is related to the Australian Kurrajongs and the African Dombeyas. It has a rather short, crooked trunk, but skyward-pointing branches which may reach a height of 20 m (60 ft). These spread into a wide crown, decked with long-stalked, rather heart-shaped leaves ranging in length from 15 to 30 cm (6 to 12 in). These are softly coloured in a restful grey-green. In perfect harmony the tree produces loose masses of showy pink blossom at its branch tips throughout the summer and autumn.

Kleinhovia is grown from cuttings of young shoots struck in sand. It is an ornamental for sub-tropical or coastal gardens only.

Kleinhovia hospita
Guest Tree

KOELREUTERIA
(kurl roi teer' ee ə)

Golden Rain Tree, Pride of China

FAMILY: SAPINDACEAE

Useful specimen trees for all types of soil and all sorts of climates short of the purely tropical, the decorative Golden Rain Trees are natives of China and Korea, with one species apparently native to Fiji as well. One can only assume it was carried there by early migrants.

131

They are propagated from seeds or root cuttings, and grow rapidly to a height of 15 m (50 ft), though only half that in cooler areas. Full sun and shelter from prevailing wind are their main requirements, and they are no good at all near the coast, being badly damaged by salt breezes.

The botanical name is *Koelreuteria*, after a German professor of natural history, and young trees often adopt a picturesque shape which has led to another popular name, Willow Pattern Plate Tree.

Koelreuteria paniculata
Golden Rain Tree. blossom

Koelreuteria paniculata
seed pods, autumn

The branches are decked with 45 cm (18 in) compound leaves, pinnate with toothed leaflets in the species *K. paniculata*, fully bipinnate in the species *K. bipinnata* and *K. elegans*.

In summer all three species bear branched, terminal panicles of tiny yellow flowers that scatter as they fall. These are superseded by papery, bladder-like seed pods that persist for months and may be pink, brown or even blood red, according to variety.

K. paniculata is quite frost-resistant, and I have seen it blooming in Europe, the United States and even sub-tropical Queensland. In cooler areas it gives a creditable show of golden autumn colour.

LABURNUM
(lə bur' nəm)

The Golden Chain Tree
FAMILY: LEGUMINOSAE

The spring glory of cool-climate gardens where it contrasts to perfection with pink and white blossom of peach and apple, the graceful *Laburnum* or Golden Chain Tree is a native of central Europe and parts of Asia Minor.

Laburnum is its old Roman name, and there's a certain amount of confusion about the precise nomenclature of popularly grown species. Most of them seem to be hybrids between the Scotch Laburnum, *L. alpinum* from southern Europe, which bears 40 cm (16 in) Wistaria-like racemes of golden pea flowers in early summer, and the earlier flowering *L. anagyroides* from further north.

Laburnum X Vossii
Golden Chain

Laburnums are small deciduous trees of slim, graceful habit and compound leaves, each consisting of three leaflets covered with silky hair on the reverse side. The chains of golden pea flowers (very variable in their brightness) are followed by simple brown pea-type pods.

All species and varieties grow well in almost any position and in any type of soil, provided the winters are cold and the atmosphere moist. They self-sow from seed, but named varieties are normally budded, just like roses.

All parts of the tree are poisonous, and this must be taken into account in country gardens, positioning them out of reach of stock.

LAGERSTROEMIA
(lah gur stroh' mee ə)

The Crepe Myrtles

FAMILY: LYTHRACEAE

Native to South-East Asia and some islands of the western Pacific, the showy Crepe Myrtles, *Lagerstroemia*, include some fifty species of the most ornamental flowering trees in the world. Yet in temperate gardens they are so often represented only by hard-pruned, shrub-size specimens of *L. indica*, which seems a great pity.

The key to Crepe Myrtle culture is that they flower only on the new season's wood, so it's in your hands whether you lop them back hard and get a compact flower display or let them have their heads and end up with a gracefully branched tree with sumptuously mottled bark and a floral canopy out of reach of flower arrangers. I prefer the latter.

Lagerstroemia speciosa
Queen Crepe Myrtle

Three species only are commonly grown, with a number of colour varieties among them. They are:

L. indica, the Chinese Crepe Myrtle, a deciduous slim tree to 7 m (20 ft), with four-sided small branches and smooth oval leaves not more than 5 cm (2 in) long. These put up a good autumn colour display in cool districts. The flower panicles develop at branch tips only, each flower about the size of a peach blossom. On every flower there are six round, wrinkled petals on narrow bases, a mass of gold stamens and a glossy green calyx. There are named flower varieties in red, purple, pink, mauve and white.

L. speciosa, the Queen Crepe Myrtle or Pride of India, is found naturally in a wide belt from India, through southern China and Papua New Guinea to Australia. It is a strong-growing tree to 25 m (80 ft) with leathery leaves up to 30 cm (12 in) long. The flowers are borne on long-stemmed panicles, each about the size of a Camellia; generally a pleasing rosy mauve, but sometimes white. The calyx is greyish-pink and downy, and the flowers are followed by round, woody seed capsules that sometimes persist for months. It is a valuable source of durable red timber, sometimes used as railway sleepers in the tropics. It must have a minimum winter temperature of −4°C (25°F).

L. subcostata, the White Crepe Myrtle, grows to around 20 m (60 ft), has the same small leaves as *L. indica*, and spidery white and yellow flowers of no particular value. Its star quality is in the magnificent trunk and branches with smooth, decorative bark in many shades of grey and beige.

The *Lagerstroemias* are named for Magnus Lagerstroem, a friend of the great botanist Lin-

Lagerstroemia speciosa
Queen Crepe Myrtle

133

naeus. All species can be grown from seed, but more reliably from cuttings. A pruning in winter and another after flowering will give you two flower displays a year.

LAGUNARIA
(lah goo neə' ree ə)

The Norfolk Island Hibiscus

FAMILY: MALVACEAE

First discovered on the lonely Pacific penal colony of Norfolk Island in 1792, *Lagunaria patersonii* has a seaside ancestry stretching back thousands of years, and has proven to be one of the few trees that can really cope with the salt-laden air of coastal gardens.

Propagated easily from seed, it grows quickly in a warm climate to a handsome pyramidal shape, with a maximum height of 16 m (50 ft) on old trees. The leaves are simple 10 cm (4 in) ovals of a greyish shade, almost white on their reverses. Throughout the warm weather, the trees are decked with pretty rose-pink flowers exactly like small Hibiscuses, to which the tree is closely related. These are followed by a rough, inedible fruit about the size of a pingpong ball, and lined with barbed hairs which can be irritating to both man and beast. Early colonists called it the Cow Itch Tree, and it is also known both as Pyramid Tree and Whitewood.

Lagunaria was subsequently rediscovered on equally remote Lord Howe Island, and in a slightly variant form on parts of the Queensland coast.

Lagerstroemia indica
Chinese Crepe Myrtle

Lagerstroemia subcostata
White Crepe Myrtle

Lagunaria patersonii
Norfolk Island Hibiscus

In spite of its predilection for growing in sandy soil, it is not drought-resistant; and the flowers vary widely from a deep rose to almost white, sometimes with a tendency to mauve.

Lagunaria is named for Andres Laguna, a Spanish botanist of the sixteenth century.

Lagunaria patersonii
detail of flower

LARIX
(la' riks)

The Larches

FAMILY: PINACEAE

Popular conifers for re-afforestation in cold winter parts of the world, the Larches are no gloomy evergreens, like their cousins the Pines and Firs and Spruces, but charming lacy trees that celebrate every season with a brand new outfit.

In spring, the long weeping branchlets are decked with a lime-green fuzz of new needles; in summer they show the cool, restful green of other conifers, but are dotted here and there with tiny red female flowers; in autumn they turn a glowing gold and brown; and finally in winter, when other deciduous trees are stark, their spidery web of twigs and branchlets are decked with small brown cones, like tiny wooden roses.

But the Larch is a cold-climate tree, found naturally in mountainous areas of Europe, North America and Asia where the drainage is particularly good. It grows fast, but cannot abide wet feet or scorching summer heat.

There are ten species in the botanical genus *Larix*, which was what the Romans first called them. All are fairly similar, except in size. For instance, the European Larch (*L. decidua*) has been measured to 50 m (160 ft) in forests of Central Europe, whereas the Japanese Larch (*L. leptolepis*) never exceeds 30 m (100 ft), and the American Larch or Tamarack (*L. laricina*) is even smaller at about 20 m (60 ft). *L. decidua* has oval cones, about 4 cm (1½ in) long. Those of the Japanese tree are round and slightly smaller, and their scales roll back like the petals on an opening rosebud. The American's cones are much smaller still.

On all species the needles, approximately 3 cm (1¼ in) long, are arranged in rosettes on the small spurs of every branchlet.

Larch species hybridize indiscriminately when they are planted near one another and all of them can be propagated from seed. Their tall, straight trunks are milled into a tough timber, greatly valued in ship building. From the wood of the European Larch, valuable Venetian turpentine is distilled.

Larix decidua
European Larch

LATANIA
(la tan' ee ə)

The Latan Palm

FAMILY: PALMAE

A small genus of three palm species from Mauritius and the Mascarene Islands, *Latanias* are much planted in humid tropical areas everywhere for their handsome, fan-shaped fronds.

Propagated from seed only, they reach 17 m (50 ft) in nature, but probably only half that in cultivation. The trunk is grey and ridged, topped with a cluster of 2 m (5 ft) fan-shaped leaves on stems of the same length.

These are greyish-blue in the Blue Latan Palm, *L. loddigesii*; reddish with red stems on young leaves of the Red Latan, *L. lontaroides*; and golden green when young on the Yellow Latan, *L. verschaffeltii*.

The name *Latania* was adapted from the native name of these graceful trees, which bear male and female flowers on separate plants, the male flowers in cylindrical spikes up to 2 m (5 ft) in length.

Laurus nobilis
Sweet Bay, Laurel

Laurus nobilis
spring flowers and foliage

Latania loddigesii
Blue Latan Palm

LAURUS
(lou' rəs)

The Sweet Bay Tree

FAMILY: LAURACEAE

What do the bay leaves in your kitchen have in common with the Laurel wreaths that crowned triumphant Roman heroes? The answer of course is everything, for they are identical, both being the leathery, fragrant foliage of the Sweet Bay Tree, *Laurus nobilis*, that grows throughout southern Europe.

So often do we see the Bay clipped and shaped to within an inch of its life that we sometimes forget it is in nature a handsome tree of up to 17 m (50 ft) and more, crowned with its own dense wreaths of deep, glossy-green leaves. In spring the entire tree is decked with sprays of tiny greenish-yellow, four-petalled flowers, followed by shiny black berries.

Laurus is easily propagated from half-ripened cuttings, and deserves a place in any garden where it can enjoy both full sun and well-drained soil.

It is often regarded as the Aspidistra of the tree world, seemingly able to survive astonishing neglect, and making itself right at home in almost any climate short of the purely tropical with wet summers. It will even survive several degrees of frost.

Laurus was its original Roman name.

LEPTOSPERMUM
(lep toh spurm' əm)

The Tea Trees

FAMILY: MYRTACEAE

Since Captain James Cook brewed a beverage from tiny leaves of a New Zealand *Leptospermum*, the whole genus has been blessed with the name of Tea Tree, though nobody these days seems eager to repeat the experiment.

The New Zealand species *L. scoparium* is the parent of the hybrid, shrubby types seen in so many gardens, with their flower colours varying from white right through the range of pinks to deep red; single or double.

But the really useful and decorative tree species is Australian, *L. laevigatum*, the Coastal Tea Tree, found in sandy coastal areas of Tasmania, Victoria, New South Wales and well up into Queensland. It is salt and wind-resistant and of tremendous value both as a windbreak in coastal gardens and for stabilizing the movement of drifting sands.

The Coastal Tea Tree grows to 10 m (30 ft) and more in a sheltered position, but is more often seen in a variety of contorted shapes, sometimes quite horizontal from its exposure to gales. The bark is stringy, grey and picturesque, the foliage fine and often quite dense. Its oblong, pointed leaves are only about 2.5 cm (1 in) long. The flowers are stalkless, and borne singly in the leaf-axils, making quite a display at many times of the year. Each consists of five rounded white petals surrounding a pale-green ovary which develops into a brown woody seed capsule after fertilization. These capsules often persist on the tree for years.

The botanical name *Leptospermum* is from the Greek *leptos* meaning slender, and *sperma* meaning seed, in reference to the fine seeds contained in each capsule. The Tea Trees grow readily from seed or more commonly from cuttings of half-ripened wood.

Leptospermum laevigatum
detail of flowers and foliage

Leptospermum laevigatum
Coastal Tea Tree

137

LIGUSTRUM
(li gus' trəm)

The Privets
FAMILY: OLEACEAE

Ligustrum lucidum
Chinese Privet

I do not greatly care for Privets myself, having once spent a year or so hauling them out of a neglected garden to which I had moved. The trunks were like cast iron, the roots like a strangling boa constrictor with a grip on everything in sight. And for years afterwards my every gardening effort was thwarted by a crop of tiny new trees from long discarded berries.

I sometimes wonder why so many garden books waste space on how to propagate them —in my experience propagation is the least of its problems. How do you tell them to stop?

Yet in spite of all this I must admit that the Chinese Privet, *Ligustrum lucidum* is a handsome tree. Smooth trunked and evergreen, with glossy, pointed leaves up to 15 cm (6 in) long, it is especially beautiful in early summer when the entire tree is frosted with panicles of tiny creamy four-petalled flowers like white lilac. It is when these fall and the berries ripen that the trouble starts; although again, these tiny fruits are a wonderful glossy purple-black.

If you do want to grow this tree the ideal is a fairly neglected part of the garden away from cultivated areas. Just watch those berries, sweep them up before they take hold. Check with your local agricultural authorities too —some areas of Australia and possibly other countries have declared this ubiquitous Chinese invader a noxious pest. Its rampant reproductive habits tend to upset the local ecology.

Ligustrum is its ancient Latin name. There are several smaller-growing, coloured-leaf varieties which are easier to manage.

LIQUIDAMBAR
(lik wid am' bah)

The Sweetgum
FAMILY: HAMAMELIDACEAE

Liquidambar formosana
Chinese Sweetgum

Ligustrum lucidum
detail of fruit

138

Liquidambar styraciflua
Sweetgum

The mellifluous name *Liquidambar styraciflua* has been given to one of the great specimen trees of the world, the North American Sweetgum. Native to a large belt from Texas to lower New York State, and right through the Smoky Mountains, it is strangely disappointing in its native haunts, looking somewhat gaunt and crushed as it struggles for survival among more pushy, widely spreading trees. But get it out on its own in a lawn with access to a good supply of water and up it shoots, straight as a die for 25 even 40 metres (75 to 120 ft), an elongated pyramid up to 15 m (45 ft) in diameter at ground level. The grey bark is deeply furrowed, hanging in cork-like flaps from almost every branch. The greenish flowers appear in small clusters at the end of twigs, developing as they are fertilized into globular burr-like fruit on long stems.

But the foliage is *Liquidambar's* special glory. The leaves are rather star-shaped with five or seven serrated lobes. They are a bright green, turning an incredible range of colours in autumn. One tree may become palest gold and pink, another purple, so dark it is almost black; still others scarlet, gold and orange. Good varieties are propagated true to colour only from root-cuttings of an individual tree.

Liquidambars are greedy feeders. Nothing will grow around them and they'll even send marauding roots up into nearby pots in search of water. Their timber is used in many types of furniture and for decorative inlays and veneers.

Far away in southern China and Taiwan, its only close relative, the Chinese Sweetgum, *L. formosana*, is of similar appearance in all respects but two — the leaves are three-lobed only, and the bark does not hang in decorative folds. It is altogether an inferior tree, though very useful in its native land.

Liquidambars are quite frost-resistant when mature, but equally suited to warm coastal climates so long as they are not in range of flying salt spray.

The name *Liquidambar* is not an allusion to the tree's autumn colour, but to a resin prepared from the Chinese species.

Liquidambar styraciflua
spring flowers and foliage

LIRIODENDRON
(li ree oh den' drən)

The Tulip Tree
FAMILY: MAGNOLIACEAE

Closely related to the Magnolias, the Tulip Tree, *Liriodendron*, is native to the entire eastern seaboard of the United States except for the northern New England states and southern Florida. A fast grower, but slow to flower, it may reach a respectable 7 m (22 ft) in as many years, and ultimately the arrow-straight trunk may top 25 m (80 ft). In its cool native forests it has been measured to twice that height!

The deciduous leaves are unique. Long-stemmed and four-lobed, with the appearance of having been lopped off at the apex, they unfurl quite late in spring, well after the Maples, and turn to a blaze of molten gold in autumn.

Liriodendron tulipifera
Tulip Tree

Liriodendron tulipifera 'Aureo-Marginatum'
Variegated Tulip Tree

The name Tulip Tree is in reference to the handsome flowers, which are indeed like Tulips. They are coloured a rich lime-green with orange centres, and appear well after the foliage, often at too great a height to pick. After the petals drop, a cone-shaped seed cluster is revealed, which persists until the branches are bare in winter; then the casing falls apart and the seeds float away on a single wing.

There are exquisite varieties with the leaves beautifully margined in yellow, although the lighter areas tend to darken in late summer.

Its botanical name is *Liriodendron tulipifera* meaning the tulip-bearing lily tree. The timber is a useful, close-grained hardwood, if you could bear to cut it down.

LITCHI
(lai' chee)

The Lychee

FAMILY: SAPINDACEAE

Surely 800 million Chinese can't be wrong when they select the Lychee as their favourite fruit? My personal idea of heaven includes a basket of these delectable morsels, fresh from the tree and lightly chilled on a summer's day. I peel away their thin lobster-like shells one by one and slip the cool, refreshing pulp into my mouth.

Liriodendron tulipifera
detail of flowers and foliage

Litchi sinensis
Lychee, fruit

Litchi sinensis
Lychee

LIVISTONA
(liv is toh' nə)

The Cabbage Palms

FAMILY: PALMAE

A relatively large Palm genus found from southern China through Malaysia to Australia and Papua New Guinea, the *Livistonas* were named after a botanist's home town of Livingstone, Scotland. No more than half a dozen of the twenty-odd species are in cultivation. The most important of these are:

L. australis, the Cabbage-tree Palm, the only Palm found naturally in Victoria (as well as other parts of eastern Australia). It has been measured at up to 26 m (80 ft) in the wild, but is usually much smaller in cultivation. The great pleated fronds are basically round in shape, about 1.3 m (4 ft) in diameter and spiny stemmed. Each leaf splits radially into as many as seventy segments, each with a drooping tip. The flowers are not spectacular, but are followed by purple-black fruits. Aboriginal people used the cabbage-like heart of young leaves as food; and in colonial times the leaves were woven into summer hats. The hard trunk-wood is still used for building.

L. chinensis, the Fountain Palm or Chinese Fan Palm, grows to 10 m (30 ft) and more in its native Malaysia and southern China, but is usually seen in gardens as a stunted dwarf with enormous kidney-shaped bluish fronds.

L. mariae, the Red Inland Palm, is a rare species from central Australia that has blood-red stalks on young foliage, which also has a reddish cast.

The tree they come from is native to southern China, India and the Philippines and is known botanically as *Litchi sinensis*, from its old Chinese name. It is a graceful tree, generally slim-trunked and growing as tall as 15 m (50 ft) in a cool, deep soil with plenty of moisture. Though tropical in origin, it is able to stand a few degrees of frost when well established, and may start to bear as early as five years from seed. But the seed must be sown within a few days of picking, or it is no longer viable. Trees are raised commercially by air-layering or inarched grafting of superior varieties.

The spreading crown consists of evergreen compound leaves, each made up of two to four pairs of drooping, pointed leaflets. These are palest green, gold, or even pink when young. The tiny yellowish flowers are borne in terminal panicles, and have no petals. The 4 cm (1½ in) oval fruit appear in dangling clusters, green at first, then deep red and finally brown at maturity. Each has a thin, warty shell surrounding a mass of delicately fragrant pulp rather the texture of a grape. This contains one large seed.

Lychees can be eaten fresh or dried, when they look and taste something like an oversized raisin. Huge quantities of them are canned and exported from South-East Asia every summer.

Livistona australis
Cabbage-tree Palm

141

MACADAMIA
(ma kad' ə mee ə)

The Queensland Nut

FAMILY: PROTEACEAE

Carrying coals to Newcastle is nothing compared to the way Australian tourists pour back from Hawaii clutching all sorts of containers of the delicious 'Hawaiian Nuts' they've been sold. The nuts grow on a tree called *Macadamia* and it comes from Queensland, Australia, whence it was first taken to Hawaii in 1890.

Macadamia tetraphylla
detail of flowers and foliage

Macadamia integrifolia
Queensland Nut, ripe nuts

Three species of *Macadamia* are grown, all of them handsome, evergreen trees for the sub-tropical and temperate garden.

Macadamias are propagated from grafted cuttings and grow fast. I have one that fruited in

its fifth year, and now, at eight years is about 7 m (20 ft) tall. The nuts ripen in late summer in a temperate climate, but the trees flower and fruit continuously in the tropics.

They are named for John Macadam, an Australian doctor.

MACLURA
(mak loo' rə)

The Osage Orange

FAMILY: MORACEAE

Whoever originated the popular name of this extraordinary North American tree must have been somewhat mixed-up. *Orange* indeed! The fruits don't resemble citrus in size, shape or colour, and certainly not in flavour. But believe it or not *Maclura* is actually most closely related to the mulberries (see *Morus*) and the tropical breadfruit (see *Artocarpus*).

Native to the southern central United States, *Maclura pomifera* has become naturalized all over that nation, and is occasionally found in old country gardens of Australia, a handsome deciduous tree that can grow as tall as 20 m (65 ft), but usually settles for much less. It will grow in particularly impoverished soil, and in drier parts of Europe it is sometimes seen pruned as a spiny, tallish hedge-plant.

The green flowers are not impressive; the large, irregularly-shaped fruits are of curiosity value only. They are quite inedible, secrete a great deal of poisonous milky juice and are about the size of a grapefruit.

The botanical name *Maclura* commemorates an American geologist.

Maclura pomifera
Osage Orange

MAGNOLIA
(mag nol' ee ə)

The Yulan and Bull Bay

FAMILY: MAGNOLIACEAE

Through a tremendous range of climates from cold temperate to sub-tropical, the ultimate flowering tree is a *Magnolia* of one sort or another. This is thanks to the fact that the genus has two homelands — the cold far west of China in the vicinity of the Himalayas, and the southern USA and Central America surrounding the warm gulf of Mexico. Two more disparate climates could not be imagined, particularly in winter.

Generally speaking, the Chinese species are deciduous and spring flowering, those from America are evergreen and bloom in summer.

The most commonly seen species in temperate climates is undoubtedly the giant American Bull Bay or Southern Magnolia, *M. grandiflora*, which may reach 25 m (80 ft) where the winters are warm enough. It is evergreen, with very large simple leaves that look as if they have been lacquered on top and sprayed with brown flock beneath. The dinner-plate sized flowers, with six to twelve petals, open continuously in the warm weather, spreading a rich citrusy perfume all around.

The deciduous Chinese species grow particularly well in acid, woodsy soil of hill areas, where one of the most commonly seen is *M. denudata*, the Yulan, a gorgeous, rounded tree that grows to 13 m (40 ft) and produces white goblet-shaped flowers on its bare branches almost at the end of winter. These are the diameter of a saucer, and superbly perfumed.

Magnolia denudata
Yulan, detail of flowers

Magnolia grandiflora
detail of flower

Where you see the Yulan, you're also likely to find its hybrid *M. X soulangeana*, the result of a cross with *M. liliflora*, a dark purple-pink flowering species that blooms later, well after its foliage has developed. *M. X soulangeana* is available in a wide range of shades from almost white to almost purple. These must of course be propagated from cuttings, but are slow-growing and often seen at leggy shrub size. Given the right climate though, they can easily match the height and spread of their Yulan parent. CV *'Rustica Rubra'* is a particularly vivid variety.

The giant of the family is the Chinese Tulip Tree, *M. campbellii*, reaching an unbelievable 50 m (160 ft) in its home mountains, but so slow-growing that we still have no idea of its ultimate size in cultivation. It is not likely to flower in much under twenty years, so is a real heirloom plant, but what an heirloom! Great velvety 25 cm (10 in) leaves, and spreading flowers of pale pink and deep rose, marvellously perfumed. Even in the autumn it is decorative with coloured leaves and spikes of scarlet seeds. It does not like frost.

Magnolias are so named for Pierre Magnol, a director of French Botanic Gardens in the eighteenth century.

Magnolia grandiflora
Bull Bay, Southern Magnolia

Magnolia liliflora
Lily Magnolia

Magnolia grandiflora
foliage and flower buds

Magnolia campbellii X *lennei*
Chinese Tulip Tree

MALUS
(mal' us)

The Apples and Crabs

FAMILY: ROSACEAE

If the cost of medical insurance continues to rise it may pay us to remember the old saying 'an apple a day keeps the doctor away' and plant an apple tree in our own gardens. That is, if we are prepared to take the trouble to combat such hazards as fruit fly and the codling moth.

Alternatively we could plant one of the many lovely varieties of flowering Crabapples or crabs, and feed our souls on the beautiful spring blossom and enjoy the tangy crabs later.

From the vast number of Apples and Crabapples listed it is hard to believe that they are all varieties of only twenty-five species. The rest are all cultivars including over a thousand named varieties of the eating apple, *Malus domestica*, alone. Apples are all native to the temperate zone of the northern hemisphere, though they are now grown in cooler climates everywhere. They are deciduous members of the rose family, a fact which isn't surprising if you look closely at their flowers and leaves. Apple fruits are only a larger, juicier version of rose hips.

The original European Crab, *M. sylvestris*, has white flowers and is rather thorny. A reason perhaps it is not seen much in cultivation, though it is a handsome 13 m (40 ft) tree in Europe and Asia Minor. The introduction of the Japanese Crab, *M. floribunda*, in 1862 quickly put an end to the European species' popularity. The Japanese Crab is a graceful, heavily flowering tree that scarcely reaches 8 m (25 ft), an ideal size for the average garden. Its buds are a deep carmine, opening to rosy flowers which finally turn almost pure white. Usually all three colours are displayed at once.

The Prairie Crab, *M. ioensis* is an American species, 10 m (30 ft) in the wild, but often quite dwarfed in cultivation. It has rather hairy, often lobed leaves, and gorgeous semi-double pink and white flowers, rather like Cherry blossom. Each bloom is up to 5 cm (2 in) in diameter.

M. hupehensis is from China and grows to 8 m (25 ft). The leaves are long and slender, the single flowers white and the charming red fruit on long stems are quite miniature.

M. X purpurea 'Eleyi' is the Purple Crab, a decorative small tree with bronzy leaves and flowers of deep purple-pink, often variable.

Other species are grown more for the decorative effect of the fruits than for their floral display. These include the cultivar *'Gorgeous'* with vivid scarlet crabs, and *'Golden Hornet'* in which the fruits are orange-yellow.

Malus, the botanical name of both Apples and Crabs, is the original Roman name of the wild European species.

Malus floribunda
Japanese Crab

Malus X 'Gorgeous'
Hybrid Crab

Malus ioensis
Prairie Crab

MANGIFERA
(man gif' ur ə)

The Mango
FAMILY: ANACARDIACEAE

Sometimes known as the Peach of the Tropics, *Mangifera indica* is hailed in its native India as King of Fruits, and is the subject of many legends. A handsome, tropical tree, preferring a warm, dry winter to produce well, the Mango may reach 30 m (100 ft) in South-East Asia and the Philippines, but rarely half that in warm temperate to sub-tropical climates. In both areas, however, its spread may be very wide.

The leaves are narrow, leathery and up to 33 cm (13 in) long. Dark green and stiff when mature, they are often brightly pink and hanging as new foliage, having a distinct odour of turpentine when crushed.

In mid-winter, the Mango tree is very picturesque, as curved, upright-pointing panicles of tiny pink four-or five-petalled flowers appear at every branch tip. These are followed by the great 15 cm (6 in) fruit that soon pull the stems down under their weight. In tropical areas these continue to ripen from spring right through to autumn, according to variety.

Malus domestica
Apple

Mangifera indica
Mango

146

Mangifera indica
detail of fruit

MANILKARA
(man il kah' rə)

The Sapodilla or Chicle Tree

FAMILY: SAPOTACEAE

This tall, dark and handsome tree from Mexico and Central America is so decorative, its hidden talents come as something of a surprise. Though it may stretch to 35 m (120 ft) in its native forests, it does not achieve half that height in the sub-tropical garden.

The leaves of *Manilkara zapota* are simple, elliptical and dark glossy green, up to about 12.5 cm (5 in) long and clustered in rosettes towards the end of twigs. The single, white, six-petalled flowers appear on long, rusty stems at the leaf axils and are only about 1 cm (½ in) in diameter. But they are followed by furry round fruits that look like and are the size of brown tennis balls. These are full of a translucent yellowish pulp with tiny black seeds, something like a Kiwi fruit, and equally delicious. Known as Sapodillas, they are one of the favourite dessert fruits of tropical America and other warm areas.

Manilkara's wood is hard, glossy-red and used for many decorative and practical purposes. Its sap, known as chicle, after much refining and flavouring, becomes the chewing gum so many of us enjoy. Great forests of them are cultivated in South America, and tapping the sap of wild trees is quite a cottage industry. A single tree can yield up to 15 gallons of chicle in just a few hours —that's over 68 litres, and a lot of gum by any standards.

Manilkara can be propagated from seed, but grafted seedlings grow quicker. Its names seem to be South American in origin.

Improved varieties must be propagated from cuttings, but do not bear so well as ordinary seedlings. Consequently the fruit seen most commonly on the market is from the more commercially practical seedling trees, and often fibrous and turpentine flavoured. Superior named varieties are quite free of fibre.

The botanical name is an extraordinary hybrid of Latin and Hindustani! *Mango* being the original Indian name and *fero* meaning to bear in Latin.

Mangifera indica
flowers, new foliage

Manilkara zapota
Chicle, Sapodilla

147

MELALEUCA
(mel a loo' k ə)

The Paperbarks

FAMILY: MYRTACEAE

One of the best loved Australian genera world-wide, the decorative *Melaleucas* now flourish in every sub-tropical to temperate area of the world, often where other trees kick up their heels. There are over a hundred species, known mostly for their decorative peeling barks and colourful flower spikes on which hundreds of long-stamened flowers are arranged in the form of a bottlebrush, generally white or cream in all of the tree-sized species.

Most common is the ubiquitous *M. quinquenervia*, known as the Broadleaf Paperbark or Cajeput tree. A handsome, spreading giant growing to 25 m (75 ft) high when planted on its own in damp ground, it is more often seen crowded in brackish swamps as a collection of slim, white-trunked saplings, with all the character of a field of clothes props. In this guise it has become unpopular in the state of Florida, where it may well succeed in taking over the famous Everglades.

In contrast, the Hong Kong Government plants it widely to help stabilize swampy farming areas of the New Territories. Like it or loathe it, everyone agrees the tree's regular display of cream bottlebrushes makes it one of the most reliable flowering trees in the world.

A second worthwhile species is the decorative Snow in Summer, *M. linariifolia*, which never outgrows its welcome. Rarely above 7 m (20 ft), it has a spreading habit, inclining towards multiple trunks. This species has the spongiest, flakiest bark of all, and really does look as if a snowstorm hit it in warm weather, when all the flowers open at once.

In the Bracelet Honeymyrtle, *M. armillaris*, the leaves are modified to needle-form, and the bark more furrowed than flaking. The dense flower-spikes are almost pure white and about 7.5 cm (3 in) long. *M. armillaris* may grow to 10 m (30 ft) and is particularly dense-foliaged. It is often seen group-planted as a windbreak in exposed positions, for single specimens are inclined to be shallow-rooted and top-heavy.

The West Australian *M. parviflora* really comes into its own in sandy coastal areas, where it may reach 7 m (20 ft), and adopt a graceful habit. It has dark tapered leaves rarely above 1 cm (½ in) long and slightly recurved, and fluffy, shorter cream bottlebrushes with an occasional dusting of red and pink.

Melaleucas are propagated from cuttings, and the botanical name is a combination of the Greek words *melos* meaning black and *leukos* meaning white. This presumably refers to the extreme tonal contrast between dark and light sections of the tree.

Melaleuca quinquenervia
flowers and foliage

Melaleuca quinquenervia
Cajeput Tree, Broadleaf Paperbark

Melaleuca parviflora
detail of flowers

148

Melaleuca linariifolia
Flaxleaf Paperbark

MELIA
(mel' ee ə)

The Chinaberry or White Cedar

FAMILY: MELIACEAE

Chinaberry, Pride of India, Persian Lilac, Texas Umbrella Tree, Syrian Bead Tree, Japanese Bead Tree, Australian White Cedar — a partial catalogue of popular names collected by the decorative *Melia azederach* only serves to underline the confusion as to its original home.

Probably it was somewhere to the north of India, but we must presume the distribution took place a long time ago, for it has many localized varieties with distinct differences in detail of the flowers, fruit and leaves. Today, there is hardly a country on earth where it is not known and grown for both its useful and its decorative qualities.

In tropical climates it shoots up to 20 m (60 ft) and more, with a wide spreading crown that provides useful shade for most of the year. In Texas, Australia and Persia it is not half as tall, and grows usually wider than its height.

In all areas it bears handsome twice-pinnate leaves that range from 20 to 90 cm in length (8 to 36 in) and resemble those of the European Ash Trees whose ancient Greek name it has been given. In cool areas these leaves turn bright yellow before falling in the autumn.

In spring with the new foliage, *Melia* produces loose sprays of lilac and purple flowers, five- or six-petalled and fragrant. These are followed by a mass of berries, green at first but turning orange as the summer warms up. They persist long after leaf fall, giving the bare tree a most attractive appearance.

Melia grows in any soil but is of particular use in dry, semi-desert areas, though it will also withstand several degrees of frost. The soft, light timber is used in cabinet-making, but does not last long outdoors.

The berries are poisonous to pigs and human beings, but cattle and birds seem to enjoy them, and in country areas the trees are often planted to shade poultry runs in summer.

Melia is easy to propagate from seed or cuttings.

Melia azederach
Persian Lilac

Melia azederach
Chinaberry, Bead Tree

149

MESPILUS
(mes' pil əs)

The Medlar

FAMILY: ROSACEAE

Outside of Europe the Medlar is probably the least commonly grown fruit tree of the Rose family (Apples, Pears and Quinces are others), and hasn't been very much in demand since refrigeration and canning have made a year-round fruit supply possible.

But in the Middle Ages it was greatly valued as the last fruit to hold on the tree until well into winter. It was not in fact regarded as fit to eat until it was frost-bitten and half rotten. Today they are picked early and stored on racks in an airy place waiting for the critical moment when they can be eaten, just before they go 'off'.

Mespilus germanica is the botanical name of the curious twisted tree it grows on, *Mespilus* being the original Latin label. The tree grows to about 7 m (20 ft), is sometimes spiny, and unlike others of the Rose family its leaves turn a rich, rusty brown in autumn. The fruit is a little larger than a golf ball, and has a fuzzy brown surface and five seeds.

From these seeds the Medlars are propagated, although a better method is to graft them on Quince or Hawthorn stock.

Mespilus germanica
Medlar, Mespilo

METASEQUOIA
(me tə see kwoy' ə)

The Dawn Redwood

FAMILY: TAXODIACEAE

Metasequoia glyptostroboides
Dawn Redwood

From a Western point-of-view probably the newest tree in cultivation, the lovely deciduous conifer *Metasequoia glyptostroboides* was discovered as recently as 1941 in China's Szechuan province. Previously, like the Ginkgo, it had only been known from fossil imprints.

An overnight sensation as a new relative outside America of Florida's swamp-cypresses (*Taxodium*, which see) and California's *Sequoias*, it was rushed into cultivation, seed being distributed worldwide in 1948. Now you can see them in all good botanic gardens, and small trees are readily available.

In nature, the Dawn Redwood grows to 35 m (120 ft) and has already reached 8 m (25 ft) in cultivation. It is a light and airy conical tree with palest-green feathery foliage. This turns pink and amber before dropping in the autumn. *Metasequoia* has a deeply fluted red trunk and bears small cones which hang on long stems. It is happiest in a damp waterside position in deep, rich soil.

The botanical name means 'related to the Sequoias' (see *Sequoia*).

METROSIDEROS
(met roh sid' ur os)

The Ironwood and Pohutukawa

FAMILY: MYRTACEAE

Scattered about the islands of the Pacific is a splendid group of trees and shrubs related to the Australian Eucalypts; their generic name is *Metrosideros*, meaning heart of iron, a tribute to the glorious red heartwood which was used for idol-making in the pagan days.

To the New Zealand Maori, these trees were known as *rata*, to their Tahitian cousins *puarata*; the Hawaiians called them *lehua*.

Most splendid of all is *M. excelsa* (syn. *M. tomentosa*), aptly called by the Maori Pohutukawa, or 'sprinkled with spray' for its habit of clinging to sea-washed cliffs or growing with its roots actually in salt water. It is both salt - and sand-resistant and in an exposed position will become gnarled and picturesque, trailing a tangle of aerial roots from every branch. Its dark, leathery, 10 cm (4 in) leaves have silver reverses, and in mid-summer (Christmas time in the southern hemisphere), it bursts into dazzling bloom as masses of scarlet-stamened pincushion flowers open on white woolly stalks.

Taller, with flowers of a duller red, is the Northern Rata, *M. robusta*, from forests of New Zealand's North Island.

A third New Zealand species, also with rounded leaves, is *M. kermadecensis*, sold in a number of variegated leaf forms.

Less useful in coastal gardens, but at home in humid, mountain areas is *M. collina*, the *Ohi'a Lehua*, found naturally high up on the slopes of Tahiti and the Hawaiian Islands, where it has been recorded up to 35 m (120 ft) in height. Its spreading shape, crowned with a blanket of vivid red blossom, caused the Hawaiians to declare it sacred to Pele, goddess of the Volcanoes.

Metrosideros excelsa
Pohutukawa

Metrosideros kermadecensis
Variegated Ironwood

Metrosideros collina
Ohi'a Lehua

Metrosideros robusta
Northern Rata

MICHELIA

(mi shel' ee ə)

The Champaks

FAMILY: MAGNOLIACEAE

Evergreen, and closely related to the Magnolias
(which see), the fifty-odd Asiatic species of
Michelia are commonly represented in Western
gardens only by shrubby *M. figo*, the Port Wine
Magnolia or Banana Shrub.

But in gardens of Asia, Hawaii, South America
and Africa, several of the tree species are among
the most beloved of garden ornamentals.

Three of these trees are generally available
and worth seeking out. They are:
M. alba, the Pak-lan, a handsome, pale-trunked
tree of 10 m (30 ft) with slender, pointed,
apple-green leaves to 25 cm (10 in) long. The
snowy-white flowers are about the size of a Gardenia, though with narrow petals of irregular
length. They are very fragrant.
M. doltsopa, the Wong-lan, is a fast-growing,
pyramidal tree to 13 m (40 ft), with pointed
leaves of a darker green. Its 6 cm (2¼ in) flowers
do not open well. They are a pure daffodil-
yellow, fragrant at first but developing an unpleasantly heavy perfume after a day. *M. champaca*, the Cham-pak, is a larger-growing tree
from Tibet and Yunnan. It may reach 30 m (100 ft)
in nature, but much less in the garden. The
fragrant, often twelve-petalled flowers are 7.5
cm (3 in) wide and a creamy-buff shade.

All *Michelias* bear their flowers in the leaf axils
(unlike the Magnolias).

The botanic name *Michelia* commemorates a
seventeenth-century Italian botanist, Pietro
Micheli.

Michelia alba
detail of flower and foliage

MORINDA

(mor ind' ə)

The Indian Mulberry

FAMILY: RUBIACEAE

A small tree with brilliantly shining foliage, the
Indian Mulberry, *Morinda*, is found naturally in
South-East Asia, Australia and the Pacific Is-
lands.

Morinda citrifolia is quite popular in sub-
tropical gardens, not only for the decorative,
shiny foliage, but for the many-flowered heads
of white, five- to seven-petalled blossom which
develop into a curious, compound fruit, rather
like a small Breadfruit or large Mulberry.

The ancient Polynesians (who called it *noni*),
extracted dyes of several colours from parts of
the plant. They even ate the fruit in hard times,
for they are edible if rather unpalatable.

The botanical name *Morinda* is merely a con-
traction from the Latin *morus* meaning mulberry, and *indica* meaning Indian. However, it is
actually related to the Gardenia rather than the
Mulberry.

Morinda citrifolia
Noni, Indian Mulberry

MORUS

(mor' əs)

The Mulberries

FAMILY: MORACEAE

'With patience, the mulberry leaf becomes a
silken robe,' says an old Chinese proverb, and
that about sums up the most important quality
of the *Morus* or Mulberries, a deciduous genus
principally found in the Americas and Asia. They
are cultivated as food for silkworms, and the
species *M. alba*, the White Mulberry, is preferred for the purpose because it grows faster, up
to 25 m (80 ft) in China, and thus produces more,
though smaller, leaves.

Morus nigra
Black Mulberry

Morus nigra, the Black Mulberry, is a fruit of a different colour! Native to Persia and nearby areas, it is a slow grower with nobbly bark, and often develops a wide-spreading, picturesque shape without any help from the gardener. Rarely above 10 m (30 ft) in height, its large, rough-textured, coarsely-toothed leaves are somewhat heart-shaped and all of 20 cm (8 in) long. The drooping flower catkins are uninteresting, but are followed in late spring by incredibly juicy, acid-sweet fruits that resemble blackberries. These are red at first, ripening to

almost black. Mulberry fruits stain faces, hands and everything in sight, but the stains can be removed with the juice of a green mulberry.

A third species, *M. rubra*, the Red Mulberry, is native to North America and rarely grown elsewhere because its fruits are inferior.

Mulberries can be propagated from very large cuttings, even whole branches.

NEPHELIUM
(ne fee' lee əm)

The Rambutan

FAMILY: SAPINDACEAE

Found in many parts of tropical South-East Asia, and even in the north of Australia, the genus *Nephelium* includes about seventy species, many of them valued locally for their fruits.

Only the following two species are grown much away from their native areas.

The Pulasan (*N. mutabile*), a Javanese tree of some 15 m (45 ft) with compound evergreen leaves and rather nobbly red fruit resembling the Lychee.

The Rambutan (*N. lappaceum*) is seen universally in tropical gardens. It grows to roughly the same size, has leathery, bay-like leaves and in late summer bears masses of 5 cm (2 in) fruits covered with soft, curling spines. These are green at first, ripening to red, and filled with delicious translucent pulp.

The botanical name *Nephelium* is from the Greek, meaning little cloud, presumably in reference to the masses of small, whitish summer flowers.

Morus rubra
detail of fruit, foliage

Nephelium lappaceum
Rambutan

NOTHOFAGUS
(noh thoh fae' gəs)

The Southern Beeches

FAMILY: FAGACEAE

The handsome Beech trees of the northern hemisphere (see *Fagus*), have a similar looking group of close relatives in the southern hemisphere. They are named *Nothofagus*, meaning False Beeches, and like many other southern genera are scattered about Australia, New Zealand and South America, pointing to a common origin, perhaps in prehistoric Antarctica.

There are at least twenty-five species growing about the southern half of the globe in climatic areas varying from cold temperate to almost tropical.

The Southern Beeches are most variable in habit, ranging from dwarf, almost scrubby plants in windy Tierra del Fuego to giant timber trees in the forests of Australia and New Zealand. The Tasmanian species *N. cunninghamii* has been recorded up to 70 m (230 ft) in height.

The foliage of Southern Beeches is much like that of their northern cousins, though more usually evergreen. The seeds (or Beech Nuts) are also very much alike.

Nothofagus moorei
Negrohead Beech, foliage

NUYTSIA
(noit' see ə)

The Fire Tree, Golden Bough

FAMILY: LORANTHACEAE

Although none of us will ever grow a Fire Tree, never even see one in flower unless we happen to be in West Australia during the hot season around Christmas, it could not be omitted from this book.

It is one of the most beautiful trees in the world, and also one of the world's great botanical mysteries — a mystery whose secrets have been broken one by one over the years, but which remains as far from final solution as ever.

Nuytsia floribunda is the botanical name of this remarkable tree, called after the Dutch Navigator Pieter Nuyts, who first discovered the part of Australia in which it grows. That is *grows*, but cannot *be* grown. For it is a root parasite, a gigantic tree-size relative of the humble mistletoe that has no means of feeding except through the roots of established nearby host plants with which it has grown to maturity.

It is found growing in large numbers in limited areas of sandy bushland, where it spreads by suckers from its own underground stems. But when the nearby bushland is cleared for development, the *Nuytsia* will most likely fade away too.

You can sow the seed and it will sprout, but stay at seedling size for years. In nature it will send feeding stems for literally hundreds of metres in every direction, battening on every plant in sight from grass to towering tree, and partaking delicately from each of their life support systems, a true vegetable Dracula. It is sometimes called the Golden Bough, or West Australian Christmas Tree.

Nothofagus obliqua
Roblé Beech

Nuytsia floribunda
Fire Tree, Golden Bough
(photo by Douglass Baglin)

NYSSA
(nis' sə)

The Tupelo or Black Gum

FAMILY: NYSSACEAE

Nyssa was a water nymph, and her name has been commemorated in a whole genus of water-loving trees, the Tupelos, native to eastern parts of both North America and Asia.

The commonly cultivated species is the deciduous *Nyssa sylvatica*, an ideal and decorative specimen tree for damp or ill-drained positions. Of a vertical, pyramidal habit, it may grow to 20 m (60 ft) in a really moist waterside position, and have a branch spread of 5 m (15 ft), though generally less.

The 10 cm (4 in) leaves are shiny, smooth-margined and slightly wider towards the tip than the base. In autumn they turn to wondrous fiery red, reflecting superbly in nearby water. The uninteresting greenish flowers appear on long stems originating in the leaf axils, and are succeeded by brilliant deep-blue fruits, about 1 cm (½ in) long, and a stunning colour contrast to the autumn foliage. The bark is a rich brownish grey, usually broken up into tile-like slabs on older trees.

Another member of the genus is *Nyssa aquatica*, the Water Tupelo from southern USA. This is a similar tree, but usually grows right in swamps or shallow water, developing a buttressed trunk. The oval fruits may reach 2.5 cm (1 in) in diameter, and the leaves are sometimes slightly toothed.

Nyssa sylvatica
detail of autumn foliage, fruit

Nyssa sylvatica
Tupelo, Black Gum

155

OLEA

The Olives
(ol' ee ə)

FAMILY: OLEACEAE

In Western civilization at least, the Olive is undoubtedly the oldest tree in continuous cultivation, valued for its many gifts to man throughout the Mediterranean area since time immemorial.

Its botanical name *Olea* is the ancient Roman word for oil, and the oil pressed from its ripe fruits is the principal reason for its popularity.

In modern times, when we think of olive oil merely as an ingredient of salad dressing or soap, it is difficult to imagine its importance to the ancient world. It was the basis of perfumes and cosmetics; it was their only method of lubrication; it provided precious lighting at night, and a valuable foodstuff by day. Greek legend tells us that the ancient city of Athens was named for the goddess Athene after she presented the olive tree to man.

The Common Olive, *Olea europaea,* is not a large tree, rarely exceeding 8 m (25 ft), but it can become enormously gnarled and thick with age, living to 1,500 years and more. Its slender leaves are silver-backed, its flowers tiny and yellowish, and the oil-rich fruits are up to 4 cm (1½ in) in diameter, glossy black when ripe.

More commonly seen away from the Mediterranean is the similar *Olea africana,* found naturally over a wide area from Africa to China. Its leaves are slightly larger, often backed with gold rather than silver. The tiny privet-like flowers are decorative in late spring, and the round fruits rarely exceed 1 cm (⅜ in) in diameter. They too contain oil, but the tree is rarely cultivated for this purpose. It is often seen as a street tree, being extremely well suited to dry pavement conditions.

Olea europaea
Common Olive

Olea africana
detail of fruit, foliage

Olea africana
mature tree in summer blossom

OREOCALLIS
(o ree oh kal' lis)

The Red Silky Oak or Tree Waratah

FAMILY: PROTEACEAE

Much of the world seems unaware of Australia's gorgeous *Oreocallis wickhamii.* A tree-sized relative of Chile's famous Fire Bush, *Embothrium,* it is rarely seen in cultivation and has certainly not achieved the popularity it deserves. Native to the moist Kurrajong forests of Queensland and New South Wales, it is actually quite amenable to garden use, provided it can be given a position sheltered from wind by large trees, and with an ample supply of the moisture it needs at

156

all times. A position where it can rise above established shrubs would be ideal, for it cannot abide its roots being disturbed by normal cultivation. Like so many Australian natives, it is a member of the family Proteaceae, with single, tough, leathery leaves which may be heavily lobed and up to 65 cm (26 in) long.

The flower display has brought it a number of popular names including Fire Tree, Red Silky Oak, and Tree Waratah, the latter seeming most appropriate for the inflorescence does rather resemble that of the New South Wales State floral emblem.

Oreocallis may be raised from seed, but like the related *Macadamia* and *Stenocarpus* it will not commence blooming until it is reasonably adult, after about seven or eight years. In maturity it rarely exceeds 10 m (30 ft) in height.

The splendid timber of *Oreocallis* once led to its being known as Red Silky Oak, but is rarely cut these days.

Ostrya carpinifolia
Hop Hornbeam

But in the cooler climates they love, and in good soil, they'll easily reach 20 m (65 ft) in height, and are particularly cultivated for their splendid show of autumn colour. The popular name is Hop Hornbeam, which describes them perfectly. The handsome toothed leaves resemble those of the Hornbeam (*Carpinus*, a tree not included in this book), while the hanging fruit clusters greatly resemble those of the edible Hop (*Humulus*, used in the brewing of beer).

The European species *O. carpinifolia* is most commonly seen, while American gardens are home to *O. virginiana*, sometimes known as Ironwood.

OXYDENDRUM
(ok see den' drəm)

The Sourwood or Sorrel Tree

FAMILY: ERICACEAE

The beautiful *Oxydendrum arboreum*, or Sourwood, from the south-eastern United States, resembles nothing so much as a tree-sized species of Andromeda (*Pieris* spp.), and so it was at first classifed (as *Andromeda arborea*). Rarely growing above 7 m (21 ft) in cultivation, it may reach four times that height in the wild, and in both situations needs acid soil and the shelter of other larger, denser trees to do well.

In late summer the entire tree is decked with drooping 25 cm (10 in) panicles of white bell-shaped blossom at branch tips, each individual flower less than 1 cm (⅜ in) long. These are delightfully fragrant, honey rich, and most attractive to bees. The tree's special glory, however, is later in the autumn, when the deciduous foliage turns a brilliant blood-red.

Oreocallis wickhamii
Tree Waratah, Red Silky Oak

OSTRYA
(os' tree ə)

The Hop Hornbeams

FAMILY: BETULACEAE

A small genus of decorative, deciduous trees found on all three continents of the northern hemisphere, the *Ostryas* (their ancient Greek name) are rarely, if at all, seen south of the equator.

Oxydendrum arboreum
Sourwood or Sorrel Tree

Oxydendrum is easily propagated from cuttings, layers or seed, and its botanical name is a combination of the old Greek words *oxys* meaning sour, and *dendron* meaning tree, a reference to its bitter-tasting sap.

PANDANUS
(pan dan' əs)

The Screw Pines

FAMILY: PANDANACEAE

Popularly known as either Screw Pines or Walking Palms, the genus *Pandanus* is neither a pine nor a palm, but was once thought to be related to the Pineapple!

There are several hundred species, with an almost infinite number of colour varieties of foliage, and they are found naturally from Madagascar right through the Indian Ocean to South-East Asia and Australia, and out into the Pacific Islands, where they are commonly seen right on the water's edge, holding themselves out of reach of the surf on stiff, aerial roots.

Today they are merely a decorative asset in seaside gardens of warm climates, grown for their profuse fountains of spirally arranged, razor-edged leaves. But in older times they were the very staff of life to many island cultures. The tough, fibrous leaves were used for house thatching and the weaving of sails, clothing, floor mats and baskets. The famous grass skirts of the island belles were often made of split, bleached *Pandanus* leaves. The branched spikes of tiny white flowers are both decorative and fragrant, and are followed by large conglomerate fruit-heads about 20 cm (8 in) in diameter, and with very much the appearance of a pineapple.

The commonly seen *P. odoratissimus* reaches 8 m (25 ft) and may spread even wider, the stiff branches supporting themselves on stilt-like masses of aerial roots. They are propagated by means of suckers or from the tough seeds which should be soaked for twenty-four hours before planting.

The botanical name *Pandanus* is a variation of the tree's old Malaysian name, *pandang*.

Pandanus veitchii
Variegated Screw Pine

Pandanus odoratissimus
Walking Palm, fruit and foliage

PARROTIA
(pa rot' ee ə)

The Persian Witchhazel

FAMILY: HAMAMELIDACEAE

Untidily shaped in cultivation and tending more to the habit of a large shrub than my idea of a tree, the Persian Witchhazel, *Parrotia*, makes a splendid autumn feature in a good year, but needs a sheltered position.

Parrotia persica
Persian Witchhazel, blossom

Parrotia persica
autumn foliage

PAULOWNIA
(por lof' nee ə)

The Princess Trees

FAMILY: BIGNONIACEAE

Named for a princess, and a true princess among trees, China's noble *Paulownias* are sometimes mistaken for the American Catalpa (see *Catalpa*), and they are closely related. The principal similarity is in the green, heart-shaped, fuzzy leaves which may reach 30 cm (12 in) in length and almost as much across. Both tree genera bear large trumpet-shaped flowers in clusters, but those of the *Paulownia* are carried in vertical spikes. Another difference is in the seeds. Catalpa carries them in hanging pea-type pods; in *Paulownia* they are in pointed, oval capsules about 3 cm (1¼ in) across, and borne on the same spikes as the flower.

Paulownias flower best in a cooler-than-average climate, and will happily survive a winter minimum of –12°C (10°F), so they are most often seen in high-country gardens where they are sometimes known as Mountain Jacaranda, from their upright panicles of mauvish flowers.

P. tomentosa is the commonly seen species, reaching 13 m (40 ft) in a good position and bearing 5 cm (2 in) mauve flowers, spotted violet and very fragrant. The buds appear in late summer and persist through winter to open in spring.

Paulownias are deciduous and were named for Anna Paulowna, daughter of a Russian Tsar. They are propagated from seed.

In its native Persian mountains, it is said to grow tall and straight with a broad crown, and to reach 17 m (50 ft), but all the garden specimens that I have seen have favoured much shorter multiple trunks and low, often weeping, branches. The deciduous leaves are rather splendid at almost any time of year, oval and blunt ended with rather rippled edges and a distinctly quilted effect on the upper surface. They are about 12.5 cm (5 in) long and unfold in the earliest spring, just after the flowers, which are rather uninteresting clusters of blood-red stamens that pop out of a pair of woolly brown bracts.

P. persica was named after the German naturalist F.W. Parrot, and is a particularly useful tree in alkaline soils. It is easily propagated from seed, layers or cuttings, and has no particular use beyond its decorative qualities.

Paulownia tomentosa
Princess Tree, blossom

159

Paulownia tomentosa
Princess Tree

PERSEA
(pur see' ə)

The Avocado

FAMILY: LAURACEAE

The delicious Avocadoes of which so many of us are fond ripen on a handsome 15 m (50 ft) tree with glossy foliage. Evergreen in tropical areas, semi-deciduous elsewhere, it demands good drainage at all times.

Persea americana
Avocado, Butterfruit

It is claimed that some four hundred named varieties of *Persea americana* are in cultivation; but all would be hybrids of local variants of the original species, which is naturally scattered about Central America and the West Indies. To the home fancier, any one of them would be a treasure, whether its fruit was round, oval or pear-shaped, and whether the skin was green, purple or black at the time of ripening.

All types of fruit contain the same sumptuous lime-green pulp, rich in oils and iodine.

Those of us in cooler temperate climates must be content with summer-ripening varieties. But as one goes further towards the tropics, a wider range becomes possible, with varieties that ripen in any season of the year.

The average home Avocado tree is grown from the large seed and requires at least seven years to fruit. Orchardists prefer to graft specific named types to maintain quality. The best advice is to buy only a guaranteed bisexual graft from your nursery.

Avocadoes bear fuzzy panicles of yellowish bisexual flowers at branch tips, sometimes annually, sometimes in alternate years, and many trees lose much of their foliage at this time.

Persea is an old Greek name.

Persea americana
Alligator Pear

160

PHOENIX
(fee' niks)

The Date Palms

FAMILY: PALMAE

'Honour the Date Palm,' said the prophet Mahomet to his followers, 'for it is your mother.' And indeed, whole races have depended on this single tree genus since time immemorial. In the desert fringe that runs across North Africa, through the Middle East to Pakistan, the Date is *life!*

Its presence in the desert waste signals an oasis and water beneath the sand; but more than that, the tree itself provides food, timber, shelter, stock fodder, wine, sugar and oil — some seven hundred uses have been listed for various parts of the plant.

Phoenix dactylifera is a handsome specimen most at home in dryish areas of all continents (for it can make do with less water than almost any other tree) rising to 30 m (100 ft) where it enjoys life, and suckering with great abandon to form a clump or oasis of its own. The striking blue-grey fronds push stiffly out to as far as 7 m (20 ft) and are spiny near their bases. The tiny flowers (in clusters of as many as ten thousand each) develop among the fronds, each sex on a different tree. The fruits or dates are as much as 5 cm (2 in) in length and contain a hard, grooved seed. They are orange-red and sticky sweet and must be sun-dried before packing.

More commonly seen in areas with normal rainfall is the Canary Island Date Palm, *P. canariensis,* a shorter, heavier tree with a trunk up to 1 m (3 ft) in diameter. The fronds are large, deep green and more densely borne than on the Date, and it does not develop the suckering habit. The stems of orange fruit are its most obvious feature for much of the year, but they are scarcely edible.

The Senegal Date Palm, *P. reclinata,* is a slender, more delicate tree, reaching 7 m (20 ft) and with trunks only a finger-length in diameter. It suckers madly, rapidly developing into a dense clump. The fronds are 3 m (9 ft) long. The oblong fruits are fingernail size and of no particular use.

P. roebelinii, the Pigmy Date Palm, is an Asiatic representative of the genus, popular all over the world both as an indoor plant and for decorative landscaping use. It rarely grows above head-height, and the delicate soft green fronds are about 1 m (3 ft) long. Its tiny fruit are black.

All Date varieties may be propagated from seed. Their botanical name *Phoenix* has been in use since the days of ancient Greece.

Phoenix dactylifera
Date Palm

Phoenix canariensis
Canary Island Date Palm

Phoenix reclinata
Senegal Date Palm

PHYLLANTHUS
(fil lan' thəs)

The Myrobalan and Otaheite Gooseberry
FAMILY: EUPHORBIACEAE

The very large genus *Phyllanthus* (over five hundred listed species), is represented in warm-climate gardens by two small trees grown for both their decorative appearance and their edible fruits. These are *P. acidus*, the Otaheite Gooseberry, and *P. emblica*, the Myrobalan, both from South-East Asia.

Both trees reach 10 m (30 ft) and both are deciduous with a foliage arrangement that gives the appearance of pinnate leaves but is actually single stalk-less leaves arranged in a flat plane along each twig. (The difference is that only the individual leaves fall, rather than the entire twig of leaves.)

Each species bears many petal-less flowers, red on the Gooseberry, yellow on the Myrobalan. In the former, they appear on separate branchlets below the foliage, directly from the main branches; in the latter, they are clustered in the leaf-axils.

The late-summer fruits of *P. acidus* are curiously ribbed and bright yellow, clustering around the trunk and branches; those of *P. emblica* are pale green, smooth, and the size of a marble. Both may be enjoyed stewed with sugar, or made into jams and pickles.

The two *Phyllanthus* species are propagated from seeds or green cuttings, and in the case of the Myrobalan from layers as well. They have no frost resistance whatever and are suited to warm-climate coastal gardens. The name *Phyllanthus* is from the Greek *phyllon* meaning leaf, and *anthos*, meaning flower; since some other smaller species flower directly from the edge of phyllodes, or twigs that have developed a leafy shape.

PICEA
(pai' see ə)

The Spruces
FAMILY: PINACEAE

Picea abies
Norway Spruce

If the genus *Picea* contained only one tree, and that was the wonderful Colorado Blue Spruce (*P. pungens Kosteriana*), it would still be listed among the most important tree groups in the world.

But fortunately there are between thirty and fifty species scattered all over the northern hemisphere, and at least four times as many beautiful cultivars from which to make a choice.

Phyllanthus acidus
Otaheite or Indian Gooseberry

Picea X standishii
Weeping Blue Spruce

162

All of them are native to a high-altitude, cooler climate zone running from Europe through Asia Minor northward to Siberia and Japan, and right across North America.

In nature, the trees are generally of a tall pyramidal habit with stiff, starchy, upward-pointing branches that droop only with the weight of age. They are often confused with the Firs (*Abies*) but vary in several important minor details of interest to the botanist. First, the leaves, which are spirally arranged, leave peg-like bases on the twig when they fall, making branchlets rough to the touch. Second, their mature cones always hang *downwards*.

Picea abies
detail of cones

Spruces are far more tolerant of pollution and climatic variation than the Firs, but do not transplant well and should be started out as young as possible. Moist, acid soil is preferred, but many of them can cope with a degree of lime.

There are three giant species in the genus: *P. abies*, the Norway Spruce of north and central Europe; *P. sitchensis*, the Sitka Spruce of north-east America; and *P. spinulosa*, the Sikkim Spruce of the Himalayas. Any of these may commonly reach 70 m (230 ft) in their native forests, and they are all regarded as valuable timber trees.

Spruces with weeping branches include: *P. breweriana*, Brewer's Weeping Spruce from California; *P. omorika Pendula*, the Serbian Spruce from Jugoslavia; and the hybrid *P. standishii* with blue foliage. All grow to around 30 m (100 ft).

Picea glauca
White Spruce

The North American White Spruce, *P. glauca*, is grown commercially for pulping into newsprint, but its dwarf cultivar *P. g. Albertiana Conica* is one of the most popular small specimen trees for landscaping in the cooler climate, rarely exceeding 3 m (10 ft).

Picea glauca CV *Albertiana Conica*
Dwarf Spruce

163

Picea pungens CV *Kosteriana*
Colorado Blue Spruce

P. orientalis from the Caucasus and *P. jezoensis* from Japan are popular specimen trees, neither topping 35 m (100 ft). But most widely grown for this purpose is the Colorado Spruce, *P. pungens*, generally in one of its blue-leafed forms such as the CVs *Argentea, Glauca, Kosteriana* and *Moerheimii*.

All Spruce species are fragrant with the resin from which they take their botanical name, *Picea* (from the Greek *pix,* meaning pitch or resin).

PIMENTA
(pai men' tə)

Allspice and Bay Rum Trees

FAMILY: MYRTACEAE

Pimenta dioica
Allspice, berries

'Take me to Jamaica where the rum comes frum' were the words of a once-popular song, and they might have applied equally to the Bay Rum Tree, one of a small genus of West Indian trees grown commercially for their aromatic parts.

Called *Pimenta* botanically (the old Spanish name) they are closely related to the Australian Eucalypts and Lillypillies and other members of the Myrtle family, Myrtaceae.

Pimenta acris, the Bayberry or Wild Clove, is a 10 m (30 ft) evergreen with leathery leaves, typical white myrtle flowers; the pea-sized berries are used in cooking.

More highly valued are ripened, dark-brown berries of *P. dioica,* which have a flavour reminiscent of nutmeg, cinnamon and cloves. They are called Allspice and ground to make a popular culinary additive.

P. racemosa, the Bay Rum Tree, is the source of Oil of Bay (the base of many hair products and much male perfumery) which is extracted both from leaves and twigs.

All are propagated from half ripened cuttings, and grow best in gardens of hot climates.

PINUS
(pai' nəs)

The Pines

FAMILY: PINACEAE

Most widespread and instantly recognizable of the conifers, the Pines have lent their old Roman name not only to a genus, *Pinus,* but to an entire botanical family Pinaceae that includes the other principal coniferous genera of the northern hemisphere as well (*Abies, Cedrus, Larix, Picea* and many other groups).

There are actually only about eighty species of Pine, all of them native to the northern continents, but their climatic range stretches from beyond the Arctic Circle to sub-tropical regions near the equator. Some of them are mountain trees; some actually flourish in almost pure sand by the seashore. But the vast majority will grow in conditions any sensible tree would reject out of hand, clinging like grim death to rocky hillsides, hanging over gorges or sprouting on windy promontories stretching way out into the ocean.

Several species including the European *P. pinaster* and the American *P. radiata* have been naturalized in the southern hemisphere where they grow better than the native conifers and better than in their own home areas.

Pines, as mentioned previously, are instantly recognizable, if only by their leaves, which have evolved into a needle-shape, often perfectly rounded and appearing in bunches of two, three or five according to species, each bundle wrapped in a sheath-like membrane. The needles may be less than 2.5 cm (1 in) long as in the

Pinus ponderosa
Western Yellow Pine

Pinus densiflora
Japanese Red Pine

Japanese *P. parviflora*, or up to 45 cm (18 in) long as in the American *P. palustris*.

The young growth of Pines is in the form of a vertical spike known as a 'candle'. Growth of small trees can be directed or modified by twisting these candles right off. Male Pine flowers appear in a ring of small cylindrical, upright catkins around the new growth. They vary from red to yellow in colour, and scatter pollen abundantly in early summer in an effort to fertilize the female cones elsewhere on the same tree.

Fertilized female flowers develop into cones, which may be borne singly or in clusters, again according to species. These take two years to develop fully on the average, after which the overlapping scales open to discharge their seeds in early autumn.

There is a Pine for almost every type of soil, and the selection of the right one is an important branch of forestry. The timber of most species is both soft and fragrant, and of great importance in the building and paper industries. The trees are also the source of important oils and resins and are highly flammable.

The general habit of most European and North American Pines is conical when young, but with a development of high, spreading branches on older trees. Exceptions are several alpine species.

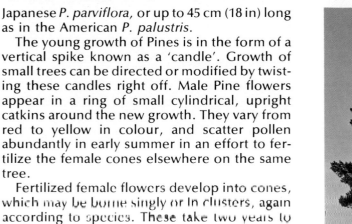

Pinus radiata
Monterey Pine

Pinus pinaster
detail of spring flowers

Pinus pinaster
Maritime Pine

Pinus palustris
Long-leaf Pine

Pinus peuce
Macedonian Pine

Pinus laricio
Corsican Pine, bark pattern

Pinus thunbergii
Japanese Black Pine

166

PISONIA
(pi son' ee ə)

The Lettuce Tree

FAMILY: NYCTAGINACEAE

Tree-loving visitors to the Philippine Republic cannot help but notice the striking colour of a tree widely planted in the airport's landscaping. Its foliage is a remarkable light lettuce-green, and therefore it was with no great surprise I learned it is known locally as the Lettuce Tree.

Native to Malaysia and the southern Philippine area, its botanical name is *Pisonia alba,* and it is closely related to the Bougainvilleas. Not a large tree, rarely reaching 5 m (16 ft), its leaves are deciduous, slightly furry and shaped like an elongated heart. Though the timber is spongy and useless, the leaves are supremely edible and eaten both raw and cooked.

I have been unable to locate any information about its flowers or fruits, but there is a closely related species *P. grandis,* the Puka, in the Pacific Islands, which is also valued for its edible foliage.

Pistacia vera
Pistachio (photo by Tess Mallos)

Pistacia chinensis
Chinese Pistachio

Pisonia alba
Lettuce Tree

PISTACIA
(pis tae' shee ə)

The Pistachios

FAMILY: ANACARDIACEAE

Species of the small genus *Pistacia* are found in many places around the temperate zone of the northern hemisphere, on all continents. They take their name from *pistake,* a word the Greeks had for the succulent nuts borne by the European species, *P. vera.* These are still popular cocktail snacks in all countries, and of great value commercially in the Middle East. They ripen on a small 7 m (20 ft) tree with compound leaves of five leaflets each.

Far more decorative and commonly grown all over the world is its oriental cousin, *P. chinensis,* a much larger deciduous tree which may reach 25 m (80 ft) in a suitable position. Its leaves consist of ten or twelve slender leaflets, but alas, the tiny blue fruits and red flowers are scarcely worth worrying about.

But for autumn colour the tree is hard to beat. The glossy leaves begin to turn quite early in cool climates, developing a veritable rainbow of tints ranging from yellow to scarlet, with an occasional patch of purple. The colour persists for many weeks.

Pistachios enjoy full sun and are not particularly fussy about soil.

167

PITHECELLOBIUM
(pith ə sel loh' bee əm)

The Opiuma or Manila Tamarind
FAMILY: LEGUMINOSAE

Originally from Central America, *Pithecellobium dulce* was distributed worldwide through the old Spanish Empire, and receives its popular name Manila Tamarind from one of the many countries in which it has naturalized.

A tree of many uses, it thrives on neglect and is grown for both ornamental and practical purposes. So spiny that even hungry stock avoid it, it can be safely used for shade and shelter in the paddocks, or trimmed into a spiky and impenetrable hedge. But left to its own as a specimen tree it may reach 20 m (65 ft) and looks fresh and attractive at any time of the year.

The bark is a decorative pale grey and the foliage most unusual. Each leaf consists of one pair of divided leaflets, four leaflets in all. The flowers are whitish puffballs, like an albino *Acacia*, and very attractive to bees which help them develop into long, twisted seedpods throughout the late spring and early summer.

These contain a sweetish pulp which is used for food, beverage and stock fodder in various parts. The timber of the large trees is strong and flexible, and almost every part of the tree is used medicinally.

The most valued and decorative variety is one in which the leaves are variegated with white. This is called Opiuma in Hawaii, and the contrast of its white foliage and red pods is most attractive.

Opiuma naturalizes readily from seed wherever it is planted, so propagation suggestions are hardly needed. Its botanical name is from *pithecos* meaning ape, and *lobos* meaning ear, a rough translation of its old native name.

PITTOSPORUM
(pit tos' por əm)

Victorian Box, Mockorange, Tarata
FAMILY: PITTOSPORACEAE

Pittosporum undulatum
detail of winter fruit

To pronounce on which of the many *Pittosporum* species might be the most attractive would be rather like repeating the infamous Judgement of Paris. Whichever way you choose, you're bound to engender jealousy somewhere, for national feelings tend to run high in such matters.

Let me say merely that the *Pittosporum* are a genus of about seventy-five handsome evergreens with flowers fragrant as orange blossom, and seed capsules which hold the seeds embedded in a mass of sticky resin. In fact, the botanical name is compounded from *pitta* meaning pitch, and *sporus* meaning a seed, in reference to this important characteristic. All

Pithecellobium dulce
Manila Tamarind or Opiuma

Pittosporum tobira
Mockorange, Tobira

Pittosporum eugenioides Variegatum
Silver Tarata

Pittosporum undulatum
Native Daphne, Victorian Box

the *Pittosporums* are found in an area centring on Australia, but with outlying species in East Africa, Japan, South-East Asia, New Zealand and Hawaii.

New Zealand's big entry in the contest is blonde: *P. eugenioides Variegatum*, a striking tree with cream margined grey-green leaves, yellow flowers and a height of 13 m (40 ft). It is known locally as the Silver Tarata.

Japan throws into the ring the universally popular *P. tobira* or Mockorange, a 7 m (20 ft) shrubby tree with blunt-ended, leathery leaves, fragrant cream blossom and bright yellow seed capsules.

Australia has two main contenders: the Queensland Pittosporum, *P. rhombifolium*, standing 10 m (30 ft), with glossy rhomboid leaves, slightly toothed small white flowers and a mass of vivid orange fruits in autumn. A most decorative street tree! Its companion *P. undulatum*, the Victorian Box or Native Daphne, grows taller, has pointed leaves of a little shinier, pale green with rippled margins, and creamy-white blossom in 7.5 cm (3 in) terminal clusters.

Across the Pacific in Hawaii is a rank outsider, the striking *P. hosmeri* or Ho'awa. A small tree found on old lava flows, it produces wonderfully wrinkled 15 cm (10 in) leaves, shiny above, furry beneath, and fragrant cream flowers.

I'll leave it to someone else to make the judgement between them, and in a cowardly fashion just suggest that though they are all beautiful, they are best kept away from paths. Those sticky fruits get on everyone's feet and into everybody's carpet.

Needless to say, all *Pittosporums* grow easily from seed.

Pittosporum rhombifolium
Queensland Pittosporum

PLATANUS
(pla tan' us)

The Planes and Sycamores

FAMILY: PLATANACEAE

Most widely planted street tree in the world, the gracious London Plane, *Platanus X acerifolia* is propagated by the million in both the northern and southern hemispheres. It satisfies all the criteria of life in the big city, growing tall and fast, spreading strong and wide, and presenting a decorative appearance at all times of the year. Its winter-flaking bark is coloured grey and beige; the handsome maple-like leaves are an attractive dull green and up to 25 cm (10 in) wide; and the fruits are arranged in rough ball-shaped structures on long hanging stems. Kids everywhere call them conkers and find them handy weapons for aggressive games.

The London Plane is a hybrid between two original species, the Chinar (*P. orientalis*) from Asia, and the Buttonwood (*P. occidentalis*) from the USA. It has the heat resistance of one and the cold hardiness of the other. It can easily reach 25 m (80 ft) in a good rich soil, and I have one in my own garden that has shot up to 10 m (30 ft) in six years and spreads almost as wide. The London Plane is of course deciduous, dropping the deposit of a year's atmospheric pollution with its leaves every autumn. There is a variety, *P. X a. Pyramidalis,* with a tall conical habit, but the normal hybrid takes readily to shaping, and has remarkable powers of healing over the scars of lopped branches in no time. It is often planted in double rows (*allées*) and trained to provide summer shade over paths.

Platanus orientalis Insularis
Cyprus Plane

Platanus X acerifolia
London Plane, bark detail

The Chinar, *P. orientalis*, is the great tree of near-East gardens, seen in perfection in the Vale of Kashmir. Its leaves are more deeply lobed than those of the London Plane, and in the variety *P. o. Insularis*, the Cyprus Plane, the lobes are cut almost to the stem.

In California and Mexico the Sycamore, *P. racemosa*, is more often seen. A slightly smaller tree, with a slimmer trunk often picturesquely twisted in exposed positions, its deeply lobed leaves are thick, with distinctly woolly reverses; the fruit balls appear as many as seven on a single hanging stem. It is the best species for dryish soils and climates.

Platanus is from the Greek *platys* meaning flat. All species strike easily from cuttings.

Platanus racemosa
detail of young foliage

Platanus X *acerifolia*
London Plane

Platanus X *acerifolia*
London Plane

Platanus racemosa
Sycamore, Western Plane

PLUMERIA
(ploo meer' ee ə)

Frangipani or Graveyard Tree
FAMILY: APOCYNACEAE

While it is often found planted about Asiatic Temples and burial grounds, there is nothing really sinister in the *Plumeria's* common name of Graveyard Tree. It has been honoured by the Buddhists for centuries as a symbol of immortality, and in Sri Lanka it is sometimes known as the Tree of Life.

Both of these popular epithets are due to its remarkable ability to continue flowering even when not in the ground, as any gardener who has ever forgotten to plant a large cutting can testify.

Though seen throughout the warm climates of the world, it seems all *Plumerias* were originally natives of Central America and were presumably carried to the East by Spanish traders. There is a great deal of confusion about their nomenclature, but modern study suggests that the myriad colour varieties are all hybrids among five recognized species.

These species are: *P. acuminata* — cream and yellow flowers, pale pointed leaves; *P. alba* —small white and yellow flowers, paddle-shaped leaves; *P. bahamensis* — white flowers, narrow, dark leaves; *P. obtusa* — large, rounded white flowers, dark, evergreen leaves with rounded tips; and *P. rubra* — red flowers, shorter, rounded leaves.

In really tropic areas they grow into quite large trees. I have seen them in the Philippines to 13 m (40 ft) in height and with a trunk as thick as a barrel.

Plumeria acuminata Lutea
Common Yellow Plumeria

Plumerias grow readily from cuttings of any size, thoroughly dried out before planting. They can also be raised from seed, though the colour of the resulting flowers would be anybody's guess.

In tropical climates the richly fragrant flower clusters appear directly from the bare, blunt ends of the branches, and continue to open all year. In more temperate zones, the new foliage appears first and flowering does not begin till late spring.

Plumerias were named in honour of Charles Plumier, a seventeenth century French botanical writer, but in Australia they are more usually called Frangipani.

Plumeria acuminata hybrid
Frangipani

Plumeria obtusa
Singapore White Plumeria

PODOCARPUS
(poh doh kah' pəs)

Fern Pines and Yellowwoods

FAMILY: TAXACEAE

Though fairly widespread in nature, the graceful coniferous genus *Podocarpus* is relatively unknown to the cooler climate gardeners of the northern hemisphere except in China and Japan, where the dark-leafed Buddhist Pines, *P. macrophylla* and *P. nagi* are very much part of the ornamental landscape.

But in the southern hemisphere they really come into their own, for the principal species are natives of South America, New Zealand and South Africa. They are in fact the only conifers found naturally in the southern half of the African continent, and known there as Fern Pines or Yellowwood. *Podocarpus* are related more to the Yews than the Pines, and their fruits, while technically cones, look more like a large berry sitting on a fat stalk. The botanical name *Podocarpus* in fact means footed-stalk.

In South Africa several species are among the most important timber trees. These are: *P. elongatus*, the African Yellowwood, a 25 m (80 ft) tree with fine 5 cm (2 in) needle leaves and fruits on red stalks; *P. falcatus*, the Oteniqua Yellowwood, a large tree that may reach 50 m (160 ft) and has thin, shedding bark. Its leaves are as little as 2 mm (^{1}/$_{12}$ in) wide and the fruits bluish-green or yellow. Finally, *P. latifolius*, a 30 m (100 ft) tree with broader leaves, 0.5 cm (¼ in) wide. Its fruits are also blue-green.

Podocarpus macrophyllus Maki
Buddhist Pine

New Zealand species are rarely seen outside that country, but are among the most striking. They include the Totara, *P. totara*, a 30 m (100 ft) giant with a tall, straight trunk and very small, spiny leaves. The fruit is green on a red stalk. The red timber is superbly figured and greatly in demand for all types of cabinet work.

None of the genus is really frost hardy; all of them can be grown from seeds or summer cuttings, and they are most attractive trees in the temperate garden, having generally a wide-branched, spreading shape.

Podocarpus falcatus
detail of foliage, fruit

Podocarpus macrophyllus Angustifolia
Kusamaki

173

POPULUS
(pop′ yoo ləs)

Poplars, Aspens, Cottonwoods
FAMILY: SALICACEAE

I doubt if it had occurred to me before I began serious research for this book, separating the old gardener's fancy from the cold botanical fact, just how closely the Poplars were related to the Willows (see *Salix*).

They are both included in the family Salicaceae to be sure, but one's thinking is so clouded by the appearance of the tall, spire-like Lombardy Poplar (*P. nigra Italica*), that any family similarity had never struck home. And yet the Lombardy Poplar (a hybrid cultivar) is the most untypical of all Poplars, resembling only the upright Humboldt Willow (*Salix humboldtii*) among the whole Willow family.

Like Willows, the Poplars are waterside plants, sharing a terrible thirst and a predilection for the banks of streams and low, waterlogged ground on which they grow like rockets, producing a light, fragrant timber quicker than any other genus of tree. They are native to all continents of the northern hemisphere, where they are generally found in cool, temperate areas.

Populus trichocarpa
Black Cottonwood

The Willow relationship appears again in this light timber, in the often colourful catkins of spring blossom produced at the leaf axils and in the resinous nature of budsheaths. The fertilized catkins of many species produce a mass of seeds tangled in cottony thread. American species are popularly known as Cottonwood from this characteristic.

Populus nigra Italica
Lombardy Poplar

Populus alba
White Poplar

174

Populus X *Canadensis*
Golden Poplar

POSOQUERIA
(pos oh kweə' reè ə)

The Needle-Flower Tree

FAMILY: RUBIACEAE

Rivalling the perfume of the Frangipani in gardens of warm climates is the exotic Needle-Flower Tree, *Posoqueria latifolia,* whose white blossoms open throughout the spring season. Related to the *Gardenia* it is native to Brazil and reaches tree size only in hot climates.

It is decorative in any place you find it, with brilliantly glossy 20 cm (8 in) evergreen leaves putting on a show at all times.

The flowers are really extraordinary: long 15 cm (6 in) tubes tipped with pointed buds that spring open as dainty white reflexed flowers, sometimes with projecting anthers. These appear in densely-crowded clusters at branch tips, and continue to open for months.

The trees do not bear much fruit, since fertilization of the long flowers presents a difficulty to most insects, but when the flowers are fertilized, yellow plum-sized fruits occasionally appear. These are edible, but rarely encourage you to try them a second time.

Posoqueria is normally propagated from cuttings, and grows rapidly in the deep rich soil it likes. It is hardy down to about 3°C (27°F).

Posoqueria is an approximation of its native name in the Guianas.

Species from all continents grow easily from cuttings, and rapidly form dense thickets from root suckers. For garden use, they are normally grafted on non-suckering stock, and are of great value in landscaping for the brilliant yellow colouring of their autumn foliage.

Populus is the old Roman name of the trees, which have been in cultivation for several thousand years.

Populus deltoides
Cottonwood, catkins

Posoqueria latifolia
Needle-Flower Tree

PRUNUS
(proo' nəs)

The Peaches, Plums and Cherries

FAMILY: ROSACEAE

'Roses by many other names' might be the simplest way to describe the hundreds of *Prunus* species in a single sentence. For they are members of the Rose family, and they do all bear flowers with a passing resemblance to Roses. But beyond that it takes a really creative imagination to spot the relationship between say, a flowering Cherry (*P. serrulata*) and an evergreen Cherry Laurel (*P. laurocerasus*).

For horticultural purposes, one really has to make a totally artificial division of this very large genus — over 200 species and probably upwards of 2000 cultivars — all of them from the northern hemisphere.

That division is between the species grown for the delight of the appetite, and the others grown purely for eye appeal. To take them in that order, the popular edible species include: the Apricot, *Prunus armeniaca*; the Cherry, *P. cerasus*; the Plum, *P. domestica*; the Almond, *P. dulcis*; the Peach, *P. persica*, together with a host of minor species with local appetite appeal; the American Red Plum, *P. americana*; the Gean, *P. avium*; the Cherry Plum, *P. cerasifera*; the Goose Plum, *P. hortulana*; the Greengages

and Damsons, *P. institia*; the St Lucie Cherry, *P. mahaleb*; the Japanese Plum, *P. salicina*; the Sloe, *P. spinosa*; the Nanking Cherry, *P. tomentosa*; and the Almond Cherry, *P. triloba*.

Most of these are to one degree or another bushy trees, rarely above 5 m (15 ft). They need a deal of pruning or shaping to produce a satisfactory fruit crop. They are all deciduous, with attractive, single Rose-type flowers in early spring, either pale pink or white. These appear generally on small spur-like branchlets designed to take the weight of the fruit. All fruiting species may be grown from their seeds or stones, but are generally propagated by bud grafting to be certain of variety and quality.

By far the most popular group of ornamentals are the Japanese Flowering Cherries, mostly hybrids of *P. serrulata* with a number of other oriental species. These have flowers both single and double, in a wide range of colours from pure white to deep red, sometimes with variegation. Often the individual flowers are borne on long, hanging stems. In their home country of Japan, their cultivation is a way of life, and springtime Cherry Blossom viewing an annual event to which everyone looks forward.

Another popular species is the Weeping Cherry, *P. subhirtella Pendula*, whose delightful miniature blossoms may appear in autumn as well as spring. This is a great favourite, together with the Taiwan Cherry, *P. campanulata*, whose

Prunus amygdalo-persica
Flowering Peaches

Prunus blireiana
Flowering Cherry Plum

Prunus campanulata
Taiwan or Formosa Cherry

delicate trumpet-shaped red blossom is among the first to open in spring.

In Western gardens, the spring display is provided more by a range of hybrid flowering peaches, including cultivars of *P. amygdalus,* the Flowering Almond, *P. persica,* the peach, and *P. glandulosa,* the dwarf Flowering Almond Cherry.

Finally, there are a number of less common evergreen species grown as much for the beauty of their foliage as for their generally white blossom. They are sometimes pruned as hedges, or certain low-growing species are used as ground covers. The evergreen types include the Californian *P. ilicifolia;* the Versailles or Cherry Laurel, *P. laurocerasus,* and the Portugal Laurel, *P. lusitanica,* all of which are small growing.

Prunus serrulata 'Shirotae'
Mount Fuji Cherry

Prunus domestica
Plum

Prunus cerasus
Cherry

Prunus serrulata 'Shimidsu Sakura'
Double Flowering Cherry

Prunus subhirtella Pendula
Weeping Cherry

Prunus laurocerasus
Cherry Laurel

Prunus maackii
Manchurian Cherry

Prunus persica
Peach var. 'White Shanghai'

Prunus armeniaca
Apricot

PSIDIUM
(sid' ee əm)

The Guavas

FAMILY: MYRTACEAE

Though native only to the warmer parts of Central and South America, the many Guava species have spread around the globe to become perhaps the most widely grown of tropical fruits outside the Banana and Mango. The secret of their popularity lies, perhaps, in their ease of growth, for they are no trouble to propagate from cuttings, and naturalize readily once established.

Over a hundred separate species have been listed, though only three are commonly seen away from the Americas. These are: *P. cattleianum*, the Purple or Cherry Guava, a slim, leggy tree of perhaps 8 m (25 ft) with smooth, reddish bark. Evergreen, it bears dark, leathery leaves very much like those of the related Tristania (see *Tristania*). The flowers are white, solitary, rather like Eucalyptus blossoms. The summer fruits are purple-red and cherry sized. They are eaten raw, or more often made into jams and jellies.

Less popular is the closely related Yellow Strawberry Guava, *P. cattleianum* var. *littorale* which is more heavily branched and bears larger orange-yellow fruits.

This tree should not be mistaken however for the universally grown *P. guajava*, the common Apple Guava or Yellow Guava. This is a larger, heavier tree, with pink-fleshed yellow-skinned fruits the size of a small peach. They are the source of commercial Guava juice.

Guava is the native South American name. The botanical *Psidium* is from the old Greek word for Pomegranate, *psidion*.

Psidium cattleianum
Cherry Guava

Psidium guajava
Apple Guava, fruit

Psidium cattleianum
Cherry Guava, fruit

179

PTEROCARPUS
(te roh kah' pəs)

The Burmese Rosewood

FAMILY: LEGUMINOSAE

Planted more for shade than show, the Padauk or Burmese Rosewood is a great, handsome, spreading tree of 25 m (80 ft) and more. Its natural range begins in India and Burma, fanning out through southern China to the Malay Archipelago. It is also found in the Philippines, where it is called Narra, and has been officially declared the national tree of the republic.

In all of those countries, its timber is regarded as the finest furnishing wood of all, and appreciated for both its grain and its rose-like fragrance. Cabinet-makers can also take advantage of its wide variation in colouring, from red to palest pink, and through a salmon shade to yellow.

A member of the mighty pea family, Leguminosae, it has deciduous compound leaves of five to nine leaflets, and about 10 cm (4 in) long. The small yellow spring flowers appear in panicles from the leaf axils and are followed by a rather stunning crop of large seeds. These are about the size of a drink coaster and surrounded by a wavy-edged circular wing. These seeds led to its botanical name *Pterocarpus indicus,* the Indian Wing-fruit.

Pterocarya fraxinifolia
detail of flowers and foliage

The genus is found exclusively in Asia — ten species from the Caucasus to China, all of them big growers to 30 m (100 ft) and more. They are particularly beautiful near water, or on damp ground, where their appearance is overpoweringly lush and tropical. Yet they are deciduous and perfectly suited to a wide range of temperate climates.

Pterocarpus indicus
Burmese Rosewood, Narra

PTEROCARYA
(te roh ceər' yə)

The Wingnuts

FAMILY: JUGLANDACEAE

The dangling golden catkins of *Pterocarya* put one more in mind of a Wistaria than a Walnut, yet they are closely related to the latter.

Pterocarya fraxinifolia
Caucasian Wingnut

Pterocarya fraxinifolia, the Caucasian Wingnut, is the only species seen much outside its native range, and it seems a pity one usually has to visit botanic gardens of Europe and North America to see it.

PTEROSPERMUM
(te roh sperm' əm)

The Bayur Tree

FAMILY: BYTTNERIACEAE

Pterospermum acerifolium
Bayur Tree

Any account of the beautiful Bayur tree is bound to be a pretty hairy story. For that would be its most recognizable feature. Almost every part of the tree is covered with brown, rusty fuzz: flowers, fruit, leaf stems and even the young branches.

It is among the world's most spectacularly lush tropical trees, native to a wide area from India to Indonesia, yet flowering just as well (even if it does not set seed) in a warm temperate climate. The Bayur (its botanical name is *Pterospermum*, meaning winged seeds) is as important a timber tree as the Teak (see *Tectona*), but known to Westerners solely as an ornamental. It grows to 35 m (100 ft) in the wild, but mercifully much smaller in the garden, particularly away from the tropics. Anywhere, though, its attractive bright green leaves are the size and shape of a rather wilted dinner plate, and on their reverses there's that hair again! In summer the flower buds develop both at leaf axils and in small terminal clusters. They too are large, like a furry corona cigar, and you're most unlikely to see one opening, for that happens at night. But the morning after, the cigar is seen to have split into five richly-cream reflexed petals, and in the centre of this is revealed a 15 cm (6 in) fountain of white, fragrant stamens.

The flowers are very long lasting, on the tree or off, and they will open indoors if you enjoy watching that sort of thing.

Again, away from the tropics, propagation is by means of stem cuttings, struck over heat, as the seeds will not develop.

PYRUS
(pai' rəs)

The Pears

FAMILY: ROSACEAE

We all believe blind Freddie could tell the difference between an apple and a pear and we would probably all be wrong. For until recent times many trees we now know as Quince, Medlar and Crabapple were classed, with many others, as Pears, or botanically speaking as *Pyrus* species, *Pyrus* being the old Roman name. And those taxonomists who did the classifying were not blind.

Pears, for instance, are not necessarily 'pear-shaped'. Sometimes they are round, sometimes flatter than round, like a tomato. Although their white flowers look similar to those of the Apples they have a different structure and the stalks of Pear fruits are thicker than apple stalks, and do not join onto the fruit in a hollow. They are sort-of streamlined in.

Pears grow wild in Europe, Asia and Africa, but not in America. The flavour of most Pear species is distinctive, and they have a woody, granular texture when eaten, unless extremely ripe. The leaves of some species are rounder and shinier than those of an apple, more like a Poplar's perhaps. But not all species. The foliage

Pyrus pashia
summer fruit and foliage

181

Pyrus communis
Wild Pear

Pyrus pashia
Indian Pear, spring

of *P. salicifolia*, the lovely Willow-leaf Pear from Asia Minor, is long, greyish and covered all over with silver-silky hair.

The Indian Pear, *P. pashia*, has slightly toothed dark leaves and speckled round fruit.

The European Wild Pear, *P. communis*, is the ancestor of all the Pears we grow for the table. It has varieties with fruits of many colours.

Pears are propagated from seed, or by grafting of cultivated varieties on wild pear stock. They are frost hardy, and do best in a fully sunny position in well-drained soil. They grow quite large, albeit slowly. I have seen them 20 m (60 ft) and more in old Czechoslovakian gardens.

Pyrus hybrid
Bartlett Pear

Pyrus spp.
Pear blossom

QUERCUS
(kwur' cəs)

The Oaks

FAMILY: FAGACEAE

I suppose the first tree I ever planted was an Oak — well, an acorn anyway. My grandfather used to tell me that 'tall oaks from little acorns grow,' and I wanted to prove the unbelievable for myself. Miraculously, in spite of being dug up a number of times to check for progress, it did sprout, it did grow; and for all I know it is still growing, for Oaks like to take their time.

The Oak I planted was an English Oak, *Quercus robur*, often seen as a street tree in Melbourne, where I spent much of my childhood, and very popular with the squirrels which have migrated to that city.

In popular conversation, Oaks are often used as yardsticks of comparison to a number of desirable qualities like strength, patience, perseverance and age, and all with good reason. But what you think of when you say 'Oak' depends very much on where you live, for there are some 450 species of them in nature.

Some are deciduous, some evergreen; some tall, some spreading; some almost shrubby, others among the largest of trees. Most have the broad, rippled, many-lobed leaves like the English species; others are dark and shiny as holly, or slim and flimsy as a willow.

But what they all have in common is acorns. The acorn, of course, is a large seed or nut set in a cup called an *involucre*. Some are long and pointed, some flattened and squat; some have hairy cups and some are smooth, but they are all acorns.

Quercus suber
Corn Oak, bark

Quercus palustris
Pin Oak, as street trees

Quercus borealis, syn. *Q. rubra*
Red Oak, acorns

Quercus robur
English Oak

183

Quercus acutissima
Bristle-tipped Oak

Quercus palustris
autumn foliage

Oaks in general prefer deep, mellow, woodsy soil, and the leaves of deciduous species break down into the most wonderful humus of all for potting, and for feeding acid-loving plants.

The timber of many Oak species has been used in ship building for thousands of years, and is noted for its resistance to water and most pests that destroy wood. From the sixteenth to the nineteenth century, entire forests of England, France and Spain were denuded of old trees in the race for European naval supremacy.

Before the introduction of exotic tropical cabinet woods such as Mahogany, Oakwood was greatly used for long-lasting country furniture. These pieces are today much in demand for their beautiful grain with satiny streaks.

The botanical name *Quercus* has been used for the Oaks since Roman times, and they are classified in the same botanical family as the Beech trees, Fagaceae.

Quercus borealis
autumn foliage

Quercus michauxii
Water Chestnut

184

Quercus dentata 'Aurea'
Golden Daimyo Oak

Quercus velutina
Black Oak, Quercitron

Quercus salicina
Willow Oak, foliage

Quercus agrifolia
Coast Live Oak

Quercus myrsinaefolia
acorns and evergreen foliage

Quercus ilex
Holm Oak

RAVENALA
(rav ə nah′ lə)

The Traveller's Tree
FAMILY: MUSACEAE

Named anagrammatically for a one-time Queen of Madagascar, the remarkable *Ravenala madagascariensis* is widely planted throughout the world's warmer climate areas, and known as the Traveller's Tree.

It is related to the Bananas and Strelitzias, but unlike either of them, sends up an unbranched, woody trunk to 10 m (30 ft) and more. This is crowned with a great fan-shaped structure of overlapping stems, each of which develops into a 3 m (10 ft) ragged leaf, very much like those of a Banana.

Its relationship to the Strelitzia is more easily spotted in the white flowers which appear from large, boat-shaped bracts among the leaf stems. These are very much like those of the giant *Strelitzia nicolai*.

Both the flower bracts and the bases of the leaf-stems hold a great deal of fresh water in tropical areas, and have been used for centuries as an emergency water source by travellers, hence the name, Traveller's Tree. The sap is also nutritious, and rich in sugar.

In its native country, the trunks of *Ravenala* are used in house construction, the great leaves as roofing.

Ravenala is normally propagated from seed.

Ravenala madagascariensis
Traveller's Tree

RHODOLEIA
(roh doh lae′ ə)

The Silk Rose or Champara
FAMILY: HAMAMELIDACEAE

Rhodoleia championii
Silk Rose, Champara

Not really common anywhere, even in its native Hong Kong, the Silk Rose, *Rhodoleia championii* was first discovered only in 1849. But it has been distributed to all continents by garden connoisseurs and is worth seeking out as a medium-sized specimen tree for sheltered gardens. Given the protection of other, larger trees, it will reach 10 m (30 ft) and flower heavily when quite young.

The dark, leathery, oblong leaves are perfectly smooth above, greyish beneath, and crowd at the end of branchlets like those of *Tristania* (which see). The spring flowers appear in heads of five to ten, from leaf axils near the branch tips, each a wide, hanging bell of purest carmine, about 4 cm (1½ in) in diameter.

Each *Rhodoleia* blossom is actually a group of five flowers, surrounded by a common row of petals.

Rhodoleia (from the Greek *Rhodon* meaning Rose and *leios* meaning smooth) enjoys humidity, part sun and deep acid soil.

It is propagated from ripened cuttings.

RHUS
(roos')

The Sumach and Toxicodendron
FAMILY: ANACARDIACEAE

Poison Elder, Poison Ivy and Poison Oak are all common names for various species of *Rhus*, a genus which at one time went under the name of *Toxicodendron*, meaning Poison Tree.

If you detect a certain repetitive quality in those names it is with good reason, for most of the species, which number about 150, have poisonous properties which can be most unpleasant to some people — I emphasize only *some* people.

The botanical name *Rhus* which is currently adopted, was the original Greek name for European members of the genus. Most commonly seen is the lovely, but sparsely branched *Rhus succedaneus* or Wax Tree, from China and Japan. This grows rapidly to 10 m (30 ft) in a cool to warm temperate climate, producing leaflets, sometimes with a purplish hue when young, and colouring to an incredibly rich red in autumn. The yellowish flowers hang in panicles from the leaf-axils, and are followed by large hanging clusters of cherry-sized fruits. These are not edible, but are a useful source of wax.

The Stag's Horn Sumach, *R. typhina* CV *Laciniata*, from the eastern USA, is smaller, rarely above 7 m (20 ft), and has magnificently toothed foliage of a vivid lime green. The sap of *R. verniciflua*, the Lacquer Tree, from China and Japan is the base of all oriental lacquer work. Like the related Wax Tree, its yellow fruit is the source of a valuable wax used in candle making.

Propagation of *Rhus* species is no problem, as they seem to self seed all over the place, but cuttings can be taken and struck with care.

Their riotous display of autumn leaf colour is best in a sheltered sunny position.

Rhus succedaneus
Toxicodendron, Wax Tree

ROBINIA
(roh bin' ee ə)

The Black Locust
FAMILY: LEGUMINOSAE

As American as Apple Pie, all twenty species of the genus *Robinia* occur naturally within the mainland of the United States, though they have long since spread over the border in both directions, even over surrounding oceans to become naturalized in Australia, southern Europe and many other places.

They are generally thorny members of the pea family, Leguminosae, and like so many of their relatives bear fragrant pea-type flowers, and dangling pea-type pods. It was the pods in fact, that led to the popular name of Black Locust, as early colonists found they resembled those of the related Locust Tree of southern Europe (see *Ceratonia*). The botanical name *Robinia* celebrates the name of Jean Robin, a royal herbalist who first grew the trees in Paris about 1600.

The commonly seen and frequently naturalized species is *R. pseudacacia*, from central North America. It is normally a tall tree to 25 m (80 ft) in height with dark gnarled trunk and frequently picturesque branches. Its deciduous leaves are pinnate.

For garden usage, many attractive cultivars have been developed from it, including: CV *Fastigiata*, with a tall, poplar-like shape; CV *Tor-*

Rhus typhina CV *Laciniata*
Stag's Horn Sumach

187

Robinia pseudacacia
spring flowers and foliage

tuosa whose branches are layered and twisted like a Japanese fantasy; CV *Inermis*, which blessedly has no spines, but alas, precious few flowers either; and the gorgeous variety CV *Frisia*, which has scarlet spines and foliage of an almost fluorescent golden green.

Foliage of all *Robinia* species turns a pale gold before leaf fall. They are easily propagated from seed or suckers, but, of course, the fancy varieties must be grafted.

Several less commonly seen species produce flowers in various shades of pink. They too have crossed with *R. pseudacacia* to produce rose-flowered cultivars.

Robinia pseudacacia
Black Locust

Robinia pseudacacia
spring flowers and foliage

ROYSTONEA
(roi stoh′ nə)

The Royal Palms

FAMILY: PALMAE

Quaintly and patriotically named for General Roy Stone, a popular American army personality of the nineteenth century; the Royal Palms are native to the Caribbean area.

Superb specimens for the warm-climate garden, they are often seen planted in rows along the driveways of tropical administrative buildings, where their pale, rather bulging trunks lend a stately, formal effect.

There are about a dozen species, all remarkably salt-resistant and preferring rich soil and a well-drained but moist position.

Roystonea regia, the Cuban Royal Palm, is most commonly planted, and reaches about 25 m (80 ft) in the tropics, its whitish trunk rather swollen in the middle. It produces brilliant green 3 m (10 ft) fronds. The flowers develop in panicles up to a metre in length (3 ft), and have distinctive violet stamens. The fruits are similarly coloured.

The gigantic Caribbee Royal Palm, *R. oleracea*, may tower 40 m (130 ft) in the air and produce fronds twice the length of the Cuban species. Its flowers are colourless, the fruits black, and it is found naturally in Barbados and Trinidad, among other islands.

Roystoneas are propagated from seed.

Roystonea regia
Cuban Royal Palm

SALIX
(sal' iks)

The Willows and Osiers

FAMILY: SALICACEAE

Think of water, think of willows! What country stream would be the same without their gnarled old trunks to frame its rippling chatter? Try to picture the edge of any lake without waterbirds playing hide-and-seek among the fine screens of weeping greenery.

The willow is so much part of our landscapes, who'd believe it has only shared them since the eighteenth century?

The Weeping Willow, *Salix babylonica*, was so named because of a romantic belief that it was the tree under which the Jews wept by the waters of Babylon. But it was no more seen there than by the waters of Europe, of America, of Africa, of Australia. It is strictly Chinese in origin, gradually moving westward with the caravans to countries of the Middle East, from where it was carried to Europe and the rest of the world.

But like the others of its genus, it is a great survivor. Just stick a twig or branch of any willow species in damp soil, or even lay it in a pool of water, and you've a new tree in a matter of weeks. That, we believe, is how they spread about the world, from willow whips discarded by caravan drivers, woven willow baskets left along the way, broken branches carried downstream by a storm.

The world is, in fact, full of Willow species (over 250 of them, mostly in the cooler northern hemisphere) and each one shares the love of water. They are invaluable for preventing erosion of river banks, or soaking up the brackish moisture of low meadows. They are also adept at seeking out and filling water pipes and blocking drains (and do not have very civilized manners in the home garden).

Species from almost any part of the world hybridize indiscriminately, and it is probable that most of the ones we see and love are natural hybrids of some sort. Among them are:
S. alba, the White Willow of Europe and northern Asia. This is a most valuable plant, appearing in one place as a thickly branched shrub, in another as a 25 m (80 ft) tree with massive trunk. The long slim leaves have silver reverses.

Salix babylonica
Weeping Willow

Salix alba
White Willow

Salix humboldtii
Humboldt Willow

Salix discolor
Pussy Willow

S. babylonica, the Weeping Willow. A wide-crowned tree up to 15 m (50 ft), with markedly weeping branches. Will grow in hot, dry climates by permanent water.

S. X chrysocoma, the Golden Willow. A hybrid between *alba* and *babylonica* with golden stems and leaves.

S. fragilis, the Crack Willow. A giant European tree of up to 30 m (100 ft), much cultivated for its timber. Similar leaves to the Weeping Willow, but without the weeping habit.

S. discolor, the Pussy Willow. A thirsty plant with voracious roots, but otherwise ideal for growing in damp, low-lying ground. Its branches point upward, the leaves are oval, and it is often grown for the beauty of its silver, furry catkins.

S. humboldtii, the Humboldt Willow from Chile. A tall, poplar-like tree with even narrower leaves than the Weeping Willow. Grows to 10 m (30 ft).

S. matsudana CV *Tortuosa*, the Corkscrew Willow. Also from China, but suited to positions with less water. Every part of the tree is twisted corkscrew fashion, from the trunk to the tips of the finest twigs. Its leaves are like those of the Weeping Willow, but it has a generally upright habit.

Willows are all deciduous, and bear their flowers in the form of catkins, sometimes long and drooping, sometimes short and plump, and usually with the male and female flowers on separate trees.

Many of the larger Willows are grown commercially as a timber crop, for they reach felling size very quickly. The wood is generally whitish, tough and brittle.

Salix matsudana CV *Tortuosa*
Corkscrew Willow

190

SAMANEA
(sa man' e ə)

The Monkeypod or Rain Tree

FAMILY: LEGUMINOSAE

Should you ever be caught in a tropical downpour, do *not* head for shelter under the nearest Monkeypod Tree. These genial South American giants fold their leaves at the first kiss of the raindrops, and let it all fall through!

It is perhaps this quality more than any other that has endeared them to warm-climate gardeners, for their spreading branches shade exotic orchids and other tropical epiphytes without robbing them of precious rainwater. The fern-like foliage of fine bipinnate leaves is scantily borne just at the tips of branches, giving a light, dappled shade at all times. The leaves close up in the evening to let the dew fall, and drop themselves in the winter to let all the short-day sunlight through.

A popular name in many areas is Rain Tree, but botanically it is called *Samanea saman*, from its American Indian name. It may grow to 25 m (80 ft) in height, and almost double that in width, particularly by rivers, or in low-lying, waterlogged ground. It belongs to the same family as the Wattles and Albizzia (see *Acacia, Albizzia*), and produces colourful tufts of blossom all through the late spring and summer. These consist mostly of glowing pink stamens.

Samanea saman
flowers and foliage

The flowers are followed by green and black pods full of sticky pulp and seeds. These make good stock fodder in warm climates, and we presume that monkeys eat them as well. The tough, beautifully figured wood is used in the Philippines, the Pacific and South America for many decorative purposes, particularly the carving of bowls and other ornamental containers.

Monkeypods grow easily from seed, reaching their full height in a very few years.

Samanea saman
Monkeypod, Rain Tree

SAPIUM
(sap' ee əm)

The Chinese Tallow Tree
FAMILY: EUPHORBIACEAE

Rarely more than 8 m (25 ft) in cultivation, the charming Chinese Tallow Tree (*Sapium sebiferum*) is widely cultivated in temperate to tropical areas, and has become naturalized in parts of the United States.

It has a dense, many-branched habit, and in cooler climates the drooping, top-shaped leaves rarely exceed 5 cm (2 in) in length. Petal-less, yellowish flowers appear in terminal spikes during early summer, both male and female together. These are followed by 1 cm (½ in) fruiting capsules which consist of three seeds, each covered with a white vegetable wax. This is used for soap and candle-making in its native Far East, but in Western countries the tree is grown purely as an ornamental — and how ornamental it is!

In marginal warm-temperate areas, where the autumn colour of many other trees cannot be relied on, the Tallow Tree turns a wonderful mixture of red and bronze. Against this flaming background, the white, wax-coated seeds make a brilliant and unusual contrast.

Sapium is propagated easily from seed or cuttings, but should be set out as young as possible, for it is never happy about transplanting at a larger size. It should not be planted in country areas with stock access. As in many other members of the family Euphorbiaceae, all parts of the tree are poisonous.

Sapium was the Latin name of an unrelated European tree grown for its crop of resin. The specific name *sebiferum* means wax-bearing.

Sapium sebiferum
Chinese Tallow Tree

SARACA
(sa rak' ə)

The Asoka or Sorrowless Tree
FAMILY: LEGUMINOSAE

Precisely why the lovely *Saraca* should be known as the Sorrowless Tree, I have been unable to discover, although it may be something to do with the cheerful display it puts on at many times of the year.

Give it a few dry, sunny days, and suddenly it erupts into a fountain of new pinnate leaves which burst from terminal buds. At first these are like a horde of butterflies emerging from their chrysalids, brightly coloured in pink and red, but limp and seemingly without support. Then, as the sap pumps through, they stiffen up and turn green. At other times, particularly the beginning and end of the tropical dry season, these remarkable trees produce a dazzling display of flowers. These are without petals, but a tubular calyx takes their place, opening to give passage to a razzle-dazzle of gold and purple stamens. The flowers are variable in colour, often opening a pale orange, and turning red within a couple of days. They are often followed by richly purple pods.

Though a large tree in its native jungles of South-East Asia, *Saraca indica* usually remains a manageable 7 m (20 ft) in cultivation. It enjoys moist, rich soil and a humid atmosphere, and is really limited to tropical and sub-tropical areas. The colour display is greatly admired in Florida, Hawaii, the Philippines and northern Australia.

In India, *Saraca* is often called Asoka, and is sacred in many religions. Buddha is said to have been born under one.

Sapium sebiferum
fruit and autumn foliage

Saraca is propagated from seeds or air-layers, and the flowers are fragrant at night.

Related *S. declinata* is similar in every respect except that the leaflets have short stems. In *S. indica* they are stemless.

SCHINUS
(shai' nəs)

The Peppercorn and Mastic Trees

FAMILY: ANACARDIACEAE

Wherever the climate is dry and warm (Australia, California, South Africa, the Mediterranean), you'll find the picturesque Peppercorn Tree, *Schinus areira*, known variously as Pepperina, California Pepper Tree, Pirul and Peruvian Mastic. It is a native of Peru's Andean deserts, grows happily in arid, sandy soil of any temperate area, and quickly becomes the most decorative of shade trees. It is evergreen, and very variable in height according to the availability of water; anywhere from 7 to 17 m (20 to 50 ft) is within its range. The leaves are bluish-green and compound, each carrying up to thirty stemless leaflets, and hang from delicate weeping branchlets.

Peppercorn trees produce clusters of tiny yellowish flowers from tips and leaf axils, which are followed (on female trees only) by chains of round, rosy-pink peppercorns. These are not the peppercorns of commerce, but are often ground and mixed with them in blends.

A related and more colourful species is the Christmas Berry or Brazilian Mastic Tree, *S. terebinthifolius*. Much more solid, and a shorter tree altogether, it is quite without the grace of the Peppercorn. The leaflets are coarser and dark green, with up to nine on each leaf; the flowers are white, and borne in upright spikes.

Saraca indica
flowers and foliage

Schinus terebinthifolius
foliage and winter berries

Schinus areira syn. *molle*
detail of fruit and foliage

The berries that follow are larger, and vary from deep pink to a vivid scarlet. All parts of the tree are fragrant with a volatile, spicy oil.

Both species of *Schinus* are propagated from seed and naturalize readily. The botanical name is Greek, but the Greeks used it for a very different tree that had the same spicy odour.

Schinus terebinthifolius
Brazilian Mastic, Christmas Berry

194

Schinus areira
Peppercorn Tree, Pepperina, Pirul

SCHIZOLOBIUM
(shitz ə loh' bee əm)

Bacurubu or Yellow Jacaranda

FAMILY: LEGUMINOSAE

Towering 40 m (130 ft) in the air, like a gigantic tree fern, the beautiful Brazilian Bacurubu is outstanding, even in a country noted for its magnificent trees.

But elsewhere, in sub-tropical gardens of Queensland, Florida, the Philippines and other warm places, the effect is unbelievable, particularly when planted in conjunction with Jacarandas and Erythrinas.

The Bacurubu (botanically *Schizolobium parahybum*) is yet another fragrant member of the pea family. Sparsely branched, and with a smooth grey trunk, it sprouts the largest bipinnate leaves in the world, up to 2 m (6 ft) in length and arranged spirally like elaborate fern fronds. In mid-winter, these droop and fall, just before the branch tips sprout 30 cm (12 in) spikes of vivid yellow blossom.

The flowers are followed by pods, each containing one seed from which the tree is commonly propagated. And this is done for its beauty alone, for the tree has no commercial use at all.

Schizolobium means split lobes, a reference to the finely divided leaf structure.

Schizolobium parahybum
Bacurubu, Yellow Jacaranda

Sciadopitys verticillata
Umbrella Pine

SCIADOPITYS
(skee ə dop' i təs)

The Umbrella Pine

FAMILY: TAXODIACEAE

You can be sure some talented modern designer would have invented *Sciadopitys* if it did not already grow wild in the mountains of Japan.

Unbelievably straight and formal, a perfect cone with needle-like leaves arranged exactly like the spokes of an umbrella, it is not a common tree in cultivation because it just refuses to grow in polluted air. But give it a sheltered, shady spot in deep, acid mountain soil, and you have a thing of beauty, a joy forever.

Just be sure to plant it out when very young (they are propagated from seed) and do not disturb it for a generation or two except for an annual top-dressing with decayed leaves.

Sciadopitys likes water, but not wet feet, and sunlight, but not hot sun, for its surface roots dry out easily.

Given time, it will reach 10 m (30 ft) but may surprise your descendants, for it has been measured at 40 m (130 ft) in the wild in Japan. The name *Sciadopitys* is Greek, from *skias* meaning a parasol, and *pitys* meaning the Fir tree.

It is not a Fir tree, in fact, though it does bear egg-shaped cones which take two years to ripen. Its common name is the Umbrella Pine.

Sciadopitys verticillata
detail of leaf arrangement

SEQUOIA
(see kwoi′ yə)

The California Redwood

FAMILY: TAXODIACEAE

Though there may have been taller trees in Australia in the nineteeth century (see *Eucalyptus*), the tallest trees of today are America's noble Redwoods or *Sequoias*. In misty coastal forests of northern California they huddle protectively together as if seeking safety in numbers, safety from the world of man that has already claimed so many of their fellows.

For the fast-growing California or Coastal Redwood is one of the world's great timber trees, its fragrant trunkwood soft and light yet almost impervious to weather. Naturally a rich, rosy red, it can be used for outside construction and roofing without any finish at all, and will weather gradually to a soft, silvery grey.

Called botanically by the lovely old Indian name *Sequoia*, the Redwood grows easily from seed, or from the shoots that sprout from dormant buds or burls around the base of felled trees.

Individual specimens in California have been measured at over 120 m (400 ft) with a trunk diameter of 8 m (25 ft), but in cultivation they are unlikely to reach a third of this.

Sequoia sempervirens
California or Coastal Redwood

The Redwood's trunk is straight and fissured, the needle-like leaves arranged in flattened layers like the related Swamp Cypress (see *Taxodium*). The cones are oval and woody, about the size of a grape.

Sequoia is not quite so cold-resistant as the closely related *Sequoiadendron*, and because of its habit of growing in dense groves, it is more difficult to cultivate unless it can be given the shelter of other trees, at least in its early stages.

Even young *Sequoias* are inclined to throw suckers from around the trunk. These should be removed as quickly as possible to give the main trunk a chance.

Sequoia sempervirens
detail of trunks in grove

Sequoia sempervirens
foliage and young cones

196

SEQUOIADENDRON
(see kwōi yə den' drən)

The Big Tree
FAMILY: TAXODIACEAE

May the king live forever! The king of trees just has to be majestic *Sequoiadendron*, the Big Tree or Giant Sequoia of California. Immense in size, immense in age, there are individual trees living in California's Sierra Mountains that were several thousand years old when Christ was born, and many of them have been gazetted as national treasures.

Unlike the related *Sequoias* (they were once lumped together in the same genus), they are loners, growing individually among mixed forests of other coniferous trees. As they do not insist on the company of their own kind, they have taken well to culture as single specimens in parks and large gardens of many temperate lands, where they actually seem to grow faster than in the wild.

Sequoiadendron giganteum
detail of cones and foliage

Sequoiadendron giganteum is raised from seed (or grafted cuttings in the case of rare fancy varieties) and grows straight as a die: a perfect, formal pyramid with horizontal, tapered branches and wonderful thick, red bark. The tiny scale-like leaves are arranged spirally on fine terminal twigs, and have a silvery sheen. The flowers are tiny catkins, and the greenish cones, very small for such a large tree, are rarely above the size of a grape.

The Big Tree is of course frost hardy, and very worthwhile planting for its good garden manners and stunning vertical effect. There are good specimens in botanic gardens of several Australian cities, and in parks all over Europe.

Their ultimate height (as measured in California) is somewhat less than that of the *Sequoia*, but the trunk is much thicker and heavily buttressed. The trunk is in effect its main feature, for some famous trees in the wild do not have a single branch below 30 m (100 ft) from the ground.

At one time, there was an attempt to name the tree Washingtonia, after America's first President; but the name had already been given to a Californian Palm tree (*see Washingtonia*). The English, in a burst of post-Napoleonic euphoria counter-suggested that the name of the Hero of Waterloo might be used as *Wellingtonia*. That idea went down in America like a lead balloon!

So *Sequoiadendron* it is and *Sequoiadendron* it will remain.

Sequoiadendron giganteum
Big Tree, Wellingtonia

197

SESBANIA
(ses ban' ee ə)

The Corkwood or Vegetable Humming Bird
FAMILY: LEGUMINOSAE

From Australia's tropical far North all the way through the Malaysian area to India, you'll find an untidy and fast-growing tropical tree often naturalized in dense groves.

Sesbania is its botanical name, but it is more often known by the popular name Corkwood, for its fast growth goes hand-in-hand with a poor, weak constitution and a tendency to frequent splitting and short life.

Though not popular in cultivation due to its inherent weaknesses, it does make an acceptable specimen in warm-climate gardens, at least until more permanent trees can grow sufficiently to take its place.

It is a member of the vast Pea family, Leguminosae, with soft green compound leaves of up to sixty leaflets, and a height rarely exceeding 8 m (25 ft). Throughout the warm months, particularly following a wet spell, remarkably handsome flowers appear at the leaf-axils, from which they hang like feeding birds.

The flowers are followed by long, flat seed pods, and the leaves, flowers and young pods are all edible.

The name *Sesbania* is a close approximation of the tree's name in Arabic.

SOPHORA
(sof' or ə)

The Kowhai and Pagoda Tree
FAMILY: LEGUMINOSAE

Scattered all about the mighty Pacific is a genus of the pea family named *Sophora*. The botanic name is an old Arabian epithet for a tree of similar appearance; but the true *Sophoras* are found only in Japan, Korea, New Zealand, Chile, Hawaii and the south-west of the United States. They are fairly typical pea members, with golden flowers; generally frost hardy and with a capacity for display rivalling the European Laburnums.

First discovered and still the most popular is the Japanese Pagoda Tree (*S. japonica*), a widely used species for tree planting in Europe, Japan and parts of the United States. It is a tall grower, to 27 m (80 ft) in height, but is often kept pruned to a more reasonable size. The deciduous foliage is dense, made up of a number of compound, pinnate leaves with up to seventeen small leaflets each. These are oval and slightly downy beneath. The tiny pea flowers are cream and appear in dense, terminal panicles, frosting the entire tree in late summer. They are followed by masses of 7.5 cm (3 in) green pods from which the tree is propagated. There is a charming variety *S. j. Pendula,* with stiffly weeping branches. This is most effective when grafted on a high standard stock.

Sesbania grandiflora
Corkwood, Vegetable Humming Bird

Sophora japonica var. *Pendula*
Weeping Pagoda Tree

Sophora japonica
autumn seed pods and foliage

In both New Zealand and Chile (similar climatic zones of the southern hemisphere) you'll find the Kowhai, *S. tetraptera*. This is a much smaller tree, rarely above 5 m (15 ft); evergreen when young, but semi-deciduous when mature. It has compound leaves with up to eighty almost round leaflets, borne sparsely on zig-zag branchlets. Many of these leaflets drop in spring, just before the flowers open. These are 7.5 cm (3 in) golden pea blossoms that droop in clusters of four to eight flowers each, from small spurs.

Sophora tetraptera
Kowhai

Kowhai is the tree's Maori name, and it has been selected as New Zealand's national tree.

A similar species, *S. chrysophylla*, the Mamane, is found at high altitudes in the Hawaiian Isles, while the south-west United States has a native species *S. secundiflora* with violet-scented mauve blossom.

All species of *Sophora* can be propagated from seed or cuttings, and do best in a mild-temperate climate.

Sophora japonica
Japanese Pagoda Tree, summer blossom

Sophora secundiflora
Mescal Bean, Frijolito

SORBUS
(sor' bəs)

Rowan, Whitebeam, Mountain Ash

FAMILY: ROSACEAE

Is there no end to the showy, fruit-bearing genera of the Rose family? After reading about the Apples, Apricots, Cherries, Hawthorns, Loquats, Medlars, Peaches, Plums and Quinces you might think that we'd done our dash, but no, there's still one of the most important Rose genera of all. *Sorbus* is the botanical name, but you'll probably recognize one or more of them better under their popular names of Mountain Ash, Rowan, Whitebeam or Service Berry.

They are all from cool temperate regions of the northern hemisphere and grow wild in North America, Europe, and northern Asia; but in the cooler southern hemisphere you'll find them only as treasured garden specimens.

The Rowan or Mountain Ash *(Sorbus aucuparia)* will probably be the most familiar. It is a tree of up to 20 m (65 ft) in forests all over Europe and the Caucasus; a handsome, slim grower with ash-like compound leaves of up to fifteen elongated leaflets. The early spring flowers are white, like Hawthorn. The 1 cm (⅓ in) summer fruits are vivid scarlet and hang in large clusters all over the tree. If the birds leave them alone, they'll still be there right up to the time that autumn turns the whole tree a brilliant golden yellow. The American Mountain Ash, *S. americana,* is very similar, but smaller.

Also from Europe is the Service Tree, *S. domestica,* a heavier, more recognizably tree-shaped plant, reaching 27 m (90 ft) in the wild. Deciduous, its leaves are coarser with up to twenty-one leaflets. The fruits are 3 cm (1¼ in) in diameter, and pale red. In Europe they are sometimes eaten when over-ripe, or brewed into a type of cider.

The Whitebeam, *S. aria,* is European as well, but a totally different type of tree, heavily clothed with single-toothed leaves of a rather long shape. It has clusters of white, cherry-blossom sized flowers, followed by masses of long-stemmed oblong fruits that ripen from green to scarlet. The Whitebeam grows to 17 m (50 ft) and has a particularly showy variety, *S. a. Majestica,* on which the leaves are neatly pleated.

The Swedish Whitebeam, *S. intermedia,* has rounder, double-toothed leaves and smaller red fruits. It is a good tree for an exposed position, and the tough wood is used to manufacture a number of small articles.

S. mougiottii is a smaller, more spectacular tree from the European Alps and the Pyrenees. Its bronzy, toothed leaves are backed with silver grey and the large orange-red fruits are borne in long, hanging clusters.

Among the Asiatic species, *S. pekingensis* is particularly attractive. Its pinnate, compound leaves are a deep purple-crimson on scarlet stems. The flowers are white, the small fruit a vivid scarlet. It grows to about 10 m (30 ft).

All eighty-five *Sorbus* species do best in cooler areas, preferably in a sunny, sheltered position. They are easily propagated from berries and many of them make stunning street trees.

There are many cultivars with coloured leaves, and also a number of variations in berry colour — white, pink, yellow and orange. These are propagated by grafting.

The botanical name *Sorbus* was an old Latin word for the fruit of the Service Berry.

Sorbus aucuparia
Rowan, Mountain Ash

Sorbus intermedia
detail of fruit and foliage

Sorbus intermedia
Swedish Whitebeam

Sorbus aria var. *Majestica*
Largeleaf Whitebeam

Sorbus domestica
Service Tree

Sorbus mougiottii
Alpine Whitebeam

Sorbus pekingensis
Chinese Service tree

201

SPATHODEA

(spa thoh' dee ə)

The African Tulip Tree

FAMILY: BIGNONIACEAE

A native of Uganda is the stunning *Spathodea campanulata*. *Spathodea* means spathe-like, a botanical description of the flowers's enlarged calyx. Its popularity has been proven by adoption as a street or specimen tree right around the warm belt of the world. It is in fact hardy down to –2 °C (28 °F), but a frost can kill it to the ground, particularly when young.

Easy to propagate from seed, *Spathodea* grows to 17 m (50 ft) in the wild. The leaves are large, 50 cm (20 in) long, ruffled and pinnate. The flowers are a vivid orange-scarlet lined with yellow and may be 10 cm (4 in) in diameter. They appear in large racemes at the ends of branches and open a few at a time, the whole display lasting months.

Spathodea goes by many popular names in many lands: Tulip Tree, African Tulip Tree, Flame of the Forest, Fountain Tree and (my own favourite, from Malagasy) Baton du Sorcier —the Sorcerer's Wand, after the old-fashioned magician's wand which used miraculously to produce flags from its innards. In *Spathodea*, the buds, shaped like a finger or small stick, split from end to end, so that the showy, flag-like petals can unfurl.

S. campanulata is seen in southern USA, the Caribbean, eastern Australia and Hong Kong.

A less spectacular species is *S. nilotica*, growing only to about 7 m (20 ft). Its leaves are similar but 40 cm (16 in) long. Flowers are a soft apricot.

Spathodea campanulata
flower buds

Spathodea campanulata
African Tulip Tree, spring blossom

Spathodea nilotica
Nile Tulip Tree

Spathodea campanulata
African Tulip Tree, Sorcerer's Wand

SPONDIAS
(spon' dee əs)

The Pomme Cythère and Mombin

FAMILY: ANACARDIACEAE

Closely related to the Mango (see *Mangifera*), the small genus *Spondias* includes about a dozen fruit-bearing trees from tropical America and the Pacific. The botanical name *Spondias* was chosen because it was Ancient Greek for the Plum which most of their fruits resemble.

They are grown universally in frost-free climates, the most commonly seen being the Hog Plum or Mombin (*S. mombin*) from Central America. This is a heavy-trunked tree of 20 m (60 ft) with compound leaves of up to seventeen pointed leaflets. The yellowish flowers appear in terminal panicles, followed by clusters of orange-yellow fruits the size of a Loquat. These are very juicy and delicious, but somewhat hard to pick due to the tree's great height.

Spondias cytherea
Vi, Otaheite Apple

Spondias cytherea
ripe fruit

Spondias mombin
Mombin, Hog Plum

The Pacific species *S. cytherea* (popularly known as Otaheite Apple, Pomme Cythère or Vi) is also a large tree, but coarser and more sparsely branched. Its bark is distinctively smooth and grey; the deciduous leaves are compound with up to twenty-three elliptical leaflets. The whitish flowers, like those of the Mango, are borne in large terminal panicles and followed by oval orange fruits that take on a purplish tone as they ripen. These are up to 7.5 cm (3 in) long, juicy and with a flavour much like a pineapple. In Tahiti and other Pacific islands, young boys have a great deal of fun knocking them down from the high branches with stones or long pieces of bamboo.

Both species enjoy a sandy soil and are propagated from cuttings.

A related species with purple fruits is *S. borbonica*, found on various islands of the Indian Ocean.

STENOCARPUS
(sten oh kah' pəs)

Wheel of Fire

FAMILY: PROTEACEAE

Australian in origin, the gorgeous Queensland Firewheel Tree seems more appreciated in California, where they have planted it in some stunning avenues.

203

Stenocarpus sinuatus
Firewheel, Wheel of Fire

Stenocarpus sinuatus, meaning narrow fruit with wavy foliage, may reach 30 m (100 ft) in its native Australian forests, but rarely half that in cultivation. It needs protection from frost when young, and grows slowly to a splendid vertical shape, reminiscent of a Lombardy Poplar. But the dark, glossy leaves with sinuate edges and deep lobes may reach 25 cm (10 in) in length.

The flowers appear in long-stalked clusters and often pop right out of the trunk or larger branches. At first green, they develop a unique wheel shape before they turn a glowing red. Finally, each series of flowers (the spokes of the wheel) splits open to reveal the golden stamens, and the whole flower takes on the appearance of a medieval crown. The warmer the climate, the more heavily the flowers are borne, generally around early autumn.

Stenocarpus sinuatus
Firewheel, foliage

Stenocarpus is a member of the family Proteaceae, which includes South Africa's *Proteas, Leucadendrons* and *Leucospermums*. Chile's *Embothrium,* and a very large number of Australian trees including *Buckinghamia, Macadamia* and *Oreocallis.* The last three named trees are dealt with elsewhere in this book, in their alphabetical order.

STERCULIA
(stur koo' lyə)

The Skunk Tree and Java Olive
FAMILY: STERCULIACEAE

Sterculia quadrifida
Scarlet Sterculia

Related to Australia's Kurrajongs and Booyongs, the *Sterculias* are a large tree genus, mostly from warm-climate areas of Asia. At one time the Kurrajongs were included among them, until reclassified as a genus of their own (see *Brachychiton*).

Useless for their timber, which is soft and light, they are planted only for shade and ornament. Most commonly seen is the Java Olive or Indian Almond, *S. foetida,* a large tree of 20 m (65 ft) with large palmate leaves of five or seven lobes. The small orange flowers appear in panicles and have an unpleasant odour; in fact the tree's botanical name is derived from *stercus*, the Latin word for dung. The seeds are sometimes roasted and eaten.

South China's *S. lanceolata* is often seen in Hong Kong and the New Territories where its decorative star-shaped clusters of seed pods are greatly admired as they change from green, through yellow to a brilliant scarlet. It is a small tree, rarely exceeding 6 m (20 ft) with simple oval leaves, rather like those of a Persimmon, and unspectacular green and pink flowers. It needs a sunny position to produce the full colour of its pods.

In Central America, a common species called *S. apetala* is known as the Panama Tree, and gave its name to that small American state. It bears large five-lobed, heart-shaped leaves, small yellowish flowers and again, the seed capsules are divided into five parts, just like *S. lanceolata*.

Sterculias are strictly for the warmer climate, and prefer a sunny, sheltered position with deep soil.

Sterculia foetida
Java Olive

SWIETENIA
(swee ten' ee ə)

The Mahogany

FAMILY: MELIACEAE

Swietenia mahagoni
Spanish Mahogany

In the early eighteenth century, the discovery of a new genus of timber tree in the Caribbean area was to revolutionize English cabinet-making. Although the genus was small, the trees themselves were towering giants of up to 50 m (160 ft) in the forests of Honduras, with heavy trunks of hard straight-grained timber coloured a rich red-brown. Seasoned properly, and cut with the grain, it could be made into furniture with a finish like glowing satin.

The trees were christened *Swietenia*, after a Dutch botanist of the period, but the exotic-sounding native name *mahagoni* was to catch European fancy and after a slight modification to Mahogany became immortalized by such famous designers as Chippendale, Sheraton, and Hepplewhite, who preferred it above all other woods for their finest work.

Today, the trees are planted all over the tropical world, for they propagate quite easily from cuttings.

Two species in particular are sought by the furniture makers of the world. *S. mahagoni*, the

205

West Indies or Spanish Mahogany, is a scaly-barked tree of 25 m (80 ft), found in many parts of the Caribbean from Florida southward. It is planted as both a shade and street tree in many warm-climate areas.

The related Honduras Mahogany, *S. macrophylla*, is the more valuable species in commerce, and requires a fully tropical climate to grow well. It is native to a hot, humid belt right down the Caribbean coast and well into the South American continent. Its timber is slightly easier to work.

The Mahoganies are both referred to as evergreen, but in Australia at least they colour well in autumn and shed almost all their foliage during the dry, tropical winter.

Syncarpia glomulifera
Turpentine

There is only one other tree in the genus, the larger-leafed Peebeen or *S. hillii*, found only on Queensland's Fraser Island.

Syncarpia is grown widely in the southern United States and Hawaii, both as a shade and timber tree.

Swietenia macrophylla
Honduras Mahogany

SYNCARPIA
(sin karp' ee ə)

The Turpentine

FAMILY: MYRTACEAE

Possibly the finest and most useful tree of Australia's east coast is the Turpentine, *Syncarpia glomulifera*, found in abundance in southern New South Wales. Often mistaken for a Eucalypt (to which it is related) the Turpentine sends up a towering trunk as high as 25 m (80 ft). This is particularly sought-after and cut for the valuable straight-grained, heavy pink timber, which is much used in underwater construction. It is completely resistant to toredo and other marine borers due to its impregnation with a turpentine-scented resin.

Syncarpia glomulifera
spring flowers and foliage

SYZYGIUM
(si zig' ee əm)

The Lillypilly, Rose Apple, etc.

FAMILY: MYRTACEAE

A taxonomist's nightmare and a great nuisance to gardeners, these lovely trees have changed names as often as Elizabeth Taylor: *Acmena, Jambosa, Phyllocladyx, Eugenia, Stenocalyx, Myrtus* and now — *Syzygium!*

The *latest* division has all species of Eugenia from the Old World (Africa, Asia, Australia) classed as *Syzygium* for reasons involving the seeds. But they are still labelled Eugenia in most of the world's major botanic gardens and dictionaries of cultivated plants.

There are between four and five hundred species, all with glossy, evergreen foliage, and often brilliantly coloured new leaves. The flowers are almost all creamy-white, a mass of stamens. They are very attractive to bees. In all the principally grown species, the flowers are followed by vividly coloured fruits, often pink, and delicately sweet. They are from warm-temperate to tropical climates, enjoy humidity and are not very resistant to frost, at least when young.

But Syzygium?

I looked it up in my trusty *Funk and Wagnalls* and all that tells me is that a *syzygy* is the point of conjunction of two heavenly bodies. The connection eludes me, but the word is a sure winner for my next game of scrabble.

Syzygium malaccense
Malay Apple

Syzygium jambos
Rose Apple, Jumbu

Syzygium paniculatum
Blue Lillypilly, Brush Cherry

Syzygium luehmannii
Water Myrtle, spring foliage

TABEBUIA
(tab ae boo' yə)

The Trumpet Trees

FAMILY: BIGNONIACEAE

Among the most beautiful of flowering trees for the warmer climate are the *Tabebuias*, all from the tropical Americas and known world-wide under a host of popular names. There are at least seventy-five species in cultivation, bearing the same spectacular trumpet flowers as the popular climbing Bignonias to which they are related.

Many of them are valuable timber trees in their home areas, and all are easily propagated from seed, cuttings or air-layers. They grow rapidly in deep, rich soil of a tropical climate, and flower while quite young.

All are showy, some quite spectacular. Among the best are:

T. argentea, the Silver Trumpet Tree from Argentina. This grows to 7 m (25 ft), has silver-grey bark, grey-green pinnate leaves covered with silver scales, and in stunning contrast, vivid chrome yellow trumpet flowers in terminal panicles. Grey fruits follow.

T. chrysantha, the Golden Trumpet Tree from Venezuela, is smaller, only 5 m (15 ft), and deciduous. Its vivid yellow blossom opens irregularly over a long period, beginning in winter.

T. pentaphylla, known variously as the Rosy Trumpet Tree, Pink Poui, Roblé Blanco and White Cedar, bears handsome, darkish pinnate leaves and rosy trumpet flowers in profusion at many times of the year.

The botanical classification *Tabebuia* is an original Indian name for these wonderful trees.

Tabebuia argentea
Silver Trumpet Tree

Tabebuia chrysantha
Golden Trumpet Tree

Tabebuia pentaphylla
Roblé Blanco, Rosy Trumpet Tree

TAMARINDUS
(tam ar in' dəs)

The Tamarind

FAMILY: LEGUMINOSAE

'Ripe Dates from India' would be a reasonable translation of this useful tree's botanical name, which is borrowed from the Arabic *tamr-i-hind*. It would also be a reasonable description of the delicious, sticky pulp for which the tree is grown.

Tamarindus indicus
detail of ripe fruit

Tamarindus indicus is the only species of the genus, and a member of the pea family Leguminosae. It is a slow-growing tree for the hot climate, whether wet or dry. Frequently seen in villages all over the tropics as a shade tree, it may reach 25 m (80 ft) and spread its branches nearly as wide. The evergreen, feathery foliage is pinnate, with from twenty to forty short, bright-green leaflets. The small red and yellow pea flowers are three-petalled and not very showy, but the long, strap-shaped pods are the tree's great feature.

They contain up to ten large seeds embedded in a thick, sticky pulp, rich in sugar and tartaric acid. The pulp is boiled and strained to make a delicious syrup used in all sorts of tropical drinks and curries. The dried pulp is sold at most Asian food stores.

TAXODIUM
(taks oh' dee əm)

The Bald Cypress, Swamp Cypress

FAMILY: TAXODIACEAE

Who can be unfamiliar with the North American Bald Cypress? For twenty years, no movie program was complete without a newsreel of water-skiing among the towering giants of Florida's Cypress Gardens. Even today, scarcely a month goes by on television without some mystery set among these ghostly conifers of the American swamps, their spreading branches festooned with eerie Spanish Moss.

Their botanical name is *Taxodium*, meaning 'like a Yew' (see *Taxus*), and they do have similarly shaped leaves. But there the resemblance ends. *Taxodiums* are found only in North America. They are water-loving trees, found beside, or actually *in* water, where they develop buttresses around the trunk, and curious conical projections called 'knees' which are raised above water level from outlying roots and enable the trees to breathe. Again, *Taxodiums* are deciduous, which Yews are not, and develop great, spreading branches. Flowers are in the form of catkins, followed by small, scaly cones, 2.5 cm (1 in) long. Bald Cypress foliage is a delicious, fresh green throughout the warm weather, and the timber is much used for its water-resistant properties. It is also resistant to termites, because of a repellent oil content.

While they prefer marshy sites, *Taxodiums* will grow happily enough in a deep garden soil. They are propagated from seed.

There are two species only:
T. distichum, the Bald Cypress, native to the south-east United States.
T. mucronatum, the Montezuma Cypress, from Mexico's Pacific coast.

Tamarindus indicus
Tamarind

Taxodium distichum
detail of trunk buttresses and 'knees'

Taxodium distichum
Bald Cypress

TAXUS
(tak′ səs)

The Yew

FAMILY: TAXACEAE

One of the oldest trees in cultivation, and certainly one of the longest-lived, the Yew or *Taxus* is that anomaly, a conifer without cones.

To see a really big one, you'd have to visit old gardens or churchyards of the northern hemisphere, for they are so slow-growing that south of the equator, they just haven't had time to push much beyond shrub size. But take my word for it, they do grow big. One famous specimen in the Scottish Highlands measured over 17 m (50 ft) in circumference!

Yews have been around so long that the Romans borrowed their botanical name *Taxus* from the Ancient Greek *taxos*. There are perhaps half a dozen species of them scattered about cooler areas of the northern hemisphere on all four continents. So greatly do they resemble each other that it has seriously been suggested that they are all the same species, modified only by local conditions. Anyway, one chooses a Yew for its habit or coloration, rather than its species.

Taxodium distichum
summer cones and foliage

Taxus baccata CV 'Pendula'
Weeping Yew

They are evergreen, with dark, narrow leaves modified almost to needle shape, and arranged spirally around the branchlets. The flowers appear in leaf-axils, male on one tree, female on another. The tiny male flowers are borne in clusters, and would not be noticeable except for the incredible amount of pollen they produce, scattering it far around. The female flower is a tiny green globule, which, when fertilized, expands into the fruit. This in itself is most eyecatching, a single green seed only partly covered by a succulent scarlet sheath or *aril*. The aril is the only part of the tree's structure that is not poisonous.

Only three cultivated *varieties* are much grown, all are varieties of the English or Irish Yew, *T. baccata*. These are:

CV *'Aurea'* with golden leaves;
CV *'Fastigiata'* with a tall, cypress-like habit;
CV *'Pendula'*, with long, weeping branches.

The original species *T. baccata* is a generally untidy-looking tree, somewhat pyramidal in youth, but later developing a spreading, horizontal crown, much like California's Monterey Cypress.

The hard wood has been used at various times for furniture-making, and of course for the famous English long-bows of medieval times. Propagate from ripe seed in spring, or from cuttings.

Taxus baccata
Irish Yew

Taxus baccata
foliage and fruit, female tree

TECTONA
(tek toh' nə)

The Teak

FAMILY: VERBENACEAE

The towering Teak trees of South-East Asia shared their days of glory with the mighty windjammers in whose construction they played so great a part. The trunks, straight as a die to 50 m (160 ft), were carved into masts that could support the fastest head of sail. Aged and sawn into planking they became decks for the finest ships afloat, and later, backing for the iron plates that clad their hulls.

Well, the days of sail have passed, and so have the largest of the Teak trees. What's left is now among the most expensive timber in the world, used for fine quality furniture and buildings that may last a thousand years.

It may seem strange to link this mighty tree with the humble flowering Verbena of cottage gardens, but they are closely related members of the same botanical family, Verbenaceae.

Tectona grandis, as the Teak is called by botanists, comes from *tekka*, the tree's old name in southern India; and it grows wild in open monsoonal forests all over southern Asia. The drooping leaves are deciduous, furry, and up to 1 m (3 ft) long and half as much across. Due

211

Tectona grandis
flowers and foliage

Tectona grandis
Teak

to their handsome appearance, Teak is often planted as an ornamental outside the truly tropical climate it needs for full development.

In late summer, the tree blossoms, producing great airy panicles of mauve and white flowers with pink calyces high on its topmost branches. These are followed by dry, papery brown fruits.

It is from these seeds that the Teak tree naturalizes in the tropics, but elsewhere it is propagated from shoots which grow at a great rate, up to 3 m (10 ft) in two years.

Teakwood is heavier than water and will sink, so in Thailand the trees are ringbarked and left to dry out for several years before felling. Then they can be floated down river to the ports.

TERMINALIA
(tur min ae′ ly ə)

The Tropical Almond or False Kamani

FAMILY: COMBRETACEAE

In tropical seaside gardens and coastal areas throughout the warm-climate world, you will often find a curious tree much wider than it is tall! Its branches are held perfectly horizontal and arranged in formal tiers. Its blunt-ended, shiny leaves are up to 30 cm (12 in) long and a few of them will be coloured a brilliant red at

Tectona grandis
Teak, young foliage

Terminalia catappa
Tropical Almond, Coast Almond

any time of the year. It is in fact completely deciduous, though it tends to disguise the fact by disrobing only partially at any one time.

The tree is called *Terminalia catappa*, from the way its leaves cluster only at the *end* of branches. It is valued not only for the deep shade it gives and for the sand-binding qualities of its vast root system, but also for its flattened, almond-like fruits, roasted or eaten, raw.

In native cultures, the *Terminalia* has many additional uses. Almost every part of the tree is used medicinally, and the reddish-coloured trunkwood is used in boat building. Very convenient, since it only grows by water!

The *Terminalia* is known by several popular names, Tropical Almond, Coast Almond and False Kamani among them.

Theobroma cacao
detail of cocoa bean

Terminalia catappa
fruit and foliage

water. It is frequently planted in conjunction with another tree, the Madre de Cacao (see *Gliricidia*).

Theobroma is evergreen, with leathery, oblong 30 cm (12 in) leaves, often tinted pink or red when young. The short-stemmed 1 cm (½ in) flowers appear at any time in dense clusters, directly from the trunk or larger branches. They are yellow with a pink calyx, and are followed by purplish-brown, ten-ribbed, woody fruits which may be any size up to that of a football. These each contain about fifty flat seeds embedded in sticky white pulp.

After picking, the seeds are fermented, roasted and ground to become chocolate.

The Cocoa tree (or Cacao, to give it the Indian name) is grown from seed, and fruits at about four years of age.

THEOBROMA
(thee oh broh' mə)

The Cocoa Tree or Cacao

FAMILY: BYTTNERIACEAE

Food for the Gods! For once a tree's botanical name comes right to the point! Food for the Gods is what *Theobroma* means, and food for the gods is what it gives, for the seeds of this fascinating Central American tree are the basis of every chocolate bar and chocolate cake produced in the world and every cup of cocoa.

The Cocoa Tree, *Theobroma cacao*, grows naturally from 5 to 12 m in height (15 to 35 ft), but is often trained to a lower, more branching shape to make picking easier. It is exclusively for warm climates, where it enjoys protection from sun and wind and deep soil with plenty of

Theobroma cacao
Cacao or Cocoa Tree, foliage

213

THEVETIA
(thae vae' tee ə)

The Yellow Oleanders

FAMILY: APOCYNACEAE

Like the related Oleanders, which they resemble in habit though not in colour, the dangerously beautiful *Thevetias* are poisonous in every part, from their milky sap to their gorgeous golden trumpets.

They are a small genus of perhaps eight species, all from the American tropics and subtropics, though cultivated in every warm-climate area of the world.

The most commonly seen is *T. peruviana*, sometimes called Be Still Tree, from the constant air movement of its spidery, short-stemmed leaves. It grows to 10 m (30 ft) in height, bears lightly-fragrant 5 cm (2 in) golden trumpet flowers, followed by angular red fruits which ripen to black. Its variety *'Aurantiaca'* has salmon-orange flowers.

The closely related *T. thevetioides* from Mexico is altogether a better plant; smaller growing to 5 m (15 ft) only, it bears much larger, more open flowers of a clearer yellow, and has poisonous fruits to 6 cm (2½ in) in diameter.

A third species *T. yccotli* (also from Mexico) has slightly hairy reverses to the leaves and apple-sized, warty green fruits.

Thevetias can be propagated from seed or cuttings and enjoy a sandy soil. Though basically tropical, they can withstand a degree of frost if planted in a sheltered position.

Thevetia thevetioides
Yellow Oleander

Thevetia peruviana
Be Still Tree

Thevetia yccotli
Mexican Oleander

214

THUJA
(thoo' yə)

Arborvitae or Western Red Cedar

FAMILY: CUPRESSACEAE

Closely related to the False Cypress (see *Chamaecyparis*), *Thuja* is a small, coniferous genus that makes up in size what it lacks in numbers. Most notable is the stunning Western Red Cedar, *T. plicata*, a towering giant that can reach up to 70 m (230 ft) and more. Found only in the moist and often mist-shrouded coastal ranges of the Rocky Mountains from California to Alaska, it is one of the world's great timber trees, source of an important softwood for internal home construction.

The Red Cedar's bark is deeply fissured, the scaly leaves arranged in flattened, horizontal branchlets. And how strange that such a big tree has such small cones! They are its trademark and are unique — the cone-scales are all hinged so that they open like a flower when ripe!

From the other side of the North American continent comes the White Cedar, *T. occidentalis*, a tree only one-third the size, but equally valued for its timber. More popular in garden use, it is genetically unstable and has produced innumerable cultivars, varying from the parent in both colour and habit.

Thuja occidentalis
White Cedar, foliage and cones

Across the North Pacific, the only three other species are found. These are *T. koraiensis* from Korea, *T. orientalis*, the Chinese Arborvitae, and *T. standishii*, the Japanese Arborvitae. All are much smaller trees and popular in horticultural use. Only the Chinese species shares the colour instability.

Thujas grow slowly, and the major species may be propagated from the fine seed.

Thuja plicata
Western Red Cedar

Thuja plicata CV 'Stoneham Gold'
Golden Cedar, foliage

TILIA
(ti' li ə)

The Lindens or Limes

FAMILY: TILIACEAE

Throughout the warmer months, the northern hemisphere's Linden or Lime Trees (*Tilia* spp.), are as attractive to bees as the south's Acacias and Eucalypts. From June right through to August (in their native lands), their branches are festooned with a delicate greenish-yellow blossom that spreads a delightful fragrance in their vicinity. They are favourite specimen trees in the larger garden, and great avenues have been planted with them, as in Berlin's famous 'Unter den Linden'.

There are about thirty species of Linden, with representative members in temperate zones of Europe, Asia and North America. They are deciduous, generally tall, with some species growing to 50 m (160 ft); the trunks are heavily buttressed and surrounded by suckers. The leaves are almost perfectly heart-shaped and slightly serrated, borne on long stems. The flowers are five-petalled and appear in long-stalked clusters from a showy greenish-white bract. They are followed by small, nut-like green fruits.

Tilia platyphyllos Aurea
Gold-leaf Lime

Limewood has been a favourite with European wood carvers from time immemorial. Pale and easily worked, it is found in more religious statues and baroque extravaganzas than any other timber, and has also been used for many practical items such as piano keys, clogs and venetian blinds.

All Linden species grow fast and well in a wide variety of soil conditions, but must have plenty of water. They are propagated from seed, layers or cuttings.

Tilia petiolaris
Pendant Silver Lime

Tilia miqueliana
Japanese Linden

In older times, the trees were favourites of the Slavic and Germanic peoples, being planted by the wells at the centre of every town. One famous tree with a trunk diameter of 3 m (10 ft) gave its name to the South German town *Neuenstadt an der grossen Linden* — Newtown by the Big Lime Tree!

TIPUANA
(tip oo ah' nə)

The Pride of Bolivia

FAMILY: LEGUMINOSAE

Found principally in mountainous Bolivia, the showy *Tipuana tipu* (an adaptation of its Indian name) has become a favourite shade tree in Mediterranean areas.

It is an untypical member of the pea family, Leguminosae, and the only one of its genus. *Tipuana* is a tall, slender grower of 30 cm (100 ft) or more in its native forests. Fortunately it remains a more manageable size in cultivation, and after a rather slow beginning tends to develop a spreading crown.

Tipuana is deciduous, producing a fresh crop of rich green leaves together with its flower display in late spring. The leaves are compound, with up to eleven pairs of leaflets, and the brilliant orange-yellow blossoms are open in shape. They appear in long sprays at branch tips, and are followed by large winged seeds or *samaras*.

In sub-tropical climates, the tree is bare for only a short period and is grown from seed.

In the grand days of Victorian cabinet-making, its wood was often sold (together with that of many other local trees) as Brazilian Rosewood, but the tree's accepted popular name is Pride of Bolivia.

Tilia cordata
Small-leafed Lime

Tilia X *europaea*
Common Lime, Linden

Young Lime foliage is a delicate chartreuse green, and older leaves of many species are silvered with fine hairs.

Tilia is the original Latin name — the French call the tree *tilleul*. Both English and German popular names Lime and Linden come from the old German *Lind*.

Tipuana tipu
Pride of Bolivia

TOONA
(toon' ə)

The Red Cedar
FAMILY: MELIACEAE

Once the glory of Australia's east coastal forests, the Red Cedar or *Toona australis* has fallen victim to its own beauty, and is now quite rare. Throughout the nineteenth century it was mercilessly hunted out and felled without a thought for the morrow.

Australian Cedar is a softwood, beautifully grained and coloured. Wonder of wonders, it is also termite resistant! It was used in colonial times for panelling, mouldings, furniture and, of course, cigar boxes.

The *Toona* tree itself is quite a curiosity — not a real Cedar of course, for Cedars are conifers, but a relative of the Chinese *Cedrelas*, and completely deciduous. The leaves are compound, pinnate with up to eight pairs of pointed leaflets, and often coloured a delicate bronze-pink when young. Small, perfumed, pink flowers hang in panicles from the end of every branchlet in spring.

The tree itself has been known to reach 70 m (230 ft) in the wild, but is slow-growing. Today you'd have to go deep into the coastal ranges to find one of any size, though there are some fine specimens as street trees in the Northern Rivers township of Bellingen, in New South Wales. To see them in the mass, you'd need to visit Hawaii, where they have been used in re-afforestation.

The *Toona* is propagated from seed, and grows fast and tall only in a warm-temperate to sub-tropical climate. It needs water aplenty.

Toona australis
foliage and seed capsules

TRISTANIA
(tris tan' ee ə)

Brush Box, Water Gum, Kanooka
FAMILY: MYRTACEAE

Named for an all-but-forgotten French botanist, Jules Tristan, the handsome *Tristanias* are a small genus found in Australia, New Caledonia and India. Only four are of any interest to the gardener, by far the most important being the Australian Brush Box, *Tristania conferta*, grown in many lands.

A good-natured giant with lofty, reddish trunk and branches, it may reach 40 m (130 ft) in a warm, moist climate, but is rather prone to frost damage when young.

The glossy, simple leaves may reach 15 cm (6 in) and are carried alternately. The flowers, borne profusely among new foliage at the branch tips in late spring, are creamy-white, five-petalled and fragrant, with masses of feathery stamens. They are followed by round seed pods, rather like the gum nuts borne by related Eucalypts. These hang on the branches all year.

Although *Tristania* is native to moist coastal forests and grows fast when young, it is surprisingly resistant to dry conditions, and has become very popular as a street tree in Australian cities. There, in a lopped, spreading shape, it is only a shadow of its tall free-growing forest cousins. There is a beautifully variegated form, *T. c. 'Aurea Variegata'*, most eyecatching against a dark background.

Second in popularity is the Australian Water Gum or Kanooka, *T. laurina*. This is a much smaller tree, rarely 20 m (65 ft) in nature, usually about 5 m (15 ft) in cultivation. Similar in most respects to the Brush Box, its leaves are nar-

Toona australis
Australian Red Cedar

Tristania conferta CV *'Aurea Variegata'*
Variegated Brush Box

rower and darker; the smaller flowers are noted for their golden colour rather than their fragrance. As its popular name suggests, it is a water-loving tree, and found wild along damp river banks of eastern Australia.

T. neriifolia (also called the Water Gum) is another even smaller tree for moist places.

Brush Box timber is popular for many home projects.

Tristania conferta
summer buds and blossom

Tristania conferta
Brush Box

Tristania laurina
Water Gum, Kanooka

TSUGA
(tsoo' gə)

The Hemlocks

FAMILY: PINACEAE

Among the crowded ranks of northern hemisphere conifers, the Hemlocks or *Tsuga* hold a unique, if negative place. They are *not* found naturally anywhere in Europe! All ten species are native to North America and eastern Asia. *Tsuga* is what the Japanese have called them for several thousand years. The popular name Hemlock is merely in reference to the leaves which vaguely resemble those of the herb which poisoned Socrates.

Tsuga canadensis
Eastern Hemlock

The Hemlocks are all valuable timber trees, resembling the Spruces, but with a softer, more graceful appearance in all their parts. Though some of them may reach 70 m (230 ft) in nature, they are generally slow-growing and have become favourite specimen trees in cool-climate gardens with acid, woodsy soil. *T. canadensis*, the Eastern Hemlock, is most commonly seen, and like other of its fellow conifers it is extremely variable in both height and colour, having produced many attractive cultivars.

Among these is the drooping *T. c. Pendula*, with weeping branches and fine bluish foliage.

Hemlocks enjoy a sheltered, shady place in the garden, and are quite frost hardy. They are propagated from the winged seeds of the small, woody female cones. .

Tsuga canadensis CV *Pendula*
Weeping Hemlock

ULMUS
(ul' məs)

The Elms

FAMILY: ULMACEAE

At the height of England's great industrial revolution, the poet Tennyson rode (or perhaps wrote) his way to the top on a wave of nostalgia for lost days of knightly chivalry and noble savagery. Patriotic pride surged on a diet of legendary heroes and spotless princesses living out their lives in an idealized English landscape.

Today, alas, it is the landscape itself that must provoke the deep nostalgia, for Tennyson's 'immemorial elms', the picturesque giants of English field and hedgerow are gone, perhaps never to return: victims of a terminal disease. Weakened by the drought of 1975-76, these monarchs of the landscape were easy prey for a fungus, *Ceratocystis ulmi*, which destroys the trees' sap system. An individual small tree might be saved by injection and spraying, some have been, but the very size of the mature English Elms (*Ulmus procera*) has been against them from the start. Trees planted in the seventeenth century had grown to 40 or 50 m (130 to 160 ft) and there was no way to treat them short of axe and fire.

Ulmus procera
English Elm
200-year-old tree killed by Dutch Elm
Disease, Kew, England

Fortunately, they have survived in the distant southern hemisphere, and other fungus-resistant species will be planted in England to help fill the gaps.

There are more than fifteen natural Elm species found around the temperate northern hemisphere, in Europe, Asia, and the eastern parts of North America, where they are the most favoured trees for shade and shelter, in both street and lawn. They are all deciduous, and mostly tall-growing with one curious feature that makes them easy to identify as a genus: their generally rough-textured, toothed leaves are quite asymmetric at the base.

Elms flower very early in the spring, in a fuzz of tiny, red-stemmed, petal-less blossom which is rarely noticed, but develops rapidly into a mass of large, single-seeded winged fruit, or *samaras*, of a delicate whitish-green. These cluster at branch tips and are often believed to be the flowers. They are even used by florists as Elm blossom.

Elms are grown easily from seed (except for the English *U. procera*, which is sterile), cuttings and the masses of suckers which appear around the trunks of many species. The preferred modern technique is to graft these on to seedling stock of sucker-free types.

Timber of many Elm species (generally a pale, light gold), has been used in the making of country furniture.

Ulmus glabra Pendula
Weeping Scotch Elm

Ulmus procera
detail of samaras, spring

Ulmus procera
English Elm

Ulmus parvifolia
Chinese Elm

Ulmus X *hollandica*
Dutch Elm

VIBURNUM
(vi burn' əm)

The Snowball Tree

FAMILY: CAPRIFOLIACEAE

Fragrant-flowered relatives of Honeysuckle, Kolkwitzia and Weigela, the enchanting *Viburnums* include a tremendous range of showy plants, all of them native to the cooler climates of the northern hemisphere, and welcome worldwide in temperate gardens.

The great majority of two hundred-odd species are shrubs, but several of them so frequently overstep the dividing line that they can rightly be classed as trees.

First among them is the gorgeous Guelder Rose, *V. opulus*, which is familiar in one variety or another in parts of North Africa, Europe and northern Asia. Growing to 5 m (15 ft) and more, it is an attractively deciduous tree with large three-lobed hairy leaves that colour marvellously in cold areas. Its spring flower display consists of flat heads of Hydrangea-like white blossom, and in the preferred variety *V. o. Sterile*, these are formed into great 7.5 cm (3 in) globular clusters that have suggested the popular name Snowball Tree.

Equally attractive in the warmer climate is the evergreen Chinese species *V. odoratissimum*, the Sweet Viburnum Tree. This has an interest-

Viburnum odoratissimum
Sweet Viburnum Tree

ing spreading shape, rather wider than its height of 7 m (20 ft). The leaves are simple ovals, shiny and leathery, and the late spring or early summer flower display is reminiscent of white Lilac.

Other tree-size *Viburnums* include the North American Arrowwood, *V. dentatum*, with deciduous, glossy, oval leaves. This grows to 5 m (15 ft) has white spring flowers and dark blue berries.

Viburnums need water and a good rich soil to look happy and flower well. They are usually propagated from cuttings of half-ripened wood.

Viburnum opulus Sterile
Snowball Tree

222

VIRGILIA
(vur jil' ee ə)

The Keurboom

FAMILY: LEGUMINOSAE

Named in honour of the Roman poet Virgil, there is a charming small tree from South Africa guaranteed to grow faster than anything else in the warm climate garden! Known as *keurboom* to the early Dutch settlers on the Cape, botanists have christened it *Virgilia capensis*.

It is a member of the Pea family, and one of the most important trees for the new garden because of its speed of growth which can be as much as 2 m (6 ft) in a year. Although its useful life may be only a decade or so, it helps fill in spaces until the main planting is established and can be eyecatching at almost any season.

Virgilia grows to 10 m (30 ft) and has small grey-green pinnate leaves with up to twenty leaflets, silver-hairy on the underside. From late spring onwards, these make a splendid contrast with the profuse display of mauve-pink blossom. This is made up of literally thousands of fingernail-sized pea flowers, many of which are followed by brown pea pods.

Virgilia is propagated from seed, and prefers a light, open soil. The only problem is, it is inclined to be shallow-rooted and can do with a little staking help in exposed positions, at least until it is well established. Keep up the water during the summer, and the flower display may continue right into the autumn.

WASHINGTONIA
(wash ing ton' ee ə)

The Petticoat Palm

FAMILY: PALMAE

It's pretty obvious that indoor-plant dealers who sell small seedlings of *Washingtonia filifera* have never visited California. The telltale white threads fringing the fan-shaped fronds may look eyecatching on a young seedling, but they should also act as a warning to the unsuspecting buyer! What you are about to buy is the granddaddy of all Palm trees: a Californian native that shoots up to 30 m (100 ft) and more, and does it fast.

The trouble, I suppose, is that the demand for indoor Palms is constantly outstripping the supply, and *Washingtonia* is among the easiest to propagate from seed.

Massive and majestic in the open air of warm climates, *Washingtonia* lines many of the grandest avenues of Los Angeles and other Californian cities, towering over other Palm species and standing out from them by reason of the dense, evenly-layered apron of dead fronds that hang a great distance down the trunk. This has brought it the popular name Petticoat Palm, but it is also known as Thread Palm or Cotton Palm from the fibrous leaf-threads referred to above.

The *Washingtonias* will grow anywhere in a warm climate, but prefer dry conditions to humid. They were named for George Washington, America's first President.

Virgilia capensis
Keurboom

Washingtonia filifera
Petticoat Palm, Thread Palm

ZELKOVA
(zel koh' wə)

The Japanese Elm
FAMILY: ULMACEAE

Zelkova carpinifolia
Caucasian Zelkova

Zelkova serrata
Japanese Elm

Splendid deciduous trees found over a wide band from Crete through the Caucasus and Asia to Japan, *Zelkovas* are closely related to the Elms and inherit their botanical name from their Russian popular name, *zelkowa*.

Only two of the five species are much in cultivation, both of them easy to grow from seeds, layers or grafts. Most commonly seen is *Z. serrata*, the Japanese Elm, a handsome, tall-grower of 30 m (100 ft) or more in its native Japanese forests, where it is an important timber tree.

In garden usage, it rarely reaches half that size, an elegant, widely branched tree with a beautifully smooth grey trunk. The leaves are shaped like a spear-head, rough to the touch.

The related *Z. carpinifolia* or Caucasian Zelkova is one of the most striking of cultivated trees for a temperate climate. Its grey, scaly trunk is relatively short, but bursts into a crowded mass of upward-pointing branches which may reach a height of 30 m (100 ft). From the tips of these the softly toothed leaves weep down on long branchlets. Neither fruit nor flowers are particularly interesting.

Both Zelkova species are frost hardy.

ZIZYPHUS
(zi' zi fəs)

The Jujube Trees
FAMILY: RHAMNACEAE

Popular fruiting trees from the Balkans eastward to India and China, the Jujubes are native mostly to warm temperate areas of the northern hemisphere, with several species found in Africa and South America. The curious botanical name *Zizyphus* is from the original Arabic name *zizouf*.

Most commonly grown by far is *Z. jujuba*, the Chinese Date, a deciduous 13 m (40 ft) tree found right across Asia. The fleshy, juicy, orange-red fruits, which ripen in late winter, are a great favourite in the Arabic countries, where they are preserved and dried and made into many sticky confections — presumably the origin of our own jujube candies.

The closely related *Z. mauritiana* or Indian jujube is similar, though usually evergreen.

According to legend, *Z. spina-christi* from North Africa and Asia Minor was the tree from which Christ's Crown of Thorns was woven. It is indeed wickedly spined and bears grape-sized fruits which are quite edible.

Zizyphus species may be propagated from seed or cuttings.

Zizyphus mauritiana
Indian Jujube

HOW TO USE THE BOOK

The trees in this book are arranged in the alphabetical order of their botanical names — names which are used and recognized throughout the world. These scientific names may be hard to remember as they are largely based on Latin and Ancient Greek, but they have the advantage of being internationally understood, which popular names in any modern language are not. Even in botanic gardens of Japan and the USSR, you will find the trees labelled with these botanical names as well as any common name in local use.

If you already know the botanical name of a tree, just turn through the alphabetically arranged pictorial sections until you find the right heading, followed by the pictures.

If you don't know the botanical name, or what the tree looks like, turn to the popular name index at the back, where you'll find the more common English-language names listed, also alphabetically, with cross-reference to the correct botanical name.

Each main entry in the pictorial section is headed with the botanical name of the tree's genus, which corresponds to your family name, e.g., *Cassia*. These generic names are printed in *italic* type everywhere in the book; in the headings they appear in *ITALIC CAPITALS*. Beneath the generic name, in parentheses, is a simple phonetic guide to its pronunciation; a key to the pronunciation guide follows.

Underneath the generic name is the English name for the whole genus, or for its most prominent member. These names have an initial capital both here and in the text.

The second heading following the generic name is in CAPITALS and is the name of the botanic family to which the tree belongs (in the case of *Cassia* it is LEGUMINOSAE, the Peas or Legumes). In botany, the family is a larger group including many related genera with similar characteristics — for example, the family LEGUMINOSAE also includes *Acacia*, *Bauhinia*, *Cercis* and *Sophora*, which all bear their seeds alternately in a long pod, just like household peas.

Within many dictionary entries, you will find reference to some of the most popular species of the genus in cultivation. Specific or species names correspond to our given or personal names. Specific names are printed in small *italic* type without an initial capital. Where several species are described, the generic name is abbreviated after its first usage to its initial capital with a full stop, to save space.

Sometimes, the generic and specific names will be followed by a third name. This is the varietal or cultivar name, which further identifies the tree when two varieties have the same generic and specific names. Varietal names are used when it is necessary to distinguish some small natural point of difference — a flower colour or leaf-marking, or a particular habit of growth that reproduces constantly from seed. Varietal names are printed in *italic* type with an initial capital, and sometimes within quotes. Cultivar names fall in the same position when it is necessary to refer to some characteristic or sport of the tree that has proved capable of cultivation only by means of cuttings (raised from seed it might revert to the original). Cultivar names are often in a modern language instead of Latin or Greek, and are prefixed with the letters *CV*.

Another word you'll run across is 'hybrid' or 'hybrida'. This is used when each of a plant's parents is of a different species. Hybrids are often raised by nurseries to produce superior new species, just as breeders of horses and cattle try to improve their stock. A hybrid is often indicated by *X* between the generic and specific names.

Individual dictionary entries give all sorts of additional information for the home gardener, such as mature height and spread, speed of growth, flowering time, country of origin, method of propagation, soil requirements, natural pests, minimum necessary winter temperature, ideal position or light intensity, popular names, uses in commerce and many other things.

Under every photograph is a brief caption giving the illustrated tree's correct botanical and popular names.

A great deal of additonal information will be found in the botanical index at the back of the book. The scientific names of all trees described or illustrated in the main text are included, and in addition, you'll discover information about many other species which could not be illustrated or included in the main dictionary section. Each and every entry in this index includes popular names, country of origin, flowering or main display season, height and speed of growth, and many other details necessary for precise identification, such as size, colouring and appearance of flowers, fruit, foliage and sometimes bark. All entries, of course, are in alphabetical order.

You will also find a separate index of popular names, cross-referenced to the main botanical index, and a glossary of botanical terms.

Key To The Phonetic Guide

Each entry in this book is headed by the tree's generic name, followed by a simple phonetic guide to its pronunciation. There are still many differences of opinion as to how these botanical names should be pronounced but the phonetic guide should help set you on the right track. Using it, the spelling will inevitably differ from the normal spelling of the generic name because the whole aim of a phonetic guide is to give *constant* pronunciation values to the symbols used.

Vowels, and some consonants, can be pronounced in many different ways in English (look at the vowel 'a' in fat, fates, father and fare or the consonant 'c' in cat and ace). A phonetic guide makes it necessary to select one special letter or group of letters to represent each specific sound, and that sound *only*. But because there are more sounds in English than there are letters in the English alphabet, we also use one extra symbol (ə) to represent the many indeterminate vowel sounds heard in words like alone, system, terrible, gallop and circus.

Beyond that, we have separated each syllable from the next by a space, and used an accent (') immediately after the syllable to be stressed. Each separate letter or letter combination is *always* pronounced according to the following.

a	fat
ae	pay, fate, sleigh
ah	mark, father
ai	ice, high, buy
ə	alone, system, terrible, gallop, circus
e	deaf, den
ee	teach, see
eə	air, dared
i	fit, tiff
o	sot, toss
oh	oath, both, crow
oi	boy, royal
oo	prove, pool, glue
or	ought, more, roar
ou	cow, crouch, slough
u	suck, son, rough
ur	err, circus
b	bat, tab
ch	chip, patch
d	do, cod
f	reef, rough, phone
g	gas, bag
h	help, ahoy
j	jaws, gem, rage
k	cat, sack
l	limb, mill
m	more, rummy
n	ton, tonight
p	pal, lap
r	rot, trot
s	sale, lace,
sh	shade, motion
t	tone, note
th	thin, both, loathe
v	vat, cave
w	win, twin
y	yellow
z	zip, toes, rose
zh	measure, invasion

Remember, the sound of each phonetic letter or letter-group remains constant. As examples, here are the first five tree entries with their generic names and the phonetic pronunciations.

ABIES	ae' bees	The Firs
ACACIA	ə kae' shə	The Wattles
ACER	ae' sə	The Maples
ACMENA	ak mee' nə	The Lillypilly
ADANSONIA	ad an soh' nee ə	The Baobab

GLOSSARY

Achene: a small, dry, one-seeded fruit with an undivided outer wall.

Acid: deficient in lime (of soil).

Acorn: the fruit and principal identifying feature of an Oak *(Quercus)*, consisting of a nut resting in a basal cup.

Acuminate: tapering with slightly concurved sides to an acute point (of a leaf).

Acute: sharp, tapering with straight sides to a point (of a leaf).

Aerial root: a root appearing above soil level, often from a branch. Used for both support and feeding.

Aggregate fruit: a compound fruit comprising several separate ripened ovaries from a single flower — as in a mulberry.

Air layering: a method of propagation which stimulates new root growth from a plant *above* ground.

Alkaline: rich in lime (of soil).

Alternate: arranged singly on different sides of the stem, and at different levels (of leaves).

Anther: the pollen bearing part of a stamen.

Apetalous: without petals.

Aphids: minute sap-sucking insects which appear in masses, often on new shoots of Citrus.

Apiculate: terminating in a short, sharp point (of leaves).

Aquatic: a plant or tree which grows naturally in water.

Aril: a fleshy sheath, partially, or sometimes completely covering a seed.

Armed: provided with thorns, spines or hooks or other sharp defence.

Asexual: without any sexual characteristics.

Asymmetrical: not evenly balanced.

Attenuate: gradually long-tapering.

Awl shaped: slender, sharp pointed.

Axil: the upper angle that a leaf stem makes with the stem from which it appears.

Axillary: in or from an axil.

Basal: at the bottom.

Berry: a pulpy fruit containing one or more seeds, but no true stone.

Bifid: forked or cleft.

Bifoliate: having two leaves.

Bigeneric: a hybrid between two *genera* of plants, as opposed to more common hybrids between species or varieties.

Bipinnate: twice pinnate, the primary leaflets are again divided into secondary leaflets, as in a jacaranda (of leaves).

Bisexual: both sexes present and functioning in the same flower.

Bloom: 1. a flower. 2. a fine, powdery coating.

Bole: the unbranched section of a tree trunk.

Bract: a modified leaf at the base of a flower, sometimes the most colourful part (see *Davidia*).

Bracteate: bearing or surrounded by bracts.

Branchlet: the finer division of a branch.

Bush: a low, thick shrub without distinct trunks.

Calcifuge: a lime-hating plant.

Calyx: the outer row of the flower, composed of separate or unified sepals.

Cambium layer: in trees, the thin layer of live growth cells between bark and heartwood.

Campanulate: bell-shaped (of flowers).

Capsule: a dry, divisible fruit composed of one or more sections.

Carpel: one of the units comprising a pistil or ovary.

Catkin: a scaly-bracted, usually flexible and hanging inflorescence.

Composite: compound.

Compound: composed usually of several leaflets (of a leaf).

Cone: a dense, often elongated construction of seed-bearing scales on a central axis, often woody, as in Pines.

Conifer: a tree bearing its seed in the form of a cone.

Cordate: heart-shaped (of a leaf).

Corolla: the inner circle of a flower, consisting of petals.

Corymb: a flat-topped inflorescence, short and broad, with the outermost flowers opening first.

Crenate: scalloped, with shallow, rounded teeth (of a leaf).

Crown: 1. the spreading mass of a tree's branches. 2. the base of a tree.

Cuneate: wedge-shaped.

Cutting: a cut section of a plant or tree which will develop new roots and become a self-sufficient plant. There are ripe cuttings (of old wood), half-ripe cuttings (new season's wood hardening off), and root cuttings.

Cyme: a type of inflorescence, usually broad and flat topped; the centre flowers opening first.

Deciduous: a tree which sheds all leaves at the one time.

Dehiscent: splitting naturally on an existing seam (of a seed capsule).

Dentate: with rather coarse and spreading teeth (of a leaf).

Digitate: compound, resembling a spread hand.

Dioecious: with unisexual flowers: male and female blossoms borne on separate plants.

Divided: separated very nearly to the base or midrib (of a leaf).

Drupe: a fruit containing one (rarely two) woody-skinned seeds.

Echinate: with bluntish prickles.

Elliptic: oblong, but narrowing to rounded ends (of a leaf).

Endemic: native to a particular, restricted area.

Ensiform: sword-shaped (of a leaf).

Entire: with a continuous, unbroken margin (of a leaf).

Espalier: 1. to train a tree or shrub in two dimensions, e.g., along a wall or house, used for ripening tender fruit in cooler climates. 2. A tree or shrub so trained.

Evergreen: having foliage that remains green throughout more than one growing season.

Falcate: sickle-shaped, strongly curved.

Fasciate: said of two main stems or other axes abnormally grown together.

Fastigiate: with branches erect and more or less parallel, as in the Lombardy Poplar.

Fertile: stamens bearing functional pollen, or fruits containing viable seeds.

Filament: a threadlike organ.

Filiform: threadlike, long and slender.

Fimbriate: fringed (of a leaf or flower).

Flaccid: weak and limp.

Floret: a very small flower.

Floriferous: flower-bearing.

Flower: an arrangement of a plant's sexual organs, consisting of pistils and stamens, usually surrounded by decorative and highly coloured petals and calyx to attract fertilizing insects.

Follicle: a dry, shelled fruit, with normally more than one seed.

Frond: leaf of a fern or palm.

Frost tender: said of a fleshy plant which may be destroyed when the unprotected sap is frozen.

Fruit: the ripened ovary, usually seed bearing.

Fungicide: a chemical preparation for the destruction of minute fungi on plants, such as mildew.

Genus: a group of closely related plant species.

Glabrous: smooth, without hairs of any kind.

Glaucous: covered with a bloom (white, grey or blue) which is easily rubbed off.

Glomerate: in a dense or compact cluster.

Glutinous: sticky.

Grafting: when a bud or shoot of one plant is joined to a rooted section of another for propagation.

Habit: general manner of growth of a plant.

Hastate: in the shape of an arrowhead, but with basal lobes turned outward.

Heeled cutting: a cutting of new wood, still attached to a portion of harder, previous year's growth.

Hermaphroditic: bisexual.

Humus: rich organic debris, resulting from the rotting of vegetable and other matter.

Husk: the outer casing of some fruits and nuts.

Hybrid: a plant resulting from parents that are genetically unsimilar.

Imbricate: overlapping, as with roof shingles.

Incised: cut, slashed irregularly and rather deeply (of a leaf).

Indehiscent: not opening along regular marked lines (of a fruit or nut).

Inflorescence: 1. the flowering part of a plant. 2. the blooming of a plant.

Involucre: one or more whorls or close groups of small leaves beneath a flower or inflorescence.

Juvenile: the second leaves to appear from seedlings, often varying a lot from the leaves of an adult plant.

Laciniate: slashed into narrow pointed lobes (of a leaf).

Lanceolate: several times longer than broad.

Lateral: 1. on or at the side. 2. a shoot arising from a stem any distance from the normal.

Latex: a colourless or whitish fluid produced by many plants.

Layering: propagation of a new plant by bending a low branch toward the ground or a pot, splitting the bark and pinning down until root growth has taken place.

Leaflet: one of the smallest units of a compound leaf.

Legume: a plant which produces pea-type seeds in a pod.

Lenticular: lens-shaped, more or less circular and flattened (of a leaf).

Lignotuber: a subterranean bulb-like storage chamber of many eucalypts, which enables them to regenerate after fire.

Linear: long and narrow.
Loam: a friable soil containing topsoil, sand, clay and silt particles, usually with decayed vegetation.
Lobe: a major segment of a petal, organ.

Membranous: thin, soft and translucent.
Monocarpic: fruiting once only and then dying.
Monoecious: a tree with unisexual flowers, but male and female flowers upon the same plant.
Mutant: a variant differing genetically and often visibly from its parent and arising spontaneously.

Natural cross: a hybrid which has occurred naturally.
Needle: a specialized, elongated leaf, as in many conifers.
Node: the position on a stem where, at a single level, one or more leaves are attached.
Nut: 1. an indehiscent, one-seeded, hard-skinned fruit. 2. the stone itself.

Oblique: slanting, with unequal sides.
Oblong: longer than wide, with the sides almost parallel.
Obovate: the opposite of ovate — broader at the outer end.
Obtuse: rounded, blunt.
Offset: a small outside division from a mature plant.
Operculum: the lid of a seed capsule, particularly in Eucalypts.
Opposite: two at each node, on opposite sides of the stem (of a leaf).
Orbicular, orbiculate: circular.
Organic: composed of live or formerly living tissue.
Ostiole: a minute opening or orifice — as in the fruit of *Ficus* spp.
Ovary: the basal, seed-developing part of the pistil in a flower.
Ovate: with a shape like that of a hen's egg, rounded both ends, but broadest below the middle.
Ovoid: egg-shaped, with the point of attachment at the broader end (of fruit).

Palmate: with three or more leaflets radiating like a fan.
Pandurate, panduriform: violin shaped — rounded at both ends, and with a waisted middle.
Panicle: a general term for a branching cluster of flowers.
Paniculate: borne in a panicle (of flowers).
Papilionaceous: literally butterfly-shaped. A typical flower of the Pea family, Papilionaceae (of flowers).
Pedicel: the stalk of an individual flower.
Peduncle: the stalk of a flower cluster.
Persistent: not falling off.
Petal: one decorative unit or segment of the corolla (in a flower).
Petaloid: an organ that has the appearance of a true petal, whether it be a stamen or a sepal (of a flower).
Petiole: the stalk of a leaf.
Phyllode: an expanded, leaf-like petiole.
Pinna, pl. **Pinnae:** the leaflets on a compound leaf.
Pinnate: like a feather; a leaf with leaflets arranged on both sides of a centre stalk.
Pip: the seed of a fruit.
Pistil: the prominent female organ of a flower.
Plicate: pleated (of a leaf).
Plumose: feather-like.
Pod: a dehiscent fruit, usually of the Pea family.
Pollen: the spores or grains borne by a flower's male anther — equivalent to mammalian sperm.

Pollination: the transfer of pollen from an anther to a receptive stigma.
Poly: prefix meaning many.
Polygamous: with both unisexual and bisexual flowers on the one plant.
Pome: the fleshy fruit typical of pears, apples and other members of the rose family.
Propagate: to reproduce a plant, generally by means of cuttings or divisions, so that it comes true to type.
Prostrate: lying flat on the ground.
Pseud- or **Pseudo-:** a prefix meaning false or untypical.
Pubescent: softly downy.
Pyriform: pear-shaped.

Raceme: an unbranched, elongated inflorescence with stemmed flowers.
Radiate: spreading from a common centre.
Rank: a vertical row.
Recurved: curved downward or backward.
Reniform: kidney-shaped.
Resinous: containing or producing resin.
Reticulate: net-like.
Rhomboid: shaped something like a parallelogram.
Rib: the primary vein, or any prominent vein (in a leaf).
Rootstock: subterranean stems.

Sagittate: shaped like an arrowhead, with the basal lobes pointing *toward* the stalk (of a leaf).
Samara: an indehiscent winged fruit or seed — as in *Acer*.
Scale: 1. a small appressed leaf or bract. 2. one of a number of plant pests, clustering on stems or reverses of leaf.
Seed: the ripened and fertilized ovule containing the enlarging plant.
Segment: one of the parts of a leaf or petal that is deeply divided.
Sepal: one of the separate units of a calyx, usually green and leaflike.
Serrate: having saw-toothed edges.
Sessile: without a stalk.
Sheath: any more or less tubular structure surrounding an organ or part.
Shrub: a woody plant, generally lower growing than a tree, and with multiple trunks (a very generalized term).
Simple: neither compound nor divided.
Sinuate: with wavy or indented margins.
Spathe: the bract which encloses the spadix.
Spathulate: spatula-shaped; oblong with the point rounded.
Species: the basic or minor unit in plant naming.
Spicate: spike-like.
Spike: a usually unbranched, elongated inflorescence.
Spine: a stiff, sharp-pointed outgrowth on any part of a plant.
Spore: the reproductive cell of a plant.
Sport: a plant variety resulting from natural mutation.
Stalk: a non-technical term for the elongated support of any plant organ.
Stamen: the male or pollen-bearing organ of a flower.
Staminate: having stamens but no pistils.
Standard: the uppermost, usually erect petal in any flower.
Stem: the main leaf or flower-bearing axis of a plant.
Sterile: 1. a plant incapable of reproduction by seed; generally a hybrid. 2. non-functional, not producing flowers.
Stigma: the tip of the female pistil which receives the pollen.
Stone: a large seed and covering, as in a peach or cherry (of fruit).

Striate: with fine longitudinal lines.
Style: the elongated point of the pistil between ovary and stigma.
Sub-: a prefix meaning 1. nearly or slightly; 2. below, under.
Subspecies: a major subdivision of a large species.
Subtropical: a plant native to areas outside the true tropics, but not able to survive cold winters.
Succulent: 1. a plant with fleshy leaves and or stems acting as water storage chambers against drought. 2. (commonly), juicy, fleshy, rather thick.
Sucker: a shoot which appears from an underground root.
Symbiosis: literally, living together. Forms of life in complete dependence on one another. For instance Figs (*Ficus* spp.) and certain wasps. The Fig provides the wasp's only feed; without the wasp, the Fig cannot be fertilized and bear seed.
Symmetrical: capable of division into identical halves.
Syncarp: a compound 'fruit' composed of the more-or-less coalesced fruits of either a single flower, or many flowers.

Taxonomy: the science of plant nomenclature.
Temperate: a mild coastal climate.
Terminal: at the end or tip.
Thorn: a sharp, woody, spine-like projection.
Thrip: a sap-sucking insect, colonies of which rapidly disfigure leaves.
Throat: the opening or orifice of the tubular part of a flower, where the tube.
Tomentose: woolly.
Tree: (commonly) a woody plant that produces one main trunk and a distinct, elevated crown.
Trifoliate: bearing three leaves to a stem.
Tropical: a plant native to the warm zone between the tropics of Capricorn and Cancer, needing a wet summer and a dry warm winter.
Tubercle: a small warty excrescence on a leaf or other organ.
Twice-pinnate: bipinnate.
Twig: the shoot of a woody plant or tree representing the growth of the current season.

Umbel: a usually flat-topped cluster of flowers growing from a common point on a stem.
Unarmed: without prickles or spines.
Undulate: having a wavy surface or edge, or both at once.
Unisexual: of one sex.
Urceolate: urn or pitcher shaped (of flowers).

Variegated: a condition of any plant when the natural green of leaves or stems is broken by other colours.
Variety: 1. the subdivision of a species. 2. a recognizably different member of a plant species capable of cultivation.
Viable: fresh, capable of germination (of
Viscid: sticky.

Whorl: a circle of three or more leaves, flowers or branches appearing around a stem, branch or trunk at the same position or level.
Windbreak: a specialized planting (generally of trees) to protect smaller and more delicate plants, or even buildings.
Woolly: with more or less matted hairs.

Xerophyte: a plant adapted to an arid habitat. Literally, a lover of dryness.

Zygomorphic: bilaterally symmetrical. Capable of being divided into two equal halves in one plane only (of flowers).

BOTANICAL INDEX

This comprehensive section is more than a mere index to the botanical names of trees illustrated in the book. Arranged in alphabetical order, the entries give many additional details for all illustrated trees; for all those mentioned in the main text; and also for many other worthwhile species of each included genus. Botanical and popular names are included; speed and habit of growth; shape, size and colour of flowers, fruits and foliage (and whether it colours in autumn); the botanical family to which each tree belongs, and its practical uses, together with other miscellaneous information which may help in identification. The regions to which each tree is native are indicated to give an idea of the climates in which they grow best.

Height of growth and spread (where given) refer to the size achieved in their natural surroundings in suitable soil. Under garden cultivation and in the average lifetime, few of them will pass half those dimensions. Similarly, descriptions of habit, e.g. 'pyramidal', 'flat-topped', refer to their shapes at maturity. Old and young trees of the same species frequently look quite different.

Speed of growth refers to growth in fairly ideal conditions and must be deliberately imprecise. For our purposes, speed of growth is shown over a 20-year period. Slow means less than 5 m (15 ft) in 20 years; medium fast 7–8 m (20–25 ft); fast 8–10 m (25–30 ft); very fast 10–13 m (30–40 ft); very very fast, over 13 m (40 ft) in 20 years. In actual garden conditions, speed of growth may vary considerably.

Size of leaves, flowers and fruit will also vary according to climate, rainfall and many other factors, but the figures quoted should help in identification.

Most entries include two or more numbers after the botanical name. The first, in light Roman type refers to the page of the main text on which reference to the tree will be found. If there is a second number in **bold** Roman type, that refers to the page on which an illustration will be found. Where an entry is not followed by any numbers, then that tree is not illustrated, and its description is found only in the Botanical Index.

All popular names used anywhere in the book are included in alphabetical order in the Popular Name Index which follows this section.

The botanical name of the genus (e.g. **ABIES**) heads each generic entry in the index; in following entries on individual species it is reduced to its initial letter (**A.**), followed by the specific name of the tree, e.g. **A. alba**, European Silver Fir.

ABBREVIATIONS
C. Central; E. East, Eastern; I. Island(s); N. North, Northern; NSW, New South Wales; NZ New Zealand; Q Queensland; S. South, Southern; SA South Australia; Tas Tasmania; Vic Victoria; W. West, Western; WA Western Australia.

ABIES 9
About 40 species of evergreen conifers, generally of tall, pyramidal habit. Single trunked, upward pointing branches with shortish, needle-like leaves, generally with two white or silver bands on reverse. Male and female flowers separately on same tree. Male flowers usually brightly coloured and clustered beneath branches. Family Pinaceae.

A. alba 9
Common Silver Fir, European Fir, Silver Fir. C. to S. Europe, cool to cold, mountainous. To 50 m (150 ft). Needle-like 2.5 cm (1 in) glossy foliage, dark green above. Pendant cones, to 20 cm (8 in), green turning brown. Fast growing. Tall, pyramidal. Used for timber.

A. cephalonica
Greek Fir. Greece, cool, mountainous. To 35 m (100 ft). Needle-like, 2.5 cm (1 in), dark green foliage; white banded reverse. Flowers in dense clusters. Glossy red-brown branchlets. Pendant cones, to 15 cm (6 in), pale green. Fast growing. Tall, pyramidal. Used for timber.

A. concolor
Colorado White Fir, White Fir. USA, Rocky Mountains, cool, mountainous. To 50 m (150 ft). Curved, greyish foliage, needle-like, to 7.5 cm (3 in). Yellow-green branchlets. Pendant cones, 12.5 cm (5 in), green or purple. Fast growing. Rounded pyramidal. Used for timber, paper pulp.

A. delavayi
Delavay's Fir. China, cool to cold, mountainous. To 30 m (90 ft). Needle-like, 2.5 cm (1 in), dark green foliage, white reverses; 2-ranked. Pendant cones, violet black, barrel-shaped, to 10 cm (4 in). Fast growing. Tall, pyramidal. Used for timber.

A. grandis
Giant Fir, Grand Fir, Lowland Fir. N.W. USA, Vancouver I. Cool temperate to cold. Will tolerate alkaline soil. To 100 m (300 ft). Needle-like foliage, to 5 cm (2 in), dark olive green, silver bands beneath. Pendant cones, purple to brown. Very fast growing. Columnar shape. Used for timber, paper pulp.

A. homolepis 9, **9**
Nikko Fir. Japan, cool to cold, mountainous. To 35 m (105 ft). Needle-like foliage, to 2.5 cm (1 in), dark shiny green, white bands beneath. Grooved branchlets. Pendant cones, to 10 cm (4 in), purple, ripening to brown. Very fast growing. Tall pyramidal. Used for timber.

A. nordmanniana
Caucasian Fir. Greece, Asia Minor, cool, mountainous. To 70 m (200 ft). Needle like, to 4 cm (1½ in), glossy bright green foliage; forward pointing. Pendant cones, to 15 cm (6 in), pale green ripening to brown. Greyish, pubescent branches. Fast growing. Conical to columnar shape. Used for timber. Many colour varieties.

A. pinsapo
Spanish Fir. Spain, temperate mountainous. Will tolerate dry and alkaline soil. Grows to 30 m (90 ft). Needle-like foliage, dull green, silver banded both sides, sometimes curved, arranged radially. Bright red male blooms in Spain. Pendant cones, to 12.5 cm (5 in), purple-green. Moderately fast growing. Narrowly conical. Used for timber

A. procera syn. **A. nobilis** 9, **9**
Noble Fir. N.W. USA, cool to cold. Dislikes alkaline soil. To 80 m (240 ft). Needle-like, to 3.5 cm (1½ in), blue-green foliage. Pendant cones, to 25 cm (10 in), blue-green to purple. Fast growing. Columnar, rounded top. Used for timber.

ACACIA 10–12
Over 700 species of highly variable trees and large shrubs, native to warm temperate areas of Australia (mostly), Asia, Africa and the Americas. Usually evergreen. Flowers bisexual, orange, yellow or white. Not frost hardy. Family Leguminosae.

A. aneura
Mulga. Australia, dry acid soil. To 6 m (18 ft). Narrow linear phyllodes to 7.5 cm (3 in). Flowers 1 cm (½ in) spikes, Spring. Oblong pods to 4 cm (1½ in). Fast growing. Bushy. Timber is the brilliantly patterned Mulga wood of many Australian souvenirs.

A. baileyana 10,**11**
Cootamundra Wattle, Bailey's Wattle. S. NSW, temperate, dry soil. To 6 m (18 ft). Silver-green or mauvish bipinnate leaves to 15 cm (6 in). Golden-yellow puffballs, 2.5 mm (⅛ in), in racemes. Winter. Pods 7.5 cm (3 in). Very fast growing. Pyramidal shape, drooping branches. Inclined to be short-lived, about 12 years.

A. confusa 12
Philippine Acacia. Philippines, Taiwan, sub-tropical to temperate. To 17 m (50 ft). Narrow linear phyllodes, bright green. 2.5 mm (⅛ in) bright yellow, solitary flowers at leaf axils. 7.5 cm (3 in) inflated green pods. Fast growing. Tall, widely branched. Ornamental; used for stock fodder.

A. dealbata
Silver Wattle, Mimosa. S.E. Australia, Tas, cool to temperate. 6–16 m (18–48 ft). Silver-grey bipinnate leaves to 15 cm (6 in). 5 mm (¼ in) golden-yellow puffballs in clusters, highly scented. Spring. Flat bluish pods 7.5 cm (3 in). Very fast growing. Spreading habit. Silver-grey branches and trunk. Flowers sold worldwide as Mimosa. A substitute for gum arabic extracted from timber.

A. decurrens 12
Black Wattle. E. Australia, warm temperate. To 20 m (60 ft). Dark green bipinnate leaves to 15 cm (6 in). Cream to yellow puffballs, 3.5 cm (1½ in). Spring. Green pods to 10 cm (4 in). Fast growing. Tall, spindly olive green trunk and branches. Ornamental, shade.

A. elata, see **A. terminalis**

A. farnesiana
Sweet Acacia, Popinac, Cassie, W. Indian Blackthorn. Pan-tropical, all continents, warm temperate to sub-tropical. To 4 m (12 ft). Dark green leaves, bipinnate, to 10 cm (4 in). 1 cm (½ in) puffball blossom in small clusters. Bright orange, very fragrant. Thick, 7.5 cm (3 in) brown pods. Fast growing. Low, spreading habit, very thorny. Extract of Mimosa (Oil of Cassie) for perfume.

A. giraffae 12
Camel Thorn. S. Africa, Zimbabwe, temperate to dry. To 13 m (40 ft). Leaves bipinnate, 5 cm (2 in), light green. Deciduous. Light yellow flowers in 6 cm (2¹/₇ in) spikes. Often appear before foliage. Curved grey pods to 12.5 cm

(5 in) long. Slow growing. Spreading habit. Vicious pointed grey spikes on branchlets.

A. glaucescens syn. **A. binervia 11**
Coast Myall, Sally Wattle. E. Australia, warm temperate. To 20 m (60 ft). Grey curved phyllodes to 15 cm (6 in). Golden-yellow flowers in 5 cm (2 in) spikes. Twisted or curved pods to 7.5 cm (3 in). Fast growing. Tall spreading habit. Foliage poisonous to stock.

A. implexa
Lightwood, Screw-pod Wattle. E. Australia, cool temperate. To 15 m (45 ft). Sickle-shaped green phyllodes to 15 cm (6 in). 5 mm (¼ in) creamy flowers in short racemes. Narrow linear twisted pods. Fast growing. Tall, pyramidal.

A. karroo 12
Karroo Thorn, African Camel Thorn. S. Africa, dry temperate. To 5 m (15 ft). Bipinnate grey foliage to 10 cm (4 in). Fragrant, pale yellow flowers in dense clusters. Narrow pods to 12.5 cm (5 in). Sharp 7.5 cm (3 in) white spines on older branches. Slow growing. Bushy, spreading.

A. koa 10, **12**
Koa. Hawaiian Islands, mountainous, tropical. To 20 m (60 ft). Greyish curved phyllodes to 15 cm (6 in). Golden flowers in short racemes. Winter. Wide brown pods to 15 cm (6 in) long. Slow growing. Twisted, spreading shape. Beautifully figured timber is one of the world's great cabinet woods.

A. longifolia 12
Sydney Golden Wattle. NSW, coastal, warm temperate. Not frost hardy. To 5 m (15 ft). Dark green lance-shaped phyllodes to 15 cm (6 in). Bright yellow flowers in loose 6 cm (2¼ in) spikes. Long flat pods to 12.5 cm (5 in). Fast growing. Dense, bushy.

A. melanoxylon
Blackwood, Australian Blackwood. Tas, SA, cool temperate. To 35 m (100 ft). Lance-shaped phyllodes to 10 cm (4 in); juvenile foliage bipinnate. 5 mm (¼ in) flowers in short racemes. Cream. Late Winter. Twisted green pods to 12.5 cm (5 in). Fast growing. Tall, spreading. A valuable timber tree. The wood, resembling teak, is marketed as Tasmanian blackwood.

A. pendula 10
Weeping Myall, Boree. E. Australia, warm temperate to dry. To 10 m (30 ft). Stiff, silver-grey phyllodes to 7.5 cm (3 in). Yellow flowers in small clusters on branches. 7.5 cm (3 in) narrow pods. Fast growing. Columnar, weeping branchlets. Violet scented timber is used for fancy inlaid work.

A. podalyriaefolia
Mt Morgan Wattle, Q Silver Wattle, Pearl Acacia. N.E. Australia, warm temperate to sub-tropical. To 7 m (20 ft). Silver, 2.5 cm (1 in) oval phyllodes. Golden-yellow puffballs, 1 cm (½ in), in long racemes. Winter. Silvery pods to 7.5 cm (3 in). Fast growing. Tall, open, often weeping branches.

A. pycnantha 10, **10**
Golden Wattle. S.E. Australia, temperate, coastal. To 8 m (24 ft). Very dark green curved phyllodes to 15 cm (6 in). 1 cm (½ in) flowers in short racemes. Brilliant yellow, very fragrant. All year but mostly late spring. Flat, narrow pods. Fast growing. Spreading, weeping branches. Australian national tree emblem.

A. saligna
Golden Wreath Wattle, Weeping Wattle. WA, dry temperate. To 5 m (25 ft). Long, curved phyllodes to 25 cm (10 in). 1 cm (½ in) pale yellow flowers in racemes.

Spring. 12.5 cm (5 in) pods. Fast growing. Bushy, weeping branches.

A. terminalis syn. **A. elata 11**
Cedar Wattle, Peppermint Tree Wattle. E. Australia, warm temperate, coastal. To 20 m (60 ft). Dark, bipinnate leaves to 20 cm (8 in); young growth golden. Cream, 1 cm (½ in) flowers in 15 cm (6 in) racemes. Dark green, 15 cm (6 in), pods. Fast growing. Pyramidal shape. Used as a shade tree and for timber.

ACER 13–14
A genus of about 200 species, mostly deciduous trees. Native to temperate regions of the northern hemisphere. Their leaves are typically palmately lobed with 3–13 lobes. Their fruit a pair of winged samaras, frequently on long stems. Probably the world's most popular genus of specimen trees. Family Aceraceae.

A. buergeranum
Trident Maple, Buerger's Maple. Japan, E. China, cool temperate. To 17 m (50 ft). Leaves 10 cm (4 in) long, 7.5 cm (3 in) wide, lightly toothed with 3 forward pointing lobes. Deep green above, paler and glaucous on reverse; red and orange in autumn. Small, yellowish flowers in a flat panicle. Samaras, 2.5 cm (1 in) long, weeping, parallel. Slow growing. Pyramidal, upward pointing branches.

A. campestre 15
Field Maple, Hedge Maple. Europe, Caucasus, temperate to cool. To 25 m (75 ft). 3–5 lobed leaves 10 cm (4 in) wide; clear yellow in autumn. Greenish flowers in upright corymbs. Samaras, 3.5 cm (1½ in) long. Wings horizontally divergent. Fast growing. Spreading, rounded head.

A. davidii
Père David's Maple. China, cool temperate. To 17m (50 ft). Leaves ovate, 17.5 cm (7 in), not lobed; purple and gold in autumn. Small yellow flowers in long, pendant racemes. Samaras, 3 cm (1¼ in) long, wings diverging at an obtuse angle. Medium fast growth. Tall, round-headed. Striped bark.

A. griseum 13
Paperbark Maple. Central China, cool temperate. To 17 m (50 ft). 7.5 cm (3 in) leaves of 3 leaflets, coarsely toothed; scarlet and orange in autumn. Yellowish flowers in small drooping cymes. Samaras, 2.5 cm (1 in) diverging at an acute to right angle. Medium fast growth. Spreading habit. Shining brown bark constantly peeling.

A. japonicum
Japanese Maple, Full Moon Maple. Japan, cool temperate. To 10 m (30 ft). Very variable leaves with 7–13 lobes to 13 cm (5 in) wide and doubly serrated. Scarlet, crimson in autumn. Small, purplish-red flowers in hanging corymbs. Samaras, to 5 cm (2 in); wings diverging at obtuse angle. Slow growing. Small and bushy. Many varied cultivars and leaf varieties.

A. monspessulanum
Montpellier Maple. N. Africa, S. Europe, Asia Minor, temperate to warm. To 15 m (45 ft). 3-lobed leaves to 7.5 cm (3 in); leathery; yellow in autumn. Greenish-yellow flowers in small corymbs. 2.5 cm (1 in) samaras, red, profuse. Medium fast growth. Tall, round-headed. Grown for seed display.

A. negundo 13
Box Elder, Ash Leaved Maple. N. America, cool to temperate. To 25 m (75 ft). Compound pinnate leaves with 3–9 serrated leaflets; yellow in autumn. Yellow-white flowers, the sexes in separate types. Samaras 3.5 cm (1½ in). Wings diverge at an acute angle. Medium fast growth. Spreading, open shape. Cultivated in many varied leaf varieties.

A. opalus 15
Italian Maple. S. Europe, temperate to warm. To 13 m (40 ft). 5-lobed leaves to 11 cm (4½ in); yellow in autumn. Yellow flowers in drooping corymbs. Samaras 3.5 cm (1½ in); wings diverging at right angles. Medium fast growth. Spreading, rounded.

A. palmatum 15
Japanese Maple. Korea, Japan, China, cool temperate to temperate. 1–16 m (3–50 ft). Foliage, small, 3m11 lobed. Autumn colours very variable. Reddish-purple flowers in small corymbs. Samaras small, glossy; wings diverged at an acute angle. Growth rate and shape variable. This species has a myriad varieties with leaf colours from white to all shades of green to dark purple. Leaves may be finely dissected, thread-like, or rippled.

A. platanoides 15
Norway Maple. Europe, Asia Minor, cool temperate. To 30 m (90 ft). Leaves 5-lobed, to 18 cm (7 in) diameter, normally glossy. Autumn colour yellow or bright red in darker leafed CVs. Greenish-yellow flowers in profuse upright corymbs. Pendulous samaras, to 5 cm (2 in) long, wings horizontal. Very fast growing. Upright, rounded head. Grown in many varieties of leaf colour, particularly the wonderful CV 'Schwedleri Nigra' with dark crimson foliage.

A. pseudoplatanus 13
Sycamore Maple, Sycamore. Europe, Asia, cool temperate. To 35 m (100 ft). Leaves 5 lobed to 12 cm (5 in) wide; variable autumn colours. Profuse yellow flowers in hanging panicles. Samaras to 5 cm (2 in) long; wings diverging at acute or right angle. Very fast growing. Spreading shape. Grown in many varieties of leaf colour particularly the slow-growing CV 'Brilliantissimum' with pink and yellow green foliage.

A. rubrum
Red Maple, Scented Maple, Swamp Maple. E. USA, cool to temperate. To 40 m (120 ft). Leaves 3—5 lobed, to 15 cm (6 in) wide; scarlet and orange in autumn. Red flowers in short, dense clusters, sexes often on separate trees. Bright red samaras to 2.5 cm (1 in) on pendulous stalks, wings diverging at acute angle. Very fast growing. Densely branched, rounded head. Var. 'Columnare' has the shape of a Lombardy Poplar.

A. saccharinum 13
Silver Maple, White Maple, Rock Maple. Canada, E. USA, cool temperate. To 45 m (135 ft). 5-lobed leaves, deeply divided, to 15 cm (6 in) wide, pale green with silver reverse; clear yellow in late autumn. Pink flowers in short dense clusters. Samaras, to 6.5 cm (2½ in) wide, wings diverging to right angle. Very fast growing. Tall, spreading head, often weeping branches. Used for commercial timber.

A. saccharum 14
Sugar Maple, Hard Maple. E. USA, cool to cold. To 45 m (135 ft). 3–5 lobed leaves, deeply cut and toothed; turning yellow, orange or scarlet, depending on season. Small, apetalous creamy flowers in corymbs on drooping long stalks, generally before foliage. Shiny samaras, to 4.5 cm (1¾ in) wide, wings slightly divergent. Very fast growing. Tall, rounded head, fluted trunk. Many colours and leaf varieties. Yields timber, maple sugar, maple syrup.

A. sieboldianum
Siebold Maple. Japan, cool to temperate. To 5 m (25 ft). 7–9 lobed leaves to 15 cm (6 in) wide. Leaves truncated at base, lobes pointed and sharply serrated. Red in autumn. Yellowish flowers on long,

downy stems. Samaras, 2 cm (³/₄ in) long, horizontally divergent wings. Moderate growth. Shrubby habit.

A. trifidum, see **A. buergeranum**

ACMENA 16

A small genus of decorative, glossy-leafed trees native to an area from Australia, up through Malaysia to S. China. Closely related to *Syzygium* and grown for their ornamental fruit display. Family Myrtaceae.

ACMENA, see also **SYZYGIUM**

A. smithii 16, **16**

Lillypilly. E. Australia, warm temperate. To 8 m (24 ft). Notably glossy, ovate to ovate-lanceolate leaves to 7.5 cm (3 in). A petal-less mass of white stamens. Early summer. Globular fruit, 1 cm (½ in) ameter, in clusters. Whitish, mauve or pale pink and edible. Fast growth in warm climate. Dense, upright, but often with weeping branches when in fruit. A good street tree.

ADANSONIA 16

A small genus, 9 species of deciduous, massively-trunked trees from Australia, Africa and Malagasy. Too large for the home garden. Family Bombacaceae.

A. digitata 16

Judas Bag, Baobab, Dead Rat Tree, Monkey Bread Tree. Africa, Madagascar, tropical, dry temperate. To 13 m (40 ft) high, 20 m (60 ft) wide. Deciduous, digitate leaves, 5—7 elliptic leaflets to 12.5 cm (5 in) long. White flowers, single, reflex petals, 10 cm (4 in) wideon long hanging stems, opening before foliage. Cylindrical, velvety, tomentose fruit to 40 cm (18 in) long on long hanging stems. Slow growing. Massive trunk, short branches. Many uses, see text.

A. gregorii

Bottle Tree, Baobab. Australia. To 20m(60 ft) high, 15 m (45 ft) wide. Otherwise similar to *A. digitata.*

AESCULUS 17

A genus of 13 deciduous species, mostly trees, from N. America, Europe and Asia. Mostly alike with upright panicles of showy spring blossom. Much hybridized. Family Hippocastanaceae.

A. californica 17

California Buckeye, California Horse Chestnut. California, temperate. To 10 m (30 ft). Leaves compound, usually with 5 ovate lanceolate leaflets 17.5 cm (7 in) long. Deciduous. Flowers to 2.5 cm (1 in) diameter in 20 cm (8 in) panicles. White or rose coloured with prominent stamens. Very fragrant. Rough textured, ovoid fruit. Medium growth. Spreading habit.

A. X carnea 17

Red Horse Chestnut. Hybrid. Cool temperate. To 20 m (60 ft). Leaves compound, dark green. 5—7 leaflets cuneate obovate to 15 cm (6 in) long. Deep rose-pink flowers in 25 cm (10 in) panicles. Medium growth. Pyramidal, becoming round-headed. Hybrid between A. *hippocastanum* and A. *pavia.*

A. glabra

Ohio Buckeye. N. America, cool temperate to cold. To 10 m (30 ft). Leaves compound, 5—7 leaflets, elliptic obovate to 16.5 cm (6½ in) long. Uninteresting autumn colour. Pale yellow flowers in 15 cm (6 in) panicles. Ovoid, prickly fruit. Medium growth. Shrubby. Used for wood pulp.

A. hippocastanum 17, **17**

Common Horse Chestnut, European Horse Chestnut. Greece, Albania, temperate. To 35 m (100 ft). Compound, 5—7 obovate leaflets to 30 cm (12 in) long; yellow in autumn. Flowers white with red patch in 30 cm (12 in) panicles. Late spring. Spherical, upright fruit 6 cm

(2½ in) diameter. Fast growing. Upright with spreading head. Used as stock feed.

A. pavia 17

Red Buckeye. S. USA, temperate. To 7 m (21 ft). Compound, 5—7 narrowly elliptical leaflets. Crimson flowers in 25 cm (10 in) panicles. Egg-shaped fruit. Slow growing. Bushy.

AGATHIS 18

A small genus of about 20 species of tall, coniferous, evergreen trees, native to the Pacific area. Various species localized in the Philippines, Australia, N.Z. and Fiji. Family Araucariaceae.

A. australis 19

Kauri Pine, Kauri. N.Z., temperate. To 35 m (100 ft). Leaves dark bronze green, elliptic, curved, 7.5 cm (3 in) long, evergreen. Separate male and female flowers on one tree, quite insignificant, axillary. Cones axillary, male, to 3 cm (1¼ in), female sub-globose to 7.5 cm (3 in) in diameter. Slow growing. Columnar. One of the world's great timber trees, a source of Kauri gum and copal varnish.

A. moorei 18

Noumea Kauri. New Caledonia, sub-tropical. To 25 m (75 ft). Evergreen, lanceolate, shelled leaves to 9 cm (3½ in). Cones to 12.5 cm (5 in) long. Medium growth. Columnar shape. Used for timber.

A. robusta 18

Queensland Kauri. N.E. Australia, temperate to sub-tropical. To 50 m (150 ft). Evergreen, dark narrow-elliptic leaves to 10 cm (4 in) long. Insignificant flowers. Female cones to 12.5 cm (5 in) long, 11.5 cm (4½ in) wide. Medium growth. Columnar. Used for timber — the most commonly cultivated species.

A. vitiensis 18, **18**

Fiji Kauri Pine, Tennis-ball Tree. Fiji, sub-tropical to tropical. To 35 m (100 ft). Evergreen leaves, dark above, pale reverses, elliptic, to 12.5 cm (5 in) long but quite variable. Insignificant flowers. Cones, to 12.5 cm (5 in), footed. Fast growing. Columnar to spreading shape. Used for timber.

AGONIS 19

A small genus of drought resistant evergreen trees all native to WA, related to the Eucalypts. Family Myrtaceae.

A. flexuosa 19, **19**

Peppermint Tree, Willow Myrtle. WA, dry temperate. To 12 m (35 ft). Leaves willow-like, lanceolate, to 10 cm (4 in) long. Flowers in axillary clusters, white, to 1 cm (½ in) in diameter, 20 stamens. Spring, summer. Small nut-like, axillary fruit. Slow growing. Spreading, weeping branches. Decorative, foliage a source of peppermint-flavoured oil.

A. juniperina 19, **19**

Small-leaf Willow Myrtle. WA, dry temperate. To 13 m (40 ft). Leaves stiff, linear, to 1 cm (½ in). White flowers in axillary clusters to .5 cm (¼ in) diameter. 10 stamens. Winter. Nut-like, axillary fruit. Slow growing. Tall, stiff branched; rough, shiny bark. Ornamental only.

AILANTHUS 20

A small genus of deciduous trees found in Asia, the Solomon Islands and Australia. Family Simaroubaceae.

A. altissima 20

Ai-lan-to, Tree of Heaven, Varnish Tree. China, cool to warm temperate. To 20 m (60 ft). Leaves compound deciduous, to 1 m (3 ft) long, with 11—14 oval leaflets. Greenish flowers, in clusters, fetid odour, sexes on different trees. Samaras, reddish-orange to 5 cm (2 in) wide on female trees only. Very fast growing. Spreading head. Grows anywhere. Good shade tree, source of copal varnish.

Naturalized worldwide.

A. excelsa

Indian Varnish Tree. India, warm temperate. To 25 m (80 ft). Curved leaves to 30 cm (12 in) long, many coarsely toothed leaflets. Greenish, small flowers on many-branched panicles. Samaras, to 5 cm (2 in) wide ripening to copper red. Fast growing. Spreading head. Shade tree, a source of varnish, bark used medicinally.

ALBIZZIA syn. **ALBIZIA** 21

A large genus of up to 150 species native to many parts of the Old World, related to the *Acacia* and mostly planted as ornamentals. All with bipinnate, deciduous foliage. Family Leguminosae.

A. distachya, see **A. lophantha**

A. julibrissin 21, **21**

Persian Silk Tree, Mimosa, Pink Siris. Persia to Japan, dry temperate. To 10 m (30 ft). Leaves fine, bipinnate, to 45 cm (18 in) long. Deciduous. Pale to deep pink flowers in terminal clusters, each flower about 2.5 cm (1 in) diameter, like an over-large Acacia blossom. Thin elongated pods to 15 cm (6 in). Fast growing. Broad, flat-topped. Widely cultivated worldwide. Many colour varieties.

A. lebbek 21, **21**

Woman's Tongue Tree, Lebbek Tree. Tropical Asia and Africa, sub-tropical to tropical. To 25 m (75 ft) high, often wide in spread. Leaves coarse and bipinnate, to 23 cm (9 in) long. Deciduous. Yellow-white puffballs on large terminal panicles. Broad pods, to 30 cm (12 in) long. Fast growing. Broad-headed. Used for stock fodder.

A. lophantha 21, **21**

Cape Wattle, Plume Albizzia. WA, temperate. To 15 m (45 ft). Leaves bipinnate, to 30 cm (12 in). Deciduous. Flowers in axillary spikes 7.5 cm (3 in) long, like a lime-coloured bottlebrush. Leguminous pods, to 7.5 cm (3 in) long. Brown. Fast growing. Bushy or spreading. Used for stock fodder.

A. odoratissima

Ceylon Rosewood. Ceylon to Thailand, tropical. To 25 m (75 ft). Coarse bipinnate leaves. Deciduous. Yellowish-white flowers in sparse panicles to 30 cm (12 in) long. Thin pods, to 23 cm (9 in) long. Fast growing. Rounded head. The fragrant timber, known as Ceylon rosewood, is used for cabinet-making.

ALECTRYON 22

A small genus of evergreen, fruiting trees found throughout the Pacific from Australia to Hawaii. Family Sapindaceae.

A. excelsa 22

Titoki. N.Z., temperate to cool. To 10 m (30 ft). Leaves unequally bipinnate, Ash-like, to 30 cm (12 in). Evergreen. Very small, cream flowers in many-branched 30 cm (12 in) panicles. Capsules, to 1 cm (½ in) long, pubescent. Medium growth. Slender, almost black bark. Timber good for cabinet-making and tool handles.

A. subcinereus 22, **22**

Native Quince, Smooth Rambutan. E. Australia, temperate to sub-tropical. To 10 m (30ft). Leaves to 20 cm (8 in) long, equally pinnate with 2—6 leaflets. Small, cream flowers in 20 cm (8 in) panicles. Smooth berries, borne in pairs, to .5 cm (¼ in) in diameter. Medium growth. Densely foliaged, spreading, often with weeping branches. Timber for minor purposes. Fruit edible, valued by Aborigines.

ALEURITES 22

A small genus of 6 tree species valued principally for the high oil content of their seeds, and for their generous shade in tropical climates. In cooler areas, they may turn deciduous. Euphorbiaceae.

A. cordata 22
Japan Wood-oil Tree. S.E. Asia, tropical. To 13 m (40 ft). Leaves ovate-cordate, usually 3–5 lobed or toothed. White flowers 2 cm (³⁄₄ in) in diameter. Warty fruit, about 2.5 cm (1 in) diameter. Medium growth. Spreading habit. Oil from seeds.

A. fordii 22
Tung-oil Tree, China Wood-oil Tree. C. Asia, temperate. To 13 m (40 ft). Leaves ovate to cordate often 3 lobed, to 12.5 cm (5 in) long. White flowers with red veins, to 2.5 cm (1 in) long. Smooth fruit, to 7.5 cm (3 in) diameter. Medium growth. Spreading habit. Seeds source of tung oil, used as a drying medium in paints and varnishes.

A. moluccana 22, 22, 23
Candlenut, Kukui, Indian Walnut, Varnish Tree. S.E. Asia to Hawaii, tropical to warm temperate. To 20 m (60 ft). Leaves ovate, to 20 cm (8 in) long, often 3 or 5 lobed, with a mealy appearance. White flowers in small panicles. Fruit 5 cm (2 in) diameter, rough textured. Medium growth. Pyramidal. Used for timber, oil, gum, pigment (see main entry).

A. montana 22
Mu-oil Tree, Mu Tree. China, Burma, temperate to sub-tropical. To 8 m (25 ft). Leaves ovate, often 3–5 lobed, to 30 cm (12 in) long. White flowers to 2.5 cm (1 in) wide. Fruit to 4 cm (1³⁄₄ in) diameter, smooth. Medium growth. Spreading habit. Oil from seeds, but quality inferior to other species.

ALNUS 23
A small genus of Birch relatives from the northern hemisphere, grown both for ornamental purposes and for their water-resistant qualities. Splendid in damp positions. Family Betulaceae.

A. cordata
Italian Alder. Corsica, Italy, temperate. To 25 m (75 ft). Leaves cordate, to 10 cm (4 in) long. Glossy, toothed. Deciduous. Male flowers in catkins to 7.5 cm (3 in) long, in clusters of 3–6. Usually before foliage. Female catkins short, rough. Erect, ovoid cones to 2.5 cm (1 in) long, in clusters. Very fast growing. Pyramidal. Used for timber, water absorption.

A. glutinosa 24
Black Alder, Common Alder. Europe, N. Africa, temperate to cool. To 25 m (75 ft). Leaves almost round, to 10 cm (4 in) long. Young growth sticky. Male catkins to 10 cm (4 in) long, greenish. Female catkins roundish. Cones oval to 2.5 cm (1 in). Very fast growing, suits boggy ground. Pyramidal to columnar. Used for timber, water absorption. Many fancy-leafed varieties.

A. jorullensis 24
Evergreen Alder. Mexico, temperate, warm temperate. To 8 m (24 ft). Leaves serrated, to 7.5 cm (3 in) long. Flowers and fruit similar to other species. Medium growth. Pyramidal shape. Used for timber. Good street tree in temperate climates. Largely, but not completely, evergreen.

A. oregana syn **A. rubra** 23
Red Alder. W. USA, temperate. To 23 m (70 ft). Leaves elliptical, serrated, to 15 cm (6 in), rusty beneath. Male catkins to 25 cm (6 in) long in clusters. Female catkins elliptical. Cones elliptical, to 2.5 cm (1 in) long. Extremely fast growing. Narrow, pyramidal, often with weeping branches. Used for timber, water absorption, erosion prevention.

A. rhombifolia 24
White Alder. W. USA, temperate to cool. To 35 m (120 ft). Leaves oblong ovate, tapering to an acute point, to 10 cm (4 in)

long. Pale beneath. Deciduous. Male catkins to 15 cm (6 in) long. Female cones rounded. Cones elliptical, to 1 cm (¹⁄₂ in) wide. Very fast growing. Pyramidal. Used for timber, water absorption. The pale grey bark is fascinatingly marked, the trunk resembling an Indian totem pole.

A. rubra, see **A. oregana**

ALOË 24
A large and popular genus of succulent plants native to the Old World, mostly in Africa. Only a few species grow tree-size and are most valuable in landscaping in dry climates. Family Liliaceae.

A. bainesii 24, 24
Tree Aloe. S. Africa, dry temperate. To 20 m (60 ft). Prickly edged, succulent leaves to 1 m (3 ft) long, curved in rosettes at branch ends. Rose-pink flowers, 3.5 cm (1¹⁄₂ in) in diameter, greenish petal tips, in 60 cm (24 in) spikes. Small capsules. Slow growing. Angular, grotesque. Trunk to 3 m (9 ft) in diameter. Decorative.

A. excelsa 24
Rhodesian Tree Aloe. S. Rhodesia, temperate. To 7 m (21 ft). Spiny-edged 20 cm (8 in) leaves with recurved points in terminal rosettes. Branches with persistent dead foliage. Crimson flowers, 1 cm (³⁄₈ in) in crowded panicles to 1 m (3 ft) high. Small capsules. Slow growing. Angular, grotesque. Decorative.

A. plicatilis 24
Smooth Tree Aloe. S. Africa, temperate. To 8 m (25 ft). Strap-shaped leaves to 30 cm (12 in) long, in two ranks along branches. Largely smooth-edged. Scarlet flowers to 6 cm (2¹⁄₄ in) long in racemes to 50 cm (20 in) high. Small capsules. Slow growing. Angular, many-branched. Decorative.

A. speciosus 24
S. Africa, temperate. To 8 m (25 ft). Red-edged ensiform leaves to 80 cm (32 in) long, with small red teeth. Arranged in rosettes. Greenish flowers to 3 cm (1¹⁄₄ in) long in dense, cylindrical racemes to 50 cm (20 in) high. Small capsules. Slow growing. Many-branched, angular, with old foliage persisting on branches. Decorative.

AMHERSTIA 25
A genus of a single species. A Burmese tree regarded by many as the most beautiful flowering tree in the world. Family Leguminosae.

A. nobilis 25, 25
Pride of Burma. Burma, tropical. To 13 m (40 ft). Evergreen pinnate leaves to 1 m (3 ft). New growth highly coloured and flaccid. 10 cm (4 in) pink flowers, marked vermilion and yellow on a hanging raceme. Crimson pods to 17.5 cm (7 in) long, widest at apex. Medium growth. Spreading, lightly branched. Decorative only.

ANDROMEDA arborea, see **OXY-DENDRUM arboreum**

ANGOPHORA 25
A small genus of perhaps half a dozen tree species, all native to E. Australia, and frequently mistaken for Eucalypts, among which they grow. The botanical difference is in the seed capsules, which are ribbed, unlike gumnuts. Small petals are also present in the largely staminal blossom. Family Myrtaceae.

A. cordifolia 25, 25
Dwarf Apple Gum. NSW, temperate. To 4 m (12 ft). Young leaves bright red. Mature leaves long, heart-shaped. Cream flowers resembling Eucalyptus blossom, but with small petals. 4 cm (1¹⁄₂ in) in diameter, in clusters of 3. Ribbed capsules, especially apically dehiscent, 2 cm (³⁄₄ in) long. Slow growing. Dwarf,

spreading, the branchlets reddish, hairy. Bark rough, loose.

A. costata 25
Smooth-barked Apple Gum. E. Australia, temperate. To 27 m (80 ft). Young leaves cordate, pale. Adult leaves lance-shaped to 12.5 cm (5 in). Cream flowers, 2.5 cm (1 in), in panicles. Ribbed capsules 1.5 cm (¹⁄₂ in) long. Medium fast growth. Tall, rounded head. Bark reddish, smooth.

ANNONA 26
A large genus of about 100 fruiting trees, all from S. America. Grown in all sub-tropical to tropical areas. Family Annonaceae.

A. cherimolia 26, 26
Custard Apple, Cherimoya. Peru, sub-tropical, high altitude. To 7 m (20 ft). Leaves simple, elongated oval to 25 cm (10 in), velvety. Flowers uninteresting, yellow-brown and fuzzy, to 2.5 cm (1 in). Summer. Fruit pale green, sub-globose to conical with a warty tubercular surface. To 12.5 cm (5 in) long. The yellow pulp resembles a slightly curdled custard. Medium fast growth. Spreading, branches often weeping. The best table species.

A. muricata 26, 26
Soursop, Prickly Custard Apple, Guanabana. Tropical America. To 7 m (20 ft). Leaves evergreen, simple, to 15 cm (6 in) long. Yellow flowers to 2.5 cm (1 in). Green, heart-shaped fruit, spines to 20 cm (8 in) long. Medium fast growth. Spreading. The pulp makes acid, refreshing drinks and ices.

A. reticulata 26
Bullock's Heart, Custard Apple. Tropical America. To 10 m (30 ft). Leaves simple, lanceolate, to 20 cm (8 in). Yellowish flowers to 2.5 cm (1 in) in leaf axils. Heart-shaped, reddish-brown fruit to 12.5 cm (5 in) diameter with a patterned, reticulated surface. Medium fast growth. Columnar, rounded head.

A. squamosa 22, 26
Sugar Apple, Sweetsop. Tropical America. To 7 m (20 ft). Leaves evergreen, lanceolate, to 11 cm (4¹⁄₂ in). Green flowers to 2.5 cm (1 in). Yellow-green, glaucous, warty fruit, to 9 cm (3¹⁄₂ in) across. A delicious dessert fruit. Medium growth. Spreading.

ARAUCARIA 27–8
A genus of more than a dozen handsome conifers, usually dioecious. All native to the southern hemisphere from S. America through the Pacific Islands to Australia. Often popular indoor plants in juvenile form. Family Araucariaceae.

A. araucana 27
Monkey Puzzle, Chilean Pine. Argentina, Chile, cool temperate. To 35 m (100 ft). Scaly, triangular, yellow-green leaves to 5 cm (2 in), densely arranged around shoots. Male flowers in drooping terminal catkins to 15 cm (6 in). Female globular on upper surfaces of branches. Cones — male elliptical, erect, to 12.5 cm (5 in). Female round, to 17.5 cm (7 in) wide, taking several years to mature. Medium fast growth. Pyramidal, sparse. Used for timber, edible seeds. The sparse branches are arranged in whorls around the trunk. This is the only Araucaria that is frost hardy and grows in a cool climate.

A. bidwillii 27, 27
Bunya Bunya. Temperate to sub-tropical. To 50 m (150 ft). Scaly, sharp, tough, overlapping leaflets to 5 cm (2 in) in juvenile form, only 1 cm (¹⁄₂ in) on adult trees. Flowers as in A. araucana. Cones upright, round, to 30 cm (12 in) long and as wide. Like a large green pineapple. Slow growing. Columnar, spreading top. The branches weeping except at top of tree. Used for timber. The red seeds are

an Aboriginal delicacy in Australia.

A. columellaris 28, **28**
Cook Pine, New Caledonia Pine. New Caledonia and nearby islands, temperate to sub-tropical. To 70 m (200 ft). Leaves small, scaly and densely overlapping, in adult form only 5 mm (¼ in) long. Flowers — as other species. Male cones cylindrical to 6 cm (2½ in) long. Female cones to 15 cm (6 in) long and almost as wide. Medium fast growth. Exaggeratedly columnar, like an abbreviated Norfolk Island Pine, loses lower branches which are replaced with fuzzy twigs. Used for timber.

A. cookii, see **A. columellaris**

A. cunninghamii 28, **28**
Hoop Pine, Moreton Bay Pine. N.E. Australia, New Guinea, sub-tropical/warm temperate. To 70 m (200 ft). Juvenile leaves needle-like, adult leaves awl-shaped, overlapping to 1 cm (½ in) long. In dense tufts at end of bare branches giving the tree a fuzzy appearance. Flowers as in other species. Both male and female cones rarely exceed 7.5 cm (3 in), the female being wider. Medium fast growth. Columnar/pyramidal. An important timber tree.

A. excelsa, see **A. heterophylla**

A. heterophylla 28, **28**
Norfolk I. Pine, Star Pine. Norfolk I., temperate. To 70 m (200 ft). Leaves bright green, scaly, rough, overlapping, to 2 cm (¾ in) long. Flowers — as other species. Cones about 10 cm (4 in) in both length and diameter. Fast growing. A perfectly shaped conical Conifer with horizontal branches arranged in whorls. Used for timber, prevention of erosion. It has many varieties of habit and leaf colour.

ARBUTUS 29
A small genus of decorative trees scattered from California to the Mediterranean area, with outlying representatives in the Canary Islands, Ireland and C. America. Family Ericaceae.

A. andrachne 29
Strawberry Tree. E. Mediterranean, temperate. To 13 m (40 ft). Leaves oval, to 10 cm (4 in), smooth, serrated edges. Cream flowers, like lily of the valley, in erect terminal clusters. Orange fruit, granular surfaced, to 1 cm (½ in) wide, edible but insipid. Slow growing. Spreading habit.

A. X andrachnoides
Hybrid between *A.andrachne* and *A.unedo*.

A. canariensis 29, **29**
Canary Island Strawberry Tree. Canary Islands, temperate. To 10 m (30 ft). Leaves oblong, serrated, to 12.5 cm (5 in). Green and pink flowers in erect terminal panicles. Orange, warty fruit, to 1 cm (½ in), edible. Slow growing. Spreading habit.

A. menziesii 29, **29**
Madrone, California Strawberry Tree. W. Canada, USA and Mexico, temperate. To 30 m (100 ft). Leaves oval/oblong, serrated, to 15 cm (6 in). White flowers in pyramidal panicles. Spring. Round, smooth, orange-red fruit, to 1 cm (½ in) wide. Medium fast growth. Open, rounded head. Timber used for furniture making, bark for tanbark.

A. unedo 29
Irish Strawberry Tree, Cane Apple. Ireland, S. Europe, temperate to cool. To 10 m (30 ft). Leaves elliptical, pointed, serrated, to 10 cm (4 in) long. White or pink flowers in hanging terminal panicles. Autumn. Fruit round, red, granular surface, to 2 cm (¾ in) diameter. Medium fast growth. Rounded head. Bark used for tanning, fruit for jams and fermented for alcoholic beverage. Several leaf and flower varieties.

ARCHONTOPHOENIX 30
A small genus of Palms popular for both indoor use in their juvenile form, and for outdoor landscaping due to their fast growth. The same handsome pinnate fronds are found on all species, distributed about Australia and Malaysia. Family Palmae.

A. alexandrae
Alexandra Palm, King Palm. NQ, sub-tropical. To 27 m (80 ft). Leaves pinnate, drooping, short-stalked, to 2 m (6½ ft) long, greyish reverse to leaflets. Juvenile leaves fish-tailed. White or cream, unisexual flowers in drooping, many-branched spadix, surrounded by two spathes. Bright red fruit, to 1 cm (½ in). Very fast growing. Slender shape, trunk spineless but ridged with scars of fallen branches.

A. cunninghamiana 30
Bangalow Palm, Piccabeen, Illawarra Palm. N.E. Australia, temperate to sub-tropical. To 20 m (60 ft). Drooping, pinnate leaves to 3 m (10 ft). Purplish flowers in 45 cm (18 in) drooping spadix. Green to red fruit, over 1 cm (½ in) diameter. Very fast growing. Slender; spineless trunk; sometimes cut for timber. Seeds very easy to germinate.

ARECASTRUM 30
A single species of decorative Palm from sub-tropical S. America, with very long, somewhat ragged fronds. Frequently sold (incorrectly) as *Cocos plumosa*. Family Palmae.

A. romanzoffianum 30, **30**
The Queen Palm. Brazil, Argentina, sub-tropical, down to 20°C (68°F) for mature trees. To 13 m (40 ft). Drooping, pinnate leaves, to 5 m (15 ft), on long stems. Yellow flowers in drooping spadix to 1 m (3 ft) long. Yellow fruit, up to 4 cm (1½ in) long, but often smaller. Fast growing. Slim trunk, often bent, greyish-brown. Very long branches. Ornamental use only.

ARTOCARPUS 31
A genus of some 50 tropical trees of the Mulberry family, native to many parts of Polynesia and tropical Asia; cultivated for both fruit and timber. Family Moraceae.

A. altilis 31, **32**
The Breadfruit. Malaysia/Polynesia, tropical. To 17 m (50 ft). Magnificent oval leaves, deeply and variably incised and lobed, to 1 m (3 ft) long. Evergreen. Male flower on a stiff green spike, 30 cm (12 in) long. Female is a round green head. Brown and green fruit with a tough, warted rind, to 20 cm (8 in) diameter. Full of greyish pulp which may be baked or fermented into a paste. Fast growing. Rounded head. Many uses, see text. Propagated only from root sprouts.

A. heterophyllus 31
Jakfruit. Malaysia, India, tropical. To 5 m (15 ft). Dark green oval leaves to 15 cm (6 in) with downy reverses. Evergreen. Greenish inconspicuous spikes of flowers produced directly from branches or main trunk. Fruit green, turning brown, oblong, densely covered in sharp green points. May reach 1 m (3 ft) in length. Fast growing. Tall, rounded head. Used for timber, edible fruit. Grown from seed, does well only in deep, rich soil.

A. incisus, see **A. altilis**

A. integrifolius, see **A. heterophyllus**

AVERRHOA 32
Two species only of tropical evergreen trees, grown for their unusual and interesting fruits. Both native to S.E. Asia. Family Oxalidaceae.

A. bilimbi 32
Cucumber Tree, Bilimbi, Blimbing. Malaysia, tropical. To 17 m (50 ft). Evergreen leaves, compound with 23-25 leaflets. Red and white flowers in 15 cm (6 in) panicles from trunk or branches. Greenish-yellow fruit, cylindrical, to 7.5 cm (3 in) long, faintly 5-sided. The acid flesh is edible either raw or pickled. Late summer. Fast growing. Densely foliaged, short-trunked.

A. carambola 32, **32**
Carambole, Star Fruit, Country Gooseberry, 5-Corner Fruit. Indo-Malaysian area, tropical. To 10 m (30 ft). Compound leaves, 5-11 leaflets. White and purple flowers in small panicles on trunk and branches. Yellow to orange fruit with 5 concave sides to 12.5 cm (5 in) long. Late summer. Fast growing. Upright, rounded head. Used for timber, edible fruit and a striking ornamental. Propagated from seeds.

BACKHOUSIA 33
A small genus of evergreen Australian trees closely related to the Eucalypts and Lillypillys. 3 species only cultivated. Family Myrtaceae.

B. anisata 33
Aniseed Tree. NSW, temperate. To 13 m (45 ft). Dark, ripple-edged lanceolate leaves to 10 cm (4 in), aniseed-scented. Small, cream flowers in sparse axillary or terminal clusters. Small capsules. Medium fast growth. Rounded head.

B. citriodora 33, **33**
Lemon-scented Myrtle, Tree Verbena, Sweet Verbena Tree. Q, warm temperate. To 10 m (30 ft). Pointed lemon-scented leaves to 10 cm (4 in). Evergreen. White flowers with persistent green calyces, in 5 cm (2 in) clusters. Summer. Small capsules. Medium fast growth. Slender, pyramidal. Foliage crushed for volatile oil.

B. myrtifolia
Grey Myrtle. NSW, temperate. To 13 m (40 ft). Hastate 5 cm (2 in) leaves. Evergreen. White flowers in clusters of 4 or 5. Small capsules. Medium growth. Rounded head.

BANKSIA 33, 34
A genus of 50 species, mostly shrubs, but including 5 decorative trees, all native to Australia, with one in New Guinea as well. All evergreen with bottlebrush-type inflorescences, and suited to sandy soil. Grown in S. USA and California. Family Proteaceae.

B. ericifolia 34, **34**
Heath-leafed Banksia. NSW, temperate. To 5 m (15 ft). Needle-like leaves to 1 cm (½ in), notched at apex. Orange-yellow flowers, in a 25 cm (10 in) inflorescence. Seeds in cone-like spike. Fast growing. Shrubby. Ornamental.

B. grandis 34, **34**
Bull Banksia. WA, dry temperate. To 10 m (30 ft). Evergreen, narrow leaves to 30 cm (12 in) long, deeply saw-toothed, woolly reverses. Pale yellow flowers in a 15 cm (6 in) inflorescence. Seeds in a cone-like spike. Fast growing. Spreading, downward pointing branches.

B. integrifolia 34, **34**
Coast Honeysuckle. E. Australia, coastal, temperate. To 10 m (30 ft). Evergreen, mostly smooth-edged, dark leaves, 20 cm (8 in) long, 2.5 cm (1 in) wide, silver reverses. Lemon-yellow flowers, turning orange, in a 15 cm (6 in) inflorescence. Seeds in a cone-like spike. Fast growing. Rounded head.

B. menziesii 34
Menzies' Banksia. WA, dry temperate. To 13 m (40 ft). Leathery evergreen leaves to 30 cm (12 in) long. Saw edged, blunt-ended. Red and silver-grey flowers, ripening to orange, in a 12.5 cm (5 in) inflorescence. Seeds in a cone-shaped spike. Slow growing. Round-headed, shrubby.

B. serrata 33, **33**
Saw Banksia, Red Honeysuckle. Coastal Australia, temperate. To 10 m (30 ft). Dark, leathery evergreen leaves to 15 cm (6 in) long. Saw-edged with woolly reverses. Silver-grey flowers, ripening to yellow, in a 15 cm (6 in) inflorescence. Seeds, as other species. Irregular growth rate. Gnarled, picturesque in coastal situations. Used for timber.

BARKLYA 35
An Australian genus of a single species, very colourful in warm-climate gardens. Family Leguminosae.

B. syringifolia 35, **35**
Gold Blossom Tree. N.E. Australia, warm temperate to sub-tropical but withstands cold down to −2°C (28°F). To 13 m (40 ft). Dark, evergreen, heart-shaped leaves to 10 cm (4 in). Orange-yellow pea blossom in dense 22.5 cm (9 in) terminal panicles. Small pods. Slow growing. Pyramidal to round-headed.

BARRINGTONIA 35–6
A large genus of tropical evergreens from the Old World, few of which are in cultivation. Family Barringtoniaceae.

B. acutangula 36
Indian Oak. India to WA, tropical. To 13 m (40 ft). Leaves evergreen, obovate, finely toothed, to 12.5 cm (5 in) long. Red, 4-petalled flowers in hanging 30 cm (12 in) racemes. Oblong, quadrangular fruit to 3.5 cm (1½ in). Fast growing. Broad-headed.

B. asiatica 35-6, **35, 36**
Hotu, Fish Poison Tree. India, Pacific Ocean areas, tropical. To 5 m (15 ft) but often much wider. Dark, evergreen, stemless, obovate to 37.5 cm (15 in) long. New foliage glossy, often colourful. Flowers are a globular mass of pink-tipped, white stamens with 4 white petals, to 15 cm (6 in) across. Green, top-shaped, 4-sided fruit to 10 cm (4 in) across. Slow growing. Squat-trunked, monumental, lives to a great age. Fruit used as fishing floats, or grated to stun fish. Timber used for carving.

B. racemosa 36
Barringtonia. Malaysia and Pacific Islands, tropical to temperate. To 16 m (45 ft). Dark, evergreen leaves, to 25 cm (10 in), often slightly rippled. Flowers generally white, in drooping 45 cm (18 in) racemes. Ovoid fruit, slightly four-angled, to 3.5 cm (1½ in) long. Medium growth rate. Rounded head.

B. samoensis, see **B. acutangula**

BAUHINIA 36-8
A very large genus (some 300 species) of tropical plants; 7 or 8 species widely grown in warm-climate gardens. The large flowers are pea-like, the leaves uniquely twin-lobed. Mostly deciduous, tend to look untidy when festooned with the persistent pea pods. Family Leguminosae.

B. blakeana 37, **36**
Hong Kong Orchid Tree. Hong Kong, sub-tropical. To 13 m (40 ft). Twin-lobed 20 cm (8 in) deciduous leaves. Vivid reddish-purple flowers to 15 cm (6 in) in long racemes. Winter. No fruit. A sterile hybrid. Fast growing. Open, spreading habit. Decorative. Must be propagated vegetatively.

B. carroni
Q Ebony. SA to Q, tropical. To 10 m (30 ft). Twin-lobed 2.5 cm (1 in) leaves. Deciduous. White, often purple-edged, flowers, 2 cm (¾ in). Pods to 15 cm (6 in). Fast growing. Rounded head.

B. corniculata 37
White Orchid Tree. S. America, tropical. To 7 m (20 ft). Twin-lobed leaves to 15 cm (6 in) long. Deciduous. White

flowers, to 15 cm (6 in) wide, long twisted petals. Long thin pods. Fast growing. Spreading habit.

B. hookeri 37
Orchid Tree, Mountain Ebony. Q, tropical. To 16 m (50 ft). Small twin-lobed leaves 2.5 cm (1 in) long. White flowers edged crimson, 3.5 cm (1½ in) long. Long thin pods. Fast growing. Rounded head.

B. monandra 37, **37**
Butterfly Flower, St Thomas' Tree, Jerusalem Date. Burma, tropical. To 7 m (20 ft). Twin-lobed 15 cm (6 in) leaves, yellow-green. Pale pink flowers, 10 cm (4 in), in terminal racemes. Pods. Fast growing. Spreading habit.

B. purpurea 37
Butterfly Tree, Orchid Tree. India to Malaysia, tropical. To 7 m (20 ft). Twin-lobed 15 cm (6 in) leaflets. Variably coloured pink to violet flowers, 12.5 cm (5 in) diameter with overlapping petals. Long pods. Fast growing. Broad-headed, untidy.

B. variegata 36-7, **38**
Mountain Ebony, Orchid Tree. India/China, temperate to tropical. To 17 m (50 ft). Twin-lobed leaves to 15 cm (6 in) across, grey-green. 5-petalled flowers, to 12.5 cm (5 in) diameter, rosy purple to yellow, but with many colour variations. Pods, to 10 cm (4 in) long. Fast growing. Shrubby, untidy, needs pruning to shape. Notable colour variation is B. variegata 'Candida' — The White Orchid Tree.

BEAUCARNEA 38
Small genus of trees or, more accurately, tree-like plants found naturally in desert areas of Mexico and Texas. Popular indoor plants in juvenile form. Family Agavaceae.

B. recurvata 38, **38**
Ponytail Tree, Bottle Ponytail, Elephant Foot Tree. Mexico, dry temperate. To 10 m (30 ft). Foliage in terminal rosettes. Lanceolate leaves to 2 m (6 ft) long, 1 cm (½ in) wide. Thin, curving, grass-like. Greenish-white flowers in long spikes. 3-winged capsules, long-stemmed. Very slow growing. Bulbous trunk, sparsely branched. A popular potted plant when small.

BETULA 39
A popular genus of deciduous trees, all native to the northern hemisphere, and mostly similar in appearance. They grow naturally in moist, shady locations by swamps or riverbeds and are closely related to the Alders. Widely cultivated for their timber which is used for furniture and household articles, particularly in Scandinavia. Most, but not all, species easily identified by their peeling bark. Family Betulaceae.

B. alba, see **B. pendula**

B. lenta 40
Cherry Birch, Sweet Birch, Mountain Mahogany. E. USA, temperate to cold. To 25 m (75 ft). 12.5 cm (5 in) leaves, silky beneath, deciduous; yellow in autumn. Typical catkins. Cones, oblong-ovoid to 3.5 cm (1½ in). Medium fast growth. Upright, round-headed. A valuable timber tree, oil of wintergreen extracted from twigs and bark.

B. lutea, see **B. allegheniensis**

B. nigra
Black Birch, River Birch, Red Birch. S.E. USA, temperate. To 35 m (100 ft). Needle-like leaves, rhomboid, to 7.5 cm (3 in), pale beneath; yellow in autumn. Typical catkins. Cylindrical 3.5 cm (1½ in) cones. Medium fast growth. Pyramidal. Timber used for cottage carpentry. Reddish-brown, ragged bark.

B. papyrifera 40
Paper Birch, Canoe Birch. Canada, N.

USA, cold temperate. To 35 m (100 ft). Coarsely serrated, pointed oval leaves to 10 cm (4 in); yellow in autumn. Typical catkins to 10 cm (4 in). Drooping cones to 3.5 cm (1½ in). Fast growing. Upright, open-headed, short limbs. Important timber tree, Indian canoes were once covered with its thick snow-white bark, which falls away in sheets.

B. pendula 39, **39, 40**
White Birch, European Birch. Europe, Asia, temperate. To 20 m (60 ft). Doubly toothed, angular ovate leaves to 6 cm (2½ in); yellow in autumn. Typical catkins. Fruiting cones, cylindrical, to 2.5 cm (1 in). Very fast growth but short-lived. Upright, open, weeping branchlets. A popular timber tree in N. Europe. Bark white, but black towards tree base. Several decorative forms are cultivated including: B. p. 'Dalecarlica', the Swedish Birch. Weeping branches, leaves deeply lobed and pointed; B. p. 'Youngii', a CV with rounded head, weeping branches.

BISCHOFIA 41
A single tropical species of tree, much grown in Asia for its valuable timber. Family Euphorbiaceae.

B. javanica 41, **41**
Toog, Koka. Malaysia to Polynesia, tropical. To 23 m (70 ft). Semi-deciduous compound leaves with 3 leaflets, each to 12.5 cm (5 in) long. Greenish flowers, small and without petals, borne in many-flowered racemes. Spring. Pea-sized berries, many colours in same cluster. Fast growing. Trunk smooth, open-headed. An important timber tree.

BIXA 41
A genus of one species, much grown as an ornamental in warm-climate gardens, but an important commercial tree in the tropics for the bright yellow dye which is extracted from the seeds and used as a food colouring, particularly in margarine. Family Bixaceae.

B. orellana 41, **41**
Lipstick Tree, Annatto, Achiote. Amazon Basin, tropical. To 10 m (30 ft). Pointed, heart-shaped evergreen leaves to 17.5 cm (7 in). Delicate pink or rose flowers, 5 petalled, in panicles. 5 cm (2 in) brown capsules, softly spiny, containing up to 50 seeds with a bright red, waxy coating. Fast growing. Shrubby, densely foliaged. Ornamental, source of red and yellow pigment.

BLIGHIA 42
A very small genus including 4 species only of evergreen trees from tropical Africa. They are grown for their edible fruit and will resist a degree of frost. Family Sapindaceae.

B. sapida 42, **42**
Akee Apple. Guinea, tropical to temperate. To 13 m (40 ft). Curved dark leaves with 6-10 graduated leaflets. Small greenish-white flowers in axillary panicles. Compound, apricot to ruby pink fruit, splitting into 5 segments, each containing 1 seed and pulp. Edible when ripe, poisonous when unripe. Fast growing. Spreading, open-headed. Grown for fruit and as an ornamental.

BOMBAX 42
A small genus of showy-flowered tropical trees, native variously to Asia, Africa, S. America and Australia. Great favourites in warm-climate gardens. Family Bombaceae.

B. barrigon
Barrigon. Tropical America. To 15 m (45 ft). Compound leaves to 30 cm (12 in) diameter, 7–9 leaflets. Deciduous. White flowers, many stamens. Pods to 17.5 cm (7 in) long. Fast growing. Pyramidal. Heavy, buttressed trunk.

B. ellipticum 43
Shaving Brush Tree, Pink Bombax. Mexico, tropical. To 25 m (75 ft). Deciduous, compound, digitate leaves to 45 cm (18 in) wide, consisting of 5 leaflets, coppery-red when young. Flowers to 25 cm (10 in) long consisting of 5 purplish petals which curl back to reveal a mass of white stamens. Spring. Pods or capsules, 10 cm (4 in) long, full of greenish fibre. Fast growing. Stark, heavy-branched; bark patterned in a magnificent snake-skin effect, grey and green. Pod fibre used as kapok substitute.

B. malabaricum 42, 42, 43
Red Silk Cotton Tree, Simal. S.E. Asia, tropical. To 35 m (105 ft). Leaves compound, to 50 cm (20 in) diameter, pale green. Deciduous. Scarlet flowers, to 17.5 cm (7 in) diameter clustered near ends of bare branches in early spring. Oblong capsules, to 15 cm (6 in) long. Fast growing. Stark, heavy-branched, sparsely foliaged, buttressed trunk. Used for timber, pod fibre used as kapok substitute. Flowers edible.

BRACHYCHITON 43—4
About a dozen deciduous trees, native to Australia and New Guinea. Of most variable foliage, and with showy late spring blossom. They are great favourites in warm temperate gardens worldwide. Family Sterculiaceae.

B. acerifolium 43
Illawarra Flame Tree, Flame Tree, Flame Bottle Tree. Q, NSW, warm temperate to sub-tropical. To 35 m (100 ft). Shiny, Maple-like, 3—7 lobed leaves to 30 cm (12 in) wide. Generally deciduous. Scarlet, campanulate flowers, to 1 cm (½ in), in loose panicles. Hard, woody black pods, to 10 cm (4 in), on long stalks. Full of irritating fibre. Slow growing. Tall, pyramidal, smooth grey trunk. Ornamental only, loves moisture.

B. bidwillii
Pink Lacebark. Q, sub-tropical. To 10 m (30 ft). Foliage slightly furry, heart-shaped, 3-lobed, to 3.5 cm (1½ in) long. Campanulate, deep pink flowers, to 3.5 cm (1½ in) in clusters at branch ends. Woody pods. Fast growing. Pyramidal, heavy-trunked. Ornamental.

B. discolor 44
Q Lacebark, White Kurrajong, Stunga. N.E. Australia, moist temperate to sub-tropical. To 35 m (100 ft). Leaves variable, 3—5—7 lobed, to 20 cm (8 in) wide, shiny above, woolly below. Deciduous in cooler areas. Pale pink, campanulate flowers to 5 cm (2 in) wide, clustered in leaf axils. Woody pods to 15 cm (6 in) long, reddish-brown and furry outside. Fast growing. Widely spreading branches high up on tree. Buttressed trunk. Ornamental.

B. diversifolia, see **B. populneum**

B. gregorii
Desert Kurrajong. SA, WA, dry temperate. To 12 m (35 ft). Shiny leaves, 3—5 short lobes. Deciduous. Pale yellow fragrant flowers, sometimes red margined 1.5 cm (¾ in) long, clustered in leaf axils. Woody pods to 5 cm (2 in) long. Slow growing. Pyramidal to columnar. Used for stock fodder; ornamental.

B. populneo-acerifolius 44
Pink Kurrajong. NSW, warm temperate. A natural hybrid. To 17 m (50 ft). Dense, variably shaped leaves to 7.5 cm (3 in), generally lobed, pale green. Deciduous. Campanulate, deep old rose flowers, to 1 cm (½ in) diameter, in clusters. Pods, very sparse. Slow growing. Pyramidal, densely foliaged, smooth lacy-patterned grey bark. Decorative.

B. populneum 44, 44
Kurrajong. E. Australia, temperate to dry. To 20 m (60ft). Leaves commonly heart-shaped, to 7.5 cm (3 in) long, but sometimes deeply lobed and longer. Deciduous. Flowers appear after foliage, campanulate, 1 cm (½ in), greenish-white, rusty red markings within. Long-stalked, rough woody pods to 7.5 cm (3 in). Seeds scarlet. Slow growing. Very variable shape, may be spreading or columnar. Used for shade, stock fodder. Easy to grow.

B. rupestre 44
Barrel Tree, Bottle Tree, Narrow-leaf Bottle Tree. Q, dry. To 16 m (50 ft).Variable leaves to 15 cm (6 in) long, but commonly much smaller. May be 3—6 lobed or simple Poplar shaped. Pinkish, campanulate flowers to 1 cm (½ in) long in panicles. Woody pods to 3.5 cm (1½ in). Slow growing. Has a ridiculously swollen trunk, like *Adansonia* (which see), with relatively small, light branches. Used for shade, stock fodder.

B. trichosiphon, see **B. australis**

BRASSAIA 45
A genus of some 40 species of tropical trees, native variously to the Malaysia-Philippines area, India, Australia and Hawaii. Only one species currently grown. Family Araliaceae.

B. actinophylla 45, 45
Octopus Tree, Q Umbrella Tree, Ivy Palm. Q, sub-tropical. To 13 m (40 ft). Long-stemmed leaves to 1 m (3 ft) diameter consisting of 7—16 radially oblong leaflets. Glossy, evergreen. Flowers in terminal clusters, a series of radiating curved racemes covered with small clusters of red blossom. Purple-red fruit in small racemes. Fast growing. Columnar, smooth grey trunk — often cut back to force a multiple-headed effect. A very popular house plant in juvenile form.

BROUSSONETIA 46
A very small genus of deciduous tropical trees, found naturally in E. Asia and Polynesia. The lower bark of the only cultivated species is used in making paper and, in the Pacific, tapa cloth. Family Moraceae.

B. papyrifera 46, 46
Paper Mulberry, Tapa Tree. China/Polynesia, temperate to tropical. To 1 m (30 ft). Very variable leaves, cordate or deeply 3-lobed to 20 cm (8 in) long. Male and female flowers on separate plants. Male, long greenish catkins to 7.5 cm (3 in), female greenish, fuzzy, 2.5 cm (1 in) clusters. Mulberry-like, red fruit. Fast growing. Variable shape, generally with open, spreading head. Uninteresting autumn colour. Inner bark used in paper and tapa making.

BROWNEA 46—7
Some 25 species of smallish tropical trees, notable for their showy inflorescences. Grown as warm-climate ornamentals. Family Leguminosae.

B. grandiceps 46—7, 46
Rose of Venezuela. Venezuela, tropical. To 20 m (60 ft). Compound pinnate leaves to 1 m (3 ft) long, consisting of about 22 leaflets. Young foliage flaccid, highly coloured. Cabbage-like, compound flower clusters up to 22.5 cm (9 in) diameter, borne behind branches and foliage. A vivid orange red. Small leguminous pods. Fast growing. Very handsome, rounded, with heavy, woolly branches. Ornamental.

B. macrophylla 47, 47
Panama Flame. Colombia, Panama, tropical. To 10 m (30 ft). Compound pinnate leaves to 30 cm (12 in) long, with 6—12

leaflets. Masses of small red/pink and yellow, long-stamened blossoms borne directly from trunk and branches. Fast growing. Very variable shape, often columnar, but light habit. Ornamental only.

BUCKINGHAMIA 47
A single species related to the Macadamia, Firewheel, and other tropical Australian trees. Family Proteaceae.

B. celsissima 47, 47
Ivory Curl Tree. Q, sub-tropical. To 20 m (60 ft). Dark, oblong, rippled leaves to 15 cm (6 in) long, paler reverses. Evergreen. Sometimes 3-lobed on young trees. Ivory-cream flowers in 22 cm (9 in) pendant racemes. Late summer. Follicles, about 2.5 cm (1 in) long. Slow growing. Variable, often columnar shape. Highly decorative.

BUTEA 48
A very small genus from tropical Asia, only one tree species of which is commonly grown. Though tropical, it is most useful in hard areas, frost hardy, drought resistant and will grow in brackish, saline soil. Family Leguminosae.

B. frondosa 48, 48
Flame of the Forest, Dhak Tree, Pulas. Bangladesh, tropical to temperate. To 16 m (50 ft). 20 cm (8 in) grey-blue leaves consisting of 3 leaflets with silver reverses. Deciduous. Brilliant orange-red blossoms with a silvery over-sheen, borne in 15 cm (6 in) racemes; appear spring before foliage. Silvery, 15 cm (6 in) pods. Fast growing. Angular, often grotesque with a twisted trunk. Source of 'Bengal Kino' gum.

B. monosperma, see **B. frondosa**

BUTIA 48
A small genus of monoecious, single-trunked Palms from the southern part of S. America, and thus hardy away from the tropics. Popular in landscapes. Family Palmae.

B. capitata var. **Odorata 48, 48**
Jelly Palm. S. Brazil, temperate. To 5 m (15 ft). Blue-grey arching leaves to 3 m (9 ft). Spiny-stemmed. Greenish-yellow to red flowers in 1 m (3 ft) drooping spadix. Yellow fruit, 2.5 cm (1 in) long and wider across. Jelly-like and edible. Slow growing. Single, very flaccid trunk, very persistent dead fronds.

B. yatay 48
Wine Palm, Yatay. Argentina, temperate. To 5 m (15 ft). Fronds, to 3 m (9 ft), blue-grey, silver beneath. Greenish-yellow flowers in very long, drooping spadices. Dark yellow to orange fruit, ovoid, to 3.5 cm (1½ in); edible. Slow growing. Single, swollen trunk.

CAESALPINIA 49
A medium-sized sub-tropical genus of the pea family including some 70 species of tropical trees widely grown for their colourful flower display. Commercially, they are also the source of dyes and tannin. Family Leguminosae.

C. echinata
Brazilwood. Tropical America. To 10 m (30 ft). Bipinnate leaves with many small, diamond-shaped leaflets. Yellow flowers with long stamens. Oblong pods to 7.5 cm (3 in). Fast growing. Tall, round-headed. Spiny trunk. Used for timber; source of red dye. Brazil's national tree.

C. ferrea 49, 49
Leopard Tree, Brazilian Ironwood. E. Brazil, tropical. To 17 m (50 ft). Dark, bipinnate leaves with 24—64 obovate leaflets. Yellow flowers in dense terminal panicles. Thick elliptical pods to 7.5 cm (3 in). Fast growing. Tall, round-headed, smooth trunk with bark beautifully marked in white, grey and beige. Used for timber.

C. peltophoroides
Sibipiruna, False Brazilwood. E. Brazil, tropical. To 12 m (35 ft). Bipinnate leaves with innumerable leaflets. Yellow flowers with long stamens, in densely flowered racemes. Brown pods. Fast growing. Upright, round-headed. Smooth trunk. Used for timber.

C. pulcherrima 49, 49
Barbadoes Pride, Barbadoes Flower Fence, Dwarf Poinciana, Peacock Flower. Pan-tropical. To 7 m (20 ft). Pale bipinnate leaves to 30 cm (12 in), numerous leaflets. Long spikes at end of branches with many 5 cm (2 in) scarlet flowers with yellow edges and 6 cm (2½ in) stamens. Pea-type pods to 10 cm (4 in). Fast growing. Shrubby, can be pruned as hedge; branches prickly. *C. p. Flava* is a yellow-flowered variety, but similar.

C. sappan 49
Sappan Wood. Malaysia, tropical. To 5 m (15 ft). Bipinnate leaves with many rectangular leaflets. Yellow flowers in long panicles. Sharply pointed pods to 9 cm (3½ in). Fast growing. Upright, round-headed. Spiny trunk and branches. Used for timber. Source of red dye.

C. spinosa 49
Tara. W.S. American deserts; dry temperate. To 7 m (20 ft). Bipinnate leaves with sparse leaflets. Flowers yellow, red margins, in dense racemes to 20 cm (8 in). Reddish pods to 11 cm (4½ in). Slow growing. Shrubby. Very spiny trunk. Important source of tannin.

CALLICOMA 50
An Australian genus of a single species, widely used in colonial days for home construction. Family Saxifragaceae.

C. serratifolia 50, 50
Blackwattle. N.E. Australia, temperate. To 10 m (30 ft). Long oval leaves to 15 cm (6 in), coarsely serrated. Young foliage pink and yellow. Cream, Acacia-like, puffball blossoms to 2.5 cm (1 in) wide. Capsules. Medium growth. Shrubby to tall and slender.

CALLISTEMON 51-2
Some of Australia's most popular small trees, the genus Callistemon is now widely grown in many lands with temperate climate. But the several tree species are often hard to identify with certainty for they hybridize indiscriminately. Family Myrtaceae.

C. citrinus 52, 52
Crimson Bottlebrush, Lemon-scented Bottlebrush. S.E. Australia, temperate. To 8 m (25 ft). Rigid, narrow, pointed leaves to 8.5 cm (3½ in) long, 1 cm (½ in) wide. Young foliage silvery, drooping. Flowers varying shades of red, cylindrical spike, to 10 cm (4 in). Circular seed cups that persist on old wood. Slow growing. Generally shrubby.

C. salignus 52, 52
Willow Bottlebrush. S.E. Australia, temperate. To 13 m (40 ft). Leaves lanceolate to 11 cm (4½ in) wide on thin, weeping branchlets. Young foliage bright pink. Flowers palest yellow, bottlebrush form, to 7.5 cm (3 in) long, drooping. Persistent seed cups. Medium fast growth. Upright, weeping branches. There are white, green and pink flowered varieties.

C. shiressii 51
Cream Bottlebrush. Australia, temperate. To 5 m (15 ft). Small, narrow leaves to 5 cm (2 in). Small bottlebrushes to 7.5 cm (3 in), often pink flecked. Persistent seed cups. Slow growing. Upright, spreading crown.

C. speciosus
Albany Bottlebrush, WA, temperate. To 7 m (20 ft). Leaves to 12.5 cm (5 in) long, only 4 mm (⅙ in) wide on downy stalks.

Bottlebrush inflorescence to 7.5 cm (3 in). Bright Red. Round seed cups to 5 mm (¼ in) wide. Fast growing. Upright.

C. viminalis 51-2, 51
Weeping Bottlebrush. NSW, temperate. To 8 m (25 ft). Willow-like leaves to 10 cm (4 in) long. Young foliage bronze. Bottlebrush inflorescence to 7.5 cm (3 in) long, scarlet. Round, green seed cups to 5 mm (¼ in) wide. Fast growing. Upright with a fully weeping habit. Old trees sometimes develop a spirally gnarled trunk and rounded head.

CALLITRIS 52
A small genus of evergreen Australian coniferous trees, typically found on the inland plains. Very useful garden specimens in arid areas. Family Cupressaceae.

C. columellaris 53
Murray Pine, White Cypress Pine. Australia, dry temperate. To 25 m (75 ft). Fine Cypress-like scales or leaves on flattened branchlets; brilliant green. 1 cm (½ in) cones, dark brown, split into 6 irregular segments. Fast growing. Upright, columnar. Highly marked timber used for flooring and feature walls.

C. cupressiformis 53
Cypress Pine. NSW, temperate, coastal. To 7 m (20 ft). Bluish leaf-scales, sparsely borne. Globular cones with 3 swollen segments. Fast growing. Upright, pyramidal. A useful timber tree.

C. preissii
Rottnest Island Pine. S. Australia, cool temperate. To 35 m (100 ft). Rounded leaf-scales to 2 mm (⅛ in). Sub-globose cones to 3.5 cm (1½ in), singly or in stalked clusters. Medium fast growth. Columnar.

C. rhomboidea 52
Port Jackson Pine, Oyster Bay Pine. NSW, coastal, temperate. To 13 m (40 ft). Leaf-scales, bluish, very small, 2 mm (⅛ in) long. Sparse. Spherical cones with 3 segments. Fast growing. Pyramidal.

CALOCEDRUS 53
A small genus of three monoecious conifers, native variously to W. USA, Taiwan, and S. China. They are slow growing and much valued in the Orient for their fragrant incense-perfumed timber. Family Cupressaceae.

C. decurrens 53, 53
California Incense Cedar. W. USA, temperate. To 35 m (100 ft). Flattened branchlets of modified scale-like leaves. Blue-green. Small 2.5 cm (1 in) cones. Very slow growing. Perfectly pyramidal. A valuable timber tree. Smaller cultivars are preferred for garden use.

C. formosana
Taiwan Incense Cedar. Taiwan, temperate to sub-tropical. To 30 m (90 ft). Leaves similar to *C. decurrens*. Cones to 2 cm (¾ in) long. Slow growing. Perfectly pyramidal.

CALODENDRON 54
For purposes of cultivation, this small African genus consists of a single evergreen species. In its natural habitat it is also a valuable timber tree. Family Rutaceae.

C. capense 54, 54
Cape Chestnut. S. and E. Africa, temperate. To 20 m (60 ft). Citrus-like leaves to 15 cm (6 in) long, often translucently spotted, evergreen. Pale pink flowers, 5 petals 3.5 cm (1½ in) wide, 5 red-spotted petaloids, 5 stamens. Borne on 20 cm (8 in) terminal panicles. Woody capsules, pentagonal, brown, to 5 cm (2 in) long. Medium growth. Broad, spreading head. A valuable timber tree. Needs plenty of water, protection from wind.

CANANGA 55
A genus of two tree species only, related

to the custard apples. One of them, the Ylang Ylang, is grown in tropical gardens everywhere for the perfume of its flowers. Family Annonaceae.

C. odorata 55, 55
Perfume Tree, Ylang Ylang. Burma, Malaysia, Australia, tropical. To 25 m (80 ft). Alternate, simple leaves to 20 cm (8 in) long, often with rippled edges. Lime green flowers, fading to orange, with twisted, drooping petals, to 7.5 cm (3 in) long, in axillary clusters. Heavily perfumed. Greenish, stalked fruit, to 2.5 cm (1 in) long. Fast growing. Upright habit, weeping branches. Flowers used to perfume Macassar oil.

CARICA 56
A small tropical genus from S. America, only two of which are seen in cultivation. They are short-lived, somewhat succulent plants, scarcely qualifying as trees except for their size. Family Caricaceae.

C. papaya 56, 56
Papaya, Paw Paw, Melon Tree. Tropical America. To 8 m (25 ft). Foliage arranged in rosettes at branch ends. These consist of 60 cm (2 ft) compound leaves, deeply divided into 7 main lobes which are also deeply lobed. Male and female flowers on separate trees, both cream and 2.5 cm (1 in) diameter. Male flowers in 1 m (3 ft) racemes, female in small axillary clusters. Melon-sized fruit, round to long oval according to variety; green, orange or red, many-seeded. Fast growing but short-lived, perhaps 12 years. Upright, often with an unbranched trunk, though branches do develop after frost or water damage. Edible fruit. The protein-digesting enzyme Papain, used as meat tenderizer, is extracted from fruit and stems.

C. pubescens
Mountain Papaya. The Andes, tropical, high altitude. To 7 m (20 ft). Leaves similar to *C. papaya* but downy. Green, downy flowers. Yellow-orange fruit, to 10 cm (4 in) deeply 5-ribbed, sour, must be cooked with sugar. Medium fast growth. Upright, branching, with a stout trunk. Frost hardy. Edible fruit. Hardier plant than the common Paw Paw, suited to colder climates.

CARYA 57
Closely related to the walnuts, these gigantic deciduous trees are native mostly to N. America, but with a few species in Asia and C. America. They are the source of magnificent timbers, as well as a wide variety of edible nuts, and will grow in a surprising range of climates. Family Juglandaceae.

C. cordiformis
Bitternut, Swamp Hickory. E. USA, temperate. To 30 m (90 ft). Compound leaves of 5-9 spear-shaped leaflets, 15 cm (6 in) long. Male flowers in drooping catkins, female in terminal racemes. Green. Round, smooth, grey nuts. Slow growing. Upright, spreading crown. Flaking bark. Used for timber, edible nuts.

C. glabra 58
Pignut, Small Fruited Hickory. N. America, cool temperate. To 13 m (40 ft). Compound leaves with 5 15 cm (6 in) long serrated leaflets. Flowers as in *C. cordiformis*. Oval, ridged, 2.5 cm (1 in) nuts. Slow growing. Upright, broad head. Yellow in autumn. Used for timber, edible nuts.

C. illinoinensis 57, 57, 58
Pecan. C. USA, Mexico, temperate to sub-tropical. To 55 m (100 ft). Compound leaves with 11-17 leaflets, 17.5 cm (7 in) long. Flowers as in *C. cordiformis*. Smooth, oval nuts, dark-spotted, in clusters. Slow growing. Col-

umnar, rounded head. Yellow in autumn. Splendid timber, delicious nuts.

C. laciniata 57
King Nut, Shellbark Hickory. E. USA, temperate. To 40 m (120 ft). Compound leaves of 5–9 lanceolate leaflets to 20 cm (8 in) long. Downy reverses. Flowers as in other species. Round nuts, orange in colour. Slow growing. Columnar. Yellow in autumn. shaggy bark.

C. ovata 57
Shagbark Hickory, Shellbark Hickory. N. America, temperate. To 25 m (70 ft). Compound leaves with 5 elliptical leaflets, 15 cm (6 in) long. Flowers as in other species. White elliptical nuts. Slow growing. Columnar, slender. Golden-brown in autumn. Used for timber, edible nuts.

CARYOTA 58
A small Palm genus from the tropics of S.E. Asia, distinguished by the pronounced 'fishtail' effect of the frond tips. They are monoecious and grown largely as ornamentals away from their home territory. Family Palmae.

C. mitis
Clustered Fishtail Palm. Indo-Malaysia, tropical. To 8 m (25 ft). Bipinnate fronds to 3 m (9 ft) with irregularly toothed wedge-shaped leaflets. Stalks and leaf sheaths are black. Cream flowers, 1 cm (½ in), in short, branched inflorescence. Single-seeded fruit, 1 cm (½ in) diameter. Grows fast, suckers readily. Slim 10 cm (4 in) trunk, clustering habit.

C. ochlandra
Chinese Fishtail Palm. S. China, tropical. To 5 m (15 ft). Bipinnate fronds to 3 m (9 ft). Male flowers 1 cm (½ in), cream, in long panicles. Blood-red fruit, 2.5 cm (1 in) diameter. Fast growing. Medium height, suckers sparsely. Thick trunk.

C. rumphiana 58, 58
Fishtail Palm. Philippines to Australia, tropical. To 25 m (75 ft). Bipinnate fronds with horizontal leaflets. Inflorescence to 1.5 m (4½ ft) long. Reddish-green fruit to 1.5 cm (⅝ in) diameter. Fast growing. Trunk straight, 30 cm (12 in) diameter.

C. urens 58
Wine Palm, Jaggery Palm, Toddy Palm, Sago Palm, Kittul. India, Sri Lanka, Malaysia, tropical. To 13 m (40 ft). Bipinnate fronds with wedge-shaped 23 cm (9 in) leaflets. Flowers in panicles to 7 m (20 ft) long. Reddish fruit, 2-seeded to 1.5 cm (⅝ in) diameter. Fast growing. Upright, does not sucker. Commercially raised for timber, fibre and sago. The sap is also fermented into an alcoholic drink known as toddy.

CASSIA 59-60
One of the largest genera of flowering tropical trees and shrubs, grown not only for their decorative effect, but for their commercial importance in medicine and tanning. Family Leguminosae.

C. brewsteri 60
Cigar Cassia. Q, sub-tropical. To 13 m (40 ft). Shiny pale green pinnate leaves with 4–8 oblong leaflets of 5 cm (2 in). Deciduous. Flowers in 20 cm (8 in) racemes. Buds scarlet, individual, 2.5 cm (1 in), open flowers, pale apricot with yellow stamens. Spring. Pods, to 30 cm (12 in) long. Medium fast growth. Round-headed, open.

C. fistula 60
Pudding Pipe Tree, Indian Laburnum, Golden Shower, Golden Rain. India, tropical. To 10 m (30 ft). Large pinnate leaves with 20 cm (8 in) oval leaflets in 4–8 pairs. Pale to brilliant yellow flowers in long dangling racemes to 45 cm (18 in). Plump dark brown pods to 60 cm (2 ft)

long. Fast growing. Columnar to round-headed. The source of medicinal senna.

C. X hybrida 59
Rainbow Shower. Hybrid, tropical. To 15 m (45 ft). Foliage similar to C. javanica. Flowers very variable in colour — may be yellow and white, yellow and pink, pink and orange, pink and red and white. Fruit variable. Fast growing. Very variable in shape. This is Hawaii's favourite tree and a natural hybrid between the species C. fistula and C. javanica.

C. javanica 59
Apple Blossom Cassia, Java Shower. Indonesia, tropical. To 7 m (20 ft). Grey-green pinnate leaves with 10–24 blunt 5 cm (2 in) leaflets. 3 cm (1¼ in) flowers in dense racemes, opening pale pink, brightening with age. Spring and summer. Pods to 60 cm (2 ft). Fast growing. Open and spreading to columnar, depending on situation.

C. leptophylla
Brazil Shower. S.E. Brazil, temperate to sub-tropical. To 20 m (60 ft). Long, pinnate leaves with 16–24 oval leaflets. Open lemon yellow flowers in clusters at branch ends. Summer. Green pods to 30 cm (12 in) long, persistent. Fast growing. Rounded head.

C. multijuga 60
Golden Shower. Brazil, Guyana, tropical. To 7 m (20 ft). Pinnate leaves with 36–80 oblong 2 cm (¾ in) leaflets. 5 cm (2 in) orange-yellow flowers in large panicles. Summer. Flat pods to 15 cm (6 in). Fast growing. Round-headed to columnar, often with weeping branches. Very common in Queensland.

C. spectabilis 59
Showy Cassia, Golden Shower. Tropical America. To 20 m (60 ft). Dark pinnate leaves with 16–30, 7.5 cm (3 in) leaflets, downy on the reverse. 3.5 cm (1½ in) bright yellow flowers in 60 cm (2 ft) panicles. Autumn. 30 cm (12 in) pods. Medium growth. Rounded head, branchlets downy.

C. surattensis 60
Singapore Shower. Tropical Asia, Australia, Polynesia, tropical to temperate. To 10 m (30 ft). Pinnate leaves with 12–20 3.5 cm (1½ in) leaflets. Pale yellow blossoms with 10 large anthers, borne in clusters. Flat pods to 15 cm (6 in). Slow growth away from tropics. Rounded head.

CASTANEA 61
Related to the Oaks and Beeches, these are a small genus of deciduous northern hemisphere trees easily recognized by their fruit or nuts which are enclosed in a large prickly envelope. Their timber has also been used in furnishing. Family Fagaceae.

C. crenata 61
Japanese Chestnut. Japan, temperate. To 10 m (30 ft). Closely toothed leaves to 15 cm (6 in), woolly reverses. Male blossom in catkins, female at leaf axils, both yellow. 2.5 cm (1 in) nuts in clusters of 2 or 3. Slow growing. Rounded head. A useful timber tree. Blight resistant.

C. dentata 61
American Chestnut, Sweet Chestnut. E. USA, cool temperate. To 30 m (100 ft). Tapering, coarsely toothed leaves to 25 cm (10 in) long. Yellow, unisexual flowers in catkins. Nuts, 2.5 cm (1 in) diameter, in clusters of 3. Slow growing. Upright, broad-crowned. Once valued for nuts, timber and tanbark, but now almost extinct due to Chestnut blight.

C. mollissima 61
Chinese Chestnut. China, cool temperate. To 20 m (60 in). Coarsely toothed leaves

to 15 cm (6 in), silky reverses. Flowers as in other species. 2.5 cm (1 in) nuts in clusters of 3. Slow growing. Rounded head, densely foliaged. Blight resistant.

C. pumila 61
Chinquapin, E. USA, temperate. To 15 m (45 ft). Coarsely toothed 12.5 cm (5 in) leaves, woolly reverses. Flowers as in other species. Solitary nut to 1 cm (½ in) diameter. Slow growing. Shrubby, densely foliaged. Tough timber used in railway sleepers and fencing.

C. sativa 61, 61
Spanish Chestnut, European Chestnut. S. Europe, N. Africa, Asia Minor, warm temperate. To 30 m (90 ft). Round-based, coarsely toothed, 20 cm (8 in) leaves, silky reverses. Brown in autumn. Flowers as in other species. Unpleasant odour. 1–3 nuts, each 2.5 cm (1 in) diameter. Slow growing. Spreading top, distinctive spiral bark pattern. A wonderful timber tree with delicious autumn nuts, but unfortunately susceptible to Chestnut blight.

CASTANOSPERMUM 62
A showy, sub-tropical tree, the only one of its genus. Family Leguminosae.

C. australe 62, 62
Moreton Bay Chestnut, Black Bean. E. Australia, sub-tropical. To 20 m (60 ft). Dark evergreen pinnate leaves to 45 cm (18 in) with 10–14 glossy leaflets. Red and orange, 2.5 cm (1 in), pea flowers in short sprays on old wood. Plump pods, 23 cm (9 in), containing 4 cm (1½ in) edible seeds. These pods change from green to red and finally brown. Medium fast growth. Shrubby to columnar, densely foliaged with often weeping branches. Edible nuts, timber used for furnishing.

CASUARINA 62-3
An interesting genus of trees native to Australia and the Pacific Islands. Delicate and graceful in appearance, but with a constitution as hard as their timber. Not related to any other tree, but superficially resembling the conifers. Family Casuarinaceae.

C. cunninghamiana
River Sheoke, Fire Oak. E. Australia, temperate to sub-tropical. To 23 m (70 ft). Minute leaf-scales, 8 in a whorl. Reddish-brown flowers. Sub-globose cones to 1 cm (½ in) diameter. Medium fast growth. Massive trunk, the largest Casuarina. A valuable timber tree, planted to prevent erosion.

C. equisetifolia 62
Horsetail Tree, Ironwood, Shingle Oak. India to Hawaii, tropical. To 25 m (80 ft). Leaf-scales, 6 or 7 in a whorl. Flowers as in other species. Cones longer than wide, grey. Slow growing. Pyramidal when young, round-headed in maturity, with distinctive weeping outer branchlets. A valuable timber tree, much planted as a wind-break in the tropics.

C. glauca
Grey Buloke. S. and E. Australia, temperate. To 16 m (50 ft). Leaf-scales, 14–16 in a whorl. Flowers as in other species. 1 cm (½ in) cones, sub-globose. Medium fast growth. Pyramidal to columnar. The entire tree has a blue grey appearance.

C. littoralis 62
Black Sheoke. E. Australia, Tas, temperate. To 15 m (45 ft). Leaf-scales, 6–7 in a whorl. Flowers as in other species. Dark brown to black cones, to 2 cm (¾ in) diameter. Fast growing. Light, open, pyramidal; blackish trunk. Dark timber.

C. stricta
Sheoke. S. Australia, cool temperate. To 20 m (60 ft). Leaf-scales, 10–12 in a whorl. Flowers as in other species. Sub-

globose cones, (2.5–4 cm) (1–1½ in) long; very dark. Medium fast growth. A slight tree, of weeping habit. Suckers from the roots. Valuable timber tree.

CATALPA 63
A small genus of northern hemisphere trees, deciduous and very spectacular when in flower. Family Bignoniaceae.

C. bignonioides 63
Catalpa, Indian Bean. E. USA, cool temperate. To 15 m (45 ft). Heart-shaped 25 cm (1 in) leaves, felty to the touch. Generally in groups of 3; unpleasantly perfumed. Yellow in autumn. Summer blossom in 25 cm (10 in) panicles from new wood. Flowers open, bell-shaped, white, with yellow and purple markings. Long pods, to 37.5 cm (15 in). Medium fast growth. Wide spreading at maturity. A gold-leafed variety is available.

C. fargesii
Pink Catalpa. China, cool temperate. To 20 cm (60 ft). Heart-shaped 15 cm (6 in) leaves, hairy on the reverse. Yellow in autumn. Flowers rose-pink, striped yellow. Late spring. Pods, to 45 cm (18 in) long. Medium fast growth. Spreading crown.

C. speciosa 63
W. Catalpa, Catawba, Cigar Tree. C. USA, cool temperate. To 35 m (100 ft). Large heart-shaped leaves to 30 cm (12 in) long, sharp pointed and without odour. White blossoms, spotted purple in early summer. Pods, to 45 cm (18 in) long. Medium fast growth. Very wide-crowned at maturity, with downward pointing branches.

CATHA 64
A genus of a single species from tropical Africa, much valued for the tea-like beverage prepared from its foliage. Highly decorative. Family Celastraceae.

C. edulis 64, 64
Khat, Arabian Tea Tree, Qat, Cafta, Abyssinian Tea. N. Africa, Arabia, tropical to temperate. To 7 m (20 ft), occasionally much more. Variable shiny leaves, generally elliptical to 10 cm (4 in) and slightly toothed. 5-petalled flowers in small clusters from leaf axils. Leathery capsules. Fast growing. Broad with weeping branchlets. Source of a popular stimulant in Arab countries.

CEDRELA 64
A small genus of trees native to both tropical America and S.E. Asia, valued for their fragrant, insect repellent timber, which has both practical and decorative uses. Not true Cedars in spite of their popular names. Family Meliaceae.

C. odorata 64, 65
Cigar Box Cedar, Spanish Cedar. W. Indies, S. America, tropical. To 35 m (100 ft). Evergreen pinnate leaves, 60 cm (2 ft), with 12–20 long oval leaflets. Yellowish flowers in 30 cm (12 in) panicles. Leathery capsules to 3.5 cm (1½ in) long. Fast growing. Upright, round-headed. A most important timber tree, its insect repellent wood being used for cigar boxes and to line storage cupboards of all types. Also grown as an ornamental.

C. sinensis 64, 64, 65
Chinese Toon, China Cedar. China, temperate. To 15 m (40 ft). Deciduous, onion-flavoured pinnate leaves to 75 cm (2½ ft), with 10–30 long oval leaflets, slightly serrated. Spring foliage a delicate pink and edible. Yellow in autumn. White flowers in long hanging panicles. Leathery capsules of 2.5 cm (1 in). Fast growing. Columnar, with ultimately a spreading head. Rough bark. A fine timber tree, grown as an ornamental for its spring foliage.

C. toona, see TOONA australis

CEDRUS 65–6
Four species of splendid, picturesque coniferous trees, of similar appearance. Found naturally from the Mediterranean to India. Grown in large gardens everywhere. Family Pinaceae.

C. atlantica 65, 66
Mt Atlas Cedar, Atlantic Cedar. N. Africa, temperate. To 40 m (120 ft). Needle-like leaves to 2.5 cm (1 in) long, borne in rosettes on old wood. Generally bluish-green but there are other colour varieties. Pale green to purple flowers in upright spikes. Summer. Barrel-shaped cones take 2 years to ripen. Fast growing. Pyramidal, spreading top in maturity. A good timber tree. *C. a. Aurea* has foliage of a golden green, *C. a. Glauca Pendula* is a picturesque, naturally weeping variety.

C. deodara 66, 66
Deodar, Indian Cedar. Himalayas, temperate to cold. To 70 m (200 ft). Dark green needle-like leaves to 3.5 cm (1½ in) long, often with a silvery finish. Male and female flowers on separate trees. Barrel-shaped cones to 12.5 cm (5 in) long. Fast growing. Pyramidal when young with weeping leafy shoots, broad-headed in old age. Largest of the genus. A fine timber tree. Many colour varieties.

C. libani 65–6, 66
Cedar of Lebanon. Lebanon, temperate. To 35 m (100 ft). Bright green needle-like leaves to 3.25 cm (1¼ in) long. Flowers as in *C. atlantica*. Cones to 10 cm (4 in). Fairly slow growing. Erect branches, flat-topped when mature. The biblical timber tree, has many named varieties.

CEIBA 67
Only one species of this small S. African genus is ever seen away from its native jungles. Family Bombacaceae.

C. pentandra 67, 67
Kapok Tree, White Silk Cotton Tree. S. America, now pan-tropical. To 50 m (150 ft). Palmately compound deciduous leaves, pinnate, with 5–7 lanceolate leaflets, 15 cm (6 in) long. Flowers, before foliage, white, tinted yellow or pink, about 7.5 cm (3 in) diameter. Elliptical capsules, to 25 cm (10 in) long, filled at maturity with a silky fibre which is kapok. Fast growing. Columnar, the spiny trunk with buttresses up to a fifth of its height and relatively short, horizontal branches arranged in whorls. Source of kapok.

CELTIS 68
A useful genus of handsomely foliaged Elm relatives from many parts of the northern hemisphere, much planted as street and shade trees in cooler areas. They are quite frost hardy. Family Ulmaceae.

C. australis 68, 68
Nettle Tree, Honeyberry. Mediterranean, temperate. To 27 m (80 ft). Lanceolate leaves, 15 cm (6 in), deciduous, rough textured. Yellow in autumn. Greenish, small flowers, both sexes separately on the same tree. Globose, purple fruit to 5 mm (¼ in) diameter, sweet and edible. Slow growing. Rounded head.

C. laevigata
Sugarberry, Mississippi Hackberry. S. USA, Mexico, warm temperate. To 35 m (100 ft). Thin, lanceolate leaves to 10 cm (4 in), smooth textured. Yellow in autumn. Flowers as in other species. Fruit orange, ripening purple, small. Slow growing. Spreading head, often weeping branches. Used for timber, edible fruit.

C. occidentalis 68
Nettleberry, Hackberry, Sugarberry. N. USA, temperate to cold. To 40 m (120 ft). Foliage oblong, to 12.5 cm (5 in), toothed, sometimes downy, deciduous. Yellow in autumn. Flowers as in other

species. Fruit orange, ripening dark purple, small, heavily produced. Slow growing. Rounded head. Useful timber; edible fruit.

C. sinensis 68
Chinese Hackberry, Japanese Hackberry. China, Korea, Japan, temperate. To 20 m (60 ft). Dark green wavy-toothed leaves to 10 cm (4 in), downy when young. Yellow in autumn. Flowers as in other species, but blooms early. Edible fruit, small, red or yellow. Medium fast growth. Upright, round-headed. Used for timber, edible fruit.

CERATONIA 68–9
A genus of one evergreen Mediterranean species, widely grown for its edible pods. Family Leguminosae.

C. siliqua 68, 69
St John's Bread, Carob Bean, Locust, Algarroba. E. Mediterranean, temperate. To 16 m (50 ft). Blue-green, even pinnate leaves with 4–6 orbicular leaflets, 10 cm (4 in) diameter. Small, red and white blooms in racemes directly from old branches, sexes separate on same tree. Edible pods, filled with sweet pulp and seeds, to 20 cm (8 in). Slow growing. Shrubby to round-headed. Pods source of carob flour, carob gum, substitute for chocolate, also fed to stock.

CERATOPETALUM 69
A small genus of slender evergreen trees native to E. Australia and New Guinea, two of them grown widely in moist temperate climates. Family Cunoniaceae.

C. apetalum 69, 69
Coachwood. NSW, Q, temperate/subtropical. To 20 m (60 ft). Leaves opposite, with generally 3 lanceolate leaflets to 12.5 cm (5 in) long. Calyx only, green ripening to cream and pink, 5 mm (¼ in) wide. Small seeds. Decorative silvery bark. Slow growing. Shrubby to upright with spreading head. An important timber tree.

C. gummiferum 69, 70
Redbush, NSW Christmas Bush. NSW, temperate. To 13 m (40 ft). Dark green leaves of 3 lanceolate leaflets to 3.5 cm (1½ in) long. Flowers in crowded panicles, white, 1 cm (½ in) wide. Persistent calyces which colour pink, red and even purple after flower fall. Slow growing. Shrubby, irregular form. The flowers and foliage of the species are a popular Christmas decoration in NSW.

CERBERA 70
Six small tree species native to India and Pacific Ocean areas, related to, and closely resembling, the Plumeria. Family Apocynaceae.

C. manghas 70
Sea Mango. S. Asia to Polynesia, tropical. To 7 m (20 ft). Simple dark green leaves to 30 cm (12 in) long, deeply veined and spirally arranged. Flowers to 7.5 cm (3 in) wide in terminal clusters, cream with red throat. Smooth, oval, pink to blue fruits, 10 cm (4 in) long, containing a poisonous woody stone. Fast growing. Many branched, shrubby. A medicinal oil is extracted from the seeds.

C. odollan 70
Cerbera. India to Pacific Islands, tropical. To 17 m (50 ft). Dark green leaves to 30 cm (12 in) long, heavily veined. Flowers to 6 cm (2½ in) wide, white with yellow eye, borne in compound cymes. Oval fruit to 10 cm (4 in) long, green, ripening red. Inedible. Medium fast growth. Shrubby to upright, heavily branched.

CERCIS 71
A genus of 7 small decorative tree species, scattered about N. America, S. Europe and Asia. Grown usually for their

spectacular display of vivid pea flowers which pop out of the main branches and trunk in late winter. Family Leguminosae.

C. canadensis 71, **71**
Redbud. E. USA, cool temperate. To 13 m (40 ft). Deciduous, almost circular leaves with cordate bases, to 10 cm (4 in). Yellow in autumn. Red-pink typical pea blossoms to 1 cm (½ in) long, appearing in clusters from old wood. Brownish pods to 9 cm (3½ in) long. Slow growing. Shrubby to open, upright. White and pink CVs are raised.

C. occidentalis
California Redbud, W. Redbud. California, temperate. To 5 m ((15 ft). Kidney-shaped leaves to 7.5 cm (3 in) diameter. Reddish pea flowers in clusters. 7.5 cm (3 in) pods to 2.5 cm (1 in) diameter. Slow growing. Shrubby.

C. siliquastrum 71, **71**
Judas Tree, Love Tree. S. Europe, Asia Minor, temperate. To 13 m (40 ft). Deeply cordate leaves to 12.5 cm (5 in) diameter. Yellow in autumn. Purplish-rose pea blossoms, 2 cm (¾ in) long in clusters. Persistent reddish-brown pods to 10 cm (4 in) long. Fast growing. Shrubby, round-topped.

CHAMAECYPARIS 72
The false Cypresses are an enormously popular genus of ornamental conifers in cool and temperate gardens, with innumerable colour varieties in their foliage. All are native to N. America and Asia. Family Cupressaceae.

C. lawsoniana 72, **72**
Port Orford Cedar, Lawson Cypress. Oregon, California, temperate. To 33 m (100 ft). Minute scale-like leaves arranged on drooping, frond-like branchlets. Separate male and female flowers on the same tree. Thin, oblong, male cones pink or crimson, female green to brown and up to 1 cm (½ in) diameter. Very fast growing in nature. Pyramidal, becoming wide-headed in old age. A valuable timber tree in W.N. America. Smaller garden cultivars in a wide range of shapes, foliage, colours and habit. Those with gold-toned foliage are more popular.

C. nootkanensis 72, **72**
Alaska Cedar, Nootka Cypress. Alaska to Oregon, cool temperate to cold. To 33 m (100 ft). Leaf-scales, minute, dark green, in drooping branchlets. Male flowers yellow. Female cones green, tinged purple, to 1 cm (½ in) diameter. Grows very fast in nature. Pyramidal, occasionally wide-headed in age. A valuable timber tree. Less inclined to sport, but there are dwarf, columnar and weeping forms.

C. obtusa 72
Hinoki Cypress, Japanese False Cypress. Japan, temperate. To 40 m (120 ft). Leaf-scales glossy above, whitish lines beneath, on flattened frond-like branches. Leaves in unequally sized pairs. Male flowers minute. Female cones green, ripening orange, 1 cm (½ in) diameter. Fast growing in nature. Broadly conical. The timber is highly prized in Japan. There are a myriad foliage varieties in cultivation.

C. thyoides 72
White Cedar, Swamp White Cedar. E. USA, temperate. To 30 m (90 ft). Tiny paired leaf-scales, bright green and sharply pointed, on flattened branchlets. Male flowers, dark brown, minute. Small purplish cones. Medium fast growth. Conical. A good timber tree in the E. USA.

CHIONANTHUS 73
A very small genus of 4 deciduous trees, 2 from Asia, 2 from N. America. Frost hardy in nature. Family Oleaceae.

C. retusa 73, **73**
Chinese Fringe Tree. China, temperate to cold. To 7 m (20 ft). Single elliptical leaves to 10 cm (4 in). Small white flowers with strap-shaped petals in showy terminal panicles, to 10 cm (4 in) long. Blue oval drupes, 1 cm (½ in) long. Slow growing. Spreading head. No commercial importance, but very decorative in cool temperate gardens.

C. virginiana 73
Fringe Tree, Old Man's Beard. S.E. USA, temperate. To 7 m (20 ft). Oblong leaves, to 20 cm (8 in). Yellow in autumn. White flowers with strap-like 2.5 cm (1 in) petals, in 20 cm (8 in) lateral panicles. Blue fruit. Slow growing. Shrubby, spreading.

CHORICARPIA 73
An Australian genus of a single species. Family Myrtaceae.

C. leptopetala 73, **73**
Brush Turpentine. E. Australia, temperate. To 16 m (48 ft). Leatery, wavy-edged leaves to 15 cm (6 in) long. Shiny with rusty reverse; young foliage rusty. Creamy-yellow puffballs to 2.5 cm (1 in) diameter in drooping clusters. Small capsules. Fast growing. Upright, weeping branches. Ornamental, good shade tree.

CHORISIA 74
Two species of deciduous trees from S. America, highly decorative and curious in that the flowers of no two specimens are *exactly* alike. Family Malvaceae.

C. insignis 74, **74**
Spicy Chorisia. Peru, temperate. To 17 m (50 ft). Palmately compound leaves with 12.5 cm (5 in) oblong serrated leaflets. White or yellow Hibiscus-type blossoms 15 cm (6 in) diameter. 12.5 cm (5 in) capsules. Medium fast growth. Viciously spined trunk to 2 m (6 ft) diameter, relatively slender branches.

C. speciosa 74, **74**
Floss Silk Tree. Brazil and Argentina, subtropical to tropical. To 17 m (50 ft) or more. Palmately compound leaves with 12.5 cm (5 in) serrated leaflets. Deciduous. Flowers pink to red or violet, sometimes yellow or apricot, to 12.5 cm (5 in) diameter. Often on bare wood. Capsules, 20j cm (8 in). Very fast growth. Upright, with a high crown and spiny trunk. Pod fibre used as a substitute for kapok.

CHRYSOPHYLLUM 75
A large genus of evergreen, tropical fruiting trees distributed about the Americas, S.E. Asia and Australia. Only two species are widely cultivated. Family Sapotaceae.

C. cainito 75, **75**
Star Apple, Caimito. Tropical America. To 17 m (50 ft). Simple 15 cm (6 in) elliptical leaves, shining green above, silky golden-brown beneath. Evergreen. Small mauve flowers in clusters. Green berries, 10 cm (4 in), ripening to red-violet, with a distinct star-shaped pattern in section. Fast growing. Upright, round-headed, weeping branches.

C. oliviforme
Satinleaf, Jamaica Plum. The Caribbean, tropical. To 10 m (30 ft). Simple 7.5 cm (3 in) shiny elliptical leaves, silky and reddish beneath. Small white blossoms in clusters. Purple berries, 2 cm (¾ in) long. Fast growing. Shrubby to broad-crowned.

CINNAMOMUM 76-7
A very large genus of aromatic-foliaged evergreens occurring naturally from Asia to Australia, source of many valuable oils and spices. Family Lauraceae.

C. burmanii 76, **76**
Padang Cassia. S.E. Asia, tropical. To 20 m

(60 ft). Opposite leaves to 10 cm (4 in), oblong, acuminate. Young foliage red. Flowers in panicles, very small and greenish-white. Green berries. Fast growing. Rounded head. The red bark is an inferior source of cinnamon.

C. camphora 76, **76**
Camphor Laurel, Camphor Tree. China, Japan, Taiwan, sub-tropical to temperate. To 35 m (100 ft). Alternate leaves to 12.5 cm (5 in), ovate, acuminate, colouring pink in spring when the tree is briefly deciduous. Tiny yellow-green flowers in small axillary panicles. Black berries, about 5 mm (¼ in) diameter. Very fast growing. Stout-branched, round-headed, rough grey bark. Light weight timber is very popular as Camphorwood. Camphor distilled from parts of the tree.

C. cassia 76
Cassia, Chinese Cinnamon. Burma, tropical. To 15 m (45 ft). Opposite leaves, lanceolate, to 15 cm (6 in). Greenish flowers in panicles as long as leaves. Small blackish berries. Fast growing. Rounded head. The bark is ground for cinnamon blends, cassia is prepared from other parts of tree.

C. loureirii 76, **77**
Saigon Cinnamon, Cassia Flower Tree. S.E. Asia, tropical. To 20 m (60 ft). Alternate or opposite leaves to 12.5 cm (5 in). Elliptic. Small, greenish-yellow flowers in short panicles. Small berries, green to black. Fast growing. Upright, round-headed. Bark ground for cinnamon blends.

C. zeylanicum 76, **76**
Cinnamon, Ceylon Cinnamon. Sri Lanka, tropical. To 10 m (30 ft). 7.5 cm (3 in) ovate-lanceolate leaves, coloured pink when young. Small yellowish flowers in panicles. Berries, green to black. Medium fast growth. Spreading, round-headed. The best quality cinnamon is prepared from the dried bark.

CITHAREXYLUM 77
A genus of small, densely foliaged trees from the tropical Americas. The evergreen leaves colour attractively in winter and they are widely planted as ornamentals. Family Verbenaceae.

C. fruticosum
Fiddlewood. W. Indies, sub-tropical. To 17 m (50 ft). Smooth, elliptical leaves to 15 cm (6 in). Colouring gold in winter. Flowers like white Lilac in 12.5 cm (5 in) racemes. All year. Small, berry-like drupes, separating into 2 parts. Fast growing. Shrubby to pyramidal. A popular timber tree in the Caribbean.

C. quadrangulare 77, **77**
Jamaica Fiddlewood. W. Indies, tropical. To 17 m (50 ft). Elliptical, 20 cm (8 in) leaves, shiny, often coarsely toothed. Colouring pinkish in winter. Small white flowers in slender racemes to 30 cm (12 in) long. Fruit similar to *C. fruticosum*, in dangling chains. Fast growing. Shrubby to pyramidal. A useful cabinet wood.

C. spinosum, see **C. quadrangulare**

CITRUS 78
The *Citrus* genus includes some 16 species of small to medium-sized decorative trees, all with dark coloured bark and evergreen, glossy foliage. The leaves are quite distinctive. Originally compound, they have developed into a single leaflet supported by a curiously winged stem or petiole, more obvious in some species than others. The fragrant blossom, white, cream or purple, is highly fragrant and arranged in axillary cymes. The *Citrus* fruits (too well known to need description) are botanically classed as an aromatic, leathery-skinned berry. The flesh divides into 8-15 segments.

Most commercially grown *Citrus* are hybrids of several original species and are listed below.

The popular dwarf Kumquats are not classed as trees, and are not true *Citrus*. Their tiny white flowers appear singly at leaf axils. Botanically they are classed separately as *Fortunella*.

As the growth and appearance of the many *Citrus* species and hybrids is similar, they are detailed below only by the difference in their fruits and foliage.

All are from S.E. Asia, and sub-tropical, though some species are more resistant to cold than others. Family Rutaceae.

C. aurantiifolia 79
Lime. Leaves elliptic-ovate to 7.5 cm (3 in) with narrowly winged petiole. White flowers in racemose clusters. Greenish-yellow fruit with a pronounced nipple at end. Thin-skinned, acid and frost tender. Varieties of this species include Mexican Lime, Persian Lime, Tahiti Lime, W. India Lime. Source of commercial lime juice. The tree is spiny.

C. aurantium 78, 79
Seville Orange, Bitter Orange, Bigarade. Ovate oblong leaves to 10 cm (4 in), petioles broadly winged. Fruit globose, to 8.25 cm (3¼ in) diameter, orange to reddish. Juice sour and acid. Fruit used for marmalade; oil of Neroli expressed from flowers. Varieties include *C. a. myrtifolia*, the Chinotto Orange, with small diamond-shaped leaves and bitter fruits. *C. a. bergamia*, the Bergamot Orange, from which the perfume Oil of Bergamot is prepared. These trees are spiny.

C. decumana
The Pomelo, Shaddock or Pamplemousse. Leaves single, elliptic, to 20 cm (8 in) long, the petioles *very* broadly winged. Very large fruits, to 15 cm (6 in) diameter, may weigh up to 9 kg (20 lb). Usually pear-shaped, and from green to orange-yellow in colour. Not seen much away from the tropics. The tree is almost spineless.

C. grandis, see C. decumana
C. limon 79
Lemon. Leaves to 10 cm (4 in), dark green and *without* winged petioles. Blossom is sometimes pink in bud. Fruit usually ovoid or oblong, yellow and with a terminal nipple. To 12.5 cm (5 in) long, except for the CV 'Ponderosa' which may grow to double the size. Juice acid to sweet, refreshing. Source of lemon oil, citric acid, citrate of lime. Usually with heavy spines. Varieties include 'Eureka', without spines. 'Lisbon', pale foliage, long, pointed fruit. 'Meyer', round, orange-yellow thin-skinned, frost-hardy, may be a lemon/orange cross. 'Ponderosa', gigantic fruit, thick skin. 'Rough', round, rough, thick skin. 'Villafranca', dark foliage, densely spined. All are small trees rarely above 7 m (20 ft).

C. X limonia
Rangpur Lime, Mandarin Lime. Dull green leaves without petioles. Purplish buds and blossom. Flatly globose fruit to 5 cm (2 in) diameter. Acid pulp. Like a small, acid mandarin. This is believed to be a mandarin/lemon cross.

C. maxima, see C. decumana

C. medica
Citron. Leaves are slightly serrated, to 20 cm (8 in) long, and without winged petioles. Flowers mauve in bud, up to 5 cm (2 in) diameter. Round to oblong fruit and may be 25 cm (10 in) diameter, warty with a very thick skin and insipid pulp. The tree has very large spines, the fruit is used for candied peel. CV 'Etrog' is shaped like a very elongated lemon.

C. X nobilis
Tangor. Lanceolate leaves, 11 cm (4½ in), petioles almost wingless. Reddish-orange fruit, flattened globose; the skin is easily removable. This is an orange/mandarin cross. CV 'Ellendale' is a popular CV. CV 'Temple' – the 'Temple Orange'. This species is almost thornless.

C. X paradisii 79
Grapefruit. Ovate leaves, to 18.5 cm (7½ in) long, the petioles broadly winged. Flowers in clusters. Fruit also in clusters of 2–20, pale yellow to orange-yellow, up to 12.5 cm (5 in) diameter. Pulp sweet to acid. The grapefruit, believed to be a cross between the pomelo and sweet orange, does not occur in nature. Popular CVs include CV 'Marsh's Seedless', nearly seedless; CV 'Ruby', with pink to red flesh, pale skin; CV 'Wheeny', very juicy.

C. reticulata 78
Mandarin Orange, Tangerine, Satsuma Orange. Oval lanceolate leaves to 3.5 cm (1½ in) long, petioles slightly winged. Flattened globose fruit to 7.5 cm (3 in) diameter, smooth, loose skin. A small spiny tree. Popular CVs include 'Clementine', fruit almost round; 'Dancy', fruit almost round.

C. sinensis
Sweet Orange, Navel Orange. Oblong ovate leaves to 10 cm (4 in), petioles narrowly winged or wingless. White flowers, 1–6 in a cluster. Globose fruit, very variable, size according to variety. Cultivars of this species are generally heavily spiked and include all the most popular orange varieties such as CV 'Valencia' (the important juice orange) late season, CV 'Washington Navel', and also sub-species such as *C. s. Melitensis*, the Maltese blood orange, and *C. s. Moro*, the crimson-fleshed 'Moro Orange' of S. Italy.

C. X tangelo 79
Tangelo, Ugli. Leaves to 15 cm (6 in) petioles broadly winged. Highly coloured, red or yellow according to CV. Delicious sweet juice, skin moderately loose. Shape from flattened globose to ovoid. These delicious fruit are a cross between the pomelo and mandarin, or between the grapefruit and mandarin. There are many popular CVs including: CV 'Minneola' with red, long-necked fruit; CV 'Orlando', round, orange, juicy; CV 'Seminole', large, red, acid juice; CV 'Ugli', large flattened, yellow, sweet, loose-skinned.

COCCOLOBA 80
A large genus from the American tropics, including vines, shrubs and trees. Two tree species are grown. Family Polygonaceae.

C. uvifera 80, 80
Sea Grape, Platterleaf, Kino. C. American coasts, sub-tropical to tropical. To 7 m (20 ft) or more. Almost circular, cordate leathery leaves with red veins to 20 cm (8 in) diameter. White, small flowers in dense 25 cm (10 in) racemes. Fruit like small purple grapes. Edible. Medium fast growth. Spreading, many-branched, often grotesque. Planted for edible fruit and as dense windbreak.

COCHLOSPERMUM 80–1
A small genus of trees from dry-climate tropical areas of Asia and C. America. Notable for showy winter blossom. Family Cochlospermaceae.

C. vitifolium 81, 80
Buttercup Tree, Maximiliana. Mexico, C. America, dry tropical. To 13 m (40 ft). Alternate, deeply lobed leaves to 30 cm (12 in), 3–7 lobes, green and slightly hairy. Flowers to 10 cm (4 in) diameter, bright buttercup yellow with many stamens, in terminal clusters.

Winter. Flowers on bare wood. Velvety green capsules to 7.5 cm (3 in) long. Slow growing. Slender, upright. A double cultivar is also grown.

COCOS 81
A single species of pan-tropical palm, probably originating in C. America or Melanesia. An important cash crop in many parts of the world. Other Palms sold as Cocos belong to the genera *Arecastrum*, *Butea*, and *Syagrus*. Family Palmae.

C. nucifera 81, 81
Coconut Palm, Coco. Tropical. To 27 m (80 ft). Long pinnate fronds to 7 m (20 ft), individual pinnae to 1 m (3 ft), the petiole smooth and fibrous, concave on the upper side. Male and female blossoms together in 1 m (3 ft) inflorescence among the leaves. Hard-shelled nuts to 30 cm (12 in) long, containing white flesh (copra) and coconut milk. Slow growing. Single trunk, often arching with fronds in terminal rosettes. See main text for many uses of the tree and its fruit.

C. plumosa, see ARECASTRUM romanzoffianum

COFFEA 82
Shrubs and trees from the Old World tropics, the genus *Coffea* have handsome glossy leaves like a *Gardenia* to which they are related. Grown commercially for the seeds or 'coffee beans'. Only one species is of any importance. Family Rubiaceae.

C. arabica 82, 82
Coffee, Arabian Coffee Tree. Africa, tropical. To 5 m (15 ft). 15 cm (6 in) elliptical leaves, a glossy dark green and often rippled. Pure white fragrant blossoms to 2 cm (¾ in) diameter, borne in axillary clusters. Winged red berries, 3.5 cm (1½ in) diameter with two seeds. Fast growing. Upright, conical, often with weeping branches. Grown in many tropical areas as a cash crop, elsewhere as an ornamental.

CORDIA 82
A large tropical genus spread around the globe and containing some 300 species, several of which are trees. Family Boraginaceae.

C. sebestena 82, 83
Geiger Tree, Bird Lime Tree, Kou Haole. Caribbean, tropical. To 10 m (30 ft). Ovate, 12.5 cm (5 in) leaves, rough, hairy, with undulate margins. Flowers in terminal clusters, vivid orange-scarlet. White drupes to 2 cm (¾ in) long. Medium fast growth. Upright, round-headed. Ornamental.

C. subcordata 82, 82
Kou. Africa to Polynesia, tropical. To 10 m (30 ft). Ovate, glossy leaves to 10 cm (4 in) on stems almost as long, sometimes with undulate edges. Open, pale orange blossoms, 5 cm (2 in) diameter, in short-stalked clusters. Globose fruit, green to yellow, about 2.5 cm (1 in) diameter. Fast growing. Smooth grey trunk, wide spreading crown. The Polynesians have many uses for both the timber and fruits of this tree. See main text.

CORNUS 83
A small genus of decorative trees and shrubs, mostly from the northern hemisphere, their small flowers surrounded by an involucre of showy bracts. Popular species are deciduous and limited to cool temperate gardens. Family Cornaceae.

C. capitata 83, 84
Himalayan Strawberry, Bentham's Cornel. Himalayas, cool temperate. To 13 m (40 ft). Elliptic, leathery, dull green, 10 cm (4 in) leaves, partly evergreen. Small

flowers in dense composite head, surrounded by 4−6 petal-like bracts. Deep pink fruit, fleshy, like a strawberry. Medium fast growth. Bushy.

C. controversa 83
Giant Dogwood. China, temperate. To 20 m (60 ft). Alternate, ovate leaves to 12.5 cm (5 in) long, silvery beneath. Small flowers in 12.5 cm (5 in) cymes. Blue-black berries in late spring. Fast growing. Pyramidal, horizontal branches.

C. florida 83, 83, 84
Flowering Dogwood. USA, temperate. To 13 m (40 ft). Deciduous, ovate leaves to 15 cm (6 in) long. Scarlet in autumn. Flowers in dense head surrounded by 4 petal-like bracts, obovate, notched, and darkly marked at end. Scarlet berries in a cluster. Slow growing. Shrubby to slender. Several cultivars with white, rose or deep pink bracts, or with variegated leaves, one with yellow fruits.

C. kousa 83
Kousa, Japanese Dogwood. Japan, Korea, cool temperate. To 8 m (25 ft). Elliptic-ovate leaves to 10 cm (4 in) long, pointed tips. Bronze to crimson in autumn. Minute flowers in clusters surrounded by 4 showy white pointed bracts. Pinkish-red fruit in a globose head. Slow growing. Shrubby. Pink flowered, variegated, and yellow-fruited CVs.

C. mas 83
Cornelian Cherry, Sorbet. Europe, W. Asia, temperate. To 8 m (25 ft). Oval, pointed leaves to 11.5 cm (4½ in) long, dull green. Purple-red in autumn. Small yellow flowers in 2 cm (¾ in) umbels. Dark red fruit, ellipsoid, to 2 cm (¾ in) long. Edible. Medium fast growth. Bushy, densely branched. Grown for edible fruits in S. Europe. Cultivars with yellow or violet fruit, coloured leaves.

COUROUPITA 85
A small American genus of some 20 species, represented in tropical gardens everywhere by the stunning C. guianensis. Family Lecythidaceae.

C. guianensis 85, 85
Cannonball Tree. Guyana, tropical. To 17 m (50 ft). Obovate 30 cm (12 in) leaves, slightly serrated. Flowers in 1 m (3 ft) racemes. Apricot-orange and asymmetrical. Globose, woody capsules to 20 cm (8 in) diameter. Fast growing. Columnar with lightly spreading head.

CRATAEGUS 86−7
An enormous genus of decorative trees from the N. temperate zones, many of them valued for their edible fruits. Family Rosaceae.

C. crus-galli 86−7
Cockspur Thorn. E. N. America, cool temperate. To 10 m (30 ft). Obovate leaves to 7.5 cm (3 in) long, rounded apically, cuneate base, shiny and toothed. Red in autumn. White flowers to 1.5 cm (⅝ in) diameter. Dull red berries to 1 cm (½ in) long. Medium growth. Spreading head. Spines 7.5 cm (3 in) long.

C. ellwangeriana 86, 87
Giant Hawthorn. N.E. N. America, cool temperate. To 8 m (25 ft). Foliage to 10 cm (4 in), elliptic, serrated, often with 8−10 lobes. Flowers 2 cm (¾ in) wide, white with red anthers, in corymbs. Fruit to 4 cm (1½ in) diameter, red. Slow growing. Upright, open-headed.

C. laevigata, see **C. oxyacantha**
C. mexicana, see **C. stipulacea**
C. monogyna 86, 86
English Hawthorn, May. Europe, Asia, Africa, temperate. To 10 m (30 ft). Foliage ovate, deeply 3−7 lobed. Flowers white with red anthers, to 1 cm (½ in) diameter, in large corymbs. Fragrant. Bright red berries only 5 mm (¼ in) wide. Fast growing.

Shrubby, spreading head in old age. Many 2.5 cm (1 in) thorns. Several cultivars with variations in flower colour, foliage and fruit.

C. oxyacantha 86, 86
Hawthorn, White Thorn. Europe, Africa, Asia, temperate. To 8 m (25 ft). Foliage obovate to 5 cm (2 in) long with 3−5 shallow lobes. Flowers to 1 cm (½ in) diameter. Medium growth rate. Spreading. Many thorns. Many CVs with single and double, white, rose, deep pink or carmine blossoms.

C. X smithiana 87, 86
Hybrid Thorn, Red Mexican Thorn. Hybrid. Temperate. To 10 m (30 ft). Elliptic, serrate-crenate foliage to 8 cm (3¼ in) long. Flowers 2 cm (¾ in) wide, in a corymb. Vivid globose fruit to 2 cm (¾ in) diameter. Fast growing. Rounded head.

C. stipulacea 86, 87
Mexican Thorn. Mexico, temperate. To 10 m (30 ft). Foliage, elliptical, to 8 cm (3¼ in) long, serrate-crenate. Flowers white, single, to 2 cm (¾ in) diameter, in corymbs. Fruit yellow, shading orange, 2.5 cm (1 in) diameter. Fast growing. Shrubby. Fruit quite edible.

C. submollis 86
Canada Thorn. N.E. N. America, cool temperate. To 10 m (30 ft). Foliage coarsely serrated, oval to elliptic. Flowers white, to 2.5 cm (1 in) diameter, yellow stamens, in loose corymbs. Pear-shaped berries to 1 cm (½ in) diameter, bright red. Fast growing. Open, spreading.

CRESCENTIA 87
A single species of tree from tropical America, grown for its fruits, which are used for utensils in primitive societies. Family Bignoniaceae.

C. cujete 87, 87
Calabash Tree. Tropical America. To 13 m (40 ft). Oblanceolate 15 cm (6 in) leaves clustered at nodes. 5 cm (2 in) flowers, creamy-yellow with purple veins. Smooth fruit, 30 cm (12 in) diameter. Fast growing. Broad-headed. The fruit shell is used for many utensils and fine musical instruments; timber in boat building.

CRYPTOMERIA 88
A coniferous genus of a single species, but innumerable varieties in foliage, size and shape. Family Taxodiaceae.

C. japonica 88
Sugi, Japanese Cedar. E. Asia, temperate to cool. To 50 m (150 ft). Needle-like scales, forward pointing and curved, bluish-green. Male cones spicate, female globular. Fast growing. Pyramidal. In cold areas, the foliage turns a rich brown in winter, greens up in spring. Many cultivars with twisted foliage, weeping branchlets, fasciation and colour variations.

CUNNINGHAMIA 89
A genus of 3 species closely related to Cryptomeria and to the N. American Taxodium. For warm temperate climates. Family Taxodiaceae.

C. kawakamii 89
Taiwan. To 33 m (100 ft). Not in cultivation.

C. konishii 89
Taiwan Fir. Taiwan, warm temperate. To 33 m (100 ft). Stiff long triangular leaves to 4 cm (1½ in) long, spirally arranged. Male flowers in a cluster. Female cones, ovoid, to 2.5 cm (1 in) long. Fast growing. Pyramidal.

C. lanceolata 89, 89
China Fir. S. China, sub-tropical. To 40 m (120 ft). Fine needle-like leaves to 6.5 cm (2½ in) long, arranged in two ranks. Flowers in a cluster. Female cones, to 5 cm (2 in) long. Fast growing. Pyramidal,

weeping branch tips. Timber highly valued in China.

CUPANIOPSIS 90
A large genus of evergreen trees from Australia and Oceania, only one species widely grown. Family Sapindaceae.

C. anacardioides 90, 90
Tuckeroo. Australia, warm temperate. To 13 m (40 ft). Large, alternate, compound leaves of 5−10 leaflets, each to 15 cm (6 in) long. Evergreen. White flowers in long, dangling panicles. Orange-yellow capsules, 2 cm (¾ in) diameter, divided into 3 lobes. Medium fast growth. Slender, broad-headed, often weeping branchlets. Used for timber. Seeds are an Aboriginal delicacy.

C. anacardiopsis, see **C. anacardioides**
CUPRESSUS 90−1
An important genus of coniferous trees and shrubs with great variation in both size and shape. They are found in many parts of Europe, Asia and N. America. Family Cupressaceae.

C. arizonica, see **C. glabra**
C. glabra 91, 92
Arizona Cypress. Arizona, temperate. To 17 m (50 ft). Scale-like leaves of a distinctive blue-green. Female cones, to 2.5 cm (1 in) wide, globose. Slow growing. Tall, conical. The old bark peels annually, leaving smooth, red, inner bark.

C. lusitanica 91, 91
Cedar of Goa, Mexican Cedar, Portuguese Cedar. C. America, warm temperate to sub-tropical. To 25 m (75 ft). Blue-green leaf-scales in weeping branchlets. Female cones, glaucous, to 1 cm (½ in) diameter. Medium fast growth. Broad-headed, upward pointing branches, weeping branchlets.

C. macrocarpa 91
Monterey Cypress. California, temperate. To 26 m (80 ft). Leaf-scales obtuse, bright green. Female cones, purple-brown, to 4 cm (1½ in) diameter. Slow growing. Columnar, becoming wide-headed with age. Picturesquely twisted in natural coastal position. Not frost hardy. A superb coastal tree. Several CVs in leaf-colour, and habit.

C. sempervirens Stricta 91, 91, 92
Italian Cypress. S. Europe, Asia Minor, temperate. To 27 m (80 ft). Leaf-scales obtuse, dark green. Female cones, to 4 cm (1½ in) diameter. Medium fast growth. Columnar − great for landscaping effects. Many colour and foliage varieties, notably the Australian 'Swanes Golden'.

C. torulosa 91
Bhutan Cypress. Himalayas, temperate to sub-tropical. To 50 m (150 ft). Bright blue-green leaf-scales in drooping branchlets. Female cones, brown, to 1 cm (½ in) diameter. Fast growing. Upright, broad-headed in age. Not frost hardy.

CYDONIA 92−3
A genus of 2 species, fruiting members of the Rose family, Rosaceae.

C. oblonga 92, 92, 93
Quince. W. Asia, temperate. To 7 m (20 ft). Simple ovate leaves to 10 cm (4 in) long, distinctly woolly beneath. Deciduous. Pale pink, 5-petalled flowers to 5 cm (2 in) wide, borne singly on new growth. Late spring. Large 10 cm (4 in) fruit, generally asymmetrical, but roughly apple-shaped, rich yellow and fragrant, the skin woolly. Supremely edible when cooked. Slow growing. Shrubby, spreading head. Fruit sold commercially.

DACRYDIUM 93
A very small genus of evergreen conifers native exclusively to the Pacific area in the southern hemisphere. Dioecious and

of extremely slow growth. Family Podocarpaceae.

D. cupressinum 93, **93**
Rimu, Red Pine, Imou Pine. N.Z., temperate. To 33 m (100 ft). Scale-like leaves to 2 mm ($^1/_8$ in) on weeping branchlets. Male cones spike-like; female cones to 2 mm ($^1/_8$ in) long with few scales. Slow growing. Pyramidal when young, with weeping branchlets. Upright with rounded head at maturity. An important timber tree.

D. franklinii 93
Huon Pine. Tas, cool temperate. To 33 m (100 ft). Bright green scale-like leaves to 1 mm ($^1/_{16}$ in) long on weeping branchlets. Very small nut-like cones with 4−8 scales. Very slow growing. Upright pyramidal, short horizontal branches, weeping branchlets. An important waterproof timber. Source of Huon Pine Wood Oil. Mature specimens now rare.

DAVIDIA 94
Genus of a single decorative species, related to the Dogwoods. Discovered in the 20th century. Family Nyssaceae.

D. involucrata 94, **94**
Dove Tree, Handkerchief Tree, Ghost Tree. W. China, temperate. To 20 m (60 ft). Broad ovate leaves to 15 cm (6 in) long, toothed, pointed, silky beneath. Deciduous. Small unisexual blooms in a dense head, subtended by two large unequal white bracts, drooping to 20 cm (8 in) or more. Late spring. Pear-shaped drupes containing a hard nut. Medium fast growth. Open habit, rounded head.

DELONIX 94
A small genus of 3 species, one of which has become a tropical favourite, worldwide, for its showy summer blossom display and unusual horizontal shape. Family Leguminosae.

D. regia 94, **94**, **95**
Poinciana, Flamboyant, Peacock Flower, Royal Poinciana. Madagascar, tropical. To 10 m (30 ft) high and several times as wide. Pale green, bipinnate leaves to 45 cm (18 in) long, with up to 40 pinnae and many 5 mm ($^1/_4$ in) leaflets. Deciduous. Open, bright scarlet flowers to 10 cm (4 in) in diameter, one petal heavily spotted in white. Long woody pods to 75 cm (2$^1/_2$ ft) long. Fast growing. Buttressed trunk, low horizontal branches, a dense canopy. Used for stock fodder.

DILLENIA 95
A medium-sized genus of 60 evergreen tropical trees with edible fruits. Family Dilleniaceae.

D. alata 95
Wormia. Indonesia, tropical. To 10 m (30 ft). Dark green obovate leaves to 10 cm (4 in). Deep pink flowers to 7.5 cm (3 in), in clusters. Globose, green fruit to 7.5 cm (3 in). Fast growing. Dense foliaged, spreading head.

D. indica 95, **95**
Simpoh, Elephant Apple, Chulta. India to Java, tropical. To 10 m (30 ft). Oblong, pleated, pale green leaves to 7.5 cm (3 in) long. White, gold-stamened blossoms to 20 cm (8 in) across, borne singly, downward pointing. Globose, indehiscent fruit to 10 cm (4 in) diameter. Edible. Used for curries and jellies. Fast growing. Dense foliaged, spreading head.

DIOSPYROS 96
A widely distributed genus of trees, largely from the northern hemisphere, valued both for their delicious autumn fruits and for their brilliantly marked timber. Includes the ebony of commerce. Family Ebenaceae.

D. ebenum 96
Ebony, Macassar Ebony. India, Sri Lanka, tropical. To 13 m (40 ft). Elliptical, leathery leaves to 10 cm (4 in). Deciduous. Flowers of both sexes on same tree, white. Male flowers in clusters, female solitary to 2 cm ($^3/_4$ in) wide. Globose fruit, 2 cm ($^3/_4$ in) diameter. Fast growing. Upright, slender, very hard timber with cream stripe. A valuable cabinet wood.

D. kaki 96, **96**
Kaki, Japanese Persimmon, Date Plum, Keg Fig. Japan, China, temperate to subtropical. To 13 m (40 ft). Obovate leaves to 17.5 cm (7 in) long, pubescent on reverse. Deciduous. Yellow white flowers, 2 cm ($^3/_4$ in) diameter. Male in clusters, female solitary. Fruit to 7.5 cm (3 in) diameter, variable shape from ovoid to flattened globose. Very acid when unripe. Moderately slow growth. Upright, usually with weeping branches. Vivid autumn colour, red, orange, yellow. An excellent cabinet timber. A favourite dessert fruit.

D. lotus
Hog Plum, Date Plum. W. Asia, temperate. To 15 m (45 ft). Elliptical to oblong leaves to 12.5 cm (5 in) long, broadly cuneate at base, pubescent reverses. Deciduous. Reddish or green leaves to 5 mm ($^1/_4$ in) diameter. Globose fruit to 2 cm ($^3/_4$ in) long. Yellow, turning orange then purple. Edible. Medium fast growth. Open shape, drooping branches. Popular fruit in the Orient.

D. virginiana 96, **96**
Possumwood, Possum Apple. E. USA, temperate. To 13 m (40 ft). Elliptic leaves to 15 cm (6 in) long, glossy and dark. Deciduous. Male flowers 1 cm ($^1/_2$ in) diameter in clusters. Female larger, solitary. Cream-yellow. Oval fruit to 5 cm (2 in) diameter, yellow-orange. Edible when softened by frost. Medium fast growth. Upright with pendulous branches. Good timber tree.

DIPLOGLOTTIS 97
A small Australian genus of which the Native Tamarind is a decorative species from the warm east coast. Not much cultivated elsewhere. Family Sapindaceae.

D. cunninghamii 97, **97**
Native Tamarind. E. Australia, sub-tropical. To 17 m (50 ft). Pinnate, fern-like leaves to 54 cm (21 in) long. Small yellow flowers in panicles. Yellow fruit to 1 cm ($^1/_2$ in) divided into 3 sections. Delicious red pulp used in jam making. Fast growing. Upright, rounded head.

DOMBEYA 97−8
A large genus of 300 species from Africa and islands of the Indian Ocean. Mainly ornamental. Family Byttneriaceae.

D. natalensis, see **D. tiliacea**
D. spectabilis 97, **98**
Wild Pear. S.E. Africa, Madagascar, temperate to sub-tropical. To 15 m (45 ft). Ovate deciduous leaves to 17.5 cm (7 in) long, cordate, sometimes with toothed edges. Flowers in paniculate cymes, pink or white, to 2 cm ($^3/_4$ in) diameter, fragrant; on bare wood. 3-celled dehiscent capsules. Fast growing. Upright, with weeping branches. Ornamental.

D. tiliacea 97, **97**
Natal Cherry. S. Africa, temperate. To 8 m (25 ft). Cordate ovate leaves to 8 cm (3$^1/_2$ in) long, pointed, irregularly toothed. Semi-deciduous. Open white flowers to 3 cm (1$^1/_4$ in) across, in 2−6 flowered cymes, subtended by two bracts. Persistent after fading. Autumn. 5-celled capsules. Fast growing. Open, many-trunked; bark blackish-brown.

D. wallichii 97−8, **98**
Mexican Rose, Manila Rose, Pink Ball. E.

Africa, Madagascar, tropical. To 10 m (30 ft). Broadly heart-shaped and toothed leaves to 30 cm (12 in) long, or more. Deep pink flowers 3.5 cm (1$^1/_2$ in) across in a many-flowered, pendent umbel, roughly globular. Subtended by downy 8.5 cm (3$^1/_2$ in) bracts. Winter. Dehiscent capsules. Fast growing. Shrubby.

ELAEOCARPUS 98
A genus of slender trees native to several areas of the sub-tropical and temperate zones, mostly in the southern hemisphere. Valued for their decorative blue fruits. Family Elaeocarpaceae.

E. dentatus, see **E. denticulatus**
E. denticulatus 98
Hinau. N.Z., temperate. To 20 m (60 ft). Leaves elliptical to lanceolate 10 cm (4 in) or larger. Lightly serrated. White bell flowers, 1 cm ($^1/_2$ in) diameter, drooping, in axillary racemes. Flat greyish-purple fruit to 1 cm ($^1/_2$ in) long. Fast growing. Columnar with spreading head. Foliage only at branch tips.

E. grandis 98
Silver Quandong. NSW, Q, temperate. To 20 m (60 ft). Lanceolate leaves to 15 cm (6 in), lightly serrated. Greenish-white bell flowers with fringed petals to 2.5 cm (1 in) long in 10 cm (4 in) clusters. Blue, 2.5 cm (1 in) berries. Slow growing. Slender, round-headed.

E. kirtonii 98
Pigeonberry Ash. Australia, temperate. To 8 m (24 ft). Lanceolate leaves to 20 cm (8 in), lightly serrated. White bell flowers to 2.5 cm (1 in) long in clusters. Blue berries. Fast growing. Columnar, drooping branches.

E. reticulatus 98, **98**, **99**
Blueberry Ash. E. Australia, temperate. To 20 m (60 ft). Elliptic to lanceolate leaves 10 cm (4 in) or more, serrated. White or pink bell flowers to 2 cm ($^3/_4$ in), serrated, in loose panicles. Bright blue berries to 1 cm ($^1/_2$ in). Fast growing. Upright, spreading head in maturity.

ERIOBOTRYA 99
An Asiatic genus of several evergreen trees, raised for their edible spring fruits. Family Rosaceae.

E. deflexa 99
Nakai. Taiwan, warm temperate. To 7 m (20 ft). Oblong-elliptic leaves to 25 cm (10 in) long, coarsely serrated. Flowers white, 1.5 cm ($^5/_8$ in) diameter, in a rusty, 12.5 cm (5 in) inflorescence. Orange fruit, about 2 cm ($^3/_4$ in) diameter. Fast growing. Upright, drooping branches.

E. japonica 99, **99**
Loquat, Japanese Medlar, Japan Plum. China, Japan, temperate. To 8 m (25 ft). 25 cm (10 in) leathery leaves, woolly beneath. White flowers, to 2 cm ($^3/_4$ in) across, in terminal panicles. Oval, yellow-orange fruit to 4 cm (1$^1/_2$ in) long. Fast growing. Round-headed. A popular fruit tree in the Orient and Australia.

ERYTHRINA 100
A popular genus of deciduous, tropical trees, flowering brilliantly on their bare wood in cooler weather. Family Leguminosae.

E. caffra 100, **101**
Kaffirboom, Coral Tree. S. Africa, temperate. To 20 m (60 ft). Trifoliate leaves with three leaflets, to 17.5 cm (7 in) across. Vermilion pea flowers with reflexed standard, 5 cm (2 in) wide, in short racemes. Leguminous woody pods, to 11.5 cm (4$^1/_2$ in) long. Fast growing. Broadly spreading. The City Tree emblem of Los Angeles.

E. crista-galli 100, **101**
Cockscomb Coral, Crybaby Tree. S. America, tropical. To 7 m (20 ft). Trifoliate leaves with 7.5 cm (3 in) elliptic leaflets.

Scarlet pea blossoms in loose terminal racemes. Leguminous pods, to 38 cm (15 in) long. Slow growing. Trunk and main branches gnarled, picturesque, often trimmed back to shrub size to stimulate dense flowering.

E. falcata 101
Coral Tree. S. America, sub-tropical. To 13 m (40 ft). Trifoliate leaves with oblong leaflets. Scarlet blossoms in long sparse panicles. Leguminous pods to 15 cm (6 in). Fast growing. Upright, open-headed.

E. indica, see E. variegata

E. speciosa 100
Corallodendron. Brazil, tropical. To 5 m (15 ft). Trifoliate leaves with three diamond-shaped leaflets to 22.5 cm (9 in) long. Scarlet-pink flowers in terminal racemes. Leguminous pods to 30 cm (12 in) long. Fast growing. Shrubby.

E. variegata 100, 100, 101
Coral Bean, Tiger Claw. Philippines to Australia, temperate to tropical. To 20 m (60 ft). Large trifoliate leaves with 15 cm (6 in) leaflets, almost round. Dense 15 cm (6 in) racemes of scarlet blossoms, each to 7 cm (2¾ in) long, with split calyx and broad standard. 30 cm (12 in) pods. Very fast growing. Heavy trunk and branches, broad-headed, often picturesque. Several colour varieties are grown: *E. v. 'Alba'* with white flowers, *E. v. 'Parcellii'* with variegated leaves.

E. vespertilio 100
Gray Corkwood, Batswing Coral. N. Australia, tropical. To 10 m (30 ft). Trifoliate leaves with three highly variable 12.5 cm (5 in) leaflets, often fan-shaped and resembling a bat's wing when seen at an angle. 4 cm (1½ in) salmon-red pea blossoms in an erect raceme. Fast growing. Shrubby to open-headed.

EUCALYPTUS 102–3
An enormous genus of over 600 species in Australia, with a few other species in Indonesia, New Guinea and the Philippines. They are the most noticeable feature of any Australian landscape, and have become popular in dry-climate areas throughout the world. Precise identification of many varieties is very difficult, partly because the leaves of young plants are often quite different from those produced at maturity. *Eucalyptus* species are highly localized and description has been attempted only in the case of a few nationally or internationally favoured species. Family Myrtaceae.

E. caesia 104
Gungunnu. WA, dry temperate. To 8 m (25 ft). Alternate, lanceolate leaves with a distinctly bluish cast. Rose-pink flowers, 4 cm (1½ in) diameter in 3-flowered umbels. Urn-shaped bluish capsules, to 2 cm (¾ in) diameter. Slow growing. Upright, often with weeping branches. Bark peels in strips, underbark green.

E. camaldulensis 103
River Red Gum, Murray Red Gum. All Australia except Tas, temperate. To 50 m (150 ft). Leaves lanceolate, thin, to 20 cm (8 in). Flowers white, in 5–10 umbels. Summer. Hemispherical, stemmed capsules. Fast growing. Wide spreading. Smooth, ash coloured bark.

E. citriodora 103, 103
Lemon-scented Gum. Q, temperate to sub-tropical. To 17 m (50 ft). 15 cm (6 in) lanceolate leaves, strongly lemon-scented, drooping. White blossoms in umbels of 3–5, on long panicles. Urceolate capsules, to 5 mm (¼ in) across. Fast growing. Slender, upright, distinctive grey-white bark that peels in patches, giving an interesting 'camouflage' effect. Source of essential oils.

E. deglupta 103, 105
Mindanao Gum. S. Philippines, tropical. To 33 m (100 ft). Dark lanceolate leaves to 15 cm (6 in) long. White flowers. Hemispherical capsules. Fast growing. Upright with spreading head at maturity. Bark striped in a decorative combination of pink, gold and apple green.

E. erythrocorys 104
Illyarie, Red-cap Gum. WA, temperate. To 10 m (30 ft). Opposite, sickle-shaped leaves. Yellow-green flowers in deep green calyx with scarlet 4-angled cap. Autumn-spring. Broadly campanulate capsules, to 5 cm (2 in) diameter. Slow growing. Upright, smooth bark, peeling occasionally in thin flakes. Frost-tender, better near the coast.

E. ficifolia 105
Red Flowering Gum, Scarlet-flowered Gum. WA, temperate. To 10 m (30 ft). Alternate, broad-lanceolate leaves. Flowers to 4 cm (1½ in) across, very variable in colour from white to crimson, but normally orange-scarlet. These are borne in umbels of 3–7 in very large panicles or masses. Ovoid-urceolate nuts, to 3 cm (1¼ in) wide. Medium fast growth. Spreading crown, rough bark. The showiest flowering gum.

E. globulus
Blue Gum, Tas Blue Gum. Tas, temperate. To 70 m (200 ft). Alternate, sickle-shaped lanceolate leaves to 45 cm (18 in) long, blue-green. White solitary flowers in racemes. Top-shaped capsules, to 3 cm (1¼ in) diameter. Very, very fast growing. Columnar to upright with spreading head, sometimes with weeping branches. Bark smooth, flaking, bluish. The most widely cultivated Gum in the world. Important for building, paper pulp, farm implements. Oil of Eucalyptus extracted from leaves.

E. haemastoma
Scribbly Gum, NSW, temperate. To 15 m (45 ft). Alternate, thick, 15 cm (6 in) leaves, lanceolate, sickle-shaped. White blossoms, 6–12 in an umbel, in terminal panicles. Hemispherical, top-shaped nuts, to 5 mm (¼ in) diameter. Fast growing. Thick, twisted trunk, heavy branches, irregular crown. As the smooth grey bark flakes, it reveals a series of scribbly marks on the trunk, the tracks of insects which live under the top layer.

E. leucoxylon 104
Whitewood, White Ironbark. SA, cool temperate. To 8 m (24 ft). Alternate leaves, narrow to broad lanceolate. White, pink or purple flowers, according to variety, in 3-flowered peduncles. Long, pointed nuts, to 1 cm (½ in) across, twice as long. Medium fast growth. Round-headed, deciduous bark in blue, white and yellowish patches. *E. l. 'Rosea'* is a popular pink-flowered variety.

E. mannifera ssp. Maculosa 102
Red-spotted Gum. NSW, Vic, temperate. Dullish lanceolate leaves to 15 cm (6 in) long. Creamy flowers in umbels of 3–7. Hemispherical nuts, to 5 mm (¼ in) diameter. Fast growing. Upright, sometimes multiple trunked. Grown for the beauty of its smooth, white bark. Frost-hardy.

E. marginata
Jarrah. WA, temperate. To 50 m (150 ft). Lanceolate leaves to 12.5 cm (5 in) long. White spring blossom in umbels of 4–8. Pear-shaped nuts, to 5 mm (¼ in) diameter. Fast growing. Upright, broad-headed. The principal timber tree of WA.

E. microcorys 104
Tallow-wood. Q, NSW, temperate. To 33 m (100 ft). Thick, alternate, lanceolate leaves to 10 cm (4 in). Small white flowers in axillary umbels or terminal

panicles. Winter. Cylindrical nuts to 5 mm (¼ in) diameter. Fast growing. Upright, broad-crowned. An important timber tree.

E. nicholii
Narrow-leaf Black Peppermint, Willow Peppermint. NSW, Q, temperate. To 33 m (100 ft). Very narrow grey-green leaves to 7.5 cm (3 in) long, with a purple bloom on young foliage. Small, sparse, whitish flowers in umbels of 5–8. Hemispherical nuts, to 2 mm (³⁄₁₆ in) diameter. Fast growing. Upright, relatively stout branches, weeping foliage. One of the most handsome Eucalypts in street and garden planting. Brown persistent bark.

E. niphophila, see E. pauciflora

E. pauciflora ssp. Niphophila 103
Snow Gum. Australian alps, alpine, cold. To 7 m (20 ft). Sickle-shaped, lanceolate, glaucous, thick leaves to 12.5 cm (5 in) long. White flowers, in 3–7 flowered umbels. Globose fruit, 5 mm (¼ in) diameter. Slow growing. Spreading, often picturesque. The most frost hardy of the Eucalypts.

E. pilularis
Blackbutt. E. Australia, warm temperate. To 23 m (70 ft). Glossy, sickle-shaped leaves to 17.5 cm (7 in) long. White blossoms in 6–12 flowered umbels. Hemispherical nuts, to 1 cm (½ in) diameter. Fast growing. Straight trunk, upright, spreading head. Fibrous bark, dark and persistent on lower trunk. Timber cut for phone poles and bridge construction.

E. racemosa 104
Narrow-leaf Ironbark, Showy Gum. NSW, Q, temperate. To 33 m (100 ft). Long, narrow, sickle-shaped leaves. White summer blossom in 16–20 flowered umbels. Hemispherical nuts, to 5 mm (¼ in) diameter. Medium fast growth. Upright, with weeping branches and dark, deeply furrowed persistent bark. A very popular specimen.

E. regnans 102
Mountain Ash, Giant Gum. Tas, Vic, cool temperate. To 100 m (300 ft) and more. Sickle-shaped, lanceolate leaves to 15 cm (6 in) long. White summer blossom in umbels of 7–12. Short-stemmed ovoid nuts, to 5 mm (¼ in) diameter. Fast growing. Very upright, a vast trunk with rough bark to 10 m (30 ft) from the ground, smooth thereafter. The tallest hardwood in the world, and a very important timber tree.

E. X rhodantha 104
Rose Gum, Rose Mottlecah. WA, dry temperate. To 3 m (9 ft). Orbicular to cordate silver leaves, 10 cm (4 in) long. Single, rose-red flowers to 10 cm (4 in) diameter. All year. Capsules with pointed cap, to 5 cm (2 in) diameter. Slow growing. A shrubby, dwarf tree, sometimes almost horizontal habit.

E. sideroxylon Pallens 105
Mulga, Pink-flowered Ironbark. SA, Vic, temperate. To 17 m (50 ft). Greyish lanceolate leaves. Pale pink flowers in 3–7 umbels. Urceolate nuts, to 5 mm (¼ in) diameter. Fast growing. Black, deeply furrowed, persistent bark. Upright habit with weeping branches.

E. torquata
Coral Gum, Coolgardie Gum. WA, temperate. To 7 m (20 ft). Lanceolate, glaucous leaves. Red or pink blossom in 3–8 flowered umbels. Spring-summer. Narrowly urceolate nuts, to 1 cm (½ in) diameter. Fast growing. Pyramidal, weeping branchlets. May flower at 2 years of age, very decorative.

EUGENIA, see SYZYGIUM

EUPHORIA 106
A small Asiatic genus of 15 species, one

of which, the Loong Ngan, is grown for its delicious fruit. Family Sapindaceae.

E. longan 106, **106**
Dragon's Eye, Loong Ngan. China, sub-tropical. To 13 m (40 ft). Evergreen pinnate leaves to 30 cm (12 in) with 4–10 elliptic leaflets, very glossy. Small, yellow-white flowers in axillary or terminal panicles. Round green fruit, ripening yellow-brown, 2.5 cm (1 in) diameter, with juicy edible flesh. Fast growing. Pyramidal when young, rounded head on mature tree. In China, the fruit is second in popularity only to the Lychee.

FAGUS 106–7
Though among the most widely seen trees in Europe, N. America and Asia, there are only a handful of Beech species worldwide. They are particularly valuable because they grow in alkaline soil. Family Fagaceae.

F. americana, see **F. grandifolia**
F. crenata 107
Japanese Beech. Japan, temperate. To 30 m (90 ft). Ovate, rhomboid leaves to 7.5 cm (3 in). Both sexes on same tree, male flowers in clusters, female in pairs. 3-angled nuts in a spiny casing. Fast growing. Upright, rounded head. Used for timber.

F. grandifolia 107
American Beech. N. America, cool temperate. To 35 m (100 ft). Ovate-oblong leaves to 12.5 cm (5 in), coarsely toothed, hairy when young. Flowers and fruit as in other species. Fast growing. Pyramidal. Yellow in autumn. A valuable timber tree.

F. sylvatica 106, **106**, 107
European Beech. Europe, temperate. To 40 m (120 ft). Ovate 10 cm (4 in) leaves, shiny and often rippled. Veins and stalks often silky. Flowers and fruit as in other species. Very fast growing. Upright, pyramidal, depending on position. Often weeping branches. Red-brown in autumn. An important timber tree, the nuts are a valuable stock food. Many varieties in leaf and habit are grown, particularly the purple-green foliaged *F. s. Purpurea.*

FICUS 108–9
A very large genus of trees with milky sap, otherwise quite variable. They are native to the tropics, have leathery evergreen leaves and are mostly too large for the home garden. Family Moraceae.

F. australis, see **F. rubiginosa**
F. benghalensis
The Banyan, East Indian Fig. India, Pakistan, tropical. To 20 m (60 ft) and several times as wide. Leathery, broad-ovate leaves to 20 cm (8 in). Figs in axillary pairs, orange-red, to 1 cm (½ in) diameter. Very fast growing. Horizontal, spreading by aerial roots into a clump. Fruit edible.

F. benjamina 108, **109**
Weeping Fig, Chinese Banyan, Weeping Banyan, Benjamin Tree. Asia to Australia, tropical. To 10 m (30 ft), several times as wide. Thin, leathery, elliptical, pointed leaves to 12.5 cm (5 in) long. 1 cm (½ in) figs in axillary pairs, red, globose. Fast growing. Tall, round-headed to horizontal, depending on climate. Rarely produces aerial roots. Slender weeping branchlets. *F. b.* CV *Exotica* has a more drooping habit and leaves with long, twisted points.

F. carica 108, **109**
Common Fig, Fiku. Mediterranean, temperate to tropical. To 10 m (30 ft). 3-lobed leaves, rough on upper side, to 20 cm (8 in) long. Deciduous in cool climates. Figs variable in colour, singly from leaf axils, to 7.5 cm (3 in) long. Medium fast growth. Shrubby, spreading. The favourite eating fig.

F. elastica 108, **108**
Indiarubber Tree, Rubber Plant. Nepal to Burma, tropical. To 35 m (100 ft) and wider. Thick elliptical leaves to 30 cm (12 in) long. 1 cm (½ in) figs in axillary pairs, oval, greenish-yellow. Very fast growing. Spreading, with buttressed trunk and aerial roots. Many coloured leaf varieties. Sap is a source of an inferior rubber, called Caoutchouc. A popular indoor plant in juvenile form.

F. hillii, see **F. microcarpa**
F. lyrata 108, **108**
Fiddle Leaf Fig. Africa, tropical. To 13 m (40 ft). Leaves fiddle-shaped, brittle, to 37.5 cm (15 in) long. 4 cm (1½ in) figs, solitary or in pairs. Green, spotted white. Slow growing. Upright, irregular head. Popular indoor plant.

F. macrophylla 108
Moreton Bay Fig, Australian Banyan. E. Australia, sub-tropical. To 70 m (200 ft). Oval, leathery leaves to 25 cm (10 in) long, shiny dark green above, rusty reverses when young. 2.5 cm (1 in) figs, purple with paler dots. Medium fast growth. Spreading, but with few aerial roots. Planted for shade in tropics, occasionally as a rather weeping tree along broad avenues, but has an invasive root system.

F. microcarpa 'Hillii'
Hills' Weeping Fig. Q, temperate–tropical. To 13 m (40 ft). Leaves oval, about 7.5 cm (3 in), light green. Figs very small, rarely seen, 7 mm (⅓ in), white spotted. Fast growing. Spreading, but with few aerial roots, often weeping branches. Popular indoor plant; much planted in Sydney streets and parks.

F. religiosa 109
Bo Tree, Peepul, Sacred Fig. India, tropical. To 30 m (90 ft). Foliage round-ovate, to 17.5 cm (7 in) with a long terminal point. Pale green, fluttering on 12.5 cm (5 in) stems. 1 cm (½ in) purple figs. Fast growing. Upright, round-headed with a few aerial roots. A smooth grey trunk. Milky sap used for toothache and gum massage. Shellac made from secretions of the twigs.

F. retusa 109
Malayan or Chinese Banyan, Laurel Fig, Glossy-leaf Fig. Malaysia, Indonesia, Australia, tropical. To 20 m (60 ft). Broad elliptic leaves to 10 cm (4 in) long. Blunt-ended, short-stemmed, glossy. Figs in axillary pairs, pink to purple, 1 cm (½ in) diameter. Fast growing. Round-headed. The most popular indoor fig in America, often clipped and trained to formal shape. Hybridizes with *F. benjamina.*

F. rubiginosa 109
Port Jackson Fig, Rusty Fig. NSW, temperate. To 20 m (60 ft). Blunt-tipped, 10 cm (4 in) oval leaves, brown and hairy on reverse and leaf stems. Figs in axillary pairs, 1 cm (½ in), globose and warty. Fast growing. Wide spreading with a weeping crown and may form secondary trunks from aerial roots. Resembles *F. macrophylla*, but smaller in all parts.

F. sycomorus
Sycamore, Mulberry Fig. Africa, Asia Minor, temperate to tropical. To 20 m (60 ft). 15 cm (6 in) broad ovate leaves, cordate bases. 2.5 cm (1 in) globose figs borne densely in clusters on leafless twigs from trunk and branches. Fast growing. Upright, spreading head. No aerial roots. The Sycamore of the Bible.

FLINDERSIA 110
A genus of 20 evergreen trees found from Indonesia through N. Australia to New Caledonia. Mostly valuable timber trees. Family Rutaceae.

F. australis 110, **110**
Australian Teak, Crow's Ash. Q, NSW,

temperate–sub-tropical. To 33 m (100 ft). Compound Ash-like leaves with 3–13 elliptic leaflets. Small white flowers in a densely branched head. Prickly, 7.5 cm (3 in) pods splitting into 5 segments. Fast growing. Tall, round-headed. Not frost-hardy. An important timber tree.

F. maculosa 110
Leopard Wood. Q, NSW, temperate–dry. To 13 m (40 ft). Leaves simple, single, to 15 cm (6 in). 5 mm (¼ in) white flowers in an open spray. 4 cm (1½ in) pods splitting into 5 segments. Slow growing. Shrubby at first, later round-headed with patchy, spotted bark.

F. pubescens 110
Silver Ash. Q, warm temperate. To 33 m (100 ft). 37.5 cm (15 in) leaves with elliptic glossy leaflets. Cream, 1 cm (½ in) flowers in large clusters. Very fragrant. Small pods. Fast growing. Upright, round-headed. A good street tree in warm climates.

F. schottiana 110, **110**
Bumpy Ash, Cudgerie. NSW, Q, temperate. to 50 m (150 ft). Large compound leaves. White, small flowers in branching clusters. Very fragrant. 10 cm (4 in) prickly pods in 5 segments. Fast growing. Tall, round-headed. Smooth grey bark with bumps from fallen branches. A good timber tree.

FRAXINUS 110–11
A popular genus of deciduous ornamental trees found all over the northern hemisphere, even into the tropics. They are valuable timber trees, noted for their elegant, compound foliage. Family Oleaceae.

F. americana 111
White Ash, American Ash. E. USA, temperate. To 40 m (120 ft). Compound, pinnate leaves with 5–9 oval leaflets 15 cm (6 in) long, greyish and downy on reverses. Small apetalous flowers in a raceme. Winged samaras, to 5 cm (2 in) long. Fast growing. Upright, round-headed. Gold, with traces of red and purple in autumn. A good timber tree.

F. excelsior 110, **111**
European Ash. Europe, Asia Minor, temperate. To 45 m (140 ft). Compound pinnate leaves with 7–11 lanceolate leaflets. Small, petal-less, creamy white flowers. Winged samaras, to 4 cm (1½ in). Fast growing. Pyramidal to broad-headed. A fine timber tree. Many cultivars are raised, especially with golden foliage, or branches that trail on the ground.

F. ornus 111
Manna Ash. S. Europe, Asia Minor, temperate. To 20 m (60 ft). Compound leaves with · 7 leaflets, to 7.5 cm (3 in) long. Small, dull white petal-less flowers in clusters. Winged samaras, to 4 cm (1½ in), turning red and purple in autumn. Fast growing. Foliage turns purple in autumn.

F. oxycarpa 'Raywoodii' 111
Claret Ash. Hybrid. Temperate. To 10 m (30 ft). Compound, pinnate leaves with 7–9 narrow 6.5 cm (2½ in) leaflets, sharply toothed. White petal-less flowers. Winged samaras, to 4 cm (1½ in) long. Fast growing. Compact, round-headed. Foliage turns a splendid claret colour in autumn.

F. X 'Raywoodii', see **F. oxycarpa**
F. uhdei 111, **111**
Evergreen Ash, Shamel Ash. Mexico, dry temperate. To 17 m (50 ft). Dark compound leaves with 5–9 lanceolate leaflets, evergreen or largely so. Petal-less flowers in long panicles. Winged samaras, to 4 cm (1½ in). Fast growing. Upright, round-headed. A popular street tree in Los Angeles.

FREMONTODENDRON 112
Showy N. American member of the Bombax family with a flower display that rivals any of the tropical species. Family Bombacaceae.

F. californicum 112, **112**
Tree Poppy, Fremontia. California, Arizona, dry temperate. To 8 m (25 ft). 3-lobed leaves on short spurs, mostly 5 cm (2 in) long or less, densely woolly on reverse. Evergreen. 6.5 cm (2½ in) yellow, 5-petalled flowers. Ovoid, 4 cm (1½ in) capsules. Slow growing. Shrubby to spreading. The flower display is spectacular as the whole tree bursts into flower at once, several times a year.

F. mexicanum 112, **112**
Mexican Tree Poppy. Mexico, dry temperate. To 6 m (18 ft). 5-lobed leaves. Orange-yellow flowers to 9 cm (3½ in). Slow growing. Spreading, shrubby. Smaller and shorter than the Californian variety.

GEIJERA 113
A small evergreen genus from Australia and New Caledonia. Very useful in a dry, Mediterranean climate. Related to the Citrus. Family Rutaceae.

G. parviflora 113, **113**
Wilga. Australia, dry temperate. To 8 m (25 ft). Linear 15 cm (6 in) leaves on drooping branchlets. Small creamy flowers in airy panicles. Bluish seeds in a small capsule. Fast growing. Slender, weeping habit. Timber very hard, useful.

G. salicifolia 113
Scrub Wilga. NSW, Q, dry temperate. To 20 m (60 ft). Oval to slender leaves, blunt tipped, to 10 cm (4 in). White, small flowers in 7.5 cm (3 in) sprays. Black seeds in small capsule. Medium fast growth. Round-headed, dense foliage.

GINKGO 113–14
A unique species extinct in the wild – the only one of its genus. A very hardy street tree for a wide range of climates. Family Ginkgoaceae.

G. biloba 113, **114**
Maidenhair Tree, Ducksfoot Tree. E. China, temperate. To 40 m (120 ft). Deeply cleft, fan-shaped leaves to 7.5 cm (3 in) wide. Deciduous; yellow in autumn. Small, scarce, yellow flowers. Long-stemmed 2.5 cm (1 in) drupes. Fast growing. Wide-headed, to slender pyramidal, or even with drooping branches — there are a number of cultivars. Edible fruit and seeds; useful timber.

GLEDITSIA 114–15
A small genus of the pea family distributed worldwide, valued both for their hard timber and decorative qualities. The latter use is limited, due to their heavy spines. Family Leguminosae.

G. caspica 115
Caspian Locust. Iran, cool temperate. To 12 m (36 ft). Compound, pinnate leaves with 12–20 pinnate, oval leaflets. Sometimes bipinnate. Greenish flowers in spikes. Long, curved, thin fruit to 20 cm (8 in). Medium fast growth. Rounded head. Very spiny. Yellow in autumn. Useful hard timber.

G. japonica 115
Japan Locust. Japan, China, temperate. To 23 m (70 ft). Compound, pinnate leaves with lanceolate leaflets. Deciduous. Yellow-green, small, male and female flowers on separate spikes. Long, twisted pods to 25 cm (10 in). Fast growing. Pyramidal to columnar, spiny trunk, purplish young branchlets. Yellow in autumn. Useful hard timber.

G.triacanthos 114, **114**, 115
Honeyshuck, Honey Locust, Sweet Locust. E. USA, temperate. To 50 m

(150 ft). Dark pinnate leaves with 20–30 lanceolate leaflets, 3 cm (1¼ in) long, or bipinnate with 8–14 pinnae and smaller leaflets. Deciduous. Yellowish-green flowers in 7 cm (2¾ in) racemes. Flat pods to 4 cm (1½ in) long. Fast growing. Broad, open shape, with spiny trunk and branches. Yellow in autumn. Useful hard timber.

GLIRICIDIA 115
A small S. American genus with showy pea blossoms. One species commonly grown with the Cocoa plant as a source of nitrogen. Family Leguminosae.

G. sepium 115, **115**
Madre de Cacao, Nicaragua Cocoa Shade. America, tropical. To 10 m (30 ft). Compound pinnate leaves with 8–14 7 cm (2¾ in) leaflets. Small pink and yellow pea flowers clustered in a 10 cm (4 in) raceme. Woody pods to 15 cm (6 in) long. Fast growing. Slender, open shape. All parts of the tree are poisonous.

GREVILLEA 116
A large Australian genus of several hundred, mostly shrubby species. The few Grevilleas of tree stature, however, are among the showiest trees in the world. Family Proteaceae.

G. banksii 116, **116**
Banks' Grevillea, Red Silky Oak. Q, warm temperate. To 7 m (20 ft). Pinnately cut, dark, 10 cm (4 in) leaves with 3–11 linear segments, the whole silky grey beneath. Scarlet to ruby-red flowers in a dense, terminal one-sided raceme to 15 cm (6 in) long. Boat-shaped capsules. Very fast growing. Shrubby, dense.

G. robusta 116, **116**
Silky Oak, Silk Oak. Q, NSW, temperate. To 50 m (150 ft). Fern-like tapered pinnate leaves with many lanceolate leaflets. Semi-deciduous. Orange, honeysuckle-like flowers in a one-sided raceme, often from bare wood. Boat-shaped capsules. Very fast growing. Columnar to spreading. A fine cabinet timber.

GUAIACUM 116–17
A small genus found in drier parts of the American tropics, notable for producing the world's densest timber. Also quite decorative. Family Zygophyllaceae.

G. officinale 117
Lignum Vitae. C. and S. America, temperate-dry tropical. To 10 m (30 ft). Compound pinnate leaves to 8.5 cm (3¼ in) long, with 4–6 15 cm (6 in) leaflets. Small 1 cm (½ in) flowers in woolly terminal clusters, pale blue or white. Yellow, obovoid capsules to 2 cm (¾ in) long. Slow growing. Slender, weeping branchlets. A useful tree for warm-climate seaside planting. Dense, valuable timber. Source of Guaiacum, a medicinal resin.

HAKEA 117
A large genus of Australian plants, mostly shrubby, but with a few tree species grown for their showy flower display. Family Proteaceae.

H. acicularis
Needle Hakea. Tas to NSW, temperate. To 5 m (15 ft). Sharp, rigid needle-like leaves to 7.5 cm (3 in). Evergreen. Cream or pink toned honeysuckle flowers in stalkless axillary clusters. Beaked, woody capsules. Fast growing. Open, straggly habit.

H. laurina 117, **117**
Pincushion Hakea, Pincushion Tree, Sea Urchin Tree. WA, temperate. To 10 m (30 ft). Simple, lance-shaped, blue-green leaves to 15 cm (6 in). Evergreen. Glowing crimson flowers in a globose, stalkless cluster, punctuated with cream styles twice as long as the petals. Woody capsules. Fast growing. Shrubby, compact to columnar with weeping branches. Frost-

hardy, a popular tree in many countries.
H. sericea, see H. acicularis
H. ternifolia, see H. acicularis
HARPEPHYLLUM 117
A single species of S. African tree with dark, dense foliage, much planted as a street specimen in warm climates. Family Anacardiaceae.

H. caffrum 117, **118**
Kaffir Plum. S. Africa, temperate − subtropical. To 10 m (30 ft). Compound pinnate leaves with many dark, lanceolate 6.5 cm (2½ in) leaflets. Greenish-white flowers in small axillary panicles. Red, oval fruit to about 2.5 cm (1 in), in clusters. Medium fast growth. Round-headed, dense foliage. Juicy, edible fruit used in jams.

HARPULLIA 118
A decorative genus of warm-climate trees found from Madagascar through S. E. Asia to Australia. Family Sapindaceae.

H. arborea 118
Philippine Tulipwood. India to the Philippines, tropical. To 12 m (36 ft). Pale green pinnate leaves with 8–10 oblong 15 cm (6 in) leaflets. Greenish 1 cm (½ in) flowers in drooping panicles. Inflated, 2-part orange capsules about 4 cm (1½ in) long, containing two shiny black seeds. Fast growing. Upright, pyramidal. A beautiful cabinet timber.

H. pendula 118, **118**
Tulipwood. Doll's Eyes. N.E. Australia, warm temperate. To 17 m (50 ft). Pale pinnate leaves with 4–8 oblong leaflets to 15 cm (6 in). Flowers similar to H. arborea. 2-part orange capsules to 4 cm (1½ in) long. Very fast growing. Pyramidal. A magnificent cabinet wood.

HETEROMELES 119
A single, ornamental American genus of small tree, much planted for the colourful effect of its winter fruit. Family Rosaceae.

H. arbutifolia 119, **119**
Toyon, California Holly, Christmas Berry. California, temperate. To 10 m (30 ft). Oblong, elliptical leaves to 10 cm (4 in). Small white flowers in corymbose panicles. Berry-like pomes to 5 mm (¼ in) diameter in dense clusters, ripening in winter. Medium fast growth. Rounded head.

HEVEA 119–20
A small genus of evergreen, S. American trees, one of them widely cultivated as the source of commercial rubber. Family Euphorbiaceae.

H. brasiliensis 119–20, **120**
Para Rubber Tree, Caoutchouc Tree. Brazil, tropical. To 43 m (130 ft). Thin leathery trifoliate leaves with 3 elliptical leaflets, to 60 cm (2 ft) long. Small white flowers in a panicled cyme. Large capsules with 2.5 cm (1 in) seeds. Very fast growing. Columnar with spreading head. Sap tapped as commercial rubber.

HIBISCUS 120
A large genus of warm-climate plants, mostly shrubs. But several tree members are popular in sub-tropical gardens, particularly in coastal areas. Family Malvaceae.

H. elatus
Cuban Bast, Mahoe. Cuba, Jamaica, tropical. To 27 m (80 ft). Round or ovate leaves to 20 cm (8 in) long, downy reverses. Open yellow Hibiscus flowers to 12.5 cm (5 in) diameter, turning orange then red. Ovoid 5-celled capsules. Fast growing. Round-headed, densely foliaged. A good timber tree; fibrous bark has many uses in tropics.

H. kahilii
Kauai Hibiscus. Kauai, tropical. To 7 m (20 ft). Coarsely toothed ovate leaves to 7.5 cm (3 in). Open, bright red flowers

with narrow petals to 4 cm (1½ in) diameter. 5-celled capsules. Fast growing. Shrubby, open habit.

H. tiliaceus 120, **120**
Tree Hibiscus, Hau, Purau, Mahoe. Tropics. To 7 m (20 ft) Heart-shaped 20 cm (8 in) leaves, paler beneath. 7.5 cm (3 in) pale yellow flowers with overlapping petals, fading through tan to a deep red before falling. 5-celled capsules. Fast growing. Often multiple headed and tangled by the coast, but a presentable pyramidal tree elsewhere.

HOWEA 121
A popular Palm genus found naturally only on Lord Howe Island in the S. Pacific. There are two species. Family Palmae.

H. belmoreana 121
Kentia, Curly Palm, Belmore Sentry Palm. Lord Howe I., temperate. To 10 m (30 ft). Fronds to 2.25 m (7 ft) with crowded leaflets. Flowers in groups of three, (2 male, 1 female) arranged in spikes in the leaf axils. Simple, 4 cm (1½ in) fruit, green. Fast growing. Single, smoothly ringed green trunk, arching fronds with drooping leaflets.

H. forsteriana 121, **121**
Kentia, Thatch Palm, Sentry Palm. Lord Howe I., temperate. To 20 m (60 ft). Fronds to 3.5 m (10 ft) with broader leaflets. Flowers arranged in 3–6 spikes in each leaf axil. Single, 5 cm (2 in) fruit, green. Very fast growing. Single, smoothly ringed green trunk, thicker than *H. belmoreana*. The branches held horizontal.

HYMENOSPORUM 121
An Australian genus of a single species, popular in many parts of the world for its splendid flower display. Family Pittosporaceae.

H. flavum 121, **121**
Sweetshade, Native Frangipani. NSW, Q, temperate. To 17 m (50 ft). Simple obovate, shiny leaves to 15 cm (6 in) long. Evergreen. Cream 4 cm (1½ in) flowers with a long tube and often marked in red and green. Fading to orange, and borne in long panicles. Highly perfumed. 2.5 cm (1 in) capsules. Fast growing. Columnar, pyramidal, with sparse branches downward pointing and arranged asymmetrically.

IDESIA 122
An Oriental genus of but one species, a handsome deciduous tree noted for its persistent panicles of showy berries. Family Flacourtiaceae.

I. polycarpa 122, **122**
Iigiri, Wonder Tree. China, Japan, temperate. To 17 m (50 ft). Cordate 25 cm (10 in) leaves on long red stems. Small, yellow-green, many-stamened flowers without petals. In terminal panicles. Many-seeded berries, 5 mm (¼ in) diameter, green ripening to red, in 25 cm (10 in) panicles. Fast growing. Upright, with horizontal branches.

ILEX 122–3
A popular genus of largely evergreen trees or shrubs, grown for the beauty of their generally spiny foliage and showy display of colourful fruits. Mostly from cold winter areas of the northern hemisphere, but also extending through the tropics into the southern hemisphere. Family Aquifoliaceae.

I. aquifolium 122, **123**
Holly, English Holly, European Holly. Europe, N. Africa, Asia, cool temperate. To 25 m (75 ft). Oval, glossy green leaves to 5 cm (2 in) long, heavily spined on margins. Small, fragrant white blossom in clusters on old wood. Bright red, ovoid fruit to 1 cm (½ in) diameter. Slow grow-

ing. Pyramidal, dense. Wood used for decorative inlays. Many varieties in habit, leaf and fruit colours.

I. cornuta
Chinese Holly, Horned Holly. China, temperate. To 10 m (30 ft). Oblong to quadrangular leaves with 2–6 exaggerated teeth. To 5 cm (2 in) long. Yellowish flowers, in clusters, on old wood. Red globose fruit to 1 cm (½ in) diameter. Slow growing. Pyramidal, dense. Many CVs in foliage and habit.

I. opaca 123
American Holly. E. USA, temperate. To 17 m (50 ft). Thick leathery elliptical leaves to 10 cm (4 in) long. Frequently twisted and without spines. Evergreen. Creamy-white blossom in axillary cymes. Scarlet to crimson fruit to 1 cm (½ in) diameter. Persisting through winter. Very slow growing. Pyramidal to columnar. Dense. A valuable timber tree with many CVs in foliage and habit.

I. paraguariensis 123, **123**
Maté, Yerba Maté, Paraguay Tea. E. S. America, warm temperate. To 7 m (20 ft). Flat elliptical leaves to 12.5 cm (5 in), edges coarsely crenate. Flowers greenish-white on new wood. Deep red globose fruit to 5 mm (¼ in) diameter. Slow growing. Round-headed, dense habit. The tea-like beverage Yerba Maté is prepared from its dried leaves.

I. pedunculata 122, **123**
Mt Fuji Holly, Longstalk Holly. Japan, cool temperate. To 10 m (30 ft). 7.5 cm (3 in) smooth-edged, oblong-elliptical leaves. Dull green. Small whitish flowers in clusters on new wood. Pendant, small scarlet fruit to 5 mm (¼ in) wide on long peduncles. Fast growing. Columnar to pyramidal. The favourite Holly in Japanese landscaping.

I. rotunda 122, **123**
Kurogane Holly, China Holly. Japan, China, Vietnam, temperate to tropical. To 20 m (60 ft). Dark green, leathery elliptical leaves on new wood to 9 cm (3½ in) long and smooth edged. Partly deciduous. White flowers in axillary cymes of 4–6. Bright red, ellipsoid fruit to 5 mm (¼ in). Fast growing. Thick-trunked, gnarled, spreading habit. A useful timber tree.

INGA 124
A large tropical genus, mostly shrubby, but including several spectacular trees. Family Leguminosae.

I. edulis 124, **124**
Pacayer, Ice Cream Beans, Ynga. S. America, tropical. To 17 m (50 ft). Compound pinnate leaves with 6–8 elliptical 15 cm (6 in) leaflets, woolly on reverse. Masses of white stamens, to 5 cm (2 in) long, in rusty pubescent spikes. Flat 15 cm (6 in) pods. Fast growing. Round-headed, dense. Planted as a windbreak and for the edible pulp which surrounds the seeds.

INOCARPUS 124
A genus of a single species found from Malaysia to Tahiti and nearby islands, widely grown in wet positions in the tropics. Family Leguminosae.

I. edulis 124, **124**
Mapé, Tahitian Chestnut. Polynesia, Malaysia, tropical. To 20 m (60 ft). Narrow oblong, leathery leaves to 20 cm (8 in). Small, white-petalled flowers to 1 cm (½ in) long, in spikes on old wood. Ovoid pods, 6 cm (2½ in) long with one edible seed. Yellowish. Fast growing. Columnar, heavily buttressed trunk. A great timber tree, growing especially well in swampy areas. The toasted nut is an island delicacy.

IPOMOEA 125
Mostly grown for its attractive climbers

and creepers, the genus also includes a handful of tree-sized species. Family Convolvulaceae.

I. arborescens 125, **125**
Tree Morning Glory, Palo Blanco, Casahuete, Morning Glory Tree. Mexico, tropical. To 7 m (20 ft). Heart-shaped deciduous leaves to 10 cm (4 in) long, downy reverses. Smooth, circular, white flowers with crimson centres, to 10 cm (3 in) wide, in dense axillary clusters. Globose capsules. Fast growing. Round-headed, weeping branches.

ITEA 125
A very small genus of attractive small trees and shrubs from N. America and Asia. Family Saxifragaceae.

I. ilicifolia 125, **125**
Hollyleaf Sweetspire, Tassel-white. China, temperate. To 7 m (20 ft). Evergreen, spiny-toothed holly-like 10 cm (4 in) leaves. Small, greenish-white flowers in 30 cm (12 in) drooping racemes. Fruit: small superior ovary. Medium fast growth. Columnar, weeping branches.

JACARANDA 126
A splendid genus of some 50 tropical American trees, noted for their gorgeous flower display in late spring. Mostly flowering in shades of mauve-blue, there are also white and deep red species and varieties. Family Bignoniaceae.

J. mimosaefolia 126, **126**
Jacaranda, Fern-leaf Jacaranda, Brazilian Rosewood. Brazil, Argentina, dry temperate. To 17 m (50 ft). Fern-like, compound bipinnate leaves with 12 or more pinnae and innumerable leaflets. Mauve-blue, tubular flowers, to 5 cm (2 in) long. Flat, almost circular capsules. Fast growing. Spreading head, leans away from cold, prevailing winds. Timber used in cabinet-making.

J. ovalifolia, see **J. mimosaefolia**
JAMBOSA, see **SYZYGIUM**
JATROPHA 126–7
Mostly shrubby, the many species of the genus Jatropha are native to the Americas, Africa and Asia. Several tree members are popular in tropical gardens. Family Euphorbiaceae.

J. hastata 126, **126**
Rose Bay, Peregrina, Spicy Jatropha. Cuba, tropical. To 5 m (15 ft). Very variable leaf shape — may be oval, oblong, or fiddle-shaped. Velvety. Cerise or deep rose flowers in a drooping terminal cyme. Small capsules. Fast growing. Shrubby, often with drooping branches.

J. integerrima, see **J. hastata**
JUBAEA 127
The one and only species of this stout-trunked Palm is from coastal Chile, but popular in temperate gardens everywhere. Family Palmae.

J. chilensis 127
Wine Palm, Honey Palm, Coquito, Little Cokernut. Chile, temperate. To 10 m (30 ft). Silvery green 1.5 m (4½ ft) fronds with about 240 pinnae. Fronds generally upward pointing with curved tips. Maroon and yellow flowers in a drooping 1 m (3 ft) inflorescence. Fruit 4 cm (1½ in) long, yellow, like young coconuts. Slow growing. Thick-trunked, solitary. Sap processed and sold as Palm Honey.

J. spectabilis, see **J. chilensis**
JUGLANS 127–8
Probably the world's most popular bearers of edible nuts. The genus has species in Europe, Asia, and both N. and S. America. Family Juglandaceae.

J. hindsii 127, **128**
California Walnut. California, temperate. To 15 m (45 ft). Compound pinnate leaves with 15–19 10 cm (4 in) leaflets.

Aromatic. Deciduous. Male flowers greenish in hanging catkins, female in small clusters, separately on one tree. Drupe-like nuts enclosed in a smooth green husk. To 2.5 cm (1 in) in diameter. Medium fast growth. Broad-headed. A useful fruit tree. Also felled for timber.

J. nigra 127
American Walnut, Black Walnut. E. USA, temperate. To 50 m (150 ft). Compound pinnate, 60 cm (2 ft), leaves with 15—23 ovate leaflets, pubescent on reverse. Deciduous. Flowers as in other species. Strongly ridged nut in a 5 cm (2 in) capsule. Very fast growing. Upright, with round, spreading head. The best species for timber, nuts edible.

J. regia 127, 127, 128
Persian Walnut, European Walnut, Common Walnut. Europe, Asia Minor, temperate. To 35 m (100 ft). Long, compound and fragrant leaves with 7—9 12.5 cm (5 in) leaflets. Flowers as in other species. Wrinkled nuts in green 5 cm (2 in) husks. Fast growing. Squat, rounded head. A valuable cabinet wood. The best edible nuts. .

JUNIPERUS 128—9
An important coniferous genus, found in all parts of the northern hemisphere. Generally slow-growing, and with endless variations in colour and habit. Family Cupressaceae.

J. chinensis 128, 129
Chinese Juniper. China, Japan, Himalayas, temperate. To 25 m (75 ft). Juvenile leaves needle-like, modified to scales in older specimens. Male flowers in small yellow catkins, female globose. Small 2 or 3-seeded cones to 5 mm (¼ in) diameter. Medium fast growth. Conical. Many foliage and habit varieties. A good timber tree.

J. communis 128—9, 129
Common Juniper. Europe, N. America, Asia, temperate. To 12 m (35 ft). Scale-like, sharp pointed leaves. Flowers as in other species. Bluish berry-like cones with 3 seeds. To 1 cm (½ in) diameter. Slow growth. May be conical or spreading. A very variable species with dozens of cultivars. Berries used to flavour gin.

J. sabina Bermudiana 129
Bermuda Cedar. Bermuda, temperate. To 13 m (40 ft). Spiny, pointed, blue-grey, overlapping scales. Flowers as in other species. Blue, glaucous cones to 1 cm (½ in) diameter. Slow growth. Pyramidal.

J. scopulorum 129, 128
Colorado Red Cedar, Rocky Mountain Juniper. W. USA, cool temperate. To 17 m (50 ft). Scale-like leaves, blue-green, glaucous. Flowers as in other species. Purple-black 2-seeded cones to 5 mm (¼ in) diameter. Slow growth. Conical to spreading, very variable. Many CVs.

J. virginiana 129
Red Cedar, Pencil Cedar. E. and C. USA, temperate. To 33 m (100 ft). Scale-like, overlapping leaves. Flowers as in other species. Female cones 1—3 seeded, bluish-black, to 5 mm (¼ in) diameter. Fast growing. Pyramidal. Many foliage CVs. The fragrant red timber of the species is used for lining storage cupboards and boxes. Raised commercially for the pencil industry.

KETELEERIA 130
A relatively uncommon coniferous species from warmer areas of China, grown for the decorative effect of its splendidly coloured cones. Family Pinaceae.

K. davidiana 130, 130
Keteleeria. S. China to Taiwan, temperate. To 35 m (100 ft). Linear, glossy leaves, pale beneath. Erect, woody cones to 20 cm (8 in) long. Bluish-green with purple stems. Fast growing. Pyramidal.

K. fortunei 130
Fortune's Keteleeria. S. China, temperate. To 35 m (100 ft). Spiny, pointed linear leaves on orange-brown young branchlets. Green cones to 17.5 cm (7 in). Purple when young. Fast growing. Pyramidal.

KIGELIA 130—1
A small tree genus from the African tropics. Notable for probably the longest stalked fruits in nature. Family Bignoniaceae.

K. pinnata 130, 130, 131
Sausage Tree. Tropical Africa. To 17 m (50 ft). Pinnate leaves with 7—11 elliptic leaflets, each to 17.5 cm (7 in) long. Claret coloured flowers to 7.5 cm (3 in) diameter. Night-blooming, in long-stemmed, drooping panicles. Unpleasantly scented. Grey, indehiscent, sausage-shaped capsules up to 60 cm (2 ft) in length, on stems as much as 7 m (20 ft) long. Fast growing. Upright, round-headed.

KLEINHOVIA 131
A single tree species from the Indian Ocean area. Family Byttneriaceae.

K. hospita 131, 131
Guest Tree. Indian Ocean, tropical. To 20 m (60 ft). Broad-oval leaves to 30 cm (12 in) long and about as wide. Reddish-pink flowers in loose, terminal panicles. Inflated pear-shaped capsules to 2.5 cm (1 in) long. Fast growing. Wide-headed.

KOELREUTERIA 131—2
A small genus. Four species of deciduous trees from Asia and Fiji, noted for their double display of golden flowers, and papery, inflated pods. Family Sapindaceae.

K. bipinnata 132
Pride of China. S.W. China, warm temperate. To 20 m (60 ft). Bipinnate leaves, to 45 cm (18 in) long, with leaflets often serrated and hairy, Deciduous. Yellow flowers in terminal panicles to 45 cm (18 in) long. 4-petalled. Pink bladder-like capsules with 3 segments. Fast growing. Upright, flat-topped.

K. elegans 132
Flamegold. Taiwan, Fiji, tropical. To 20 m (60 ft). Bipinnate leaves to 45 cm (18 in) long, leaflets narrow. Flowers in a long terminal panicle. Yellow. 5-petalled. Rosy 4 cm (1½ in) capsules with 3 papery segments. Fast growing. Upright, flat-topped.

K. paniculata 132, 132
Golden Rain Tree, Varnish Tree, Pride of India. China, temperate. To 15 m (45 ft). Pinnate or bipinnate leaves to 45 cm (18 in) long. Yellow, 4-petalled flowers in a 45 cm (18 in) terminal panicle. Red-brown, papery 5 cm (2 in) capsules with 3 pointed segments. Fast growing. Flat-topped to rounded. The flowers are used medicinally in China.

LABURNUM 132—3
A small European genus grown for their decorative hanging chains of golden spring flowers. Family Leguminosae.

L. alpinum 132
Scotch Laburnum. C. Europe, cool temperate. To 8 m (25 ft). Trifoliate, deep green, shiny oval-pointed leaves, pale and hairy on reverse. Deciduous. Flowers in 38 cm (15 in) pendant racemes. Flat, single-winged pods. Fast growing. Short trunk, upright branches.

L. anagyroides 132
Golden Chain. C. and S. Europe, temperate. To 10 m (30 ft). Trifoliate leaves of 3 dull green oval leaflets, downy on reverse. Yellow flowers in a pendant raceme to 20 cm (8 in) long. Leguminous pods to 5 cm (2 in), downy. Fast growing. Low-branching habit.

L. X vossii 132
Golden Chain Tree, Hybrid Laburnum. Hybrid. Cool temperate climate. To 10 m (30 ft). Trifoliate leaves with 7.5 cm (3 in) elliptical leaflets. Deciduous. Yellow flowers in slender racemes to 25 cm (10 in). Pods very scantily borne, few seeded. Often sterile. Fast growing. Stiffly upright habit.

L. X watererii, see **L. X vossii**

LAGERSTROEMIA 133—4
There are over 50 species of these showy flowered trees, native to Asia and the Pacific Islands. Family Lythraceae.

L. indica 133, 134
Chinese Crepe Myrtle. China, warm temperate. To 7 m (20 ft). 7 cm (2¾ in) rounded to elliptic leaves, usually glabrous. Deciduous. Flowers 2.75 cm (1⅛ in) diameter, orbicular, crisped petals in terminal panicles. May be red, pink, purple or white. Capsules with winged seeds. Fast growing. Slender, handsome mottled bark, upward pointing branches.

L. speciosa 133, 133
Queen Crepe Myrtle, Pride of India. China, India to Australia, tropical. To 27 m (80 ft). Leathery, ovate-elliptical leaves to 30 cm (12 in) long. Flowers in a terminal panicle. Individual blooms to 5 cm (2 in) diameter. Pink or purple with about 200 stamens. Shiny green capsules. Fast growing. Round-headed. Timber used for many construction purposes.

L. subcostata 133, 134
White Crepe Myrtle. Taiwan, S.E. China, temperate. To 10 m (30 ft). Shiny ovate-lanceolate leaves to 10 cm (4 in) long. Spidery white flowers in 20 cm (8 in) panicles. Shiny capsules. Fast growing. Slender, sparsely branched tree.

LAGUNARIA 134—5
A single species of evergreen tree found in E. Australia, Lord Howe and Norfolk Islands. Family Malvaceae.

L. patersonii 134, 134, 135
Norfolk I. Hibiscus, Cow Itch Tree, Pyramid Tree, Whitewood. Australia, S. Pacific, warm temperate. To 17 m (50 ft). Single oblong-lanceolate leaves to 10 cm (4 in). Silvery grey on reverse. Pink to mauve flowers, single, at upper leaf axils, to 6.5 cm (2½ in) diameter. 5-celled dehiscent capsules. Fast growing. Pyramidal to columnar. Sometimes cut for timber. Seeds lined with irritating hairs.

LARIX 135
A northern hemisphere genus of conifers, deciduous and all native to cold winter areas. Family Pinaceae.

L. decidua 135, 135
European Larch. Swiss and Carpathian Alps, cool temperate. To 60 m (180 ft). 4 cm (1½ in) needle-like, deciduous leaves, clustered on small spurs of weeping branchlets, or spirally on new shoots. Male flowers solitary, yellow. Female in an upright cone. Cones, often brightly coloured, but persistent after seeds fall. Very fast growing. Pyramidal, usually with weeping branchlets. Brown and gold in autumn. The source of Venetian turpentine and a valuable timber tree.

L. laricina 135
Tamarack, American Larch, Hackmatack. E. USA, cool temperate. To 27 m (80 ft). 3-angled needle leaves to 4 cm (1½ in). Deciduous. Very small cones to 2 cm (¾ in). Very fast growing. Pyramidal. Yellow in autumn.

L. leptolepis, see **L. kaempferi**

LATANIA 136
Three species of tall, dioecious Palms

LATANIA

from the Mascarene Islands in the Indian Ocean. Family Palmae.

L. borbonica, see **L. lontaroides**

L. loddigesii 136, **136**
Blue Latan Palm. Mauritius, sub-tropical. To 17 m (50 ft). Fan-shaped glaucous blue fronds to 2 m (5 ft) long. Male inflorescence to 2 m (5 ft), heavily bracted, female the same length, but more lightly bracted and with larger flowers. Globose seeds to 6 cm (2³/₈ in) long. Fast growing. Stout trunk, definite bluish appearance.

L. lontaroides 136
Red Latan Palm. Reunion I., tropical. To 17 m (50 ft). Fan-shaped bracts to 2 m (5 ft) or more, grey-green, but with the stem and base of blade tinted red when young. Flowers and fruit as in L. loddigesii. Stout-trunked, solitary.

L. verschaffeltii 136
Yellow Latan Palm. Rodrigues I., tropical. To 17 m (50 ft). Fan-shaped fronds to 136 cm (4¹/₂ ft), yellow when young, yellow margined at maturity. Flower spikes drooping to 2 m (5 ft) or more in length. Globose seeds to 5 cm (2 in) long. Fast growing. Solitary, stout-trunked.

LAURUS 136–7
A famous tree from the Mediterranean region, source of the laurel garlands of ancient Greece, and the gourmet's bay leaves. Family Lauraceae.

L. nobilis 136, **136**
Sweet Bay, Bay Tree, Laurel. Mediterranean, temperate. To 13 m (40 ft). Dark, glossy green leaves to 10 cm (4 in), lanceolate to elliptic. Evergreen. Small yellow flowers in axillary umbels. Male and female on separate trees. Black or purple berries. Slow growing. Generally upright and round-headed to pyramidal. Source of culinary bay leaves, oils used in perfumery.

LEPTOSPERMUM 137
A genus of evergreen, coastal trees from the southern hemisphere. Species in Malaysia, New Zealand and Australia. Family Myrtaceae.

L. laevigatum 137, **137**
Coastal Tea-Tree. Coastal S.E. Australia and Tas, temperate. To 10 m (30 ft). Broadly oblanceolate leaves to 2.5 cm (1 in) long. White solitary flowers, to 2 cm (³/₄ in) wide, in axils. 8–10 valved woody capsules. Fast growing. Usually of picturesque wind-blown shape, with corrugated, shredding bark. A good coastal windbreak.

L. petersonii
Lemon Scented Tea-Tree. E. Australia, temperate. To 8 m (20 ft). Linear-lanceolate leaves to 5 cm (2 in). Evergreen. Solitary white flowers to 1.2 cm (⁵/₈ in) wide, borne singly at axils or terminally. 5-valved, woody capsules. Fast growing. Shrubby, flat-headed. A lemon-scented oil is extracted from the foliage.

LIGUSTRUM 138
A medium-sized genus of mostly evergreen small trees. The larger number of species are found from China, through Malaysia to Australia — but with outlying species in Africa and Europe. In many lands they are declared noxious weeds. Family Oleaceae.

L. lucidum 138, **138**
Glossy Privet, Chinese Privet. China, Korea, temperate. To 10 m (30 ft). 15 cm (6 in) glossy, acuminate leaves. Evergreen. White flowers in 25 cm (10 in) panicles. Purple-black, berry-like drupes. Fast growing. Densely branched, upright, round-headed. Many decorative varieties with colourful foliage.

LIQUIDAMBAR 138–9
A genus of 3 decorative specimen trees, one from N. America, one from S. E. Asia,

and one from Asia Minor. Family Hamamelidaceae.

L. formosana 139, **138**
Formosan Sweet Gum. S. China, Taiwan, sub-tropical. To 40 m (120 ft). 3-lobed leaves to 25 cm (6 in) wide, sometimes downy on reverse. Male flowers in terminal spikes or racemes, female separately in hanging globose heads. Fruit: a pendant, globose head with spiny persistent styles. Fast growing. Pyramidal with smooth branches. Brilliant autumn colours. An important timber tree, source of aromatic styrax, used in perfumery.

L. styraciflua 139, **139**
Sweet Gum, Red Gum, Bilsted. E. and C. USA, temperate. To 40 m (120 ft). 5 or 7 lobed leaves to 17.5 cm (7 in) wide, serrated edges. Flowers and fruit as in other species. Fast growing. Pyramidal, with corky wings on lower side of branches. Often brilliant red, yellow and purple in autumn. An important timber tree; source of styrax. Several cultivars with good autumn colour are propagated.

LIRIODENDRON 139–40
Two species of deciduous trees found a world apart — one in C. China and the other in E. N. America. Family Magnoliaceae.

L. chinense
Chinese Tulip Tree. C. China, temperate. To 17 m (50 ft). 4-lobed, squarish, 15 cm (6 in) leaves. 4 cm (1¹/₂ in) tulip flowers, dull green with yellow bases. Magnolia-like fruit, a conical mass of congested carpels. Very fast growing. Columnar.

L. tulipifera 139–40, **140**
Tulip Tree, Tulip Poplar, Yellow Poplar. E. USA, temperate. To 70 m (200 ft). Squarish, 4-lobed leaves, 12.5 cm (5 in) long, pale beneath. Deciduous. 5 cm (2 in) flowers of lime green with orange bases. 7.5 cm (3 in) carpel. Very fast growing. Columnar to flat-topped, the trunk often bare to a great height. Yellow in autumn. An important timber tree, the wood known as Yellow Poplar.

LITCHI 140–1
A small genus of which only one species is commonly cultivated for its delicious fruits. Family Sapindaceae.

L. sinensis 140–1, **141**
Lychee, Leecheenut. S. China, sub-tropical. To 13 m (40 ft). Compound, 24 cm (9¹/₂ in) evergreen leaves with 2–8 leathery leaflets. A 30 cm (12 in) inflorescence of small greenish-yellow flowers without petals. Bright red drupes with brittle, tubercled shell, 3 cm (1¹/₂ in). It contains one seed surrounded by juicy edible pulp. Fast growing. Spreading head. Source of China's favourite fruit.

LIVISTONA 141
A large genus of Palms with gigantic orbicular fronds, divided palmately. Family Palmae.

L. australis 141, **141**
Cabbage-tree Palm, Gippsland Palm. E. Australia, temperate. To 20 m (60 ft). Large orbicular or fan-shaped fronds, about 1.3 m (4 ft) diameter divided into about 70 segments with pendulous tips. A branched inflorescence with small yellow flowers in twos and threes. Purple-black fruit, to 2.5 cm (1 in) long, 2 cm (³/₄ in) wide. Fast growing. Single-trunked, drooping fronds.

L. chinensis 141
Chinese Fountain Palm, Chinese Fan Palm. China, Japan, sub-tropical. To 10 m, (30 ft). Orbicular, fan-shaped fronds, to 3 m (10 ft) diameter, deeply divided and blue-green. A branched inflorescence with flowers in clusters of six. Blue-green, ellipsoid fruit 2 cm (³/₄ in) long. Fast growing. Single-trunked, leaves arching almost

to ground on toothed petioles.

L. mariae 141
Red Inland Palm. C. Australia, dry temperate. To 33 m (100 ft). Orbicular, deeply divided fronds, bronze-red on young blades. Inflorescences similar to L. australis. Blackish, 1 cm (¹/₂ in) fruit. Slow growing. Single-trunked.

MACADAMIA 142
A genus of 10 nut-bearing trees, very important in the economy of Hawaii, but actually native to N. Australia. Evergreen, and all very similar. Family Proteaceae.

M. integrifolia 142
Macadamia, Australian Nut. Queensland Nut. N.Q, warm temperate to tropical. To 20 m (60 ft) and almost as wide. Juvenile leaves pale green, coarsely serrated; adult oblanceolate, dark, to 30 cm (12 in) and mostly smooth-edged. Small white flowers, several hundred to a 30 cm (12 in) raceme. A sweet nut contained in a hard woody shell to 3 cm (1¹/₄ in) diameter. Fast growing. Broad-headed, spreading. The principal commercial species.

M. tetraphylla 142
Rough-shelled Macadamia, Macadamia, Queensland Nut. NSW, warm temperate. To 17 m (50 ft) and wider in spread. New foliage pink, red or yellowish, finely serrated. Adult leaves oblanceolate, to 50 cm (20 in), in whorls of 4, finely serrated with 30–80 teeth. Pink or cream flowers in 45 cm (18 in) racemes. A small nut enclosed in a hard-shelled capsule to 4 cm (1¹/₂ in) diameter. Sometimes two hemispherical nuts in one husk. Fast growing. Wide spreading, round shape. A popular commercial crop.

MACLURA 142
A single species of deciduous tree from E. USA. Sometimes cultivated in Australia for the curiosity value of its inedible fruits. Family Moraceae.

M. pomifera 142, **142**
Osage Orange, Bowwood. E. USA, temperate. To 20 m (60 ft). Oblong-ovate leaves to 15 cm (6 in). Deciduous. Greenish flowers in a small raceme. Rough textured, irregularly shaped syncarp to 12.5 cm (5 in) in diameter. Fast growing. Irregularly shaped with weeping branches, often spiny. Cultivated more as a hedge plant than as a tree.

MAGNOLIA 143–4
A splendid genus of over 80 shrubs and trees from Asia, N. and C. USA. Those from Asia are deciduous, the others mostly evergreen. Grown for the great beauty of their enormous and fragrant flowers. Family Magnoliaceae.

M. acuminata
Cucumber Tree. E. USA, temperate. To 33 m (100 ft). Elliptic leaves to 25 cm (10 in) long, woolly reverses. Deciduous. Greenish-yellow flowers to 10 cm (4 in) long. Purple cones of many seed capsules. Fast growing. Pyramidal.

M. campbellii 144, **144**
Pink Tulip Tree, Chinese Tulip Tree. Himalayas, temperate. To 50 m (150 ft). Oval, elliptic, tapering leaves to 30 cm (12 in), mealy on reverse. Flowers to 25 cm (10 in) wide, pale pink with deeper reverse. Greenish-brown, twisted cones containing scarlet seeds, to 20 cm (8 in) long. Fast growing. Sparsely branched, upright. May not flower under 20 years of age.

M. conspicua, see **M. denudata.**

M. delavayi
Delavay's Magnolia. China, cool temperate. To 12 m (35 ft). Enormous grey-green ovate leaves to 25 cm (10 in) long. Evergreen. 20 cm (8 in) open white flowers, strongly perfumed. 12.5 cm

248

(5 in) green cones. Medium fast growth. Flat-topped, spreading, pale beige bark.

M. denudata 143
Yulan, Lily Tree. China, temperate. To 33 m (100 ft). Obovate 17.5 cm (7 in) leaves, downy beneath. Deciduous. Pure white, chalice-shaped flowers to 15 cm (6 in) diameter. Very fragrant, early spring. Brownish 12.5 cm (5 in) oblong cones with orange seeds. Medium fast growth. Round-headed, densely branched. Dark bark. Hairy flower buds deck tree in winter, open in earliest spring.

M. grandiflora 143, 143, 144
Bull Bay, Southern Magnolia, Laurel Magnolia. S.E. USA, warm temperate. To 33 m (100 ft). Leathery, obovate-oblong evergreen leaves to 20 cm (8 in) long; shiny surface, woolly-rusty on reverse. Open white flowers to 20 cm (8 in) diameter, fading to creamy-brown. Heavily fragrant. Rusty cone-like seed conglomerate to 10 cm (4 in) long. Medium fast growth. Pyramidal, densely foliaged.

M. heptapeta, see **M. denudata**

M. kobus
Japanese Magnolia. Japan, temperate. To 25 m (75 ft). Obovate, 15 cm (6 in) leaves. Deciduous. Cream to pink, 10 cm (4 in) erect flowers. Before foliage. Green cones. Medium fast growth. Pyramidal to round-headed. May not flower for 25 years.

M. liliflora 144, 144
Lily Magnolia. C. China, temperate. To 5 m (15 ft). Elliptic, 17.5 cm (7 in) leaves. Deciduous. Tulip-shaped flowers to 10 cm (4 in) high, pink within, purple reverse. Green oblong cones. Slow growing. Shrubby. Flowers irregularly, often after foliage in early summer.

M. sieboldii
Oyama Magnolia, Mountain Magnolia. Korea, Japan, cool temperate. To 10 m (30 ft). Lanceolate leaves to 15 cm (6 in). Deciduous. White, 10 cm (4 in) flowers with pink and red stamens. Fragrant. Summer. Crimson cones. Slow growing. Round-headed, shrubby.

M. X soulangeana 144
Soulange Bodin's Magnolia, Saucer Magnolia, Chinese Magnolia. Hybrid. Temperate climate. To 8 m (25 ft). Leaves obovate, variable in size. Deciduous. Flowers to 15 cm (6 in) diameter, tulip-shaped, pale pink, deeper without. Small greenish cones. Very slow growing. Bushy to round-headed, often many-trunked. Many named CVs of this Magnolia are sold, varying from pure white to a ruby red in colour.

M. X veitchii
Veitch's Magnolia. Hybrid. Temperate climate. To 25 m (75 ft). 22.5 cm (9 in) oblong leaves. Deciduous. White, 25 cm (10 in) flowers, flushed pink, fragrant. Small greenish cones. Fast growing. Open, rounded habit.

M. virginiana
Sweet Bay, Swamp Bay. E. USA, temperate. To 20 m (65 ft). Oblong, glossy, 12.5 cm (5 in) leaves, blue-grey beneath. Evergreen. 7.5 cm (3 in) white flowers in early summer. Red 5 cm (2 in) cones. Fast growing. Shrubby to round-headed. Often turns deciduous in cool climate.

MALUS 145
A genus of some 200 species of small, deciduous trees from the northern hemisphere. Much crossed and hybridized to produce the innumerable Apple varieties of commerce and the daintier, ornamental Crabapples. Family Rosaceae.

M. baccata
Siberian Crab. E. Asia, temperate. To 15 m (45 ft). Ovate 7.5 cm (3 in) leaves, finely serrated. White, 4 cm (1½ in) single flowers, very fragrant. 1 cm (½ in) fruit, yellow with red flush. Fast growing. Upright, densely branching.

M. domestica 145, 146
Apple, Orchard Apple, Common Apple. S. Europe, temperate. To 5 m (15 ft). Obtuse to acuminate, 7.5 cm (3 in) leaves, woolly reverses. Deciduous. White flowers, to 4 cm (1½ in). Large, sweet fruit, variable, to 10 cm (4 in) diameter. May be green, yellow or red according to variety. Fast growing. Open, round-headed. The apple of commerce with up to 1,000 named cultivars.

M. floribunda 145, 145
Japanese Flowering Crabapple, Showy Crab, Purple Chokeberry. Japan, temperate. To 12 m (35 ft). Ovate to oblong leaves, 7.5 cm (3 in) long. May be simple, sharply serrated or even 3–5 lobed. Reverses pale. Deciduous. Carmine buds, opening to rose pink. 4 cm (1½ in) flowers which fade to white. Fragrant. 5 mm (¼ in) red or yellow fruit. Fast growing. Spreading habit. Parent of many hybrid Crabapples.

M. X 'Golden Hornet' 145
A hybrid Crabapple with orange-yellow persistent fruits.

M. X 'Gorgeous' 145, 145
A hybrid Crabapple with scarlet, persistent fruits — raised in N.Z.

M. hupehensis 145
Chinese Crab. China, temperate. To 8 m (25 ft). Ovate-oblong leaves, sharply serrulate, downy beneath. Young foliage purplish. White or pale pink blossom to 4 cm (1½ in) diameter. Fragrant. Greenish-yellow fruit to 1 cm (½ in) diameter. Ripening red. Medium fast growth. Spreading, stiff-branched.

M. ioensis 145, 146
Prairie Crab, Bechtel's Crab, Wild Crab. Midwest USA, cool temperate. To 10 m (30 ft). Oblong ovate leaves to 10 cm (4 in), often with serrated lobes. Woolly reverses. Deciduous. Pale pink, semi-double flowers to 5 cm (2 in) diameter, borne in loose, flat heads. Sparse yellow and green fruits to 2.5 cm (1 in) diameter. Fast growing. Spreading habit.

M. purpurea 145
Purple Crab. Hybrid. Cool temperate climate. To 7 m (20 ft). Ovate, acute, 4 cm (1½ in) leaves, coarsely serrated, purple, deep green when young. Purple-red flowers, to 4 cm (1½ in) diameter, fading with age. Purple-red fruit to 2.5 cm (1 in) diameter. Fast growing. Pyramidal to round-headed. CVs 'Eleyi' and 'Lemoinei' are most commonly seen.

M. spectabilis
Chinese Floral Apple, China Flowering Apple. China, temperate. To 8 m (25 ft). 7.5 cm (3 in) elliptic to lanceolate leaves, sometimes pubescent. Deciduous. Bright pink, semi-double flowers, 5 cm (2 in) diameter. Borne alternate years only. Sparse, 2.5 cm (1 in) yellow fruits, very sour. Fast growing. Open shape, wide-topped in age.

M. sylvestris 145
European Crab, Crabapple. Europe, S.W. Asia, temperate. To 13 m (40 ft). 4 cm (1½ in) leaves on long petiole, oval, smooth-edged with age. Deciduous. White or pale pink flowers, 4 cm (1½ in) diameter, 4–7 in an umbellate inflorescence. 2.5 cm (1 in) wide fruit. Green, sour and sometimes red tinted. Fast growing. Upright, rounded head.

MANGIFERA 146–7
There are actually about 40 species of the genus *Mangifera*, but all those you are likely to see are CVs of *M. indica*, the Mango Tree. Family Anacardiaceae.

M. indica 146, 146, 147
Mango, King of Fruits. India to Malaysia, tropical. To 30 m (90 ft). Stiff, lanceolate evergreen leaves to 40 cm (16 in) long. Young foliage pink. Small red to pink flowers in a stiff inflorescence. Fruit commonly 12.5 cm (5 in) long, but very variable in shape, colour and size. Green, yellow, red, purple or pink. Contains a large fibrous seed. Fast growing. Spreading head to 40 m (125 ft) wide. Many CVs are sold by nurseries, 'Bowen' being the Australian favourite.

MANILKARA 147
A large genus of evergreen, tropical trees from both hemispheres. Only one species widely grown, both for its fruit, and for the sap which is tapped for chicle, the base of chewing gum. Family Sapotaceae.

M. zapota 147, 147
Sapodilla, Chicozapote, Naseberry, Nispero. C. America, tropical. Prefers alkaline soil. To 35 m (120 ft). Elliptical, glossy leaves to 15 cm (6 in) long, clustered toward end of branch tips. Evergreen. White, solitary, axillary flowers to 7 mm (⅓ in wide). Fruit to 10 cm (4 in) diameter, rusty brown skin, full of yellow, translucent flesh. Fast growing. Upright, densely foliated.

M. zapotilla, see **M. zapota.**

MELALEUCA 148
A large genus of evergreen trees in the Myrtle family, related to Eucalypts and Callistemons. Mostly native to Australia, there are several outlying species in New Guinea and Malaysia. Family Myrtaceae.

M. armillaris 148
Bracelet Honeymyrtle. S.E. Australia, temperate. To 10 m (30 ft). Narrow linear leaves to 2 cm (¾ in) long. Evergreen. White flowers in a 5 cm (2 in) bottlebrush inflorescence. Woody capsules. Fast growing. Shrubby, slight. Grey bark peeling in strips.

M. ericifolia
Swamp Paperbark. Tas, S.E. Australia, temperate. To 10 m (30 ft). Narrowly linear leaves, to 1 cm (½ in). Yellowish-white flowers in a 5 cm (2 in) terminal inflorescence. Woody capsules. Fast growing. Shrubby, tends to multiple trunks. Bark soft and papery.

M. linariifolia 148, 149
Flaxleaf Paperbark, Snow-in-Summer. Q, NSW, SA, temperate. To 7 m (20 ft). Linear-lanceolate, opposite leaves, to 4 cm (1½ in), rigid. Loose asymmetrical spikes of feathery, cream stamens to 5 cm (2 in) long. Woody capsules. Medium fast growth. Heavy-trunked, spreading. Bark spongy, thick, deciduous. A medicinal oil is extracted from foliage.

M. parviflora 148, 148
Small-flowered Paperbark. WA, dry temperate. To 7 m (20 ft). Dark, tapered, recurved leaves to 1 cm (½ in). Loose cream bottlebrushes with flecks of pink, to 4 cm (1½ in). Woody capsules. Medium fast growth. Shrubby. Whitish papery bark. A good beach tree.

M. quinquenervia 148, 148
Cajeput Tree, Broadleaf Paperbark, Punk Tree, Swamp Paperbark. E. Australia, New Guinea, New Caledonia, temperate to tropical. To 17 m (50 ft). Alternate, lanceolate, 9 cm (3½ in) leaves. Dense bottlebrush spikes of white stamens to 7.5 cm (3 in) long. Woody capsules. Very fast growing. Columnar to wide-headed depending on position. Naturalizes rapidly in swamps. White, spongy bark, peeling in sheets. Useful timber for

fences or farmyard construction. Cajeput oil extracted from foliage.

M. styphelioides
Prickly Paperbark. NSW, temperate. To 20 m (60 ft). Ovate, twisted leaves to 1 cm (1/2 in) long, with a sharp point. Dense spikes of white stamens to 5 cm (2 in) long. Woody pods. Fast growing. Round-headed, thick, spongy bark. Thrives in both swampy and dry conditions.

MELIA 149
A small genus of deciduous trees native to Asia and Australia but now naturalized throughout the sub-tropical zones of the world. One species only is widely cultivated. Family Meliaceae.

M. azederach 149, **149**
Persian Lilac, Chinaberry, Bead Tree, Texas Umbrella Tree, Pride of India, Pride of China, Paradise Tree, Indian Lilac, Japanese Bead Tree, White Cedar. Asia, temperate to sub-tropical. To 15 m (45 ft). Bipinnate, 1 m (3 ft) leaves with many toothed leaflets. Deciduous. Small, purplish, fragrant flowers in clusters, resembling Lilacs. Green, 2 cm (3/4 in) berries, turning orange and persisting after leaf fall. Fast growing. Spreading, generally flat-topped. Several named cultivars, varying in habit. The berries, poisonous to humans, contain medicinal properties. The timber is used in cabinet-making.

MESPILUS 150
A genus of a single species, within the Rose family, once valued for its late-ripening fruit. Family Rosaceae.

M. germanica 150, **150**
Medlar, Mespilo. Europe, Asia Minor, temperate. To 7 m (20 ft). Leathery opposite leaves with hairy surface, to 12.5 cm (5 in) long. Deciduous. Single, white flowers, early summer, 5 cm (2 in) diameter. Apple-shaped, brown fruit to 5 cm (2 in) diameter with pronounced calyx. Slow growing. Twisted and shrubby, with spreading head. Red-brown in autumn. Fruit edible when fully ripe, generally after frost.

METASEQUOIA 150
A single species from Szechuan, China, related to *Sequoia* but deciduous. Family Taxodiaceae.

M. glyptostroboides 150, **150**
Dawn Redwood. China, temperate. To 35 m (100 ft) and more. Linear, 2-ranked leaves to 1 cm (1/2 in) long on deciduous branchlets. Leaves much larger on young trees. Male flowers in long drooping spikes. Female cones ellipsoid, to 2.5 cm (1 in), green ripening to brown. Very fast growing. Perfectly pyramidal. Orange flaking bark on a massive trunk.

METROSIDEROS 151
A widespread genus of up to 60 evergreen species found over a wide range from S. Africa to Australia and N.Z. with outlying species in Malaysia, Hawaii and Tahiti. Family Myrtaceae.

M. collina 151, **151**
Ohi'a Lehua, Lehua, Puarata. Tahiti, Hawaii, tropical, high altitude. To 35 m (100 ft). Shiny green leaves, elliptic to obovate, to 7.5 cm (3 in) long. Orange-red to crimson flowers in dense terminal tufts. Petals almost invisible but stamens to 2.5 cm (1 in) long. Leathery capsules. Medium fast growth. Shrubby to tall with umbrella-like head. Timber known as ironwood, used for many purposes.

M. excelsa 151, **151**
Pohutukawa, New Zealand Xmas Tree, Rata. N.Z., temperate. To 10 m (30 ft). Dark, leathery, 10 cm (4 in) leaves, with silver reverses. Evergreen. Dark red flowers in terminal clusters, to 2.5 cm (1

in) long. Blooming almost exactly at Christmas in southern hemisphere. Leathery capsules. Fast growing. Many-branched, often flat-headed, sometimes with aerial roots.

M. kermadecensis 151, **151**
Kermadec Ironwood. N.Z., temperate. To 10 m (30 ft). Broadly ovate leaves to 2.5 cm (1 in) long. Red flowers in cymose clusters, shorter stems than *M. excelsa*, borne sparsely in summer. Leathery capsules. Slow growing. Densely rounded when young, becoming leggy with age. Grown most often in its coloured leaf varieties, margined or centred in gold or silver.

M. robusta 151, **151**
Northern Rata. N. N.Z., temperate. To 27 m (80 ft). Elliptic-lanceolate leaves to 5 cm (2 in) long. Dull red flowers in terminal cymes. Stamens to 2 cm (3/4 in) long. Leathery capsules. Fast growing. Upright, rounded head. A useful timber tree.

M. tomentosa, see M. excelsa

MICHELIA 152
Less well known than they deserve away from Asia, these evergreen trees are closely related to the Magnolias, and bear fragrant flowers. Family Magnoliaceae.

M. alba 152, **152**
Pak-lan, Pakalana. Java, sub-tropical. To 10 m (30 ft). Apple green, slender leaves to 25 cm (10 in). Pure-white, Gardenia-size flowers with petals of irregular length. Very fragrant. Cone-like clusters of capsules. Fast growing. Upright, round-headed. A notably pale, grey trunk.

M. champaca 152
Cham-pak, Orange Champak, Mulang. Himalayas, temperate. To 13 m (40 ft). Pointed, dull green leaves to 25 cm (10 in). Orange or yellow flowers to 6 cm (2½ in) with long narrow petals. Heavy perfume. Cone-like clusters of capsules. Fast growing. Pyramidal. Source of perfumed Champaca Oil.

M. doltsopa 152
Wong-lan. Tibet, Yunnan, temperate. To 30 m (90 ft). Elliptic, 15 cm (6 in) leaves. Fragrant, white to buff 12-petalled flowers to 7.5 cm (3 in) wide. Cone-like carpel clusters. Fast growing. Pyramidal. A valuable timber tree.

MORINDA 153
A tropical, evergreen genus of 80 species, only one of which is much in cultivation. Family Moraceae.

M. citrifolia 152, **152**
Indian Mulberry, Noni, Awl Tree. S.E. Asia/Australia, tropical. To 7 m (20 ft). Shiny leaves, oblong to broadly elliptic, 25 cm (10 in). Small, white flowers in dense terminal and axillary clusters. A compound head of almost coherent drupes to 5 cm (2 in) long. Fast growing. Shrubby. Source of red and yellow dyes. Ripe fruit edible but unpalatable.

MORUS 152–3
A well-known genus of fairly similar, deciduous fruiting trees from N. and S. America, Europe and Asia. Their fruit, known as Mulberries, is very attractive to birds. The foliage is the principal food of silkworms. Family Moraceae.

M. alba 152
White Mulberry. China, temperate. To 25 m (80 ft). Heart-shaped to ovate leaves, 10 cm (4 in), coarsely toothed, often lobed. Tiny, greenish flowers in a drooping catkin. Juicy syncarp or aggregate fruit, to 5 cm (2 in) long. May be white, pink or purplish. Slow growing. Round-headed. Often gnarled and grotesque. The principal food for silkworms.

Popular in several CVs including a weeping variety.

M. nigra 153, **153**
Black Mulberry. W. Asia, temperate. To 10 m (30 ft). Broadly ovate leaves to 20 cm (8 in), cordate, sharply toothed; may be lobed or unlobed; rough surface. Deciduous. Small, greenish flowers in a drooping catkin. A purple to black syncarp or compound fruit to 2.5 cm (1 in) long. Very slow growing. Spreading head, gnarled trunk. The best table variety.

M. rubra 153, **153**
Red Mulberry, American Mulberry. N. America, cool temperate. To 20 m (60 ft). Ovate, 12.5 cm (5 in) leaves, sharply toothed and often lobed. Rough surface, pubescent reverse. Greenish catkins. Fruit, to 2.5 cm (1 in) long, red to dark purple. Edible. Slow growing. Gnarled, grotesque — more often grown for decoration than for its fruit.

MYRTUS, see SYZYGIUM

NEPHELIUM 153
A tropical genus of some 70 species found from N. Australia well into S.E. Asia. Several species grown for their delicious fruits. Family Sapindaceae.

N. lappaceum 153, **153**
Rambutan. S.E. Asia, tropical. To 15 m (45 ft). Leathery, bay-like, 15 cm (6 in) leaves. Small whitish flowers in dense clusters. 5 cm (2 in) fruits with stiff curling spines, green to red. Fast growing. Rounded head, densely foliaged.

N. mutabile 153
Pulasan. Java, tropical. To 15 m (45 ft). Compound evergreen leaves with several leaflets. Small whitish flowers in panicles. Red, knobby fruit to 4 cm (1½ in), resembling Lychees. Fast growing. Round-headed, densely foliaged.

NOTHOFAGUS 154
Some 40 species of Beech-like trees from the southern hemisphere. Found in S. America, N.Z., Australia and up through New Caledonia to New Guinea. One of Australia's most important timber trees. Family Fagaceae.

N. cunninghamii 154
Myrtle Beech. Tas, Vic, cool temperate. To 70 m (200 ft). Small (less than 1 cm (1/2 in) long), dark, triangularly toothed leaves in fan-shaped sprays. Young leaves bronze. Deciduous. Small, greenish flowers, solitary or in threes. 4 3-angled nuts enclosed in a single involucre. Fast growing. Upright, round-headed. An important timber tree.

N. dombeyi
Coigue. Chile, Argentina, temperate. To 27 m (80 ft). Oval, evergreen leaves, to 2.5 cm (1 in) long. Small, greenish flowers. 3 triangular nuts in a single involucre. Medium fast growth. Wide-headed. Used for timber.

N. fusca
Red Beech. N.Z., temperate. To 35 m (100 ft). Coarsely toothed 4 cm (1½ in) leaves. Evergreen. Small, greenish flowers. 3 triangular nuts in a single involucre. Fast growing. Upright, round-headed. An important timber tree.

N. moorei 154
Negrohead Beech, Australian Beech. E. Australia, warm temperate. To 50 m (150 ft). Pointed, oval leaves to 7.5 cm (3 in) long, with a bronze lustre when young. Evergreen. Small, greenish-white flowers. 3 triangular nuts in a single involucre. Fast growing. Tall, broad-headed, dense foliage. Not frost-hardy.

N. obliqua 154
Roblè Beech. Chile, temperate. To 50 m (150 ft). Alternate, 7.5 cm (3 in) leaves, deeply toothed. Deciduous. Small, greenish flowers. Several 3-sided nuts in a

single involucre. Fast growing. Wide-headed.

N. solandri
Black Beech. N.Z., temperate. To 25 m (80 ft). Tiny, oval leaves about 2 cm (¾ in) long. Evergreen. Greenish, solitary flowers. Fruit as in other species. Very fast growing. Slender, tall, round-headed. An important timber tree.

NUYTSIA 154
A single species of parasitic tree found in WA, and very difficult to raise elsewhere. Family Loranthaceae.

N. floribunda 154, **155**
Fire Tree, Golden Bough, WA Xmas Tree. WA, temperate. To 9 m (27 ft). Coarse, narrow, evergreen leaves to 7.5 cm (3 in). Small, orange-yellow flowers in crowded 15 cm (6 in) racemes. Small capsules. Slow growing. Round-headed, parasitic.

NYSSA 155
A very small genus of deciduous trees from N. America and S.E. Asia. Much planted in damp ground for their water-loving quality. Family Nyssaceae.

N. aquatica 155
Cotton Gum, Wild Olive, Large Tupelo. S. USA, temperate. To 35 m (100 ft). Ovate, 25 cm (10 in), deciduous leaves, some-times toothed. Minute greenish-white flowers in axillary clusters. Dark purple berries to 2.5 cm (1 in) long. Fast growing. Pyramidal. Scarlet in autumn. Swamp-loving. Flowers attractive to bees. Valuable timber tree.

N. sylvatica 155, **155**
Tupelo, Sourgum, Pepperidge, Blackgum. S.E. USA, temperate. To 35 m (100 ft). Elliptic to obovate leaves, to 12.5 cm (5 in) long. Minute flowers in greenish axillary clusters. Deep blue fruit, to 1 cm (½ in) diameter. In clusters. Medium fast growth. Pyramidal. Bright to deep red in autumn. Important timber tree. Prefers moist positions.

OLEA 156
An eastern hemisphere genus of about 20 species, grown as ornamentals, and for their oil-rich fruits.

O. africana 156, **156**
African Olive, Wild Olive. Africa, Asia Minor, China, temperate. To 8 m (25 ft). Evergreen leaves, 9 cm (3½ in), with goldish reverses. Very small white flowers in panicles. Like privet. Globose fruit, to 1 cm (⅜ in), black. Slow growing. Gnarled, picturesque, horizontal. Minor source of olive oil. Useful street tree.

O. europaea 156, **156**
Common Olive. Olive. Mediterranean, temperate. To 8 m (25 ft). Elliptic, lanceo-late leaves, to 6.5 cm (2½ in), with silvery reverse. Small white flowers in panicles. Fruit to 4 cm (1½ in) long, ovoid, black when ripe. Slow growing. Horizontal, picturesquely gnarled, often multiple-trunked. The olive of commerce. Wood used for ornamental carving and turning.

OREOCALLIS 156–7
A very small genus of 5 evergreen trees. Found variously in Australia, S. America and Malaysia. Family Proteaceae.

O. pinnata, see **O. wickhamii**
O. wickhamii 156–7, **157**
Tree Waratah, Red Silky Oak. Q, NSW, warm temperate. To 10 m (30 ft). Pinnate leaves, variably 22.5 cm to 45 cm (9 to 18 in) long, with from 7–9 leaflets. Evergreen. Flowers bisexual, red florets in a clustered flat-topped terminal raceme about 15 cm (6 in) diameter. A one-celled follicle containing winged seeds. Fast growing. Upright, sparse, round-headed.

OSTRYA 157
A small genus of Birch relatives from Europe and N. America. Deciduous and cultivated for the autumn colour of their foliage and for their decoratively droop-ing catkins. Family Betulaceae.

O. carpinifolia 157, **157**
Hop Hornbeam. S. Europe, Asia Minor, temperate. To 22 m (65 ft). Ovate to ellip-tical leaves to 10 cm (4 in) long, deeply toothed. Male flowers in slender droop-ing catkins, female in upright spathes. A series of nutlets, each enclosed in a sepa-rate green involucre, hanging in chains. Fast growing. Round-headed. Gold to red in autumn. Useful timber tree.

O. virginiana 157
Leverwood, American Hop Hornbeam. E. USA. Useful timber tree. Very similar to O. carpinifolia, but with dark, brownish bark and larger nutlets.

OXYDENDRUM 157–8
A genus of a single species from E. USA but popular throughout the world. Family Ericaceae.

O. arboreum 157–8, **158**
Sourwood, Sorrel Tree, Titi. E. USA, tem-perate to cold. To 27 m (80 ft). Oblong-lanceolate leaves to 20 cm (8 in), serrul-ate, deciduous. White flowers, like lily of the valley, in a drooping 25 cm (8 in) panicle. 5-valved capsules, greyish. Slow growing. Slender trunk, upright, often weeping branchlets. Red in autumn. Summer flowers very attractive to bees.

PANDANUS 158
A very large genus of tree-like plants from the Old World tropics, notable for their stiff aerial roots which prop up the tree to various degrees, and their spirally ar-ranged clusters of razor-sharp leaves. Family Pandanaceae.

P. odoratissimus 158, **158**
Screw Pine, Walking Palm, Pandanus, Bread Fruit. Sri Lanka to Philippines and naturalized through Polynesia, sub-tropi-cal. To 7 m (20 ft). 1.5 m (5 ft) acuminate-caudate leaves with sharp spines on margin. Pendant at ends. Male flowers in 10 cm (4 in) spadix enclosed by white bracts; female flowers whitish in a 5 cm (2 in) globose inflorescence, yellow bracted. A multiple fruit or syncarp of orange-red, smooth segments, to 25 cm (10 in) long. Fast growing. Many-branched, flat-headed. Useful tree in warm-climate, coastal gardens.

P. veitchii 158
Variegated Screw Pine, Veitch Screw Pine. Polynesia, tropical. To 5 m (15 ft). 1 m (3 ft) leaves, pale green, striped with small reddish spines on margins. Flowers and fruit unknown. Propagated vegetatively. Fast growing. Many-branched, flat-headed. Popular as an in-door plant in its juvenile form.

PARROTIA 158–9
A single species of deciduous tree widely cultivated for its show of autumn colour. Family Hamamelidaceae.

P. persica 158–9, **159**
Persian Witchhazel, Parrotia, Ironwood. Persia, Caucasus, temperate to cool. To 17 m (50 ft). Obovate, 12.5 cm (5 in) leaves, shiny, sometimes coarsely toothed. Deciduous. Clusters of crimson stamens, without petals, spring, on bare branches. A nut-like seed capsule. Fast growing. Shrubby, multiple-trunked. Vivid red in autumn.

PAULOWNIA 159
A stunning genus of Chinese trees, deciduous, and with a remarkable flower display in early spring. Family Big-noniaceae.

P. fortunei
Fortune's Paulownia. China, temperate. To 7 m (20 ft). Oblong-ovate leaves, 25 cm (10 in), densely woolly beneath. Deciduous. 10 cm (4 in) flowers resem-bling foxgloves, oyster-white marked with purple and yellow, in upright 37.5 cm (15 in) panicles. 8 cm (3¼ in) oblong capsules. Very fast growing. Pyramidal to spreading. Not frost-hardy.

P. imperialis, see **P. tomentosa**
P. tomentosa 159, **159**, **160**
Empress Tree, Royal Paulownia, Princess Tree, Kurri. China, temperate. To 13 m (40 ft). Leaves broadly ovate, 30 cm (12 in) or more, entire or 3-lobed. Flowers in a pyramidal 30 cm (12 in) panicle, pale violet, very fragrant. Ovoid 3 cm (1¼ in) capsules. Very fast grow-ing. Pyramidal. The timber is valued for cabinet work in Asian countries.

PERSEA 160
A genus of tropical evergreen trees from Asia and the Americas, planted largely for ornamental purposes. The one big excep-tion is the C. American Persea americana, the Avocado of commerce. Family Lauraceae.

P. americana 160, **160**
Avocado, Alligator Pear, Aguacate. C. America, sub-tropical to tropical. To 20 m (60 ft). Glossy elliptical, 20 cm (8 in) leaves, often deciduous in cooler cli-mates. Small greenish-yellow flowers in terminal panicles. Quite variable, accord-ing to named cultivar. May be globose or pear-shaped, coloured pale green to pur-ple or brown, and up to 17.5 cm (7 in) long. Fast growing. Upright, densely foliaged.

P. borbonica
Florida Mahogany, Red Bay. S.E. USA, sub-tropical. To 13 m (40 ft). Lanceolate leaves, 15 cm (6 in). Evergreen. Small, yellow-green flowers in scant terminal panicles. 1 cm (½ in) blue-black fruit on red stems. Round-headed.

PHOENIX 161
A genus of Palms from Africa and Asia, the Date Palm particularly bearing an im-portant food crop in hot climates. In cooler areas, they are planted as non-fruit-bearing ornamentals. Family Palmae.

P. canariensis 161, **161**
Canary I. Date Palm. Canary I., temperate. To 20 m (60 ft). Pinnate green fronds to 7 m (20 ft) long in a heavy rosette. Old fronds persistent on the trunk, leaving broad-oval scars when they fall. Infloresc-ence to 2 m (6 ft) long bearing male and female flowers to 1 cm (½ in) diameter. Ellipsoid, orange-red fruits to 2 cm (¾ in) long in heavy clusters. Slow growing. Trunk to 1 m (3 ft) diameter.

P. dactylifera 161, **161**
Date Palm, Date. Africa, W. Asia, hot, dry. To 30 m (100 ft). Pinnate, grey-green fronds to 7 m (20 ft) with many 45 cm (18 in) leaflets. Fronds leave upright-oval scars when they fall. White perfumed flowers in a 1.25 m (4 ft) stalk. Sexes on separate trees. Oblong ellipsoid, orange, 7.5 cm (3 in) fruit. Fast growing. Slender trunk, suckers if not controlled. Edible dates.

P. reclinata 161, **161**
Senegal Date Palm. Tropical Africa. To 7 m (20 ft). Gracefully arching, pinnate fronds to 3 m (9 ft), their stems heavily spined. Flowers in 1.7 m (5 ft) inflores-cences. Elliptical, 2 cm (¾ in) fruit, red, ripening black. Fast growing. Slender trunk. Clusters rapidly from suckers.

P. roebelinii 161
Pygmy Date Palm, Dwarf Date. Laos, temperate/tropical. To 4 m (12 ft). Pin-nate fronds to 1.25 m (4 ft), with about 100 25 cm (10 in) slender pinnae. Flowers in 45 cm (18 in) inflorescences. Pea-sized fruit, orange to black. Medium fast growth. Very slender trunk, 5–15 cm (2–6 in) diameter. Popular pot plant in juvenile form.

PHYLLANTHUS 162
A very large botanical genus, mostly tropical, and containing over 500 species. Two tree species are cultivated for their edible fruits. Family Euphorbiaceae.

P. acidus 162, **162**
Otaheite Gooseberry, Gooseberry Tree. S.E. Asia, tropical. To 10 m (30 ft). Ovate-lanceolate leaves, 7.5 cm (3 in), ranged on both sides of a twig, giving the appearance of pinnate form. Tiny, reddish flowers in a dense cyme. Yellowgreen, 2 cm (¾ in) fruits, usually under branchlets. Fast growing. Round-headed. Edible fruit.

P. emblica 162
Emblic, Myrobalan. Tropical Asia. To 17 m (50 ft). Small, 2 cm (¾ in) leaves arranged in two ranks on small twigs. Small yellow flowers clustered in leaf axils. Lobed yellow fruit to 2.5 cm (2 in) diameter. Fast growing. Round-headed to pyramidal. Edible fruits.

PHYLLOCLADYX, see SYZYGIUM

PICEA 162–4
A splendid genus of over 40 coniferous species, generally of a perfect conical habit. Larger species are raised commercially for paper pulp and plywood; many of the smaller species and cultivars for decorative garden use. Family Pinaceae.

P. abies 163, **162, 163**
Norway Spruce. N. Europe, cool temperate. To 70 m (200 ft). 4-angled needle-like leaves, to 2 cm (¾ in). Dark and shiny. Female flowers small, pinkish, on older trees only. Male flowers sparse. Downward-hanging cones, to 20 cm (8 in) long. Very fast growing. Tall conical to columnar on old trees. An important timber tree with many garden CVs varying in size, shape and colour of foliage.

P. breweriana 163
Brewer's Spruce, Weeping Spruce. W. USA, cool temperate. To 35 m (100 ft). Dark green, flattened leaves to 2.5 cm (1 in) long. White-banded above. On weeping branchlets. Flowers as in other species. Light brown 12.5 cm (5 in) cones, downward pointing. Slow growing. Conical, weeping branches, flattened foliage.

P. engelmanii
Engelmann Spruce. W. USA, temperate to cool. To 40 m (120 ft). Grey-green 4-angled needle leaves to 2.5 cm (1 in) long. Flowers as in other species. 7.5 cm (3 in) cones. Medium fast growth. Conical. Cultivated for tanbark and timber.

P. glauca 163, **163**
White Spruce, Cat Spruce. Canada, N.E. USA, cool temperate. To 25 m (75 ft). Blue-green 2 cm (¾ in) leaves on drooping branchlets. Flowers as in other species. Narrow, 5 cm (2 in), pendulous cones. Very fast growing. Conical. An important tree for timber and pulping. Many garden cultivars with variations in habit and foliage.

P. glauca 'Albertiana Conica' 163, **163**
Alberta Spruce. A dwarf form of P. glauca with fine, rich green foliage and dwarf cones. Perfectly conical and rarely above bush size. Prone to red spider damage.

P. jezoensis 164
Yeddo Spruce. Japan, temperate. To 50 m (150 ft). Flattened, 2 cm (¾ in) leaves, silver-white above, dark beneath. Flowers as in other species. Crimson cones to 7.5 cm (3 in) long, downward pointing. Fast growing. Elongated conical, tips of branches upward pointing. Important timber tree in Japan.

P. omorika 163
Serbian Spruce. Jugoslavia, temperate. To 33 m (100 ft). Flattened, 1 cm (½ in) leaves, white-banded above. Flowers as in other species. Ovoid cones to 6.5 cm (2½ in) long. Fast growing. Conical.

P. orientalis 164
Caucasian Spruce, Oriental Spruce. Caucasus, temperate to cool. To 40 m (120 ft). 4-angled, glossy, 1 cm (½ in) leaves, crowded on drooping, brown branchlets. Flowers as in other species. Purplish cones, 8 cm (3¼ in), freely borne. Very fast growing. Conical. Likes a sheltered position.

P. pungens 162, 164, **164**
Colorado Blue Spruce. S.W. USA, temperate to cool. To 35 m (100 ft). Stiff, spiny-pointed, 3 cm (2¼ in) leaves, bluish-green to silver. Flowers as in other species. 10 cm (4 in) cones. Medium fast growth. Perfectly conical. Horizontal branches. A popular garden tree in its many cultivars with eye-catching foliage. These include 'Argentea', 'Aurea', 'Caerulea', 'Kosteriana' and 'Moerheimii'. These are propagated by grafting.

P. rubens
Red Spruce, He Balsam. N.E. USA, cool temperate. To 30 m (90 ft). 4-angled, dark green, 1 cm (½ in) leaves on brown branchlets. Flowers as in other species. Red-brown, 5 cm (2 in) cones. Fast growing. Naturally conical. There is a popular CV P. r. 'Virgata', the Snake Spruce, which has naturally weeping branches, without branchlets.

P. sitchensis 163
Sitka Spruce. N.E. USA cool temperate. To 70 m (200 ft). 2.5 cm (1 in) leaves, silver-white above, green on reverse. Flowers as in other species. 10 cm (4 in) cones early in winter. Very, very fast growing. Tall, conical. An important timber tree.

P. spinulosa 163
Sikkim Spruce. Himalayas, temperate. To 70 m (200 ft). Sharply pointed, 3 cm (1¼ in) needles. Flowers as in other species. 17.5 cm (7 in) green cones. Very fast growing. Conical; pendulous branches.

P. X standishii 163, **162**
A hybrid blue-foliaged Spruce with long needles on weeping branchlets: parentage unknown.

PIMENTA 164
A small genus of tropical American trees cultivated for their aromatic oils. Family Myrtaceae.

P. acris 164
Wild Clove. Caribbean, tropical. To 10 m (30 ft). Green oblong, leathery leaves, 15 cm (6 in). Small white flowers in axillary cymes. Pea-sized berries. Medium fast growth. Round-headed. Berries ground for spice.

P. dioica 164, **164**
Allspice, Pimento. C. America, Caribbean, tropical. To 13 m (40 ft). Oblong-lanceolate leaves, 15 cm (6 in), prominently veined. 5 mm (¼ in) white flowers in axillary cymes. Dark brown, 5 mm (¼ in) drupes. Medium fast growth. Round-headed. The fruit, picked green and dried, are the Allspice of the spice trade.

P. racemosa 164
Bay Rum Tree. Caribbean, Venezuela, Guyana, tropical. To 13 m (40 ft). Obovate leaves, 15 cm (6 in), finely reversed. 5 mm (¼ in) white flowers in axillary cymes. Brown 5 mm (¼ in) drupes. Medium fast growth. Round-headed. Oil of Bay, distilled from leaves and twigs, is used to perfume Bay Rum hairdressing.

PINUS 164–5
The Pines seem endless in their variety, though in fact there are probably less than 90 species of them, all found in nature in the northern hemisphere. Unlike the Firs and Spruces, their young conical profile generally becomes flat-topped in age. The principal means of identification is in their needle-shaped leaves, which come in clusters of 2, 3 or 5 depending on the species. Family Pinaceae.

P. ayacahuite
Mexican White Pine. Mexico, Guatemala, temperate. To 35 m (100 ft). Needle leaves, 15 cm (6 in), in bundles of 5, bluish-green. Cylindrical cones to 37.5 cm (15 in) long. Medium fast growth. Spreading head.

P. canariensis
Canary I. Pine. Canary I., temperate. To 35 m (100 ft). 30 cm (12 in) long, glossy light green, on weeping branchlets. 20 cm (8 in) oblong cones. Fast growing. Tall, conical.

P. contorta
Beach Pine, Shore Pine. W. USA, temperate. To 25 m (75 ft). Stiff, twisted, 5 cm (2 in) needles in pairs. Conical, 5 cm (2 in) cones. Very fast growing. Shrubby, horizontal.

P. coulteri
Big-cone Pine. California, temperate. To 25 m (75 ft). 30 cm (12 in) blue-green needles in bundles of 3. Cylindrical, drooping cones to 35 cm (14 in) long. Very fast growing. Bushy.

P. densiflora 165
Japanese Red Pine. Japan, temperate. To 33 m (100 ft). Bright green, 12.5 cm (5 in) needles, in pairs. Ovoid to oblong 5 cm (2 in) cones. Pink or purplish. Fast growing. Irregularly shaped, often twisted, even horizontal. Several CVs are raised, including P.d. 'Umbraculifera', with multiple trunks and a flat top.

P. halepensis
Aleppo Pine, Jerusalem Pine. Mediterranean, temperate. To 17 m (50 ft). Soft green, 10 cm (4 in) needles, in twos or threes. Ovoid cones to 9 cm (3½ in) in groups of 3. Fast growing. Irregularly branched, informal shape. Source of Turpentine.

P. insularis
Benguet Pine. Philippines, Burma, S. China, tropical. To 35 m (100 ft). Bright green, flexible, 25 cm (10 in) needles. 10 cm (4 in) ovoid cones. Fast growing. Conical. Useful in tropical gardens.

P. laricio (a sub-species of P. nigra) 166
Corsican Pine. Corsica, Sardinia, temperate. To 35 m (100 ft). Flexible, blue-green needles to 17 cm (6½ in) long. Ovoid cones to 9 cm (3½ in) long. Fast growing. Tall, picturesque; elegantly patterned bark.

P. massoniana
Canton Pine. S. China, sub-tropical. To 25 m (80 ft). Thin, light green, 20 cm (8 in) needles, in pairs. Brown ovoid cones to 7.5 cm (3 in) long. Fast growing. Often picturesque and horizontal or flat-topped. Valuable timber tree in China.

P. montezumae
Montezuma Pine. Mexico, temperate. To 25 m (75 ft). Drooping bluish-green needles, to 30 cm (12 in), in bundles of 5. Cylindrical, 20 cm (8 in) cones. Fast growing. Rounded and spreading. Valuable timber tree.

P. nigra
Austrian Pine. Europe, Asia Minor, cool temperate. To 35 m (100 ft). 16.5 cm (6½ in) needles, dark green and stiff. Ovoid, golden, 9 cm (3½ in) cones. Fast growing. Conical, flat-topped in age. An important timber tree. Sub-species P.n. 'Maritima', the Italian Pine, is a source of pine nuts, or pignolia.

P. palustris 165, **166**
Largeleaf Pine, Long-leaf Pine, Georgia

Pine, Pitch Pine. S.E. USA, temperate. To 33 m (100 ft). Soft, drooping needles to 45 cm (18 in) long in bundles of 3. Cylindrical, dull brown cones to 25 cm (10 in) long. Fast growing. Broad, densely foliaged.

P. parviflora syn. **P. pentaphylla** 164–5
Japanese White Pine. Japan, temperate. To 15 m (45 ft). Blue-green needles to 4 cm (1½ in) in bundles of 5, tufted at ends of branches. Small oval cones. Slow growing. Flat-headed, spreading.

P. patula
Mexican Yellow Pine. Mexico, temperate. To 15 m (45 ft). Yellow-green, drooping, 30 cm (12 in) needles in threes. Ovoid, 11.5 cm (4½ in) cones, in whorls of 2–5. Very fast growing. Spreading, widely conical. Useful timber tree.

P. peuce 166
Macedonian Pine. Balkans, temperate. To 20 m (60 ft). 10 cm (4 in) blue-green needles. 15 cm (6 in) cones, in clusters. Fast growing. Conical to columnar in age. Good timber tree.

P. pinaster 164, **166**
Cluster Pine. Mediterranean, temperate. To 35 m (100 ft). Stiff, 25 cm (10 in) needles, in pairs. Ovoid, 25 cm (10 in) cones. Very fast growing. Columnar, but often twisted picturesquely in exposed positions.

P. ponderosa 165
Western Yellow Pine, Ponderosa Pine. W. USA, temperate to cool. To 70 m (200 ft). 27.5 cm (11 in) needles, very dark green, in bundles of 3. Oblong, 20 cm (8 in) cones. Very fast growing. Narrowly conical. Highly valued timber tree.

P. radiata 164, **165**
Monterey Pine, Radiata Pine. California, temperate. To 25 m (75 ft). 15 cm (6 in) needles, bright green, in threes. Ovoid, 17.5 cm (7 in) cones, amber coloured. Extremely fast growing. Widely spreading and flat-topped. The most vigorous of Pines, widely grown for timber.

P. roxburghii
Chir Pine, Emodi. Himalayas, temperate. To 50 m (150 ft). 30 cm (12 in) light green needles in threes. 17.5 cm (7 in) cones with reflexed scales. Fast growing. Flat-topped. Bark patterned tan and grey.

P. thunbergii syn. **P. thunbergiana** 166
Japanese Black Pine. Japan, temperate. To 40 m (120 ft). Dark green, pointed, 11.5 cm (4½ in) needles in pairs. Ovoid, 6.5 cm (2½ in) cones. Medium fast growth. Irregularly crowned, often growing in a naturally picturesque shape with branches weeping almost to ground. The inspiration of Japanese Bonsai design.

PISONIA 167
A small genus from sub-tropical areas grown principally for their splendid foliage. Sometimes used as indoor plants. Family Nyctaginaceae.

P. alba 167, **167**
Lettuce Tree. Malaysia, Philippines, tropical, to 5 m (15 ft). Deciduous, 20 cm (8 in) leaves, cordate, broadly pointed, pubescent, a brilliant yellow. Fast growing. Densely shrubby when young, sparsely branched in age. Leaves edible.

P. grandis 167
Puka, Puatea. Polynesia, sub-tropical. To 5 m (15 ft). Large green leaves. Slow growing. Spreading, shrubby. Foliage edible, the soft timber has many uses.

P. umbellifera
Para Para, Bird Catcher Tree. Mauritius, Australia, N.Z., sub-tropical. To 7 m (20 ft). Oblong, 37.5 cm (15 in), glossy leaves, often variegated white. 5 mm (¼ in) flowers in small panicles, pink or yellow. Sticky, 3.5 cm (1½ in) achenes.

Slow growing. Dense foliage, shrubby. Sticky fruit, once used to catch birds.

PISTACIA 167
A small genus of very variable trees spread right across the northern hemisphere from C. America through the Mediterranean basin to Asia. Family Anacardiaceae.

P. chinensis 167, **167**
Chinese Pistachio. China to Philippines, temperate. To 25 m (75 ft). Compound, pinnate leaves with 10 or more 6.5 cm (2½ in) leaflets. Deciduous. Minute red axillary flowers, male in racemes, female in panicles. Round drupes to 3.5 cm (1½ in) diameter. Fast growing. Shrubby to round-headed. Red, yellow and purple in autumn.

P. vera 167
Pistachio, Green Almond, Pistachia Nut. Asia, temperate. To 10 m (30 ft). Compound, pinnate leaves with 2–10 rounded, downy leaflets. Deciduous. Minute, reddish, unisexual flowers. Small reddish fruit containing a yellow-green, edible nut. Slow growing. Sparsely branched, spreading. Likes a dry climate.

PITHECELLOBIUM 168
A large genus of shrubs and trees grown principally for ornamental purposes. Family Leguminosae.

P. dulce 168, **168**
Opiuma, Manila Tamarind, Huamuchil. C. America, naturalized Philippines, tropical. To 20 m (60 ft). Compound leaves with two pairs of elliptical 5 cm (2 in) leaflets. Small white puffball flowers in dense, stalkless heads. 12.5 cm (5 in) leguminous pods, scarlet, twisted. Fast growing. Shrubby to gnarled, flat-headed. A very spiny tree, often planted as hedges. Often seen with white-variegated leaves.

P. pruinosum
Snow Wood. NSW, Q, warm temperate. To 7 m (20 ft). Compound pinnate leaves with 6–8 7.5 cm (3 in) leaflets. White axillary puffball flowers in threes. Twisted orange-red leguminous pods. Fast growing. Shrubby, to sparse and slim.

PITTOSPORUM 168–9
A medium-sized genus of handsome evergreen trees from temperate and sub-tropical areas, particularly Australia, N.Z., Hawaii and S.E. Asia. Generally with extremely fragrant blossom and showy fruit. Family Pittosporaceae.

P. crassifolium
Karo. N.Z., temperate. To 12 m (35 ft). Oblanceolate, 7.5 cm (3 in), leathery leaves, whitish beneath. Small, 1 cm (½ in) reddish-purple flowers in terminal clusters. Elliptic, woolly-grey seed capsules to 4 cm (1½ in) long. Fast growing. Round-headed.

P. eugenioides 169
Tarata. N.Z., temperate. To 13 m (40 ft). 10 cm (4 in) elliptical leaves with undulate margins. Pale yellow, fragrant, 5 mm (¼ in) flowers in terminal panicles. 5 mm (¼ in) glabrous seed capsules. Fast growing. Pyramidal. Most commonly seen is its CV *P.e.Variegatum*, with cream and grey-green variegated leaves.

P. hosmeri 169
Ho'awa. Hawaii, tropical. To 10 m (30 ft). Leathery, oblong, 60 cm (24 in) leaves with brown hairy reverses. White, 1 cm (½ in) flowers in axillary racemes. Orange 5 cm (2 in) capsules. Fast growing. Sparsely branched, upright.

P. phyllyraeoides
Willow Pittosporum. Australia, temperate. To 10 m (30 ft). Linear-lanceolate 10 cm (4 in) leaves on pendulous branches. Yellow 5 mm (¼ in) flowers in sparse axillary clusters. Deep yellow

2 cm (¾ in) globose capsules. Fast growing. Upright, weeping branches.

P. rhombifolium 169, **169**
Queensland Pittosporum, Brisbane Laurel. E. Australia, temperate. To 25 m (75 ft). Rhombic-ovate leaves to 10 cm (4 in) long, coarsely toothed. White 5 mm (¼ in) flowers in dense corymbs. Elliptical, orange, 1 cm (½ in) capsules. Medium fast growth. Upright. Fine street tree.

P. tobira 169, **168**
Japanese Laurel, Mockorange. Japan, China, temperate. To 7 m (20 ft). Leathery, obovate leaves, 10 cm (4 in). 1 cm (½ in) white or lemon-yellow flowers in dense, umbellate clusters. Yellow, globose, 1 cm (½ in) capsules. Medium fast growth. Shrubby to round-headed. CV *Variegata* with yellow or white variegated leaves is popular.

P. undulatum 169, **169**
Vic Box, Native Daphne, Mock Orange. Australia, temperate. To 15 m (45 ft). Pale green, lanceolate, 10 cm (6 in) leaves with undulate margins. Cream, fragrant, 1 cm (½ in) flowers in terminal clusters. 1 cm (½ in) oval capsules, yellow to orange-brown. Fast growing. Round-headed, densely foliaged.

PLATANUS 170–1
A very small genus of broad-leafed deciduous trees, most commonly represented by the London Plane Tree, a hybrid which has become probably the most popular street tree in the world. Family Platanaceae.

P. X acerifolia 170, **170, 171**
London Plane. Hybrid. Temperate climate. To 45 m (135 ft). 3–5 lobed leaves, roughly toothed and up to 22.5 cm (9 in) diameter. Deciduous. Minute red flowers in globular, hanging clusters. Fruit in globular long-stemmed heads, usually in pairs. Very fast growing. Tall, round-headed, often with drooping lower branches. A natural hybrid between *P. occidentalis* and *P. orientalis*. A CV 'Pyramidalis' has an upright Poplar-like habit, with leaves mostly 3–lobed.

P. X hispanica, see **P. X acerifolia**
P. insularis, see **P. orientalis Insularis**
P. occidentalis 170
American Plane, Button Wood, E. Sycamore. C. USA, cool temperate. To 50 m (150 ft). 25 cm (10 in) shallowly 3–5 lobed leaves, glabrous. Deciduous. Greenish flowers in lacy clusters. A long-stemmed hanging seed cluster, usually solitary. Very fast growing. Open, broad-headed.

P. orientalis 170
Chinar, Oriental Plane. S.E. Europe to India, temperate. To 35 m (100 ft). Glabrous, 20 cm (8 in) leaves, 5–7 lobed. Greenish flowers in hanging clusters. Hanging, globular seed clusters, 2–6 on one peduncle. Fast growing. Spreading, broad-headed.

P. orientalis Insularis 170, **170**
Cyprus Plane. A local sub-species of *P. orientalis* with slighter habit and very deeply lobed leaves. Found naturally on Crete and Cyprus.

P. racemosa 170, **171**
Sycamore, California Plane. California, Mexico, temperate. To 40 m (120 ft). 3–5 lobed leaves, brownish-downy beneath. Greenish flowers in globose hanging clusters. Bristly, globose seed heads, 2–7 on each peduncle. Fast growing. Spreading, irregularly shaped.

PLUMERIA 172
A small genus of tropical trees from Mexico and the Caribbean area, grown widely in warm climates for the beauty of their perfumed flowers. Family Apocynaceae.

PLUMERIA

P. acuminata 172, **172**
Frangipani, Nosegay Tree, Graveyard Tree, Temple Flower, Pagoda Tree, Tree of Life. Mexico, tropical. To 15 m (45 ft). Variable, 50 cm (20 in) leaves, most commonly elliptical, acuminate. Deciduous. Yellow-centred cream flowers to 11.5 cm (4½ in) diameter. Two pointed pods, hanging samara-like on a single stem. Slow growing. Round-headed, ultimately very thick-trunked and untidy. There are many recognized colour varieties of this wonderful tree, with flowers varying through pink and yellow.

P. alba 172
White Plumeria. Puerto Rico, tropical. To 15 m (45 ft). 30 cm (12 in) leaves, lanceolate, long-acuminate. White, yellow-centred flowers to 7.5 cm (3 in). Double pods on hanging stem. Slow growing. Rounded head.

P. obtusa 172, **172**
Singapore Plumeria, White Frangipani. Bahamas, tropical. To 8 m (24 ft). Dark, obovate, 17.5 cm (7 in) leaves, evergreen in tropical climates. Pure white flowers, orange-yellow centre, overlapped petals, to 7.5 cm (3 in) diameter. Double pod. Slow growing. Round-headed.

P. rubra 172
Red Frangipani. This name is commonly used for varieties with deep pink to blood-red flowers, but is probably the correct specific name, including most of the paler varieties; even *P. acuminata* (which see).

PODOCARPUS 173
A genus of decorative coniferous trees, native largely to the temperate southern hemisphere, but with outlying species found at higher altitudes above the equator. The distinctive globular seed capsules are often highly coloured, and borne singly on a short stalk or foot. Family Podocarpaceae.

P. dacrydioides
Kahikatea, White Pine. N.Z., temperate. To 50 m (150 ft). Scale-like, overlapping leaves, often with a reddish tinge. Small red fruits. Fast growing. Upright with drooping branches.

P. elatus
Brown Pine, She Pine. NSW, Q, temperate. To 30 m (90 ft). Flat linear-lanceolate leaves to 11 cm (4½ in) long, but only 5 mm (¼ in) wide. A 2 cm (¾ in) blue-black fruit. Medium fast growth. Upright. A useful timber tree.

P. elongatus 173
African Yellowwood. Tropical Africa, warm temperate. To 23 m (70 ft). Linear-lanceolate leaves to 5 cm (2 in) long. 1 cm (⅜ in) fruits, blue-green on red stalks. Fast growing. Upright, round-headed. Useful timber tree.

P. falcatus 173, **173**
Oteniqua Yellowwood. S. Africa, temperate. To 50 m (150 ft). Spirally arranged needle leaves to 5 cm (2 in) long and very narrow. Globose, 1 cm (½ in) fruits, glaucous green to yellow. Fast growing. Round-headed, densely foliaged. Valuable timber tree.

P. gracilior
Fern Pine. E. Africa, warm temperate. To 20 m (60 ft). Grey-green, linear-lanceolate leaves to 10 cm (4 in) long. Oval, 1 cm (⅜ in) fruit, glaucous blue. Fast growing. Round-headed, often weeping branchlets. Useful timber tree.

P. latifolius 173
Real Yellowwood. S. Africa, temperate. To 30 m (100 ft). Rigid, lanceolate leaves to 5 cm (2 in) long. Globose, 1 cm (⅜ in) fruits: green, glaucous. Fast growing. Round-headed; upward pointing branches.

P. macrophyllus, 173, **173**
Buddhist Pine, Southern Yew. Japan, temperate. To 25 m (75 ft). Dark linear-lanceolate leaves to 11.5 cm (4½ in) long. Bluish 1 cm (⅜ in) fruits on longer stalks. Fast growing. Pyramidal habit. Var. *Angustifolius* has yellow-green leaves, is a popular street tree. Var. *Maki* has upright branches and a shorter, darker, obtuse-tipped leaf.

P. nagi 173
Broadleaf Podocarp. Japan, temperate. To 30 m (60 ft). Elliptical, 7.5 cm (3 in) leaves, to 2.5 cm (1 in) wide. Ellipsoid green fruit to 1 cm (⅜ in) wide. Medium fast growth. Pyramidal.

P. neriifolius
Blackleaf Podocarp. China to New Guinea, tropical. To 23 m (70 ft). 15 cm (6 in) leathery, lanceolate, dark leaves. Ellipsoid, 1 cm (⅜ in) green fruits. Fast growing. Upright, densely foliaged.

P. totara 173
Totara, Mahogany Pine. N.Z., temperate. To 30 m (100 ft). Linear, 2.5 cm (1 in), dark leaves. Red, 1 cm (⅜ in) fruits. Fast growing. Upright, round-headed. Valuable timber tree.

POPULUS 174–5
A genus of fast-growing, water-loving, soft-wooded deciduous trees, native to all parts of the northern hemisphere. Family Salicaceae.

P. alba 174
White Poplar, Abele, Silver-leaf Poplar. C. Europe to Siberia, temperate. To 25 m (75 ft). 12.5 cm (5 in) ovate leaves, palmately 3–5 lobed. Silvery white and tomentose beneath. Deciduous. Yellowish catkins, the sexes on separate trees. Capsules containing hairy seeds. Very, very fast growing. Spreading habit. Yellow in autumn. Likes alkaline soil. Suckers badly.

P. X canadensis 175
Carolina Poplar, Canada Poplar, Golden Poplar. Hybrid. Temperate climate. To 30 m (90 ft). 10 cm (4 in) triangular-ovate leaves. Catkins. Capsules containing hairy seeds. Very, very fast growing. Upright. Yellow in autumn.

P. deltoides 175
Cottonwood, Necklace Poplar. E. N. America, temperate. To 30 m (90 ft). 17.5 cm (7 in) heart-shaped leaves, pale reverses. Catkins, densely flowered. 20 cm (8 in) long, red and yellow. Capsules. Very, very fast growth. Tall, wide-spreading. Useful timber tree.

P. fremontii
Fremont Cottonwood. California, temperate. To 35 m (100 ft). Triangular 7.5 cm (3 in) leaves. Yellow catkins. Capsules. Fast growing. Round-headed. Yellow in autumn.

P. nigra
Black Poplar. Europe, W. Asia, temperate. To 45 m (130 ft). Diamond-shaped to oval leaves, 10 cm (4 in) long. Red catkins. Capsules. Very, very fast growth. Upright, broadly pyramidal. Yellow in autumn.

P. nigra Italica 174, **174**
Lombardy Poplar. Italy. To 30 m (90 ft). Yellow in autumn. Flowers, fruit and foliage as *P. nigra* but with columnar habit.

P. simonii
Simon Poplar. N. China, temperate. To 13 m (40 ft). Rhombic-ovate, 10 cm (4 in) leaves, whitish beneath. Green catkins. Capsules. Very, very fast growth. Upright, slender-branched. Yellow in autumn. CV *Fastigiata* has similar habit to *P. nigra Italica* but does not sucker.

P. tremula
Aspen. Europe, Asia, N. Africa, temperate.

To 35 m (100 ft). Orbicular, 7.5 cm (3 in) toothed leaves on long flattened petioles. Yellowish catkins. Capsules. Very, very fast growth. Upright, narrow, with open crown. Yellow in autumn. Loves water — suckers badly.

P. tremuloides
Quaking Aspen, Quiverleaf. W. N. America, temperate. To 33 m (100 ft). Orbicular, 7.5 cm (3 in) finely toothed leaves on flattened stalks. Short yellowish catkins. Capsules. Very fast growing. Wide spreading. Yellow in autumn.

P. trichocarpa 174
Black Cottonwood, Western Balsam Poplar. W. N. America, temperate. To 70 m (200 ft). Broadly ovate leaves, to 25 cm (10 in) long, whitish beneath, slender tipped. Strongly balsam scented. Greenish catkins. Capsules. Very, very fast growth. Pyramidal. Yellow in autumn.

P. serotina Aurea, see *P. canadensis*

POSOQUERIA 175
A small genus of tropical trees with extremely elongated flowers. Related to the Gardenia. Family Rubiaceae.

P. latifolia 175, **175**
Needle-Flower Tree. S. and C. America, tropical. To 7 m (20 ft). Elliptical, 20 cm (8 in) glossy leaves. Small white flowers with an elongated, 15 cm (6 in), tube. Globose yellow berries to 5 cm (2 in) diameter. Edible. Medium fast growth. Shrubby to slender upright.

PRUNUS 176–7
A very large genus of mostly deciduous trees and shrubs, almost all from the northern hemisphere. Grown largely for their decorative, fragrant blossom, and in many cases for the fruits, which include the Almond, Apricot, Cherry, Nectarine, Peach and Plum. Family Rosaceae.

P. americana 176
American Red Plum, Wild Plum, Goose Plum. E. N. America, temperate. To 8 m (25 ft). Lanceolate-ovate leaves to 11 cm (4½ in) long, acuminate and sharply serrated, on thorny branchlets. Deciduous. Single, 2.5 cm (1 in) flowers. Yellow or red fruits to 2 cm (¾ in) diameter. Medium fast growth. Shrubby, open habit. Shaggy bark. Many named CVs of fruit varieties.

P. amygdalus, see *P. dulcis*

P. armeniaca 176, **178**
Apricot. C. Asia, China, temperate. To 12 m (35 ft). Roundish, pointed leaves to 7.5 cm (3 in). Lightly serrated. Deciduous. Pinkish-white, 2.5 cm (1 in) flowers. Before leaves. Fleshy drupes to 7.5 cm (3 in) diameter, ovoid, pale orange flushed red. Slow growing. Spreading, open habit. The Apricot of commerce. Many named CVs.

P. avium 176
Gean, Mazzard, Bird Cherry. Europe, Asia, temperate. To 23 m (70 ft). Obovate-elliptic serrated leaves to 15 cm (6 in) long. Cup-shaped, clustered white flowers to 2.5 cm (1 in) diameter. Globose, dark red fruit to 2.5 cm (1 in) diameter on long stems. Very fast growing. Pyramidal. Red-brown, peeling bark.

P. campanulata 176–7, **177**
Taiwan Cherry, Formosa Cherry, Bell-flowered Cherry. Taiwan, cool temperate. To 8 m (25 ft). Ovate, pointed, sharply serrated leaves to 8.5 cm (3½ in) long. Campanulate, deep rose-red flowers to 2 cm (¾ in) diameter, in clusters. Very early. Ovoid, red, 1 cm (½ in) drupes. Fast growth. Upright, bushy.

P. cerasifera 176
Cherry Plum, Myrobalan. W. Asia, temperate. To 8 m (25 ft). Oval, pale green leaves to 7.5 cm (3 in) long, lightly toothed. Solitary white blossoms to

2.5 cm (1 in) diameter. 2.5 cm (1 in) yellowish globose fruit, red flushed. Fast growing. Upright, wide, slender, thorny branches, round-headed in age. Variety 'Pissardii', the Pissard Plum, has young foliage ruby-red, fading to purple, and sparsely produced purple fruits.

P. cerasus 176, **177**
Sour Cherry. W. Asia. To 12 m (35 ft). Doubly serrated, ovate 7.5 cm (3 in) leaves. Deciduous. Clustered, white to pink flowers, 2.5 cm (1 in) diameter. Bright red, 2 cm (¾ in) fruit on long stems. Sour. Fast growing. Spreading. Variety *P. c. Austera* is the Morello Cherry.

P. domestica 176, **177**
Plum, European Plum. Europe, N. America, temperate. To 10 m (30 ft). Ovate, 10 cm (4 in) serrated leaves. Whitish, 2.5 cm (1 in) flowers in sparse clusters. Drupes, to 7.5 cm (3 in), variously coloured. Fast growing. Upright, open-headed.

P. dulcis 176
Almond. W. Asia, temperate. To 10 m (30 ft). Lanceolate, 12.5 cm (5 in) leaves, serrulate. White or pink flowers, to 4 cm (1½ in) long. Fruit on oblong, flattened drupe to 6 cm (2½ in) long, inedible, but containing the edible seed, or almond. Fast growing. Broad-crowned. There are ornamental CVs with double blossom in many colours, commonly known as flowering Peaches.

P. hortulana 176
Goose Plum, Hortulan. C. USA, temperate. To 10 m (30 ft). 10 cm (4 in) lanceolate, long pointed leaves. 1 cm (½ in) white flowers. 2.5 cm (1 in) drupes, red and yellow. Fast growing. Upright, round-headed. Many named CVs of fruit varieties are grown.

P. ilicifolia 177
Holly-leaf Cherry, Evergreen Cherry, Islay. California, temperate. To 8 m (25 ft). Coarsely toothed 5 cm (2 in) evergreen leaves. Sparse 5 mm (¼ in) flowers in racemes. Red, ellipsoid drupes to 1 cm (½ in) long. Fast growing. Round-headed, densely foliaged.

P. institia 176
Damson, Bullace. Europe, N. Africa, temperate. To 7 m (20 ft). Hairy, elliptic 7.5 cm (3 in) leaves, coarsely serrated. White, single, 2.5 cm (1 in) flowers. Ovoid, blue-black fruit, to 4 cm (1½ in) long. Medium fast growth. Spreading, round-headed. *Prunus institia* var. *Italica* is the green-fruited Greengage or Reine Claude. *Prunus institia* var. *Syriaca* is the yellow-fruited Mirabelle.

P. laurocerasus 177, **178**
Cherry Laurel, Versailles Laurel. Europe, Asia Minor, temperate. To 13 m (40 ft). Dark, evergreen lance-shaped leathery leaves to 17.5 cm (7 in) long. Many 5 mm (¼ in) cream flowers in spikes or ascending racemes. Purple-black, ovoid, 1 cm (½ in) fruits. Fast growing. Densely foliaged, wide spreading. There are many named CVs with different leaf shapes and growth habits, some quite low and shrubby.

P. lusitanica 177
Portugal Laurel. Spain to Canary I., temperate. To 20 m (60 ft). Oblong, shiny, evergreen, finely toothed leaves on red stems. Tiny cup-shaped white flowers in slender 25 cm (10 in) racemes. Oval, purple fruits to 1 cm (½ in) long. Fast growing. Shrubby, densely foliaged.

P. maackii 178
Manchurian Cherry. E. Asia, temperate. To 17 m (50 ft). Elliptic-ovate leaves, to 7.5 cm (3 in) long, sharply serrated. White, 5 mm (¼ in) flowers on racemes. Black, ovoid, currant-sized fruits. Fast

growing. Wide spreading with shiny, orange-brown bark.

P. mahaleb 176
St Lucie Cherry, Perfumed Cherry. Europe, W. Asia, temperate. To 10 m (30 ft). Round, ovate leaves to 7 cm (2½ in) long, toothed. 1 cm (½ in) white flowers in clusters of 4–10. Very fragrant. Ovoid fruits to 5 mm (¼ in), almost black. On long stems. Fast growing. Spreading shape, slender green branches.

P. persica 177, **178**
Peach. China, temperate. To 8 m (25 ft). Pale, lanceolate, 15 cm (6 in) leaves, lightly serrated and pointed. Deciduous. Pink and red flowers, 4 cm (1½ in) across. Globose, pale green fruit, to 7.5 cm (3 in), flushed red when ripe. Medium fast growth. Spreading. The Peach of commerce. *Prunus persica* var. *Nucipersica* is the Nectarine. Many named CVs both in flower and fruit variety.

P. salicina 176
Japanese Plum. China, temperate. To 8 m (25 ft). Shining, oblong-ovate, pointed leaves to 10 cm (4 in) long. White, 2 cm (¾ in) flowers in threes, on slender pedicels. Yellow or light red pointed fruits. Fast growing. Spreading.

P. serrulata 176, **177**, **178**
Japanese Flowering Cherry. E. Asia, temperate. To 20 m (60 ft). Pale green, narrow ovate, toothed leaves to 12.5 cm (5 in) long. The species flowers are white, 4 cm (1½ in) diameter, not fragrant. Black, pea-sized fruit. Fast growing. Spreading. Literally dozens of named CVs are grown. These are often smaller trees, with flowers in every shade and combination of white, pink, red and green. Some are double, some single, some on long pendant stems.

P. subhirtella 178
Rosebud Cherry, Higan Cherry. Japan, temperate. To 8 m (25 ft). Lanceolate, doubly serrated leaves to 7.5 cm (3 in) long. Small pale pink flowers with notched petals. Borne very freely. Currant-sized black fruit. Fast growing. Densely branched. *P. s.* var. *Autumnalis* begins to flower in autumn and continues through to spring. *P. s.* var. *Pendula* has heavily weeping branches, sometimes double flowering.

PSEUDOBOMBAX, see **BOMBAX ellipticum**
PSIDIUM 179
A popular genus of evergreen trees from the American tropics, including the Guavas of commerce. Family Myrtaceae.

P. cattleianum syn. **P. littorale** var. **Longipes** 179, **179**
Purple Guava, Strawberry Guava, Cherry Guava. Brazil, temperate to tropical. To 10 m (30 ft). Elliptic, leathery, shiny leaves to 7.5 cm (3 in) long. White, solitary flowers to 2.5 cm (1 in) diameter. Globose, purple-red fruits to 4 cm (1½ in) diameter. Fast growing. Slender, dense-foliaged tree.

P. guajava 179, **179**
Pineapple Guava, Apple Guava, Common Guava. Tropical America. To 10 m (30 ft). 15 cm (6 in) ovate leaves, prominently veined and pubescent beneath. Small white flowers, solitary or grouped in a slender peduncle. Pear-shaped fruit, to 10 cm (4 in) long, yellow with pink flesh. Fast growing. Spreading, round-headed.

P. littorale var. **Longipes,** see **P. cattleianum**
PTEROCARPUS 180
A large tropical genus of perhaps 100 tree species, including some of the world's finest timber trees. Family Leguminosae.

P. indicus 180, **180**
Burmese Rosewood, Narra, Padauk. India to Philippines, tropical. To 27 m (80 ft). Compound, odd-pinnate leaves with many ovate leaflets. 1 cm (½ in) yellow flowers in woolly brown calyces, borne in abundant panicles. An orbicular, indehiscent legume, 5 cm (2 in) diameter. Fast growing. Spreading, round-headed. The magnificent rosewood of Chinese furniture, red with almost black stripes.

PTEROCARYA 180–1
A small genus of deciduous Asian trees, related to the Walnuts. Family Juglandaceae.

P. fraxinifolia 181, **180**
Caucasian Wingnut. Caucasus, Persia, temperate. To 35 m (100 ft). Compound, pinnate leaves with 11–20 oblong lanceolate leaflets, each to 12.5 cm (5 in) long. Deciduous. Male and female flowers in drooping catkins, yellow-green. Winged nutlets, in a 45 cm (18 in) chain. Fast growing. Broadly spreading.

PTEROSPERMUM 181
A small genus of trees from tropical Asia. Family Byttneriaceae.

P. acerifolium 181, **181**
Bayur Tree. India to Java, tropical. To 33 m (100 ft). Ovate to orbicular leaves, 35 cm (17 in) diameter, palmately lobed. Long cream flowers in rusty, tomentose sepals, to 15 cm (6 in) long. 15 cm (6 in) capsules containing winged seeds. Fast growing. Tall, broad-headed. Valuable timber tree.

PYRUS 181–2
A small genus of important fruiting trees in the Rose family (Rosaceae), all from the northern hemisphere.

P. communis 182, **182**
Common Pear. Europe, W. Asia, temperate. To 20 m (60 ft). Leathery, oblong-ovate leaves, to 6 cm (2½ in) long, sharp pointed. Deciduous. White to pink flowers, 2.5 cm (1 in) diameter. Variable fruit, mostly pear-shaped, to about 7.5 cm (3 in) long. Fast growing. Pyramidal. Wood used for turning domestic articles. Many named CVs with fruit in various colours, brown, green and yellow, sometimes globose.

P. pashia 182, **181**, **182**
Indian Pear. N. India, temperate. To 12 m (35 ft). Ovate, 10 cm (4 in) leaves, long, finely toothed. Dense clusters of white, 2 cm (¾ in) flowers, pink in bud. Globose fruit, speckled brown, to 4 cm (1½ in) diameter. Fast growing. Pyramidal.

P. salicifolia 181–2
Willow-leaf Pear, Weeping Silver Pear. S.E. Europe to Caucasus, temperate. To 10 m (30 ft). Willowy, silver, tomentose leaves. White, 2 cm (¾ in) flowers in tight, flat heads. Pear-shaped yellowish fruits to 2.5 cm (1 in) long. Fast growing. Pyramidal.

QUERCUS 183–4
A very large tree genus, the Oaks, with both evergreen and deciduous species found all over the northern hemisphere and occasionally in the high-altitude tropics. Very variable, their only common feature being the acorn. Family Fagaceae.

Q. acutissima 184
Bristle-tipped Oak, Sawtooth Oak. Japan, China, temperate. To 17 m (50 ft). Oblong, shiny leaves to 17.5 cm (7 in) with bristle-tipped teeth. Deciduous. Profuse yellow catkins. Long-stemmed acorn almost hidden in the cup. Medium fast growth. Spreading, broad-headed.

Q. agrifolia 185
Coast Live Oak, California Live Oak. Mexico, California, temperate. To 35 m (100 ft). Evergreen elliptic leaves, 7.5 cm (3 in) rather pubescent, spiny edges, pale

beneath. Flowers in short clusters. A stalkless cone-shaped acorn, less than one-third covered by the cup. Medium fast growth. Wide spreading, smooth dark bark.

Q. borealis syn. **Q. rubra 183, 184**
Red Oak. E. USA, cool temperate. To 27 m (80 ft). Oblong, 22.5 cm (9 in) leaves, deeply lobed with 7−11 lobes. Catkins. 3 cm (1¼ in) acorns, one-third enclosed by cup. Fast growing. Round-topped, broad. Scarlet and orange in autumn; brilliant.

Q. cerris
Turkey Oak. S. Europe, Asia Minor, temperate. To 35 m (110 ft). Oblong, 12.5 cm (5 in) leaves with 6−16 toothed lobes, greyish beneath. Deciduous. Catkins. 3 cm (1¼ in) acorns in fuzzy cup enclosing half nut. Generally in pairs or fours. Very fast growing. Pyramidal to spreading.

Q. chrysolepis
Canyon Oak, Maul Oak, California Live Oak, Golden Cup Oak. W. USA, temperate. To 30 m (90 ft). Elliptic, spiny toothed leaves to 10 cm (4 in) long. Deciduous. Short catkins. 2.5 cm (1 in) acorns, less than a quarter enclosed by a downy cup. Slow growing. Broadly spreading with squat trunk.

Q. dentata 185
Daimyo Oak. Japan, China, Korea, temperate. To 25 m (75 ft). Ovate, 30 cm (12 in) leaves with 8−18 rounded lobes. Deciduous. Catkins. Small acorns only half enclosed by cup. Medium fast growth. Round-headed. CV *Aurea* has golden foliage.

Q. engelmannii
Engelmann Oak. California, temperate. To 20 m (60 ft). Oblong, 5 cm (2 in) evergreen leaves, pale beneath. Small catkins. Small acorns half enclosed by cup. Slow growing. Wide spreading, often picturesque shape.

Q. ilex 185
Holm Oak, Holly Oak. Mediterranean, temperate. To 20 m (60 ft). Dark, ovate/lanceolate, 7.5 cm (3 in) evergreen leaves, yellowish tomentose beneath. Small whitish catkins. 2 cm (¾ in) acorns half enclosed by cup. Generally in threes. Slow growing. Rounded head, upright or spreading.

Q. lobata
California White Oak. California, temperate. To 33 m (100 ft). 7.5 cm (3 in) obovate leaves with an odd number of obtuse lobes. Greyish beneath. Deciduous. Small catkins. Small acorns, quarter enclosed by cup. Slow growing. Spreading.

Q. michauxii 184
Basket Oak, Water Chestnut, Swamp Chestnut. S. USA, temperate. To 35 m (100 ft). Coarsely toothed obovate leaves. Catkins. 4 cm (1½ in) stalked acorns. Fast growing. Round-headed, a compact shape. Prefers a wet position.

Q. myrsinaefolia 185
E. Asia. To 20 m (60 ft). Lanceolate, acuminate, lightly toothed, 12.5 cm (5 in) leaves. Evergreen. Small catkins. Very small acorns half enclosed by cup. Fast growing. Compact, rounded head.

Q. nigra syn. **Q. aquatica**
Water Oak, Possum Oak. S. USA, temperate. To 27 m (80 ft). Obovate, 7.5 cm (3 in) leaves, bluish-green, 3−lobed at apex. Deciduous or evergreen. Catkins. Acorns, 1 cm (½ in) across, a quarter enclosed by cup. Fast growing. Pyramidal.

Q. palustris 183, 184
Pin Oak, Spanish Oak. N.E. USA, cool temperate. To 40 m (120 ft). 12.5 cm (5 in) elliptical leaves with an odd number of toothed lobes. Deciduous. Catkins. Slender, small acorns, barely resting in shallow cup. Fast growing. Pyramidal. Brilliant red autumn colour, but dead leaves persist on tree until spring. Important timber tree.

Q. petraea
Durmast Oak. Europe, W. Asia. To 35 m (100 ft). An important timber tree. Very similar to *Q. robur* but leaves have longer stems and acorns are stemless.

Q. robur 183, 183
English Oak, Common Oak. Europe, Asia Minor, N. Africa, temperate. To 35 m (100 ft). 12.5 cm (5 in) obovate leaves with 6−14 rounded lobes. Yellowish catkins. 4 cm (1½ in) ovoid acorns, on long stalks, generally several together. Deciduous. Very fast growing. Squat trunk, generally broad, open head with massive branches. Brown in autumn. Important timber tree.

Q. rubra, see **Q. borealis**

Q. salicina 185
Willow Oak. Japan, temperate. To 20 m (60 ft). Slender lanceolate, 10 cm (4 in) leaves, white on reverse. Evergreen. Small greyish catkins. Tiny flattened acorns in shallow cups. Fast growing. Compact, round-headed, densely foliaged.

Q. suber 183
Cork Oak. S. Europe, N. Africa, temperate. To 20 m (60 ft). 7.5 cm (3 in) toothed, ovate leaves, greyish on reverse. Evergreen or deciduous. Small catkins. Single, 1 cm (½ in) acorns, half enclosed by cup. Slow growing. Wide spreading, heavily branched with a thick, spongy bark which is stripped and made into cork.

Q. velutina 185
Quercitron, Black Oak, Yellow-bark Oak. E. USA, temperate. To 35 m (100 ft). 25 cm (10 in) oblong leaves with 7−9 broad lobes. Catkins. 2 cm (¾ in) acorns in fringed, pubescent cups. Fast growing. Dense foliaged, rounded head. Vivid scarlet in autumn. Bark source of the yellow dye, Quercitron.

Q. virginiana
Live Oak, Southern Live Oak. Cuba, Mexico, S.E. USA, temperate. To 20 m (60 ft). 12.5 cm (5 in) elliptical leaves, woolly white beneath. Evergreen. Small catkins. Oval, 2.5 cm (1 in) acorns, quarter hidden by cup. Slow growing. Flat-topped; spreading, horizontal branches.

RAVENALA 186
A genus of one species only, a stunning tree from Malagasy with Palm-like trunks — sometimes mistaken for *Strelitzia nicolai* in its juvenile form. Family Musaceae.

R. madagascariensis 186, 186
Traveller's Tree, Traveller's Palm. Malagasy, sub-tropical. To 10 m (30 ft). 3 m (9 ft) banana-like leaves, overlapping in a fan-shaped cluster. Evergreen. Large white flowers with up to 10 bracts in each axillary inflorescence. 3-valved capsules containing many seeds. Fast growing. Single-trunked, Palm-like, but suckers readily. Useful for timber, thatch. The sap is edible.

RHODOLEIA 186
A small genus of evergreen Asiatic trees, resembling *Rhododendrons* but not related to them. Family Hamamelidaceae.

R. championii 186, 186
Silk Rose, Champara. Hong Kong, temperate. To 10 m (30 ft). Leathery, elliptic-ovate leaves to 9 cm (3½ in). Evergreen. 4 cm (1½ in) carmine blossoms, crowded in heads of 5−10 at branch tips. Cluster of 5 radiating capsules. Fast growing. Leg-

gy, sparsely branched. Needs a sheltered position.

RHUS 187
A large genus of shrubs, trees and vines, almost all of them having poisonous properties. The tree species are valued for their stunning autumn colour. Family Anacardiaceae.

R. succedaneus 187, 187
Wax Tree. E. Asia, temperate. To 10 m (30 ft). Compound, pinnate leaves with 9−15 oblong, 10 cm (4 in) leaflets. Deciduous. Small yellow-green flowers in panicles. A cluster of cherry-sized, whitish drupes, turning through green to brown. Very fast growing. Sparsely branched, open. Autumn colours of scarlet, purple and gold. Often very late. Wax extracted from fruits.

R. typhina CV **laciniata 187, 187**
Stag's Horn Sumach, Velvet Sumach. E. USA, temperate. To 10 m (30 ft). Large compound pinnate leaves, consisting of 11−31 deeply toothed pale green leaflets. Deciduous. Small greenish flowers in a terminal panicle. Male and female on separate trees. Crimson hairy drupes, also in terminal panicles. Fast growing. Wide-spreading, sparsely branched. Vivid red, orange and purple. Important source of tannin.

R. verniciflua 187
Varnish Tree, Lacquer Tree. E. Asia, temperate. To 20 m (60 ft). Compound, pinnate leaves with up to 15 ovate leaflets to 20 cm (8 in) long. Deciduous. Small whitish flowers in loose, axillary panicles. Sexes on separate trees. Small, yellowish fruits. Fast growing. Tall, round-headed. Rich red in autumn. Cultivated in Japan as the principal source of lacquer.

ROBINIA 187−8
An exclusively N. American genus of flowering trees, many of them now naturalized worldwide. Family Leguminosae.

R. X ambigua 'Bella Rosea'
Pink Locust. Hybrid. Temperate climate. To 20 m (60 ft). Compound, pinnate leaves with 12−20 leaflets. Deep, rose-pink pea flowers in sparse racemes. Reddish-brown 10 cm (4 in) pods. Fast growing. Upright, sparsely branched. Slender habit. Only lightly spined. A hybrid between *R. pseudacacia* and *R. viscosa*.

R. pseudacacia 187, 188
Black Locust, False Acacia. E. and C. USA, temperate. To 27 m (80 ft). Compound, pinnate leaves with generally 18 elliptic, 4.5 cm (1¾ in) leaflets. Deciduous. White, fragrant pea flowers in dangling 20 cm (8 in) racemes, very like white *Wisteria*. Reddish-brown 10 cm (4 in) glabrous pods, persistent through winter. Very fast growing. Upright, sparsely branched. Very spiny. Yellow in autumn. Hard timber with many uses. A number of CVs are seen: CV *Frisia* has golden-green foliage, orange branches, red spines. CV *Tortuosa* has spirally twisted, shorter branches.

ROYSTONEA 188−9
A genus of Palms from the Caribbean and coastal S. America, generally with pale, swollen trunks. Family Palmae.

R. oleracea 188
Caribbee Royal Palm. Trinidad, Venezuela, tropical. To 40 m (120 ft). 7 m (2 ft) pinnate fronds, ascending, pinnae in a flat plane. Small white flowers on a stalk well below the leaves. Ellipsoid, blackish fruit to 2 cm (¾ in) long. Fast growing. Upright, semi-globular crown of fronds appearing flat on bottom. White swollen-based trunk.

R. regia 188, 189
Cuban Royal Palm. Cuba, tropical. To

25 m (75 ft). Bright green 3.5 m (10 ft) fronds, the older ones drooping. Small white and violet flowers in a 1 m (3 ft) inflorescence. Dull red or purple fruits, globose to 1 cm (½ in) diameter. Fast growing. Upright, globose crown, white trunk swollen in middle. All parts of the tree are used in its native area.

SALIX 189–90
A very large genus of water-loving deciduous trees, mostly from the northern hemisphere. Often with slender, lanceolate leaves and flowers in soft woolly catkins. Family Salicaceae.
S. alba 189, **189**
White Willow. Europe, N. Africa, Asia, temperate. To 25 m (75 ft). Slender 10 cm (4 in) leaves, finely toothed and silvery beneath. Deciduous. Soft catkins appearing with leaves. Small capsules. Very very fast growing. Shrubby, spreading or upright. Very variable. Yellow in autumn. Soft, but useful timber. Twigs used for basket-making.
S. babylonica 189, **189**
Weeping Willow. China, temperate. To 15 m (45 ft). Leaves narrow-lanceolate, 15 cm (6 in), finely toothed, pale green. Deciduous. Catkins with leaves. Small capsules. Very very fast growing. Rounded head, upright branches, weeping branchlets. Yellow in autumn. Has several cultivars with variant foliage.
S. chilensis, see **S. humboldtii**
S. X chrysocoma 190
Golden Willow. France, temperate. To 17 m (50 ft). Slender lanceolate pale green leaves on long branchlets. Deciduous. Male and female flowers in same catkin. Small capsules. Very fast growing. Weeping branches, yellow branchlets, similar to *S. babylonica* of which it is a hybrid. Yellow in autumn.
S. discolor 190, **190**
Pussy Willow. E. USA, temperate. To 12 m (35 ft). 10 cm (4 in) dark leaves, glaucous reverse and with wavy toothed margins. Deciduous. Soft, silvery upright catkins, before the leaves. Winter. Small capsules. Very very fast growing. Shrubby, low-branched. Yellow in autumn.
S. fragilis 190
Crack Willow. Europe, Asia, temperate. To 35 m (100 ft). Lanceolate, toothed, light green, 17.5 cm (7 in) leaves. Deciduous. Catkins with leaves. Stalked capsules. Very fast growing. Wide spreading, deeply furrowed trunk. Brittle branchlets. Yellow in autumn.
S. humboldtii syn. **S. humboldtiana, S. chilensis** 190, **190**
Humboldt Willow. Chile, temperate to warm tropical. To 15 m (45 ft). Linear lanceolate leaves, pale green, to 15 cm (6 in). Evergreen in warmer climate. Small catkins. Small capsules. Fast growing. Generally seen in an upright, columnar shape, like a Lombardy Poplar.
S. matsudana 190
Peking Willow. N. Asia. To 15 m (45 ft). Narrow lanceolate leaves, to 7.5 cm (3 in) long, sharply toothed. Catkins appearing with leaves. Small capsules. Generally resembling *S. babylonica* but smaller in all parts. Commonly seen in its CV *S. m. Tortuosa*, the Corkscrew Willow or Dragon Claw Willow, which has spirally twisted branches and branchlets.
SAMANEA 191
A small genus of leguminous trees from Africa and the S. American Tropics, only one of which is widely cultivated. Family Leguminosae.
S. saman 191, **191**
Rain Tree, Monkey Pod, Saman, Zamang. Tropical America. To 25 m (75 ft). Compound bipinnate leaves, consisting of up to 12 pinnae, each bearing to 16 obovate leaflets to 6 cm (2½ in) long. Deciduous in cooler areas. A dense, umbellate head of pink stamens. 20 cm (8 in) leguminous pods. Very fast growing. Squat, heavy trunk, horizontal branches, may spread half again as wide as its height. A popular shade tree in the tropics where the timber is greatly valued for ornamental carving.

SAPIUM 192
A genus of generally tropical small trees, though often found at cooler, high altitudes. One species, the Chinese Tallow Tree, colours well in warm climates. Family Euphorbiaceae.
S. sebiferum 192, **192**
Chinese Tallow Tree, Wax Tree. China, Japan, warm temperate. To 13 m (40 ft). Rhombic-ovate leaves, 7.5 cm (3 in), sharply pointed. Deciduous. Small apetalous flowers on a 10 cm (4 in) spike. 1 cm (½ in) fruit consisting of 3 seeds covered in white wax. Fast growing. Upright, densely foliaged to shrubby. Deep glossy red and orange in autumn. A good street tree. Wax processed from seeds.

SARACA 192–3
A genus of small trees native to the tropics of S.E. Asia, greatly valued for the masses of showy blossoms produced on older branches. Family Leguminosae.
S. indica 192–3, **193**
Asoka, Sorrowless Tree. India, Malaysia, tropical. To 10 m (30 ft). Bipinnate leaves with 6–12 oblong-lanceolate leaflets to 22.5 cm (9 in) long. Young foliage pink and bronze. Evergreen. Orange-red, long-stemmed flowers in a dense, 10 cm (4 in) corymb. 25 cm (10 in) black pods. Fast growing. Untidy, irregularly shaped, inclined to be spreading.

SCHEFFLERA, see **BRASSAIA**
SCHINUS 193–4
A small genus of S. American trees, widely naturalized in warm, dry climates. Family Anacardiaceae.
S. areira syn. **S. molle** 193, **194**
Peppercorn Tree, Pepperina, Molle, Pirul, California Pepper Tree, Peruvian Mastic. Peru, warm temperate. To 17 m (50 ft). Compound pinnate leaves with 15–41 leaflets, linear-lanceolate and 7 cm (2½ in) long, on weeping branchlets. Evergreen. Minute, yellowish flowers in many-branched terminal panicles. Very small, bright pink berries in dangling chains. Fast growing. Rounded head, gracefully drooping branches and dark, picturesquely furrowed bark.
S. molle, see **S. areira**
S. terebinthifolius 193, **194**
Christmas Berry, Brazilian Pepper Tree, Brazilian Mastic, Wilelaiki. Brazil, tropical. To 7 m (21 ft). Compound leaves with 5–13 leathery dark green leaflets, 6 cm (2½ in) long. Small white flowers in a terminal spike. Pink and bright red currant-size fruits. Fast growing. Shrubby to round-headed, branches *not* drooping. Berries used for Christmas decorations in warm northern hemisphere.

SCHIZOLOBIUM 194
A small genus of showy, S. American trees with brilliant yellow blossom, flowering at the same time as *Jacaranda*. Family Leguminosae.
S. excelsum, see **S. parahybum**
S. parahybum 194, **194**
Bacurubu, Yellow Jacaranda, Fern Tree. C. America to Brazil, tropical. To 35 m (100 ft). Compound bipinnate leaves, to 1 m (3 ft) long, with 20 pinnae each consisting of up to 40 narrow leaflets. Deciduous in cooler climates. 2 cm (¾ in) bright yellow flowers in erect terminal panicles. Brown pods to 12 cm (4¾ in) long. Fast growing. Upright, spreading head, relatively unbranched to a great height.

SCIADOPITYS 195
A single decorative coniferous species from Japan. Family Taxodiaceae.
S. verticillata 195, **195**
Umbrella Pine, Japanese Umbrella Tree. Japan, temperate. To 33 m (100 ft). Linear needle leaves, 12.5 cm (5 in), arranged in whorls of 20–30. Female cones, to 10 cm (4 in) long. Medium fast growth. Perfectly conical. Grown only away from cities, not tolerant of air pollution.

SEQUOIA 196
A single, gigantic coniferous tree from N. California, not often seen away from that area except in large parks, for it needs the company of other trees. Family Taxodiaceae.
S. sempervirens 196, **196**
Sequoia, California Redwood. California, temperate. To 100 m (300 ft). Linear, 2.5 cm (1 in) leaves in two ranks. Evergreen. Male and female 'flowers' on same tree. Broadly oblong cones, to 4.5 cm (1¾ in) long. Very very fast growth. Roughly conical to columnar. An incomparable timber tree.

SEQUOIADENDRON 196
Another single-species genus of conifer from California, more often seen in public gardens. Family Taxodiaceae.
S. giganteum 197, **197**
Big Tree, Giant Sequoia, Wellingtonia. California, cool temperate. To 85 m (250 ft). Short, blue-green needle leaves, turning brown after several years. Cones, to 8.5 cm (3½ in) long, persisting up to 20 years. Very very fast growth. Narrowly pyramidal. No branches to a great height on mature trees. Probably has the broadest trunk of any tree. Bark alone may be 60 cm (24 in) thick.

SESBANIA 198
A most valuable warm-climate genus of ornamental plants, mostly of shrub size, but with several eye-catching tree species. Family Leguminosae.
S. grandiflora, syn. **Agati grandiflora 198**
Corkwood, Vegetable Hummingbird, Wistaria Tree. India to Australia, sub-tropical. To 13 m (40 ft). 30 cm (12 in) even-pinnate leaves with up to 60 leaflets. 10 cm (4 in) pea flowers in groups of 2–4 at leaf axils. Generally white, sometimes pink or red. Flat, 50 cm (20 in) pods. Fast growing. Untidy, spreading. Very soft, brittle timber. Many parts used medicinally. A short-lived tree.

SOPHORA 198–9
A widespread genus of decorative trees in the Pea family (Leguminosae), mostly from temperate areas.
S. chrysophylla 199
Mamane. Hawaii, sub-tropical. To 13 m (40 ft). Odd-pinnate leaves with up to 18 leaflets, obovate, to 3 cm (1¼ in) long. Bright yellow, 2 cm (¾ in) pea flowers in axillary racemes. 12.5 cm (5 in) 4-winged pods. Fast growing. Most variable, from an erect tree to a sprawling, horizontal shrub.
S. japonica 198, **199**
Japanese Pagoda Tree, Chinese Scholar Tree. China, Korea, temperate. To 27 m (80 ft). Compound pinnate leaves with up to 16 ovate leaflets, 5 cm (2 in) long. Deciduous. 1 cm (½ in) yellow-white pea flowers in loose 38 cm (15 in) panicles. Green, pointed pods, to 7.5 cm (3 in). Fast growing. Round-headed, often picturesque tree with three popular CVs: CV *Pendula*, the Weeping Pagoda Tree, with pendulous branches. CV *Tortuosa*, with twisted branches. CV *Violacea*, with flower petals tinged purple.

S. secundiflora 199, **199**
Frijolito, Mescal Bean. Texas, Mexico, temperate. To 15 m (45 ft). Pinnate leaves, with up to 10 silky 5 cm (2 in) leaflets. Evergreen. Mauve, 2.5 cm (1 in) pea flowers, violet-scented. Woody, 20 cm (8 in) pods containing scarlet seeds. Medium fast growth. Shrubby to tall, sparsely branched.

S. tetraptera 199, **199**
Kowhai. N.Z., temperate. To 13 m (40 ft). 15 cm (6 in) pinnate leaves with up to 40 leaflets, silky-hairy, and 3 cm (1¼ in) long. Deciduous. Golden yellow 5 cm (2 in) pea flowers. Broadly winged 20 cm (8 in) pods. Medium fast growth. Shrubby to pyramidal. Yellowish young branchlets. There is a variety, S. t. Microphylla, with 5 mm (¼ in) leaflets.

SORBUS 200–1
A medium-sized genus of the Rose family (Rosaceae) containing over 80 species of decorative trees from all points of the northern hemisphere, mostly grown for their showy, sometimes edible fruit.

S. americana 200
Dogberry, Roundwood, Missey-Moosey, American Mountain Ash. E. USA, cool temperate. To 10 m (30 ft). Pinnate, 25 cm (10 in) leaves with up to 17 narrow leaflets. Deciduous. Dense corymbs of 5 mm (¼ in) white single flowers. Bright red 5 mm (¼ in) pomes in dense corymbs. Persistent to winter. Fast growing. Round-headed, narrow.

S. aria 200
Whitebeam, Chess Apple. Europe, temperate. To 17 m (50 ft). Simple, elliptic, 12.5 cm (5 in) serrated leaves. Deciduous and with white tomentose reverses. 1 cm (½ in) white flowers in broad inflorescences. Heavily scented. Ellipsoid, scarlet fruits to 1.25 cm (⅝ in) diameter. Fast growing. Spreading habit. Var. Majestica, the Largeleaf Whitebeam, has 17.5 cm (7 in) leaves, brown spotted red fruits.

S. aucuparia 200, **200**
Mountain Ash, Rowan, Quickbeam. Europe, Asia Minor, temperate. To 20 m (60 ft). Pinnate, 25 cm (10 in) leaves with up to 15 oblong leaflets. Deciduous. 5 mm (¼ in) white flowers in a dense inflorescence. Oval, scarlet fruits, densely borne. Fast growing. Spreading to upright. Yellow in autumn. Fruit edible. Many CVs with foliage variation.

S. domestica 200, **201**
Service Tree, Sorb. Mediterranean, temperate. To 20 m (60 ft). Coarse, pinnate leaves with up to 21 leaflets. 1 cm (½ in) white flowers in dense clusters. Rosy-green 2.5 cm (1 in) fruits, ripening to brown. Edible. Fast growing. Open; spreading branches, somewhat round-headed. Pink, red in autumn.

S. intermedia 200, **200**, **201**
Swedish Whitebeam. N.W. Europe, cool temperate. To 12 m (35 ft). Simple, broadly ovate, 10 cm (4 in) leaves, sometimes lobed. Deciduous. 10 cm (4 in) flat inflorescences of white, single blossoms. 1 cm (½ in) ellipsoid orange-red fruits. Fast growing. Upright, wide-headed.

S. mougiottii 200, **201**
Alpine Whitebeam. European Alps, Pyrenees, cool temperate. To 12 m (36 ft). Simple, round-ovate, 10 cm (4 in) leaves, serrated and lobed, pale grey on reverse. Deciduous. Small white flowers in a dense, woolly, inflorescence. Bright red fruits to 1 cm (½ in) diameter. Medium fast growth. Rounded head, shaggy bark.

S. pekingensis 200, **201**
Peking Serviceberry, Chinese Service Tree. N. China, temperate. To 10 m (30 ft). Purple-red pinnate leaves on

scarlet stems. Small white flowers in a cluster. 1 cm (½ in) fruits, vivid scarlet. Medium fast growth. Pyramidal, slightly drooping branches. Scarlet in autumn.

SPATHODEA 202
Perhaps two species of showy, evergreen trees from tropical Africa, popular everywhere in warm climates. Family Bignoniaceae.

S. campanulata 202, **202**
African Tulip Tree, Fountain Tree, Flame of the Forest, Baton du Sorcier. Uganda, sub-tropical. To 17 m (50 ft). Compound, 45 cm (18 in) leaves with 9–19 broad-lanceolate leaflets. Evergreen. Orange-scarlet, 12.5 cm (5 in) trumpet flowers emerging from hairy buds. Oblong, 20 cm (8 in) capsules. Very fast growing. Tall, spreading head.

S. nilotica 202, **202**
Nile Tulip Tree. Sudan, tropical. To 7 m (20 ft). Pinnate leaves, 40 cm (6 in). Evergreen. Soft apricot to yellow-edged flowers. Fast growing. Heavily branched, bushy.

SPONDIAS 203
A small genus of tropical trees from Asia and the Americas. Greatly valued for their fruits in many warm areas. Family Anarcardiaceae.

S. cytherea 203, **203**
Pomme Cythère, Vi, Wi, Golden Apple, Ambarella, Otaheite Apple. Society I., tropical. To 20 m (60 ft). Compound pinnate leaves with 11–23 oblong, 8.5 cm (3½ in) leaflets. Semi-deciduous. Small white blossoms in terminal panicles. Ovoid, 7.5 cm (3 in) drupes, orange-yellow, edible. Fast growing. Tall, heavily branched, round-headed.

S. mombin 203, **203**
Hog Plum, Mombin, Jobo. Tropical America. To 20 m (60 ft). Compound pinnate leaves with up to 17 lanceolate, 10 cm (4 in) leaflets. Semi-deciduous. Small, palé yellow flowers in loose, terminal panicles. Ovoid, 2.5 cm (1 in) fruits, very juicy, edible. Fast growing. Upright, round-headed, grey furrowed bark, almost vertical branches.

STENOCALYX, see SYZYGIUM
STENOCARPUS 203–4
A small genus of spectacular evergreen trees, native to the Malay archipelago and down through Australia to New Caledonia. Family Proteaceae.

S. sinuatus 204, **204**
Firewheel, Wheel of Fire. Q, NSW, sub-tropical. To 35 m (100 ft). Dark glossy sinuate leaves, to 25 cm (10 in), often deeply lobed. Evergreen. Tubular, bright red, 2.5 cm (1 in) flowers in wheel-shaped umbels, appearing directly from trunk and branches. Leathery follicles. Fast growing. Upright, Poplar-shaped, often with weeping branches.

STERCULIA 204–5
A large genus of tropical trees grown principally for their showy, scarlet seed pods — related to the Australian Brachychiton. Usually deciduous. Family Sterculiaceae.

S. apetala 205
Panama Tree, Bellota. C. America, temperate. To 15 m (45 ft). Palmately 5–lobed, heart-shaped leaves to 50 cm (20 in) across. Deciduous. 2.5 cm (1 in) yellow flowers, purple spotted, in axillary panicles. 5 tomentose, 10 cm (4 in) seed follicles arranged in star-form. Fast growing. Round-headed, densely foliaged. Medicinal properties.

S. foetida 204–5, **205**
Java Olive, Skunk Tree, Kelumpang. S.E. Asia, Africa, tropical. to 20 m (60 ft). Palmately compound 30 cm (12 in) leaves, divided generally into 11 pointed

leaflets. 1 cm (½ in) red and yellow flowers in terminal panicles. Bad odour. 5 scarlet, tomentose, 10 cm (4 in) seed follicles arranged like a 5-pointed star. Fast growing. Rounded, heavily branched. Many medicinal uses.

S. lanceolata 205
Hong Kong Sterculia. S. China, sub-tropical. To 7 m (20 ft). Simple oval leaves, to 10 cm (4 in). Small green and pink flowers in a terminal panicle. 5 scarlet pods in the form of a star. Fast growing. Untidy, loosely branched. Medicinal uses.

S. quadrifida 204
Four-fruit Sterculia. NSW, Q, warm temperate. To 20 m (60 ft). Heart-shaped, sharply pointed, 7.5 cm (5 in) leaves. Deciduous. Small yellowish flowers in terminal panicles. 4 scarlet, tomentose, boat-shaped, 7.5 cm (5 in) seed follicles arranged as a 4-pointed star. Fast growing. Sparsely branched, roughly pyramidal.

SWIETENIA 205–6
A very small genus of less than half a dozen species of tropical evergreen trees — source of commercial Mahogany. Family Meliaceae.

S. macrophylla 206, **206**
Honduras Mahogany. Tropical America. To 50 m (150 ft). Compound, pinnate 35 cm (14 in) leaves with up to 12 lanceolate leaflets. Small flowers in axillary and terminal panicles. Large dehiscent woody capsules to 15 cm (6 in) long. Fast growing. Many-branched, round-headed. Source of finest Mahogany timber. Evergreen in tropics, semi-deciduous in cooler climates.

S. mahagoni 205–6, **205**
Spanish Mahogany, Madeira Redwood, W. Indies Mahogany. Florida, Caribbean, tropical. To 25 m (75 ft). Pinnately compound leaves, 20 cm (8 in), with up to 10 ovate leaflets. Evergreen. Flowers in small panicles. Woody dehiscent capsules to 12.5 cm (5 in) long. Fast growing. Tall, spreading. Source of Mahogany timber; popular street tree in sub-tropical climates.

SYNCARPIA 206
A small genus of Eucalypt-like evergreen trees found exclusively in E. Australia, but now grown in many countries. Family Myrtaceae.

S. glomulifera 206, **206**
Turpentine. NSW, Q, temperate. To 25 m (75 ft). Elliptic-oblong leaves, to 7.5 cm (3 in). Dark green, silvery pubescent on underside. Dense globose heads of cream-stamened blossom, on 2.5 cm (1 in) peduncles. Dehiscent capsules with 2–3 sections. Fast growing. Pyramidal to columnar. Dark grey heavily grooved bark. Valuable dark pink timber is resistant to marine borer.

S. hillii 206
Peebeen. Fraser Island, Q. Similar to S. glomulifera, but with leaves to 15 cm (6 in) long.

SYZYGIUM 207
An extremely large genus of trees, formerly called Eugenia, mostly from the Old World tropics. Perhaps 500 species with showy, staminate blossom and colourful, often edible fruits. family Myrtaceae.

S. aromaticum
Clove Tree. Moluccas, tropical. To 10 m (30 ft). Elliptical, glossy, clove-scented leaves. Small yellow puffball flowers in sparse terminal panicles. Small, pea-sized fruits. Fast growing. Round-headed. The dried flower buds are the cloves of commerce.

S. jambos 207
Malabar Plum, Rose Apple, Jumbu. S.E.

Asia, sub-tropical. To 13 m (40 ft). Glossy lanceolate 20 cm (8 in) leaves. Evergreen. Greenish-white 7.5 cm (3 in) puffballs in terminal, sparse clusters. 4 cm (1½ in) pale yellow fruit, very fragrant. Fast growing. Round-headed, often with weeping branches. The insipid fruit are candied or made into jellies.

S. luehmannii 207
Water Myrtle, Cherry Alder, Small-leaf Lillypilly. NSW, Q, temperate. To 27 m (80 ft). Small, pointed, 5 cm (2 in) glossy leaves. Evergreen. Young foliage pink-bronze. Very small white staminate flowers, lightly borne. 1 cm (½ in) bright red-pink berries, pear or egg-shaped. Fast growing. Round-headed to horizontal.

S. malaccense 207
Malay Apple, Rose Apple, Pomerac. Malaysia, tropical. To 17 m (50 ft). Ovate, oblong, 30 cm (12 in) leathery leaves. Showy, staminous, 2.5 cm (1 in) flowers in clusters, directly from old wood and branches. Purple-pink. Pear-shaped, 5 cm (2 in) berries, green ripening to pink. Fast growing. Round-headed to upright. Fruit very popular raw, cooked or made into wine.

S. paniculatum syn. **Eugenia australis 207**
Brush Cherry. Australia, temperate. To 15 m (45 ft). Glossy, lanceolate leaves, 7.5 cm (3 in), flushed pink when young. Evergreen. Creamy-white, 1.5 cm (½ in) staminate blossom in sparse panicles. Ovoid red-violet berries to 2 cm (¾ in). Fast growing. Round-headed to upright. Densely foliaged, often weeping branches. Sometimes trained and clipped into hedges. The fruit is made into jams and jellies.

S. samarangense
Jumbool, Java Apple, Wax Apple. Malaysia, tropical. To 10 m (30 ft). Short-stemmed, elliptic-oblong leaves to 15 cm (6 in) or more. 4 cm (1½ in) white puffball flowers in dense clusters. Deep pink to red egg-shaped berries. Edible. Fast growing. Shrubby to broad-headed.

TABEBUIA 208
A large genus of showy, flowering trees from tropical America, generally seen as ornamentals, but often the source of valuable timber in their home territory. Family Bignoniaceae.

T. argentea 208, 208
Silver Trumpet Tree, Tree of Gold, Paraguay Trumpet Tree. Paraguay, Argentina, sub-tropical. To 8 m (25 ft). Palmately compound silver-grey leaves with 5–7 oblong 15 cm (6 in) leaflets. Semi-deciduous. Chrome yellow 6 cm (2½ in) trumpet flowers in terminal racemes. Grey 10 cm (4 in) capsules. Fast growing. Open-headed, spirally twisted with silver-grey bark. Useful timber tree.

T. avellanedae
Argentina Trumpet Tree. Argentina, Paraguay, warm temperate. To 20 m (60 ft). Palmately compound leaves with 5 leaflets, to 15 cm (6 in) long. Red or purple-pink trumpet flowers, to 4 cm (1½ in) long. Pendant capsules, to 30 cm (12 in) long. Fast growing. Round-headed. Valuable timber tree.

T. chrysantha 208, 208
Golden Trumpet Tree. C. America, Venezuela, sub-tropical. To 7 m (20 ft). Palmately compound leaves with 17.5 cm (7 in) lanceolate leaflets. Deciduous. Bright yellow 7 cm (2¾ in) trumpet flowers in dense clusters. Pendant capsules to 30 cm (12 in) long. Fast growing. Spreading, sparsely branched.

T. ipe, see **T. avellanedae**
T. pentaphylla syn. **T. rosea 208, 208**
Rosy Trumpet Tree, Pink Poui, White Cedar, Roblé Blanco. Mexico to Ecuador,

tropical. To 27 m (80 ft). Palmately compound leaves of 3–5 elliptic leaflets, to 15 cm (6 in) long. Deciduous. Purple-pink, 8 cm (3½ in) trumpet flowers in terminal clusters. 35 cm (14 in) capsules. Fast growing. Pyramidal.

T. rosea, see **T. pentaphylla**
TAMARINDUS 208–9
A single species, one of the most popular evergreen shade trees in warm climates, and bearing a fruit that is used in a dozen ways. Family Leguminosae.

T. indicus 208–9, 209
Tamarind, Tamarindo, Wi-'awa' awa. India, tropical. To 25 m (75 ft). Dull green, compound, even pinnate leaves with up to 36 oblong, 2.5 cm (1 in) leaflets. Pale yellow, 2.5 cm (1 in) flowers in short, sparse racemes. Light brown pods to 15 cm (6 in) long, full of delicious sweet-sour pulp. Fast growing. Upright, wide-headed. Useful shade tree in humid or arid areas.

TAXODIUM 209
Two species only of water-loving conifers from N. America, their timber greatly valued for its resistance to both water and termite attack. Family Taxodiaceae.

T. distichum 209, 209, 210
Bald Cypress, Swamp Cypress. S.E. USA, temperate. To 50 m (150 ft). Flat, linear leaves, to 2 cm (¾ in) long, or spirally arranged, awl-shaped, 1 cm (½ in) long. Both types on the same tree. Deciduous. Pale green. Male cones in catkin-like clusters on branch tips, female cones globose. Fast growing. Pyramidal to upright, flat-topped, often surrounded by 'knees', curious aerating projections from the roots. Rich bronze in autumn. CV *Pendans* has weeping foliage.

T. mucronatum 209
Montezuma Cypress, Mexican Bald Cypress. Mexico. To 40 m (120 ft). Similar to *T. distichum* but leaves are evergreen.

TAXUS 210–11
A small genus of perhaps half a dozen coniferous species, although all the specimens you're likely to see in a lifetime are cultivars of the Common Yew, *Taxus baccata*. Family Taxaceae.

T. baccata 211, 210, 211
English Yew, Irish Yew, Common Yew. Europe, W. Asia, N. Africa, temperate. To 27 m (80 ft). Dark, flattened needle leaves, to 3 cm (1¼ in), yellow-green beneath. Deciduous. A single bony seed almost enclosed in a scarlet sheath or *aril*, female trees only. Slow growing. Roughly pyramidal, tending to flat-topped in extreme age. Useful for timber. Many CVs with gold, silver or variegated foliage, weeping habit or golden arils.

TECTONA 211–12
A small genus of deciduous trees from S.E. Asia, much valued for their magnificent timber, Teak. Family Verbenaceae.

T. grandis 211–12, 212
Teak, Tekka. India to Malaysia, tropical. To 50 m (150 ft). Drooping, broadly elliptic leaves, to 30 cm (12 in) or more, tomentose and deciduous. Small mauve flowers in terminal panicles. Globose, 4-lobed drupes. Fast growing. Tall, upright-pointing branches. Flat-topped in age. The valuable timber is heavier than water.

TERMINALIA 212–13
A very large genus of tropical trees from the Asian area, one of which is commonly grown in warm-climate, coastal positions throughout the world. Family Combretaceae.

T. catappa 212–13, 212, 213
Tropical Almond, False Kamani, Myrobalan, Coast Almond. Malaysia, tropical. To 25 m (75 ft). Semi-deciduous, obovate, 30 cm (12 in) leaves. Greenish-

white flower spikes to 15 cm (6 in) long. Flattened, 5 cm (2 in) drupes, green to red. Fast growing. Squat-trunked, horizontal branches. Extremely flat-topped, often wider than tall. Bright red in autumn. Edible seeds, useful timber.

THEOBROMA 213
Though more than a dozen species of *Theobroma* are known, only the Cocoa Tree is widely cultivated. Family Byttneriaceae.

T. cacao 213, 213
Cacao, Cocoa Tree. C., S. America, tropical. To 12 m (35 ft). 30 cm (12 in) leathery oblong leaves, young foliage slack, reddish. Long-stemmed, 1 cm (⅜ in) yellow flowers borne directly on trunk and branches. Large 10-angled fruit up to the size of a football, containing many ellipsoid seeds in a sticky pulp. Fast growing. Shrubby to round-headed.

THEVETIA 214
A small genus of shrubby trees from Tropical America, all noted for their golden-yellow trumpet flowers. Family Apocynaceae.

T. peruviana 214, 214
Be Still Tree, Lucky Nut. Tropical America. To 10 m (30 ft). Slender, linear-lanceolate, 15 cm (6 in) leaves, dark green and glossy. Yellow, 5 cm (2 in) wide trumpet flowers. Hard, green, 2.5 cm (1 in) drupe, ripening to red and black. Fast growing. Open, spreading shape. There are CVs with apricot or white flowers.

T. thevetioides 214, 214
Yellow Oleander. Mexico, tropical. To 5 m (15 ft). 10 cm (4 in) linear-lanceolate leaves. Evergreen. Chrome yellow, open, trumpet flowers to 7.5 cm (3 in) diameter. Green, poisonous drupes to 6 cm (2½ in) diameter. Fast growing. Shrubby.

T. yccotli 214, 214
Mexican Oleander. Mexico, tropical. To 7 m (20 ft). Linear-lanceolate leaves, hairy on reverses. Yellow trumpet flowers. Apple-sized, warty green fruits. Fast growing. Lightweight, spreading head.

THUJA 215
Five only species of evergreen coniferous trees from N. America and E. Asia. Important timber trees in their wild form. Family Cupressaceae.

T. koraiensis 215
Korean Arborvitae. Korea, temperate. To 12 m (35 ft). Scale-like concave leaves. Evergreen. Female cones 5 mm (¼ in) long. Slow growing. Conical habit.

T. occidentalis 215, 215
White Cedar, Tree of Life, American Arborvitae. N.E. and C. USA, temperate. To 20 m (60 ft). Dark green scale-like leaves, yellowish beneath, in fan-like sprays. Evergreen. Female cones, to 1 cm (½ in) long. Slow growing. Pyramidal to columnar in age. Valuable soft white timber. Several dozen CVs in shape, habit, foliage and colour.

T. orientalis 215
Chinese Thuja, Chinese Arborvitae. China, temperate. To 15 m (45 ft). Triangular scale-like leaves in flat sprays. Small cones in crowded clusters. Slow growing. Roughly pyramidal, upward pointing branches.

T. plicata 215, 215
Western Red Cedar, Giant Arborvitae. W. N. America, temperate. To 70 m (200 ft). Glossy green scale-like leaves, whitish beneath. In flat sprays. Female cones to 1 cm (½ in) long. Very fast growing. Pyramidal to columnar with ridged, red-brown bark. An important timber tree.

T. standishii 215
Japanese Arborvitae. Japan, temperate. To 17 m (50 ft). Scale-like leaves, dark grey-

green, whitish marks beneath. Female cones, to 1 cm (½ in) long. Very fast growing. Broadly conical, deep red bark. An important timber tree.

TILIA 216–17
Possibly the most outstanding deciduous tree in the northern hemisphere, about 20 species in all. Family Tiliaceae.

T. americana
Basswood, Whitewood, American Linden. E. N.America, temperate. To 45 m (130 ft). Broad-ovate 20 cm (8 in) leaves, coarsely serrated. Deciduous. Small yellow-white fragrant blossoms in a pendulous, bracted cyme. Small, nut-like fruit, green and tomentose. Fast growing. Spreading head. Yellow in autumn. Source of the inexpensive Whitewood timber used in furniture-making. Attractive to bees.

T. cordata 217
Small-leafed Lime, Linden. Europe, temperate. To 35 m (100 ft). 6 cm (2½ in) nearly round leaves, finely serrated, glaucous beneath. Deciduous. Small yellow flowers in a bracted 5–7 flowered cyme. Small globose, faintly ribbed fruit. Very fast growing. Pyramidal. A popular street tree.

T. X europaea 217
Common Lime, European Lime. Hybrid between *T. cordata* and *T. platyphyllus*. Temperate climate. To 40 m (120 ft). Broadly ovate leaves, 10 cm (4 in), cordate, serrate. Deciduous. Yellow blossom in 5–10 flowered cymes. Small round fruit, lightly ribbed. Fast growing. Upright, spreading in age.

T. miqueliana
Japanese Linden. Chinese Linden. China, temperate. To 15 m (45 ft). Triangular-ovate leaves to 8 cm (3¼ in), coarsely serrated, greyish on reverse. Deciduous. Yellowish blossom in cymes of up to 20 flowers. Five-ribbed fruit. Slow growing. Pyramidal.

T. petiolaris 216
Pendant Silver Lime, Weeping Lime. Europe, W. Asia, temperate. To 25 m (75 ft). Ovate-orbicular leaves, 10 cm (4 in), obliquely cordate and whitish tomentose on reverse. Deciduous. Yellow blossom on 10-flowered brownish woolly cymes. Very fragrant. Round, warty fruit. Very fast growing. Pyramidal, weeping branches.

T. platyphyllos 216
Large-leafed Lime, Big-leaf Linden. Britain, C. and S. Europe, temperate. To 45 m (135 ft). Roundish 12.5 cm (5 in) leaves, serrated and dull above, pubescent beneath. Deciduous. Yellowish flowers in small 6-flowered bracted cymes. Small 5-ribbed fruit, round or pea-shaped. Very fast growing. Pyramidal to columnar. CVs with variations in habit, foliage and bract colour.

TIPUANA 217
A spectacular S.American tree, widely grown in many parts of the world. Family Leguminosae.

T. tipu 217, 217
Pride of Bolivia, Rosewood. Brazil to Bolivia, sub-tropical to temperate. To 25 m (75 ft). Compound pinnate leaves with up to 22 leaflets, 4 cm (1½ in) long. Open, orange-yellow flowers in short racemes. 6 cm (2½ in) pods. Fast growing. Spreading habit. Timber sold as Brazilian Rosewood.

TOONA 218
A single species of deciduous Australian tree, valued for its fragrant red timber. Native trees now rare. Family Meliaceae.

T. australis 218, 218
Australian Red Cedar, Red Cedar. NSW, Q, warm temperate to sub-tropical. To 33 m (100 ft). Pinnate, 30 cm (12 in) leaves. Young foliage bronze. Deciduous. Small pink flowers in terminal panicles. Fragrant. Woody seed capsules. Slow growing. Tall, spreading. Australia's most valuable timber tree.

TRISTANIA 218–19
A splendid genus of evergreen trees in the Myrtle family (Myrtaceae), native to Australia and nearby countries.

T. conferta 218, 219
Brush Box, Brisbane Box. E.Australia, temperate to sub-tropical. To 50 m (150 ft). 15 cm (6 in) lanceolate leaves, alternate. Deciduous. 2.5 cm (1 in) flowers with white, plume-like petals, in cymes on young wood. 1 cm (½ in) capsules. Fast growing. Upright, often pyramidal. Valuable timber tree. A popular CV 'Aurea Variegata' has white and green variegated leaves.

T. laurifolia, see T. laurina

T. laurina 218–19, 219
Kanooka, Water Gum. Australia, temperate. To 20 m (60 ft). Lanceolate leaves, 10 cm (4 in), alternate. 1 cm (½ in) yellow flowers in axillary cymes. 5mm (¼ in) capsules. Medium fast growth. Round-headed.

T. neriifolia 219
Water Gum. Australia. To 6 m (18 ft). Almost identical to *T. laurina* except in size. The leaves also appear in opposite pairs.

TSUGA 219–20
A small genus of evergreen conifers from N. America and Asia. Valuable timber trees with many decorative garden varieties. Family Pinaceae.

T. canadensis 220, 220
Eastern Hemlock, Canada Hemlock. E. N. America, temperate. To 25 m (75 ft). 1 cm (⅜ in), linear flattened leaves, finely toothed. Evergreen. 2 cm (¾ in) stalked cones. Fast growing. Roughly conical, often with several trunks or upward pointing branches. Blackish-brown deeply furrowed bark. An important timber tree. Many garden CVs with smaller size, weeping habit or varying foliage colours.

ULMUS 220–1
Among the most beloved deciduous trees of the northern hemisphere, due largely to their marked cold-hardiness, the 18 or so species of Elm are now something of a rarity, in Europe at least, due to the ravages of the dreaded Dutch Elm Disease. So far those in the southern hemisphere have escaped destruction. Family Ulmaceae.

U. americana
American Elm, Water Elm, White Elm. E. and C. N. America, cold temperate. To 40 m (120 ft). Asymmetrical, slender, 15 cm (6 in) leaves, toothed and hairy, on slender, drooping stems. Deciduous. Inconspicuous greenish-white flowers in clusters. Flat, hairy samaras, green, fading brown. Fast growing. Upright, with a wide weeping crown. Yellow in autumn. An important timber tree.

U. fulva, see U. rubra

U. glabra 221
Wych Elm, Scotch Elm. Europe, Asia, temperate. To 45 m (130 ft). Asymmetrical, obovate, doubly serrated leaves, 20 cm (8 in), with a rough surface. Inconspicuous greenish flowers in clusters. Large, downy samaras with seed at centre. Very fast growth. Yellow in autumn. Wide spreading tree with many garden cultivars including the popular *U.g. Pendula*, the Weeping Elm.

U. X hollandica 222
Dutch Elm, Holland Elm. Hybrid. Temperate climate. To 40 m (120 ft). Asymmetrical, broadly elliptic leaves, 12.5 cm (5 in), smooth and almost glossy. Deciduous. Inconspicuous greenish flowers. Samaras with seeds to one end. Very fast growing. Spreading tree with somewhat weeping branches. Suckers badly. Yellow in autumn. Many named CVs, differing principally in habit and shape.

U. laevis
European White Elm. C. Europe, Asia, cool temperate. To 40 m (120 ft). Asymmetrical, oblong leaves, 12.5 cm (5 in), pointed, downy beneath. Deciduous. Flower and fruit as in other species. Fast growing. Upright, with open crown. Yellow in autumn. More cold-hardy than other European species.

U. parvifolia 221
Chinese Elm. China, Taiwan, Korea, Japan, temperate. To 30 m (90 ft). Ovate leaves, 5 cm (2 in), shiny above, smooth beneath, lightly toothed. Semi-evergreen. Small, greenish-white flowers. 5 mm (¼ in) samaras, brown, colouring highly in autumn. Very fast growth. Upright to broadly spreading, with weeping branches. Bark attractively mottled in grey, white, cinnamon. The most common Elm in warm climates, an attractive small tree in garden use.

U. procera 220–1, 220, 221
English Elm. Europe, temperate. To 50 m (150 ft). Asymmetrical, broadly elliptical leaves, 10 cm (4 in), rough textured and pointed. Deciduous. Inconspicuous greenish flowers. Samaras greenish-white, before foliage, seed to one end. Infertile. Very fast growing. Tall, upright, with a fountain-shaped head. Dark striated bark. Yellow in autumn. Spreads easily from suckers. CV 'Louis van Houtte' with golden foliage is popular as a garden specimen.

U. rubra syn. **U. fulva**
Slippery Elm, Red Elm. E. to C. USA, cool temperate. To 33 m (100 ft). Large, 20 cm (8 in) leaves, broadly ovate and coarsely serrated, asymmetrical. Deciduous. Greenish, inconspicuous flowers in clusters. Samaras, as other species. Slow growing. Spreading top. Dull yellow in autumn. Useful timber tree.

U. X Vanhouttei, see U. procera 'Louis van Houtte'

VIBURNUM 222
The several hundred shrubby species of *Viburnum* are among the most popular garden subjects, but there are also several tree species. Family Caprifoliaceae.

V. dentatum 222
Arrowwood. N. America, temperate. To 5 m (15 ft). Round to ovate, 7.5 cm (3 in) leaves, coarsely toothed. Deciduous. Small white flowers in 7.5 cm (3 in) cymes. Blue-black berries. Fast growing. Slender, shrubby.

V. lantana
Wayfaring Tree, Twistwood. Europe, W. Asia, temperate. To 5 m (15 ft). Ovate leaves, 12.5 cm (5 in), finely toothed and downy. Deciduous. Small cream flowers in 10 cm (4 in) cymes. Small, red drupes. Fast growing. Slender, upright habit. Crimson in autumn.

V. odoratissimum 222, 222
Sweet Viburnum. Asia, Japan, temperate. To 7 m (20 ft). Leathery, pale green, elliptic leaves, 15 cm (6 in). Evergreen. Small fragrant white flowers in 10 cm (4 in) upright panicles. Small red drupes, withering to black. Fast growing. Shrubby, densely foliaged, wider than high.

V. opulus 222, 222
Bush Rose, Whitten Tree, Snowball Tree, Cranberry. Europe, N. Africa, N. Asia, temperate. To 5 m (15 ft). 10 cm (4 in) lobed, Maple-like leaves, downy and

deciduous. White, 2 cm ($^3/_4$ in) flowers in a globose head. Scarlet drupes. Medium fast growth. Shrubby to spreading. Several CVs are grown, varying in size, foliage, fruit and colours.

VIRGILIA 223

Either one or two species (nobody is quite sure) of small flowering trees from S. Africa. Fast growing, but short-lived, they are useful in the new garden. Family Leguminosae.

V. capensis 223, **223**

Keurboom. S. Africa, temperate. To 10 m (30 ft). Dark, compound, odd-pinnate leaves, 20 cm (8 in), with up to 20 leaflets, pale and furry beneath. Mauve-pink, 1 cm ($^1/_2$ in) pea flowers in a panicle. Summer-autumn. 7.5 cm (3 in) pods. Very fast growing. Shrubby to pyramidal.

V. divaricata

May only be a sub-species of V. capensis, or a clone that flowers briefly in early spring.

V. oroboides, see V. capensis

WASHINGTONIA 223

Two gigantic Palms from the S.W. USA and Mexico, notable for their great height and persistent 'petticoats' of dead fronds. Family Palmae.

W. filifera 223, **223**

Petticoat Palm, Desert Fan Palm, Thread Palm. California, Arizona, temperate. To 28 m (85 ft). Grey-green palmate fronds to 2 m (6 ft) diameter, on 2 m (6 ft) toothed stems. Blades have weeping tips. The old fronds persist below the crown of new foliage. Small white flowers on a hanging stalk, to 4 m (12 ft) in length. Oval, 1 cm ($^1/_2$ in) green fruit. Slow growing. Thick, dead-straight trunk, to 1 m (3 ft) diameter. Edges of fronds decked with loose white fibres.

W. robusta

Mexican Fan Palm, Cotton Palm. Mexico, warm temperate. To 33 m (100 ft). Bright green palmate fronds, to 2 m (6 ft) diameter, on 2 m (6 ft) toothed stems. Fronds *without* loose fibres. Flowers and fruit as in *W. filifera*. Medium fast growth. A more slender trunk than *W. filifera*, less inclined to be draped with dead foliage. Not frost hardy.

WELLINGTONIA, see SEQUOIA-DENDRON

ZELKOVA 224

A very small genus of Elm relatives from W. Asia and Japan. Family Ulmaceae.

Z. carpinifolia 224, **224**

Caucasian Zelkova, Elm Zelkova, Zelkova. Caucasus, temperate. To 27 m (80 ft). Elliptical pointed leaves, 5 cm (2 in), with wavy teeth, downy beneath. Deciduous. Small, greenish, inconspicuous flowers. Male flowers clustered, female single. Small asymmetrical drupes. Fast growing. Short trunk, upward pointing branches, weeping branchlets.

Z. serrata 224, **224**

Japanese Zelkova, Zelkova, Saw-leaf Zelkova, Japanese Elm. Japan, temperate to cool. To 35 m (100 ft). Oblong-ovate leaves, 12.5 cm (5 in), sharply pointed and toothed. Small greenish flowers, male in clusters. Persistent woody fruits. Fast growing. Upright habit, the branches in fountain pattern. Yellow-brown in autumn. Important timber tree in Japan.

ZIZYPHUS syn. ZIZIPHUS 224

A genus of curious fruiting trees from warm and sub-tropical regions of both hemispheres. Family Rhamnaceae.

Z. jujuba 224

Chinese Date, Common Jujube. S.E. Europe to China, temperate. To 15 m (45 ft). Oblong-elliptic leaves, obtusely serrated and with two light spines on stem. Deciduous. Small creamy flowers in axillary clusters. Fleshy, ovoid drupes, to 3 cm ($1^1/_4$) long. Sweet. Fast growing. Shrubby to spreading. The fruits are greatly valued in desert areas, raw or cooked.

Z. mauritiana 224, **224**

Indian Jujube, Cotton Jujube. India, temperate. To 10 m (30 ft). Broad elliptic, 6 cm ($2^1/_2$ in) leaves, woolly beneath. Evergreen. Heavier spines on leaf stem. Small creamy flowers in axillary clusters. Globose fruit, 2.5 cm (1 in); edible but acid. Fast growing. Shrubby to round-headed.

Z. spina-christi 224

Crown of Thorns. N. Africa, Asia Minor, dry temperate. To 10 m (30 ft). Leaves small, deciduous, the stem wickedly spined. Yellowish flowers in axillary clusters. Grape-sized edible fruit. Medium fast growth. Sparse, shrubby. According to legend, the tree from which Christ's Crown of Thorns was woven.

INDEX OF POPULAR NAMES

All popular names used anywhere in this book are listed alphabetically in this index, whether they are used in the main text, in picture captions or in the Botanical Index. Each one has a cross-reference to its full botanical name, both generic and specific names being included, e.g., European Silver Fir see *Abies alba*. Most popular names will be included in the index several times, so that if you think the tree is a Fir, but don't know which one, you may turn to Fir, and find:

    Fir, Chinese Silver
    Fir, European Silver
    Fir, Pacific Silver, etc.

Many popular tree names, such as Cedar or Cypress, are used for many different tree genera. Cedar for instance is used not only for the true Cedars (*Cedrus* spp.) but by popular usage for many trees in other botanical genera as well. For instance, under Cedar in the index you will find: *Calocedrus, Cedrela, Cedrus, Chamaecyparis, Cryptomeria, Cupressus, Juniperus, Melia, Pinus, Thuja* and *Toona*.

You may then need to turn to the Botanical Index to each of the cross-referenced genera, e.g., *Toona* — Australian Red Cedar, and proceed from there.

Many species referred to, of course, may not be illustrated, so the best idea is to turn to the Botanical Index first, look up the referred botanic name e.g. *Toona australis*, and *if* it is followed by a number in bold type, that will lead you to the text page on which the tree is illustrated.

Abele see *Populus alba*
Abyssinian Tea see *Catha edulis*
Acacia, False see *Robinia pseudacacia*
    Pearl see *Acacia podalyriaefolia*
    Philippine see *Acacia confusa*
    Sweet see *Acacia farnesiana*
Achiote see *Bixa orellana*
African Camel Thorn see *Acacia karroo*
    Olive see *Olea africana*
    Tulip Tree see *Spathodea campanulata*
    Yellowwood see *Podocarpus*
Agati see *Sesbania grandiflora*
Aguacate see *Persea americana*
Ai-lan-to see *Ailanthus altissima*
Akee Apple see *Blighia sapida*
Alaska Cedar see *Chamaecyparis*
Albany Bottlebrush see *Callistemon*
Albizzia, Plume see *Albizzia lophantha*
Alder see *Alnus* sp.
    Black see *Alnus glutinosa*
    Cherry see *Syzygium luehmannii*
    Common see *Alnus glutinosa*
    Evergreen see *Alnus jorullensis*
    Italian see *Alnus cordata*
    Mexican Evergreen see *Alnus jorullensis*
    Red see *Alnus oregana*
    White see *Alnus rhombifolia*
Aleppo Pine see *Pinus halepensis*
Alexandra Palm see *Archontophoenix*
Algarroba see *Ceratonia siliqua*
Almond see *Prunus dulcis*
Almond, Cherry see *Prunus laurocerasus*
    Coast see *Terminalia catappa*
    Flowering see *Prunus amygdalus*
    Green see *Pistacia vera*
    Indian see *Sterculia foetida*
    Tropical see *Terminalia catappa*
Aloe, Rhodesian Tree see *Aloë excelsa*
    Smooth Tree see *Aloë plicatilis*
    Tree see *Aloë bainesii*
Aloe tree see *Aloë bainesii*
Alligator Pear see *Persea americana*

Allspice see *Pimenta dioica*
Alpine Fir, Dwarf see *Abies lasiocarpa*
Alpine Whitebeam see *Sorbus mougiottii*
Ambarella see *Spondias cytherea*
American Arborvitae see *Thuja*
    Ash see *Fraxinus americana*
    Beech see *Fagus grandifolia*
    Chestnut see *Castanea dentata*
    Elm see *Ulmus americana*
    Holly see *Ilex opaca*
    Hop-Hornbeam see *Ostrya virginiana*
    Larch see *Larix laricina*
    Linden see *Tilia americana*
    Mountain Ash see *Sorbus americana*
    Mulberry see *Morus rubra*
    Plane see *Platanus occidentalis*
    Red Plum see *Prunus americana*
    Walnut see *Juglans nigra*
    White Elm see *Ulmus americana*
Anise Magnolia see *Magnolia salicifolia*
Aniseed Tree see *Backhousia anisata*
Annatto see *Bixa orellana*
Apple see *Malus* sp.
    Akee see *Blighia sapida*
    Cane see *Arbutus unedo*
    Common see *Malus domestica*
    Crab see *Malus floribunda*
    Custard see *Annona cherimola*
    Elephant see *Dillenia indica*
    Java see *Syzygium samarangense*
    Malay see *Syzygium malaccense*
    Orchard see *Malus domestica*
    Possum see *Diospyros virginiana*
    Rose see *Syzygium jambos*
        see *Syzygium malaccense*
    Star see *Chrysophyllum cainito*
    Sugar see *Annona* sp.
    Wax see *Syzygium samarangense*
Apple Blossom Cassia see *Cassia javanica*
Apple Guava see *Psidium guajava*
Apple Gum see *Angophora* sp.
    Dwarf see *Angophora cordifolia*
    Smooth-barked see *Angophora costata*
Apricot see *Prunus armeniaca*
Arabian Coffee Tree see *Coffea arabica*
Arabian Tea Tree see *Catha edulis*
Arborvitae see *Thuja* sp.
    American see *Thuja occidentalis*
    Chinese see *Thuja orientalis*
    Giant see *Thuja plicata*
    Japanese see *Thuja standishii*
    Korean see *Thuja koraiensis*
Argentina Trumpet Tree see *Tabebuia*
Arizona Cypress see *Cupressus glabra*
Arrowwood see *Viburnum dentatum*
Ash see *Fraxinus* sp.
    American see *Fraxinus americana*
    American Mountain see *Sorbus*
    Australian see *Flindersia* sp.
    Blueberry see *Elaeocarpus* sp.
    Bumpy see *Flindersia schottiana*
    Claret see *Fraxinus X oxycarpa*
    Crow's see *Flindersia australis*
    European see *Fraxinus excelsior*
    Evergreen see *Fraxinus uhdei*
    Golden see *Fraxinus excelsior*
    Manna see *Fraxinus ornus*
    Mexican see *Fraxinus uhdei*
    Mexican Evergreen see *Fraxinus uhdei*
    Mountain see *Eucalyptus regnans*
        see *Sorbus aucuparia*
    Pigeonberry see *Elaeocarpus kirtonii*
    Silver see *Flindersia* sp.
    Weeping see *Fraxinus excelsior*
    White see *Fraxinus americana*
Ash-leaf Maple see *Acer negundo*
Asian Camphor Laurel see *Cinnamomum*
Asoka see *Saraca indica*
Aspen see *Populus tremula*

Aspen, Quaking see *Populus tremuloides*
Atlantic Cedar see *Cedrus atlantica*
    Blue see *Cedrus atlantica*
    Golden see *Cedrus atlantica*
Atlas Cedar see *Cedrus atlantica*
Australian Ash see *Flindersia australis*
    Banyan see *Ficus macrophylla*
    Beech see *Nothofagus moorei*
    Blackwood see *Acacia melanoxylon*
    Nut see *Macadamia integrifolia*
    Red Cedar see *Toona australis*
    Teak see *Flindersia australis*
    White Cedar see *Melia azederach*
Austrian Pine see *Pinus nigra*
Avocado see *Persea americana*

Babal see *Acacia nilotica*
Bacurubu see *Schizolobium parahybum*
Bailey's Mimosa see *Acacia baileyana*
Bald Cypress see *Taxodium distichum*
    Mexican see *Taxodium mucronatum*
Balsam see *Abies* sp.
    Poplar see *Populus deltoides*
Banana Shrub see *Michelia figo*
Bangalow Palm see *Archontophoenix*
Banjo Fig see *Ficus lyrata*
Banks' Grevillea see *Grevillea banksii*
Banksia, Bull see *Banksia grandis*
    Coastal see *Banksia integrifolia*
    Heath-leaf see *Banksia ericifolia*
    Menzies' see *Banksia menziesii*
    Saw see *Banksia serrata*
Banyan see *Ficus benghalensis*
    Australian see *Ficus macrophylla*
    Chinese see *Ficus benjamina*
        see *Ficus retusa*
    Malayan see *Ficus retusa*
Baobab see *Adansonia* sp.
Barbadoes Flower Fence see *Caesalpinia*
    Flowering Hedge see *Caesalpinia*
    Pride see *Caesalpinia pulcherrima*
Barrel Tree see *Brachychiton rupestre*
Barrigon see *Bombax barrigon*
Barringtonia see *Barringtonia racemosa*
Bartlett Pear see *Pyrus X hybrid*
Basket Oak see *Quercus michauxii*
Basswood see *Tilia americana*
Baton du Socier see *Spathodea*
Batswing Coral see *Erythrina vespertilio*
Bay, Bull see *Magnolia grandiflora*
    Rose see *Jatropha hastata*
    Swamp see *Magnolia virginiana*
    Sweet see *Laurus nobilis*
        see *Magnolia virginiana*
Bay Rum Tree see *Pimenta racemosa*
Bay Tree see *Laurus nobilis*
Bayberry see *Pimenta acris*
Bayur Tree see *Pterospermum acerifolia*
Beach Pine see *Pinus contorta*
Bead Tree see *Melia azederach*
    Japanese see *Melia azederach*
Bean, Coral see *Erythrina variegata*
Bechtel's Crab see *Malus ioensis*
Beech see *Fagus* sp.
    American see *Fagus americana*
    Australian see *Nothofagus moorei*
    Black see *Nothofagus solandri*
    Common see *Fagus sylvatica*
    Copper see *Fagus sylvatica* CV
    European see *Fagus sylvatica*
    False see *Nothofagus* sp.
    Fernleaf see *Fagus sylvatica* CV
    Japanese see *Fagus crenata*
    Myrtle see *Nothofagus cunninghamii*
    Negrohead see *Nothofagus moorei*
    Purple see *Fagus sylvatica* CV
    Red see *Nothofagus fusca*
    Roble see *Nothofagus obliqua*
Bell-flowered Cherry see *Prunus*

Bellota see *Sterculia apetala*
Belmore Sentry Palm see *Howea*
Benguet Pine see *Pinus insularis*
Benjamin Tree see *Ficus benjamina*
Bentham's Cornel see *Cornus capitata*
Bergamot Orange see *Citrus aurantium*
Bermuda Cedar see *Juniperus sabina*
Be-still Tree see *Thevetia peruviana*
Bhutan Cypress see *Cupressus torulosa*
Bigarade see *Citrus aurantium*
Big-cone Pine see *Pinus coulteri*
Big-leaf Linden see *Tilia platyphyllos*
Big-leaf Magnolia see *Magnolia*
Big Tree see *Sequoiadendron giganteum*
Bilimbi see *Averrhoa bilimbi*
Bilsted see *Liquidambar styraciflua*
Birch see *Betula* sp.
  Black see *Betula nigra*
  Canoe see *Betula papyrifera*
  Cherry see *Betula lenta*
  European see *Betula pendula*
  Paper see *Betula papyrifera*
  River see *Betula nigra*
  Swedish see *Betula pendula*
  Sweet see *Betula lenta*
  White see *Betula pendula*
  Young's Weeping see *Betula pendula*
Bird Catcher Tree see *Pisonia umbellifera*
Bird Cherry see *Prunus avium*
Bird-lime Tree see *Cordia sebestena*
Bitter Orange see *Citrus aurantium*
Bitternut see *Carya cordiformis*
Black Alder see *Alnus glutinosa*
  Bean see *Castanospermum australe*
  Beech see *Nothofagus solandri*
  Birch see *Betula nigra*
  Cottonwood see *Populus trichocarpa*
  Locust see *Robinia pseudacacia*
  Mulberry see *Morus nigra*
  Oak see *Quercus velutina*
  Peppermint see *Eucalyptus nicholii*
  Pine see *Podocarpus neriifolius*
  Pine, Japanese see *Pinus thunbergii*
  Poplar see *Populus nigra*
  Sheoke see *Casuarina littoralis*
  Walnut see *Juglans nigra*
  Wattle see *Acacia decurrens*
Blackbutt see *Eucalyptus pilularis*
Blackgum see *Nyssa sylvatica*
Blackleaf Podocarp see *Podocarpus*
Blackthorn, West India see *Acacia*
Blackwattle see *Callicoma serratifolia*
Blackwood see *Acacia melanoxylon*
Blimbing see *Averrhoa bilimbi*
Blue Atlas Cedar see *Cedrus atlantica*
  Haze Tree see *Jacaranda mimosaefolia*
  Latan Palm see *Latania loddigesii*
  Oliveberry see *Elaeocarpus grandis*
Blueberry Ash see *Elaeocarpus reticulatus*
Bluegum see *Eucalyptus globulus*
  Tasmanian see *Eucalyptus globulus*
Bo Tree see *Ficus religiosa*
Bombax, Pink see *Bombax ellipticum*
Boree see *Acacia pendula*
Bottle Ponytail see *Beaucarnea recurvata*
Bottle Tree see *Adansonia* sp.
  Flame see *Brachychiton aerifolium*
  Narrowleaf see *Brachychiton rupestre*
  Queensland see *Brachychiton rupestre*
Bottlebrush see *Callistemon* sp.
  see *Melaleuca* sp.
  Albany see *Callistemon speciosus*
  Cream see *Callistemon shiressii*
  Crimson see *Callistemon citrinus*
  Lemon-scented see *Callistemon citrinus*
  Weeping see *Callistemon viminalis*
  White see *Callistemon salignus*
  Willow see *Callistemon salignus*
Bow-wood see *Maclura pomifera*
Box, Australian Brush see *Tristania conferta*
  Brisbane see *Tristania conferta*
  Brush see *Tristania conferta*
  Variegated Brush see *Tristania conferta*
  Victorian see *Pittosporum undulatum*
    see *Tristania conferta*
Box Elder see *Acer negundo*

Bracelet Honeymyrtle see *Melaleuca*
Brazil Shower see *Cassia leptophylla*
Brazilian Ironwood see *Caesalpinia ferrea*
  Mastic see *Schinus terebinthifolius*
  Pepper Tree see *Schinus terebinthifolius*
  Rosewood see *Jacaranda mimosaefolia*
    see *Tipuana tipu*
Brazilwood see *Caesalpinia echinata*
  False see *Caesalpinia peltophoroides*
Breadfruit see *Artocarpus altilis*
  see *Pandanus odoratissimus*
Bread Tree, Malay see *Adansonia digitata*
Brewers' Spruce see *Picea*
Brewers' Weeping Spruce see *Picea*
Brisbane Box see *Tristania conferta*
  Laurel see *Pittosporum rhombifolium*
Bristle-tipped Oak see *Quercus acutissima*
Broadleaf Paperbark see *Melaleuca*
  Podocarp see *Podocarpus nagi*
Brown Pine see *Podocarpus elatus*
Brush Box see *Tristania conferta*
  Cherry see *Syzygium paniculatum*
  Turpentine see *Choricarpia leptopetala*
Buckeye see *Aesculus* sp.
  California see *Aesculus californica*
  Ohio see *Aesculus glabra*
  Red see *Aesculus pavia*
Buddhist Pine see *Podocarpus*
  see *Podocarpus nagi*
Buerger's Maple see *Acer buergerianum*
Bull Banksia see *Banksia grandis*
  Bay see *Magnolia grandiflora*
Bullace see *Prunus institia*
Bullock's Heart see *Annona reticulata*
Buloke see *Casuarina* sp.
  Grey see *Casuarina glauca*
Bumpy Ash see *Flindersia schottiana*
Bunya Bunya see *Araucaria bidwillii*
Bunya Pine see *Araucaria bidwillii*
Burma, Pride of see *Amherstia nobilis*
Burmese Rosewood see *Pterocarpus*
Bush Lemon see *Citrus limonia* CV
Buttercup Tree see *Cochlospermum*
Butterfly Flower see *Bauhinia monandra*
  Tree see *Bauhinia purpurea*
Butterfruit see *Persea americana*
Buttonwood see *Platanus occidentalis*

Cabbage Palm see *Livistona australis*
  Tree see *Livistona australis*
Cacao see *Theobroma cacao*
Cafta see *Catha edulis*
Caimito see *Chrysophyllum cainito*
Cajeput see *Melaleuca quinquenervia*
Calabash Tree see *Crescentia cujete*
Calamondin see *Citrus* sp.
California Buckeye see *Aesculus*
  Coastal Redwood see *Sequoia*
  Holly see *Heteromeles arbutifolia*
  Horse Chestnut see *Aesculus californica*
  Incense Cedar see *Calocedrus decurrens*
  Live Oak see *Quercus agrifolia*
    see *Quercus chrysolepis*
  Maybush see *Heteromeles arbutifolia*
  Pepper Tree see *Schinus areira*
  Plane see *Platanus racemosa*
  Plum see *Prunus ilicifolius*
  Redbud see *Cercis occidentalis*
  Redwood see *Sequoia sempervirens*
  Strawberry Tree see *Arbutus menziesii*
  Tree Poppy see *Fremontodendron*
  Walnut see *Juglans tindsii*
  White Oak see *Quercus lobata*
Camel Thorn see *Acacia giraffae*
Camphor Laurel see *Cinnamomum*
  Tree see *Cinnamomum camphora*
Canada Hemlock see *Tsuga canadensis*
  Poplar see *Populus canadensis*
  Thorn see *Crataegus submollis*
Canary Island Date Palm see *Phoenix*
  Pine see *Pinus canariensis*
  Strawberry Tree see *Arbutus canariensis*
Candlenut see *Aleurites moluccana*
  Remui see *Aleurites moluccana* CV
Cane Apples see *Arbutus unedo*
Cannonball Tree see *Couroupita*
Canoe Birch see *Betula papyrifera*

Canton Pine see *Pinus massoniana*
Canyon Oak see *Quercus chrysolepis*
Caoutchouc Tree see *Hevea brasiliensis*
Cape Chestnut see *Calodendron capense*
  Wattle see *Albizzia lophantha*
Carambole see *Averrhoa carambola*
Caribbee Royal Palm see *Roystonea*
Carob Bean see *Ceratonia siliqua*
  Tree see *Ceratonia siliqua*
Carolina Poplar see *Populus canadensis*
Casahuete see *Ipomoea arborescens*
Caspian Locust see *Gleditsia caspica*
Cassia see *Cassia* sp.
  see *Cinnamomum cassia*
  Apple Blossom see *Cassia javanica*
  Chinese see *Cinnamomum camphora*
  Cigar see *Cassia brewsteri*
  Padang see *Cinnamomum burmanii*
  Saigon see *Cinnamomum loureirii*
  Showy see *Cassia spectabilis*
  Flower Tree see *Cinnamomum loureirii*
Cassie see *Acacia farnesiana*
Cat Spruce see *Picea glauca*
Catalpa, Pink see *Catalpa fargesii*
  Western see *Catalpa speciosa*
Catawba see *Catalpa speciosa*
Caucasian Fir see *Abies nordmanniana*
  Spruce see *Picea orientalis*
  Wingnut see *Pterocarya fraxinifolia*
  Zelkova see *Zelkova carpinifolia*
Cedar see *Cedrus* sp.
  Alaska see *Chamaecyparis nootkaensis*
  Atlantic see *Cedrus atlantica*
  Atlas see *Cedrus atlantica*
  Australian Red see *Toona australis*
  Australian White see *Melia azederach*
  Bermuda see *Juniperus sabina*
  China see *Cedrela sinensis*
  Chinese see *Cedrela sinensis*
  Cigar Box see *Cedrela odorata*
  Colorado Red see *Juniperus scopulorum*
  Creeping see *Juniperus horizontalis*
  Deodar see *Cedrus deodara*
  Incense see *Calocedrus decurrens*
  Indian see *Cedrus deodara*
  Japanese see *Cryptomeria japonica*
  Mexican see *Cupressus lusitanica*
  Mount Atlas see *Cedrus atlantica*
  Pencil see *Juniperus virginiana*
  Port Orford see *Chamaecyparis*
  Portuguese see *Cupressus lusitanica*
  Red see *Juniperus virginiana*
    see *Toona australis*
  Russian see *Pinus cembra*
  Spanish see *Cedrela odorata*
  Western Red see *Thuja plicata*
  White see *Chamaecyparis thyoides*
    see *Melia azederach*
    see *Tabebuia pentaphylla*
Cedar of Goa see *Cupressus lusitanica*
Cedar of Lebanon see *Cedrus libani*
Cedar Wattle see *Acacia terminalis*
Cerbera see *Cerbera odollan*
Ceylon Cinnamon see *Cinnamomum*
  Rosewood see *Albizzia odoratissima*
Champak see *Michelia champaca*
  Orange see *Michelia champaca*
Champara see *Rhodoleia championii*
Cherimoya see *Annona cherimolia*
Cherry see *Prunus cerasus*
  Bell-flowered see *Prunus campanulata*
  Bird see *Prunus avium*
  Brush see *Syzygium paniculatum*
  Cornelian see *Cornus mas*
  Evergreen see *Prunus ilicifolius*
  Flowering see *Prunus serrulata*
  Formosa see *Prunus campanulata*
  Higan see *Prunus subhirtella*
  Hollyleaf see *Prunus ilicifolius*
  Japanese Flowering see *Prunus serrulata*
  Manchurian see *Prunus maackii*
  Nanking see *Prunus tomentosa*
  Natal see *Dombeya natalensis*
  Perfumed see *Prunus mahaleb*
  Rosebud see *Prunus subhirtella*
  St Lucie see *Prunus mahaleb*
  Sour see *Prunus cerasus*

Swamp see *Carya cordiformis*
Hill's Weeping Fig see *Ficus hillii*
Himalayan Strawberry see *Cornus capitata*
Hinau see *Elaeocarpus denticulatus*
Hinoki Cypress see *Chamaecyparis obtusa*
Ho'awa see *Pittosporum hosmeri*
Hog Plum see *Diospyros lotus*
  see *Spondias mombin*
Holland Elm see *Ulmus X hollandica*
Holly see *Ilex* sp.
  American see *Ilex opaca*
  California see *Heteromeles arbutifolia*
  Chinese see *Ilex cornuta*
  Chinese see *Ilex rotunda*
  Common see *Ilex aquifolium*
  English see *Ilex aquifolium*
  European see *Ilex aquifolium*
  Horned see *Ilex cornuta*
  Japanese see *Ilex pedunculata*
  Long-stalked see *Ilex latifolia*
  Kurogane see *Ilex rotunda*
  Mt Fuji see *Ilex pedunculata*
  Variegated see *Ilex aquifolium*
Holly Oak see *Quercus ilex*
Hollyleaf Cherry see *Prunus ilicifolia*
Hollyleaf Sweetspire see *Itea ilicifolia*
Hollywood Juniper see *Juniperus chinensis*
Holm Oak see *Quercus ilex*
Honduras Mahogany see *Swietenia*
Honey Locust see *Gleditsia triacanthos*
Honey Myrtle, Bracelet see *Melaleuca*
Honey Palm see *Jubaea chilensis*
Honeyberry see *Celtis australis*
Honeyshuck see *Gleditsia triacanthos*
Honeysuckle see *Banksia* sp.
  Coast see *Banksia integrifolia*
  Red see *Banksia serrata*
Hong Kong Orchid Tree see *Bauhinia*
  Sterculia see *Sterculia lanceolata*
Hoop Pine see *Araucaria cunninghamii*
Hop Hornbeam see *Ostrya carpinifolia*
  American see *Ostrya virginiana*
Horned Holly see *Ilex cornuta*
Horse Chestnut see *Aesculus* sp.
  California see *Aesculus californica*
  Common see *Aesculus hippocastanum*
  European see *Aesculus hippocastanum*
  Red see *Aesculus X carnea*
Horsetail Tree see *Casuarina equisetifolia*
Hortulan see *Prunus hortulana*
Hotu see *Barringtonia asiatica*
Huamuchil see *Pithecellobium dulce*
Humboldt Willow see *Salix humboldtii*
Huon Pine see *Dacrydium franklinii*
Hybrid Laburnum see *Laburnum X vossii*
  Thorn see *Crataegus X smithiana*
Ice Cream Beans see *Inga edulis*
Iigiri see *Idesia polycarpa*
Illawarra Flame see *Brachychiton*
  Palm see *Archontophoenix*
Illyarrie see *Eucalyptus erythrocorys*
Imou Pine see *Dacrydium cupressinum*
Incense Cedar see *Calocedrus* sp.
  California see *Calocedrus decurrens*
  Taiwan see *Calocedrus formosana*
India-rubber Plant see *Ficus elastica*
  Variegated see *Ficus elastica* CV
Indian Almond see *Sterculia foetida*
  Bean see *Catalpa bignonioides*
  Cedar see *Cedrus deodara*
  Coral Bean see *Erythrina variegata*
  Gooseberry see *Phyllanthus acidus*
  Jujube see *Zizyphus mauritia*
  Laburnum see *Cassia fistula*
  Lilac see *Melia azederach*
  Mulberry see *Morinda citrifolia*
  Oak see *Barringtonia acutangula*
  Pear see *Pyrus pashia*
  Varnish Tree see *Ailanthus excelsa*
  Wingfruit see *Pterocarpus indicus*
Irish Juniper see *Juniperus communis*
  Strawberry Tree see *Arbutus unedo*
  Yew see *Taxus baccata*
Ironbark see *Eucalyptus* sp.
  Narrowleaf see *Eucalyptus racemosa*
  Pink-flowered see *Eucalyptus*
  White see *Eucalyptus leucoxylon*

Ironwood see *Casuarina* sp.
  see *Parrotia persica*
  see *Ostrya carpinifolia*
  Brazilian see *Caesalpinia ferrea*
  Kermadec see *Metrosideros*
  Variegated see *Metrosideros*
Islay see *Prunus ilicifolius*
Italian Alder see *Alnus cordata*
  Cypress see *Cupressus sempervirens* CV
  Maple see *Acer opalus*
Ivory Curl Tree see *Buckinghamia*
Ivy Palm see *Brassaia actinophylla*

Jacaranda see *Jacaranda mimosaefolia*
  Fernleaf see *Jacaranda mimosaefolia*
  Mountain see *Paulownia imperialis*
  Yellow see *Schizolobium parahybum*
Jaggery Palm see *Caryota urens*
Jakfruit see *Artocarpus heterophyllus*
Jamaica Fiddlewood see *Citharexylum*
  Plum see *Chrysophyllum oliviforme*
Japan Locust see *Gleditsia japonica*
  Plum see *Eriobotrya japonica*
  Wood Oil Tree see *Aleurites cordata*
Japanese Arborvitae see *Thuja standishii*
  Bead Tree see *Melia azederach*
  Beech see *Fagus japonica*
  Black Pine see *Pinus thunbergii*
  Cedar see *Cryptomeria japonica*
  Cherry see *Prunus serrulata*
  Chestnut see *Castanea crenata*
  Crab see *Malus floribunda*
  Dogwood see *Cornus kousa*
  Elm see *Zelkova serrata*
  False Cypress see *Chamaecyparis obtusa*
  Flowering Cherry see *Prunus serrulata*
  Flowering Crabapple see *Malus*
  Hackberry see *Celtis sinensis*
  Laurel see *Pittosporum tobira*
  Linden see *Tilia miqueliana*
  Locust see *Gleditsia japonica*
  Magnolia see *Magnolia kobus*
  Maple see *Acer japonicum*
    see *Acer palmatum* sp.
  Medlar see *Eriobotrya japonica*
  Mountain Maple see *Acer palmatum*
  Pagoda Tree see *Sophora japonica*
  Persimmon see *Diospyros kaki*
  Plum see *Prunus salicina*
  Red Pine see *Pinus densiflora*
  Umbrella Tree see *Sciadopitys*
  White Pine see *Prunus parviflora*
Jarrah see *Eucalyptus marginata*
Java Apple see *Syzygium cumini*
  see *Syzygium samarangense*
  Olive see *Sterculia foetida*
  Shower see *Cassia javanica*
Jelly Palm see *Butia capitata*
Jerusalem Date see *Bauhinia monandra*
  Pine see *Pinus halepensis*
Jobo see *Spondias mombin*
Judas Bag see *Adansonia digitata*
  Tree see *Cercis siliquastrum*
Jujube see *Zizyphus* sp.
  Common see *Zizyphus jujuba*
  Cotton see *Zizyphus mauritiana*
  Indian see *Zizyphus mauritiana*
Jumbool see *Syzygium samarangense*
Jumbu see *Syzygium jambos*
Juniper see *Juniperus* sp.
  Chinese see *Juniperus chinensis*
  Common see *Juniperus communis*
  Golden Chinese see *Juniperus chinensis*
  Hollywood Juniper see *Juniperus*
  Rocky Mountain see *Juniperus*
  Twisted see *Juniperus chinensis* CV

Kaffir Plum see *Harpephyllum caffrum*
Kaffirboom see *Erythrina caffra*
Kahika see *Podocarpus dacrydioides*
Kaki see *Diospyros kaki*
Kanooka see *Tristania laurina*
Kapok see *Ceiba pentandra*
Karo see *Pittosporum crassifolium*
Karroo Thorn see *Acacia karroo*
Kauai Hibiscus see *Hibiscus kahilii*
Kauri see *Agathis* sp.

Kauri see *Agathis australis*
  New Caledonia see *Agathis moorei*
  Noumea see *Agathis moorei*
  Queensland see *Agathis robusta*
Kauri Pine see *Agathis australis*
  Fiji see *Agathis vitiensis*
Keg Fig see *Diospyros kaki*
Kelumpang see *Sterculia foetida*
Kentia see *Howea belmoreana*
  see *Howea forsteriana*
Kermadec Ironwood see *Metrosideros*
Keteleeria see *Keteleeria davidiana*
  Fortune's see *Keteleeria fortunei*
Keurboom see *Virgilia capensis*
Khat see *Catha edulis*
King Nut see *Carya laciniata*
King of Fruits see *Mangifera indica*
King Palm see *Archontophoenix*
Kino see *Coccoloba uvifera*
Kittul see *Caryota urens*
Koa see *Acacia koa*
Koka see *Bischofia javanica*
Korean Arborvitae see *Thuja koraiensis*
Kou see *Cordia subcordata*
Kou Haole see *Cordia sebestena*
Kousa see *Cornus kousa*
Kowhai see *Sophora tetraptera*
Kukui see *Aleurites moluccana*
Kurogane Holly see *Ilex rotunda*
Kurrajong see *Brachychiton populneum*
  Desert see *Brachychiton gregoryii*
  Pink see *Brachychiton*
  White see *Brachychiton discolor*
Kurri see *Paulownia tomentosa*
Kusamaki see *Podocarpus macrophyllus*

Laburnum, Hybrid see *Laburnum X*
  Indian see *Cassia fistula*
  Scotch see *Laburnum alpinum*
Lacebark see *Brachychiton* sp.
  Pink see *Brachychiton bidwillii*
  Queensland see *Brachychiton discolor*
Lacquer Tree see *Rhus verniciflua*
Larch see *Larix* sp.
  American see *Larix laricina*
  European see *Larix decidua*
Large Tupelo see *Nyssa aquatica*
Largeleaf
  Lime see *Tilia platyphyllos*
  Pine see *Pinus palustris*
  Whitebeam see *Sorbus aria* CV
Latan Palm, Blue see *Latania loddigesii*
  Red see *Latania lontaroides*
  Yellow see *Latania verschaffeltii*
Laurel see *Laurus nobilis*
  Brisbane see *Pittosporum rhombifolium*
  Camphor see *Cinnamomum camphora*
  Cherry see *Prunus laurocerasus*
  Japanese see *Pittosporum tobira*
  Portugal see *Prunus lusitanica*
  Versailles see *Prunus laurocerasus*
  Weeping see *Ficus benjamina*
Laurel Fig see *Ficus retusa*
Laurel Magnolia see *Magnolia grandiflora*
Lawson Cypress see *Chamaecyparis*
Lebbek Tree see *Albizzia lebbek*
Leechee Nut see *Litchi sinensis*
Lehua see *Metrosideros collina*
Lemon see *Citrus limon*
  Bush see *Citrus limon* CV
  Eureka see *Citrus limon* CV
  Lisbon see *Citrus limon* CV
  Meyer see *Citrus limon* CV
  Ponderosa see *Citrus limon* CV
  Rough see *Citrus limon* CV
  Villafranca see *Citrus limon* CV
Lemon-scented Bottlebrush see
    Callistemon citrinus
  Gum see *Eucalyptus citriodora*
  Myrtle see *Backhousia citriodora*
  Tea Tree see *Leptospermum petersonii*
Leopard Tree see *Caesalpinia ferrea*
Leopardwood see *Caesalpinia ferrea*
    see *Flindersia maculosa*
Lettuce Tree see *Pisonia alba*
Leverwood see *Ostrya virginiana*

Norway Maple see *Acer platanoides*
   Spruce see *Picea abies*
Nosegay Tree see *Plumeria acuminata*
Noumea Kauri see *Agathis moorei*
Nut, Australian see *Macadamia integrifolia*
   Hawaiian see *Macadamia integrifolia*
   Pistachio see *Pistacia vera*
   Queensland see *Macadamia integrifolia*

Oak see *Quercus* sp.
   Basket see *Quercus michauxii*
   Black see *Quercus velutina*
   Bristle-tipped see *Quercus acutissima*
   California Live see *Quercus agrifolia*
     see *Quercus chrysolepis*
   California White see *Quercus lobata*
   Canyon see *Quercus chrysolepis*
   Coast Live see *Quercus agrifolia*
   Common see *Quercus robur*
   Cork see *Quercus suber*
   Daimyo see *Quercus dentata*
   Durmast see *Quercus petraea*
   Engelmann see *Quercus engelmannii*
   Fire see *Casuarina cunninghamiana*
   Forest see *Casuarina cunninghamiana*
   Golden Cup see *Quercus chrysolepis*
   Holly see *Quercus ilex*
   Holm see *Quercus ilex*
   Indian see *Barringtonia acutangula*
   Live see *Quercus virginiana*
   Maul see *Quercus chrysolepis*
   Pin see *Quercus palustris*
   Poison see *Rhus* sp.
   Possum see *Quercus nigra*
   Red see *Quercus borealis*
   Red Silky see *Grevillea banksii*
   Sawtooth see *Quercus acutissima*
   Shingle see *Casuarina equisetifolia*
   Silk see *Grevillea robusta*
   Silky see *Grevillea robusta*
   Southern Live see *Quercus virginiana*
   Spanish see *Quercus palustris*
   Turkey see *Quercus cerris*
   Water see *Quercus nigra*
   Willow see *Quercus salicina*
   Yellow-bark see *Quercus velutina*
Octopus Tree see *Brassaia actinophylla*
Ohi'a Lehua see *Metrosideros collina*
Ohio Buckeye see *Aesculus glabra*
Old Man's Beard see *Chionanthus*
Oleander, Mexican see *Thevetia yccotli*
   Yellow see *Thevetia thevetioides*
Olive see *Olea* sp.
   African see *Olea africana*
   Common see *Olea europaea*
   European see *Olea europaea*
   Wild see *Olea africana*
     see *Nyssa aquatica*
Opiuma see *Pithecellobium dulce*
Orange see *Citrus aurantium*
   see *Citrus sinensis*
   Bergamot see *Citrus aurantium* CV
   Chinotto see *Citrus aurantium* CV
   Maltese Blood see *Citrus sinensis* CV
   Osage see *Maclura pomifera*
   Temple see *Citrus X nobilis*
   Valencia see *Citrus sinensis* CV
   Washington Navel see *Citrus aurantium* CV
   Washington Navel see *Citrus aurantium*
Orange Champak see *Michelia champaca*
Orchard Apple see *Malus domestica*
Orchid Tree see *Bauhinia purpurea*
   see *Bauhinia variegata*
   Hong Kong see *Bauhinia blakeana*
   Queensland see *Bauhinia hookeri*
   White see *Bauhinia corniculata*
Oriental Plane see *Platanus orientalis*
   Spruce see *Picea orientalis*
Osage Orange see *Maclura pomifera*
Osier see *Salix fragilis*
Otaheite Apple see *Spondias cytherea*
   Gooseberry see *Phyllanthus acidus*
Oteniqua Yellowwood see *Podocarpus*
Oyama Magnolia see *Magnolia sieboldii*
Oyster Bay Pine see *Callitris rhomboidea*

Pacayer see *Inga edulis*

Padang Cassia see *Cinnamomum*
Padang Cinnamon see *Cinnamomum*
Padauk see *Pterocarpus indicus*
Pagoda Tree see *Plumeria acuminata*
   Japanese see *Sophora japonica*
   Weeping see *Sophora japonica* CV
Pakalana see *Michelia alba*
Pak Lan see *Michelia alba*
Palm, Alexandra see *Archontophoenix*
   Bangalow see *Archontophoenix*
   Blue Latan see *Latania loddigesii*
   Cabbage see *Livistona australis*
   Cabbage Tree see *Livistona australis*
   Carribee Royal see *Roystonea oleracea*
   Chinese Fan see *Livistona chinensis*
   Chinese Fishtail see *Caryota ochlandra*
   Chinese Fountain see *Livistona*
   Clustered Fishtail see *Caryota mitis*
   Coconut see *Cocos nucifera*
   Cotton see *Washingtonia robusta*
   Cuban Royal see *Roystonea regia*
   Date see *Phoenix dactylifera*
   Desert Fan see *Washingtonia filifera*
   Fishtail see *Caryota* sp.
   Fountain see *Livistona* sp.
   Gippsland see *Livistona australis*
   Illawarra see *Archontophoenix*
   Ivy see *Brassaia actinophylla*
   Jaggery see *Caryota urens*
   Jelly see *Butia capitata*
   King see *Archontophoenix alexandrae*
   Latan see *Latania* sp.
   Mexican Fan see *Washingtonia robusta*
   Petticoat see *Washingtonia filifera*
   Pygmy Date see *Phoenix roebelinii*
   Queen see *Arecastrum romanzoffianum*
   Red Inland see *Livistona mariae*
   Red Latan see *Latania lontaroides*
   Royal see *Roystonea oleracea*
   Sago see *Caryota urens*
   Senegal Date see *Phoenix reclinata*
   Sentry see *Howea* sp.
   Thread see *Washingtonia filifera*
   Toddy see *Caryota urens*
   Traveller's see *Ravenala*
   Wine see *Butia yatay*
     see *Caryota urens*
     see *Jubaea chilensis*
   Yellow Latan see *Latania verschaffeltii*
Palo Blanco see *Ipomoea arborescens*
Panama Flame see *Brownea macrophylla*
   Tree see *Sterculia apetala*
Pandanus see *Pandanus odoratissimus*
Papaya see *Carica papaya*
   Mountain see *Carica pubescens*

Paper Birch see *Betula papyrifera*
Paper Mulberry see *Broussonetia papyrifera*
Paperbark see *Melaleuca* sp.
   Broadleaf see *Melaleuca quinquenervia*
   Flaxleaf see *Melaleuca linariifolia*
   Prickly see *Melaleuca styphelioides*
   Small-flowered see *Melaleuca parviflora*
   Swamp see *Melaleuca ericifolia*
     see *Melaleuca quinquenervia*
Paperbark Maple see *Acer griseum*
Para Rubber Tree see *Hevea brasiliensis*
Para Para see *Pisonia umbellifera*
Paradise Tree see *Melia azederach*
Paraguay Tea see *Ilex paraguariensis*
Paraguay Trumpet Tree see *Tabebuia*
Parrotia see *Parrotia persica*
Paulownia, Royal see *Paulownia*
Paul's Double Scarlet Thorn see *Crataegus*
Paw Paw see *Carica papaya*
Peach see *Prunus persica*
Peach of the Tropics see *Mangifera indica*
Peacock Flower see *Caesalpinia*
   see *Delonix regia*
Pear see *Pyrus* sp.
   Common see *Pyrus communis*
   European Wild see *Pyrus communis*
   Indian see *Pyrus pashia*
   Weeping Silver see *Pyrus salicifolia*
   Wild see *Pyrus communis*
     see *Dombeya spectabilis*
   Willowleaf see *Pyrus salicifolia*

Pearl Acacia see *Acacia podalyriaefolia*
Pecan see *Carya illinoinensis*
Peebeen see *Syncarpia glomulifera*
Peepul see *Ficus religiosa*
Peking Serviceberry see *Sorbus pekingensis*
   Willow see *Salix matsudana*
Pencil Cedar see *Juniperus virginiana*
Pendant Silver Lime see *Tilia petiolaris*
Peppercorn Tree see *Schinus areira*
Pepperidge see *Nyssa sylvatica*
Pepperina see *Schinus areira*
Peppermint, Willow see *Eucalyptus*
   Narrowleaf Black see *Eucalyptus nicholii*
Peppermint Tree see *Agonis flexuosa*
Peppermint Tree Wattle see *Acacia*
Pepper Tree, Brazilian see *Schinus*
   California see *Schinus areira*
Père David's Maple see *Acer davidiana*
Peregrina see *Jatropha hastata*
Perfume Tree see *Cananga odorata*
Perfume Wattle see *Acacia farnesiana*
Perfumed Cherry see *Prunus mahaleb*
Persian Lilac see *Melia azederach*
   Silk Tree see *Albizzia julibrissin*
   Walnut see *Juglans regia*
   Witchhazel see *Parrotia persica*
Persimmon see *Diospyros kaki*
Peruvian Mastic Tree see *Schinus areira*
Petticoat Palm see *Washingtonia filifera*
Philippine Acacia see *Acacia confusa*
   Tulipwood see *Harpullia arborea*
Piccabeen see *Archontophoenix*
Pigeonberry Ash see *Elaeocarpus kirtonii*
Pignut see *Carya glabra*
Pimento see *Pimenta dioica*
Pin Oak see *Quercus palustris*
Pincushion Hakea see *Hakea laurina*
Pincushion Tree see *Hakea laurina*
Pine see *Pinus* sp.
   Aleppo see *Pinus halepensis*
   Austrian see *Pinus nigra*
   Beach see *Pinus contorta*
   Benguet see *Pinus insularis*
   Big-Cone see *Pinus coulteri*
   Black see *Podocarpus* sp.
   Brown see *Podocarpus elatus*
   Buddhist see *Podocarpus macrophyllus*
     see *Podocarpus nagi*
   Canary Island see *Pinus canariensis*
   Canton see *Pinus massoniana*
   Chilean see *Araucaria araucana*
   Chir see *Pinus roxburghii*
   Cluster see *Pinus pinaster*
   Cook see *Araucaria columellaris*
   Corsican see *Pinus laricio*
   Cypress see *Callitris cupressiformis*
   Fern see *Podocarpus gracilior*
   Fiji Kauri see *Agathis vitiensis*
   Georgia see *Pinus palustris*
   Golden Pencil see *Cupressus*
   Hoop see *Araucaria cunninghamii*
   Huon see *Dacrydium franklinii*
   Imou see *Dacrydium cupressinum*
   Japanese Black see *Pinus thunbergii*
   Japanese Red see *Pinus densiflora*
   Japanese White see *Pinus parviflora*
   Jerusalem see *Pinus halepensis*
   Kauri see *Agathis australis*
   Largeleaf see *Pinus palustris*
   Macedonian see *Pinus peuce*
   Maritime see *Pinus pinaster*
   Mexican White see *Pinus ayacahuite*
   Mexican Yellow see *Pinus patula*
   Monterey see *Pinus radiata*
   Montezuma see *Pinus montezumae*
   Moreton Bay see *Araucaria*
   Murray see *Callitris columellaris*
   New Caledonia see *Araucaria*
   New Zealand Red see *Dacrydium*
   Norfolk Island see *Araucaria*
   Oyster Bay see *Callitris rhomboidea*
   Pitch see *Pinus palustris*
   Ponderosa see *Pinus ponderosa*
   Port Jackson see *Callitris rhomboidea*
   Radiata see *Pinus radiata*
   Red see *Dacrydium* sp.
   Rimu see *Dacrydium cuppressinum*

Sausage Tree see *Kigelia pinnata*
Saw Banksia see *Banksia serrata*
Sawtooth Oak see *Quercus acutissima*
Scarlet Flame Bean see *Brownea*
    Flowered Gum see *Eucalyptus ficifolia*
    Maple see *Acer rubrum*
    Wistaria Tree see *Sesbania grandiflora*
Schefflera see *Brassaia actinophylla*
Scotch Elm see *Ulmus glabra*
    Laburnum see *Laburnum alpinum*
Screw Pine see *Pandanus odoratissimus*
Screwpod Wattle see *Acacia implexa*
Scribbly Gum see *Eucalyptus haemastoma*
Scrub Wilga see *Geijera salicifolia*
Sea Grape see *Coccoloba uvifera*
    Mango see *Cerbera manghas*
    Urchin Tree see *Hakea laurina*
Senegal Date Palm see *Phoenix reclinata*
Senna see *Cassia* sp.
Sentry Palm see *Howea forsteriana*
Serbian Spruce see *Picea omorika*
Service Tree see *Sorbus aucuparia*
Serviceberry, Peking see *Sorbus*
Sequoia see *Sequoia sempervirens*
    Giant see *Sequoiadendron giganteum*
Seville Orange see *Citrus aurantium*
Shaddock see *Citrus decumana*
Shagbark Hickory see *Carya ovata*
Shamel Ash see *Fraxinus uhdei*
Shaving Brush Tree see *Bombax ellipticum*
She Pine see *Podocarpus elatus*
Shellbark Hickory see *Carya laciniata*
Sheoke
    Black see *Casuarina littoralis*
    River see *Casuarina cunninghamiana*
Shingle Oak see *Casuarina equisetifolia*
Shore Pine see *Pinus contorta*
Shower, Brazil see *Cassia leptophylla*
    Golden see *Cassia fistula*
    Java see *Cassia javanica*
    Rainbow see *Cassia X hybrida*
    Singapore see *Cassia surattensis*
Shower Tree see *Cassia* sp.
Showy Cassia see *Cassia spectabilis*
    Crab see *Malus floribunda*
    Gum see *Eucalyptus racemosa*
Siberian Crab see *Malus baccata*
    Elm see *Ulmus pumila*
Sibipiruna see *Caesalpinia peltophoroides*
Siebold Maple see *Acer sieboldianum*
Sikkim Spruce see *Picea spinulosa*
Silk Mulberry see *Morus alba*
    Oak see *Grevillea robusta*
    Rose see *Rhodoleia championii*
    Tree see *Albizzia julibrissin*
    Tree, Persian see *Albizzia julibrissin*
Silk-cotton Tree see *Bombax* sp.
    Red see *Bombax malabaricum*
    White see *Ceiba pentandra*
Silky Oak see *Grevillea robusta*
    Red see *Oreocallis wickhamii*
Silver Ash see *Flindersia pubescens*
    Fir see *Abies alba*
        Common see *Abies alba*
        European see *Abies alba*
        Veitch's see *Abies veitchii*
    Lawson Cypress see *Chamaecyparis*
    Maple see *Acer saccharinum*
    Quandong see *Elaeocarpus*
    Tarata see *Pittosporum eugenioides* CV
    Trumpet Tree see *Tabebuia argentea*
    Wattle see *Acacia dealbata*
    Wattle, Queensland see *Acacia*
Silverleaf Poplar see *Populus alba*
Simal see *Bombax malabaricum*
Simon Poplar see *Populus simonii*
Simpoh see *Dillenia indica*
Singapore Plumeria see *Plumeria obtusa*
    Shower see *Cassia surattensis*
    White Plumeria see *Plumeria obtusa*
Siris see *Albizzia lebbek*
    Pink see *Albizzia julibrissin*
Siris Tree see *Albizzia* sp.
Sitka Spruce see *Picea sitchensis*
Skunk Tree see *Sterculia foetida*
Sloe see *Prunus* sp.
Small-flowered Paperbark see *Melaleuca*

Small-fruited Hickory see *Carya glabra*
Small-leaf Lillypilly see *Syzygium*
Small-leaf Lime see *Tilia cordata*
Small-leaf Willow Myrtle see *Agonis*
Smooth Apple Gum see *Angophora*
    Rambutan see *Alectryon subcinereus*
    Tree Aloe see *Aloe plicatilis*
Smooth-Barked Apple Gum see
    Angophora costata
Snow Gum see *Eucalyptus pauciflora* CV
Snow in Summer see *Melaleuca linariifolia*
Snowball Tree see *Viburnum opulus*
Snowwood see *Pithecellobium pruinosum*
Sorb see *Sorbus domestica*
Sorbet see *Cornus mas*
Sorcerer's Wand see *Spathodea*
Sorrel Tree see *Oxydendrum arboreum*
Sorrowless Tree see *Saraca indica*
Soulange-Bodin's Magnolia see *Magnolia*
Sour Cherry see *Prunus cerasus*
Sourgum see *Nyssa sylvatica*
Soursop see *Annona muricata*
Sourwood see *Oxydendrum arboreum*
South American Cigar Box Cedar see
    Cedrela odorata
Southern
    Live Oak see *Quercus virginiana*
    Magnolia see *Magnolia grandiflora*
    Yew see *Podocarpus macrophyllus*
Spanish Cedar see *Cedrela odorata*
    Chestnut see *Cassia sativa*
    Fir see *Abies pinsapo*
    Mahogany see *Swietenia mahagoni*
    Oak see *Quercus palustris*
Spicy Jatropha see *Jatropha hastata*
Spiny Chorisia see *Chorisia insignis*
Spruce see *Picea* sp.
    Alberta see *Picea glauca* CV
    Brewer's see *Picea breweriana*
    Brewer's Weeping see *Picea breweriana*
    Cat see *Picea glauca*
    Caucasian see *Picea orientalis*
    Colorado see *Picea pungens*
    Colorado Blue see *Picea pungens*
    Engelmann see *Picea engelmannii*
    Norway see *Picea abies*
    Oriental see *Picea orientalis*
    Serbian see *Picea omorika*
    Sikkim see *Picea spinulosa*
    Sitka see *Picea sitchensis*
    Weeping see *Picea breweriana*
    Weeping Blue see *Picea X standishii*
    White see *Picea glauca*
    Yeddo see *Picea yezoensis*
Staghorn Sumach see *Rhus typhina*
Star Apple see *Chrysophyllum cainito*
    Fruit see *Averrhoa carambola*
    Pine see *Araucaria heterophylla*
Sterculia, Four-fruit see *Sterculia*
    Hong Kong see *Sterculia lanceolata*
    Scarlet see *Sterculia lanceolata*
Strawberry Guava see *Psidium cattleianum*
Strawberry, Himalayan see *Cornus*
    capitata
    Irish see *Arbutus unedo*
Strawberry Tree see *Arbutus* sp.
    California see *Arbutus menziesii*
    Canary Island see *Arbutus canariensis*
    Irish see *Arbutus unedo*
Stringybark see *Eucalyptus* sp.
Striped Maple see *Acer pennsylvanicum*
Stunga see *Brachychiton discolor*
Sugar Apple see *Annona squamosa*
    Maple see *Acer saccharum*
Sugarberry see *Celtis laevigata*
    see *Celtis occidentalis*
Sugi see *Cryptomeria japonica*
Sumach see *Rhus* sp.
    Stagshorn see *Rhus typhina*
    Velvet see *Rhus typhina*
Swamp Bay see *Magnolia virginiana*
    Chestnut see *Quercus michauxii*
    Cypress see *Taxodium distichum*
    Cypress, Mexican see *Taxodium*
    Hickory see *Carya cordiformis*
    Maple see *Acer rubrum*

Paperbark see *Melaleuca ericifolia*
    see *Melaleuca quinquenervia*
White Cedar see *Chamaecyparis*
Swedish Birch see *Betula pendula* CV
Whitebeam see *Sorbus intermedia*
Sweet Acacia see *Acacia farnesiana*
    Bay see *Laurus nobilis*
    see *Magnolia virginiana*
    Birch see *Betula lenta*
    Chestnut see *Castanea sativa*
    Locust see *Gleditsia triacanthos*
    Orange see *Citrus sinensis*
    Shade see *Hymenosporum flavum*
    Verbena Tree see *Backhousia citriodora*
    Viburnum see *Viburnum odoratissimum*
    Viburnum Tree see *Viburnum opulus*
Sweetgum see *Liquidambar* sp.
    Chinese see *Liquidambar formosana*
    Formosan see *Liquidambar formosana*
Sweetsop see *Annona squamosa*
Sweetspire see *Itea ilicifolia*
    Hollyleaf see *Itea ilicifolia*
Sycamore see *Platanus racemosa*
    see *Acer pseudoplatanus*
    Eastern see *Platanus occidentalis*
Sycamore Maple see *Acer pseudoplatanus*
Sycomore see *Ficus sycomorus*
Sydney Golden Wattle see *Acacia*
Syrian Bead Tree see *Media azederach*
Szechuan Fir see *Abies sutchuensis*

Tahiti Lime see *Citrus aurantiifolia*
Tahitian Chestnut see *Inocarpus edulis*
Taiwan Cherry see *Prunus campanulata*
    Fir see *Cunninghamia konishii*
    Incense Cedar see *Calocedrus*
Tallow Tree, Chinese see *Sepium*
Tallow Wood see *Eucalyptus microcorys*
Tamarack see *Larix laricina*
Tamarind see *Tamarindus indicus*
    Manila see *Pithecellobium dulce*
    Native see *Diploglottis* sp.
Tamarindo see *Tamarindus indicus*
Tambookie Thorn see *Erythrina*
    acanthacarpa
Tangelo see *Citrus X Tangelo*
Tangerine see *Citrus reticulata*
Tangor see *Citrus X nobilis*
Tapa Tree see *Broussonetia papyrifera*
Tara see *Caesalpinia spinosa*
Tarata see *Pittosporum eugenioides*
    Silver see *Pittosporum eugenioides* CV
Tasmanian Bluegum see *Eucalyptus*
Tasselwhite see *Itea ilicifolia*
Tea Tree see *Leptospermum* sp.
    Arabian see *Catha edulis*
    Coastal see *Leptospermum laevigatum*
    Lemon-scented see *Leptospermum*
Teak see *Tectona grandis*
    Australian see *Flindersia* sp.
Tekka see *Tectona grandis*
Temple Flower see *Plumeria acuminata*
    Orange see *Citrus X nobilis*
Tennis Ball Tree see *Agathis vitiensis*
Texas Umbrella Tree see *Melia azederach*
Thatch Palm see *Howea forsteriana*
Thorn, Camel see *Acacia giraffae*
    Canada see *Crataegus submollis*
    Cockspur see *Crataegus crus-galli*
    Hybrid see *Crataegus X smithiana*
    Karroo see *Acacia karroo*
    Mexican see *Crataegus stipulacea*
    Paul's Double Scarlet see *Crataegus*
    Red Mexican see *Crataegus X smithiana*
    White see *Crataegus oxyacantha*
Thread Palm see *Washingtonia filifera*
Three-lobed Red Maple see *Acer rubrum*
Tiger Claw see *Erythrina variegata*
    Variegated see *Erythrina variegata* CV
Titi see *Oxydendron arboreum*
Titoki see *Alectryon excelsa*
Tobira see *Pittosporum tobira*
Toddy Palm see *Caryota urens*
Toog see *Bischofia javanica*
Toon see *Cedrela sinensis*
Toon, Chinese see *Cedrela sinensis*
Toxicodendron see *Rhus* sp.

YELLOW-WOOD, REAL

Real see *Podocarpus latifolius*
Yerba Maté see *Ilex paraguariensis*
Yew see *Taxus* sp.
   Common see *Taxus baccata*
   English see *Taxus baccata*
   Irish see *Taxus baccata*
   Southern see *Podocarpus macrophyllus*

Weeping see *Taxus baccata* CV
Ylang-ylang see *Cananga odorata*
Ynga see *Inga edulis*
Young's Weeping Birch see *Betula*
Yulan see *Magnolia denudata*
   see *Magnolia heptapeta*

Zamang see *Samanea saman*
Zelkova, Caucasian see *Zelkova*
   Elm see *Zelkova carpinifolia*
   Japanese see *Zelkova serrata*
   Sawleaf see *Zelkova serrata*
Zelkowa see *Zelkova* sp.

ACKNOWLEDGEMENTS

Though this book has been in preparation for several years, many of the trees proved surprisingly elusive when I came to track them down with camera in hand. I am indebted to many friends, new and old, who helped locate my subjects, and often patiently took notes while I photographed, to aid in identification at a later date. They include:

in Australia
Mr Justice A. C. Beattie, Air Commodore & Mrs David Cooper, Brian Donges, Mr & Mrs Ross Field, Margaret Gill, Eddy Graham, Peter Landers, Mr & Mrs David Klippel, Dr A. North, Colin Olson, Peg Perrin, Tony Rodd, Messrs Paul & Ib Sorensen, Mr & Mrs L. Willersdorff

in Czechoslovakia
Wing Commander & Mrs B. M. Burley, Miss Lucy Burley, Dr Kvet

in France
Roderick Cameron, Mme R-P. Jeanneret, Arnaud de Vinzelles

in Hawaii
Dr Horace Clay, Arthur & Margaret Davis, Bill, Owen & Ruth Farrior, Mrs Loy Marks, Dr William Stewart

in Hong Kong
Mrs Gloria Barreto, Albert Chin, Dr S. S. Kwan, Yvonne Wong

in Japan
Hirofumi Chonan, Kazuo Iida

in Tahiti
Michel Hello, Janine Laguesse, Irene Micheli, Coco Pautu, Jacques Rentier, Teama Teriipaia

in the United Kingdom
David & Diana Garde, Richard Moody

in the United States
Lex Dampier, David & Barbara Goux, Lucille & Blake Hampton, Hugh Hefner, Ray Karras, Betty Klein, James F. Lichtman, Al & Ginny Littau, Professor Milton Meyer, Stan & Doreen Quinn, Ed Rice, Terry Scalese, John Winston, David Wittry.

The greater number of trees were photographed at:
Abbotsleigh College, Wahroonga, N.S.W.
Adelaide Botanic Gardens
Arnold Arboretum, Mass.
Bagatelle, Paris
Beauchamp Park, Chatswood, N.S.W.
Brisbane Botanic Gardens
British Embassy, Prague
Brooklyn Botanic Gardens
California State & County Arboretum, Arcadia
Chatswood Memorial Park, N.S.W.
Ching Chung Koon Temple, New Territories, H.K.
Descanso Gardens, Calif.
E. G. Waterhouse Memorial Camellia Garden, Caringbah, N.S.W.
Foster Gardens, Honolulu
Hillier Arboretum, U.K.
Hong Kong Botanic Gardens
Honolulu Academy of Arts
Hotel Lisboa, Macau
Hotel Taaone, Tahiti
Hotel Tahara'a, Tahiti
Huntington Gardens, San Marino, Calif.
Jardin Botanique de Tahiti
Jardin des Plantes, Paris
Jardin des Tuileries, Paris
Kun Ian Temple, Macau
La Brea Park, Los Angeles
La Fiorentina, St Jean Cap Ferrat
Les Cedres, St Jean Cap Ferrat
Kadoorie Farm & Botanic Garden, New Territories, H.K.
Lanyon, A.C.T.
Lou Lim Ioc Garden, Macau
The Louvre, Paris
Lyon Arboretum, Hawaii
Malmaison, Paris
Manila Hotel
Manila Zoo
Meiji Shrine, Tokyo
Milton Park, Bowral, N.S.W.
National Botanic Garden, Canberra, A.C.T.
National University, A.C.T.
The Oasis, Brisbane
Olu Pua Botanic Garden, Kauai
Pacific Tropical Botanic Gardens, Kauai
Palais des Nations, Paris
Palais Luxembourg, Paris
Philippine School of Forestry, Makiling
Prague Botanic Garden
Pruhonice Arboretum, Czechoslovakia
Pua Laki, Kauai
R.A.F. College, Cranwell, Lincs
Rainmaker Hotel, Pago Pago, American Samoa
Rancho Santa Ana Botanic Garden, Calif.
Repulse Bay Hotel, Hong Kong
Rizal Park, Manila
Royal Botanic Gardens, Kew, London
Royal Botanic Gardens, Sydney
The Royal Horticultural Society's Garden, Wisley, Surrey, U.K.
Shinjuku Go-en, Tokyo
Sospel, Leura, N.S.W.
South Coast Botanic Garden, Los Angeles
Stony Range Reserve, Dee Why, N.S.W.
The Strybing Arboretum, San Francisco, Calif.
Taihoa, Mt Irvine, N.S.W.
The Thun Palace, Prague
Tokyo Botanic Gardens
UCLA Botanic Garden, Los Angeles, Calif.
UCLA Japanese Garden, Bel Air, Calif.
United States Embassy, Prague
University of Connecticut
University of Hawaii, Honolulu
University of the Philippines, Los Banos

Photographs were also taken at:
Armidale, N.S.W.
Avarua, Cook Islands
Azusa, Calif.
Baghdad, Iraq
Bathurst, N.S.W.
Bellingen, N.S.W.
Bendigo, Vic.
Bombay, India
Botany Bay, N.S.W.
Bowral, N.S.W.
Brunswick Heads, N.S.W.
Cambridge, Mass.
Canberra, A.C.T.
Concord, Mass.
Cumbabah, Q'land
Glendora, Calif.
Grafton, N.S.W.
Lexington, Mass.
Lismore, N.S.W.
Maryborough, Vic.
Mt Canobolas, N.S.W.
Mt Irvine, N.S.W.
Mt Kosciusko, N.S.W.
Mt Tambourine, Q'land
Mt Wilson, N.S.W.
Mohonk, New York
Mystic Seaport, Conn.
Noank, Conn.
New York City, N.Y.
Noumea, New Caledonia
Orange, N.S.W.
Pasadena, Calif.
Port Macquarie, N.S.W.
Port Stephens, N.S.W.
Roanoke, Va.
Tai Po, N.T., Hong Kong
The Southern Alps of N.S.W.
Washington D.C.
Weston, Conn.
Yesilkoy, Turkey
and on the islands of Moorea, Ra'iatea, Tahaa and Tahiti.

My special thanks to the Department of Agriculture and Fisheries, Hong Kong; the Forestry Department of the Czech Democratic Republic, and the Department of Tourism, Macau, all of which provided experts and guidance to the local flora.